The Day the Laughter Stop
His first, *To Encourage the*
the British Government t
case – a case which had be
The book, which provok
Lords, and the author's
vinced many, ranging from the former
Gardiner, Lords Arran and Goodman, to authors such as Arthur Koestler, that a major miscarriage of justice had occurred. This was in the years 1970 to 1973. A new and updated edition of the book, published in 1990, has again forced the British Government to reopen the case, spearheading a renewed campaign to bring it before the public and parliament to establish once and for all the full truth of this unique and horrific story.

David Yallop's third book, *Beyond Reasonable Doubt?* led directly to the freeing of Arthur Thomas, a New Zealand farmer serving a life sentence for double murder. Prior to Yallop's investigation Thomas had been found guilty by unanimous jury decisions on two separate occasions. Following publication of Yallop's book, Arthur Thomas was granted a Royal Pardon and, after a Royal Commission had deliberated, one million dollars compensation for wrongful imprisonment.

Yallop's fourth book, *Deliver Us From Evil*, was stimulated by a desire to pull a man *into* prison, the Yorkshire Ripper. Yallop's statements to Assistant Chief Constable George Oldfield in June 1980 proved uncannily accurate. If they had been acted upon at the time, Peter Sutcliffe would have been arrested before he could have carried out a further four murderous attacks.

Yallop receives letters continuously from many parts of the world asking, demanding, pleading that he investigate this murder or that alleged miscarriage of justice. He received one particularly singular request, to investigate a very special death. The request came from within the Vatican, and the death was that of Pope John Paul I.

David Yallop then began the extensive research for his fifth book, *In God's Name* (also published by Corgi), which caused a worldwide storm of controversy and to date has sold more than 4 million copies. To this day his central conclusions concerning the murder of the late Pope and the whirlpool of corruption within the Vatican remain unanswered, and the frightening accusations still stand undisputed.

Thus, David Yallop has established a reputation not merely as 'a seeker of justice', but also as the world's greatest investigative author. Now for the first time his second book is made available in paperback.

'The definitive biography of the star who grew famous with Hollywood and did so much to make it famous in turn. It's a horrifying book. It shows precisely what a legal authority can do to wreck people's lives and foreshadowed the welter of moralizing which reached its zenith during the McCarthy "witch-hunt" of the 1950s.

'It's horrifying, too, because it shows conclusively that Arbuckle was innocent of the charges of rape and murder levelled at him by a politically ambitious district attorney. THE DAY THE LAUGHTER STOPPED is not just a biography of "Fatty" Arbuckle. It's a history of Hollywood – and a damning indictment of hypocritical "crusaders" who tore a man to pieces in the name of morality'

SUNDAY PRESS

'Lifts a stone, not just on Hollywood or Prohibition America, but on man's inhumanity to man'

DAILY MIRROR

'The zealots and reformers saw Hollywood and its works as the new Sodom. The Arbuckle scandal gave them exactly the weapon they needed . . . David Yallop's book THE DAY THE LAUGHTER STOPPED shows that there was never a real case'

THE TIMES

'David Yallop has dug up much valuable new information and is the first writer to draw extensively on the records of the trials, which he enthrallingly reconstructs'

NEW STATESMAN

'An emotive story with a passionate exploration of the facts and fantasy. David Yallop's knife-edge research has chopped through the guff and glut of the Hollywood jungle of the twenties from which censorship was born'

FINANCIAL TIMES

'It would appear that anybody attempting to correct the Arbuckle story would be fighting uphill all the way. David Yallop does just that, he battles his way to the top and arrives panting to plant the banner of Fatty's innocence . . . Tragic Roscoe, the poor bastard didn't have a chance'

NEW YORK NEWS

'Riveting . . . the full and unvarnished story of the dreadful ordeal suffered by Roscoe Arbuckle is clearly told and fully documented . . . It is a book that had to be written. It clears Arbuckle's name, though several movie moguls of the 1920s come out of the story very badly indeed'

SCREEN INTERNATIONAL

'Employing court transcripts once thought destroyed and interviews with the surviving principals, David Yallop meticulously tears apart the prosecution case. A fascinating work of film history which catches the social currents of the times'

THE NEW YORK TIMES

'Three years of fanatical research worthy of the Sacco-Vanzetti case have gone into David Yallop's angry vindication of Arbuckle. Yallop makes a convincing case that the generous woman-shy and somewhat prudish comic was victimized by a posse of women's clubs, ministers and a Hearst press hungering after circulation-boosting scandals. THE DAY THE LAUGHTER STOPPED is a grim and lurid chronicle of an age. This engrossing book signals that a revival of Fatty Arbuckle's funny and long-neglected films is overdue'

LOS ANGELES EXAMINER

'A fascinating story of a witch-hunt and a thorough vindication of a man'

PUBLISHERS WEEKLY

'As the book unreels the sense of outrage mounts'

CHICAGO NEWS

'A stunning picture not only of the trials but also of Silent Hollywood and all its excesses . . . Yallop's story gives a uniquely fascinating picture of Hollywood that is both moving and unforgettable'

MOVIE BOOK CLUB PREVIEW

Also by David Yallop

IN GOD'S NAME
TO ENCOURAGE THE OTHERS
BEYOND REASONABLE DOUBT
DELIVER US FROM EVIL

and published by Corgi Books

THE DAY THE LAUGHTER STOPPED

The True Story of Fatty Arbuckle

David Yallop

Filmography by Samuel A. Gill

CORGI BOOKS

THE DAY THE LAUGHTER STOPPED

A CORGI BOOK 0 552 13452 X

Originally published in Great Britain by
Hodder and Stoughton Ltd

PRINTING HISTORY
Hodder & Stoughton edition published 1976
Revised and updated Corgi edition published 1991

This book is set in 10/11pt Plantin by
Kestrel Data, Exeter

Corgi Books are published by Transworld Publishers Ltd, 61-63 Uxbridge Road, Ealing, London W5 5SA, in Australia by Transworld Publishers (Australia) Pty Ltd, 15-23 Helles Avenue, Moorebank, NSW 2170, and in New Zealand by Transworld Publishers (NZ) Ltd, Cnr Moselle and Waipareira Avenues, Henderson, Auckland.

Made and printed in Great Britain by
Cox & Wyman Ltd, Reading, Berks.

To Fletcher and Lucy

Saki observed '*Hors d'oeuvres* have always a pathetic interest for me: they remind me of one's childhood that one goes through, wondering what the next course is going to be like – and during the rest of the menu one wishes one had eaten more of the hors d'oeuvres.' Thank you for sharing your *hors d'oeuvres* with me.

Author's Acknowledgements

This book would not have been possible without the cooperation of many people, some of whom agreed to help me only on the strict understanding that their names not be made public. I have respected their wishes. I am grateful to them and to the following (listed in alphabetical order):

Johnny Aitchison, Addie McPhail Arbuckle, Barbara Arbuckle, Clyde Arbuckle, Doris Deane Arbuckle, Helen Arbuckle, Minta Durfee Arbuckle, DeWitt Bodeen, David Bradley, Kevin Brownlow, Herb Caen, Chief Judge Oliver Carter, Dr James D. Causey, Betty Compson, Judge Sam Conti, Jackie Coogan, Alan De Witt, Paul Durfee, Mrs Fred Fischbach, Bill Foster (official court reporter during the Arbuckle trials), Mrs Leo Friedman, Ed 'Scoop' Gleeson, Judge George B. Harris, Randolph Hearst, Babe London, Ben Lyon, Colleen Moore, Turk Murphy and Pete Chute of Earthquake Magoons (San Francisco), Marion Nixon, Adela Rogers St Johns, Judge Robert Schnocke, Mrs Kay Schmulowitz, Judge Albert Tharlorborg, Judge Stanley Theigee, King Vidor, and Judge Alphonso Zerpali.

The management and staff of the St Francis Hotel, San Fransisco; Rev. Joseph Falanga and the Catholic Church Authorities in Los Angeles (present owners of Roscoe Arbuckle's West Adams Boulevard home); G. Brokaw, Chief Customs Officer of San Francisco; port authorities in charge of Alcatraz; San Fransisco District Attorney John Jay Ferdon and his staff; the staff of the district attorney of Los Angeles; Mr Burton Hayes and Mr Joe Ruocco of the County Clerk's Office, Hall of Justice, San Fransisco; the staff and officials of the Superior Court of the State of California, City and County of San Fransisco; the staff and officials of the US District Court, Northern District of California.

The chief Librarian and staff of the University of London; the librarian and staff of the Department des Periodiques Annexe de Versailles; Tony Slide of the American Film Institute, Washington; and staffs of the following libraries and organizations: the Academy of Motion Picture Arts and Sciences,

Hollywood; the Bibliothéque Nationale, Paris; the Boston Public Library; Cinémathèque Française, Paris; the Motion Picture Country House and Lodge, California; the Museum of Modern Art, New York; the New York Public Library and the Library and Museum of the Performing Arts, New York City; the San Fransisco Public Library; and various departments and libraries of the University of California, both at Berkeley and Los Angeles.

Mr Blackbeard and the staff of the National Newspaper Archives, in San Fransisco; and the editors and staffs of *Debretts*, the Los Angeles *Examiner*, the Los Angeles *Times*, the San Francisco *Examiner*.

The filmography at the back of the book, the result of three years' intensive research, is the most comprehensive list of Roscoe Arbuckle's films ever published. Credit for this remarkable achievement goes to Samuel A. Gill, Archivist at the Academy of Motion Picture Arts and Sciences in Hollywood. Neither Sam nor I would claim that the list is complete, but that it includes 150 more titles than any previous list speaks for itself.

That this book exists at all is due very largely to three people. For their help, encouragement and commitment over a three-year period that must at times have seemed like a lifetime to them, I offer grateful thanks to my editors, Maureen Rissik and Pat McNees Mancini, and to my American publisher, Tom McCormack.

Filmographer's Acknowledgements

The filmography was compiled with the assistance and cooperation of many individuals and organizations to whom the compiler, Samuel A. Gill, expresses his gratitude: Minta Durfee, Doris Deane, Addie McPhail, King Vidor, Babe London, Mrs Al St John, Anthony Slide, Leonard Maltin, John and Dorothy Hampton, David Bradley, Kenneth Munden, Sam E. Brown, Mildred Simpson and Library Staff of the Academy of Motion Picture Arts and Sciences, American Film Institute, Kansas City Public Library, Library of Congress, The Museum of Modern Art, University of California at Los Angeles, University of Texas at Austin, and above all to his parents, Dr George L. and Florence Gill.

CONTENTS

Roscoe Arbuckle's
Suite in the St Francis Hotel
San Francisco

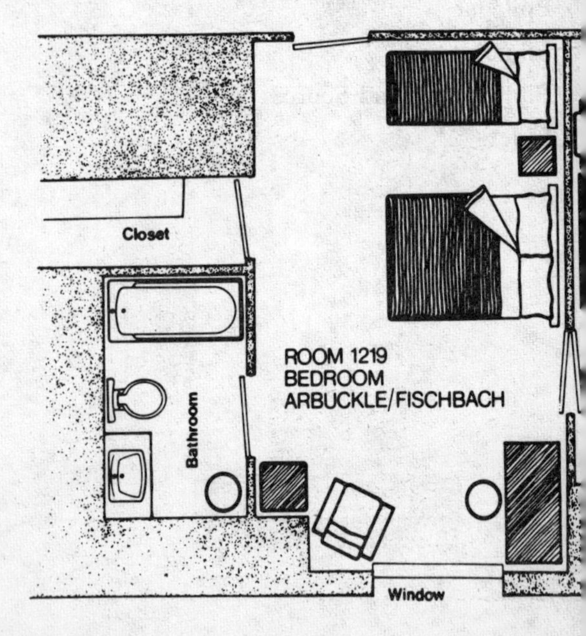

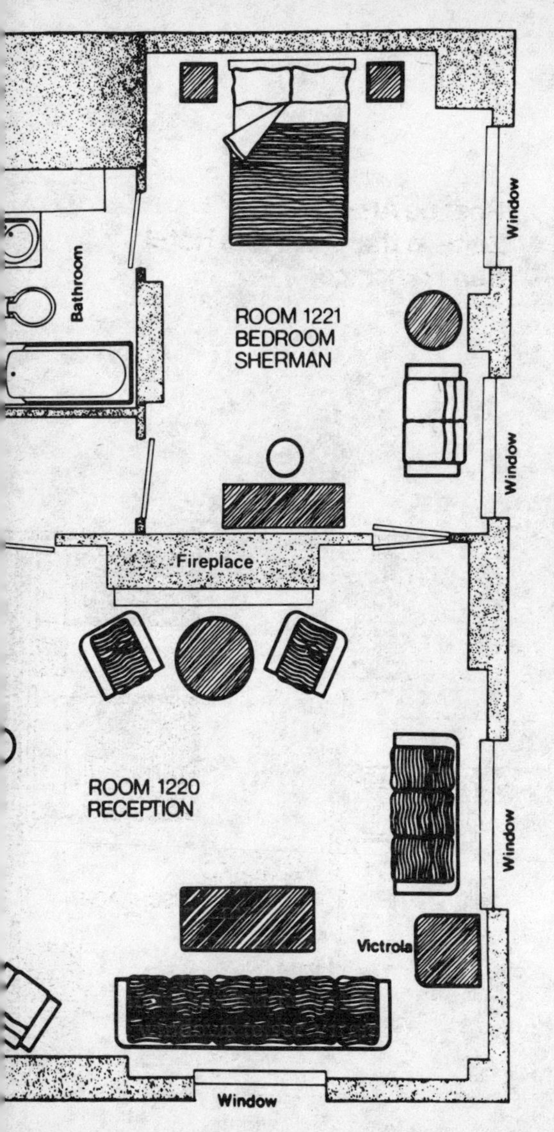
Bathroom
ROOM 1221
BEDROOM
SHERMAN
Window
Window
Fireplace
POWELL STREET
ROOM 1220
RECEPTION
Window
Victrola
Window

But one day in September 1921, all of the laughter stopped. Overnight what had been innocent fun was suddenly being denounced as 'another Hollywood drunken orgy' or 'one more shocking example of sex depravity'. The day our laughter stopped was the day that Roscoe Arbuckle was accused of having caused the death of Virginia Rappe.

—Buster Keaton

PROLOGUE

It was a hot afternoon. The date: Monday, 5 September 1921. The place: a luxury suite in the St Francis Hotel, San Francisco. A lively party was in progress. The music played loudly and guests danced with abandon to a stream of fox trots. The Roaring Twenties and the Jazz Age had just begun; with the Eighteenth Amendment, so had Prohibition. Here the guests drank freely, which meant that everyone at the party was breaking the law. Still, they were in good company – it was Labor Day, and millions of their fellow citizens were doing precisely the same. Most of those millions would pay a small price for their pleasure: a few dollars for the bootleg liquor and a hangover the following day. For a number of the guests at the St Francis party, the price would be more. Much more . . .

Film actress Virginia Rappe (pronounced Rap-PAY)[1] arrived at the St Francis Hotel just after midday. She

---

[1] One of the curiosities of the Arbuckle story is the constancy with which facts have been garbled over the years, a general carelessness that has resulted in a chaos of misspelled names. Even 'newspapers of record' such as the *New York Times* were sloppy, perhaps in their haste to beat other newspapers to a story. Rappe, in some accounts, sports an accent mark. Semnacher is just as often Seminacher. Bambina Maude is sometimes Maude Bambina. And writers have had a field day with Fred Fischbach, who is most often Fred Fishback, but is also listed as Fishbeck, Fishbach, and Fischback. Irvan Weinberg seemed an odd spelling, but when Doris Deane died, I could trace him no further. I have tried to track down the right names, but in some cases I have simply had to make an educated guess.

had been having a late breakfast at the Palace Hotel with her manager, Al Semnacher, and a friend of his, Bambina Maude Delmont, when someone called to tell her that Mr Sherman and Mr Arbuckle were at the St Francis. Excited, Virginia told her friends that they had been invited to join the two men. Virginia mused, 'I don't know what Arbuckle that may be. It may be Roscoe, but I didn't even know he was in town. But it may be he.'

As the breakfast progressed, they speculated on the possibility that the 'Mr Arbuckle' was indeed Roscoe 'Fatty' Arbuckle. It seemed unlikely that the world-famous film comedian was in San Francisco. Wherever he went and whatever he did, Roscoe was news. Scanning the papers, they found no mention of his presence in the city.

'It might be Andy Arbuckle, whom I know,' Maude Delmont remarked.

Virginia Rappe intended to find out. 'We will go over and see,' she declared.

The two women waited impatiently for Al to appear at the Palace Hotel's main entrance with his car. Eventually they walked over to the garage. There they found Al Semnacher arguing with one of the garage attendants. He had left instructions the night before that his car should be washed. It had not been done.

With Al grumbling about the inefficiency of the hotel staff, they drove to the St Francis. Virginia got out, saying, 'I'll go up first and see who it is, and you call me in five minutes, Maudie. If it's someone I don't care to bother with, I will say I will come right down. But if it's all right and I want you to come up, I'll say, "Come up." ' With that, Virginia ran up the steps to the hotel's imposing front entrance and vanished.

Obviously everything was 'all right', for when Maude phoned the luxury suite and asked for her friend, she heard Virginia's voice saying, 'Come up.' It occurred to Maude that although Virginia was obviously happy with their mysterious hosts, she might feel different. She told

Al to wait in the lobby. 'If we want to stay up there a little while, I'll have you paged, and you come up.' Twenty minutes later, Al was paged to Room 1220.

Al Semnacher must have thought he had struck gold when he entered the room. As a manager of film stars he knew better than most the importance of making influential contacts in the business. Besides Virginia and Maude, there were four men in the room, one of whom Al had never seen before. The other three were well-known to every manager in the business: actor Lowell Sherman, director Fred Fischbach, and Roscoe 'Fatty' Arbuckle, the million-dollar-a-year comedian. As befitted America's funniest man, Arbuckle exuded joy. Dressed in his pyjamas and bathrobe, he had the group roaring with laughter. There was plenty of bootleg whisky and gin, and everybody was helping himself. Maude was putting the whisky away as quickly as she could; in the space of an hour she consumed ten Scotches. During the same period, Virginia sipped orange blossoms (a mixture of gin and orange juice) and contented herself with three glasses. Inevitably, as the spirits in the bottles went down, the spirits of the partygoers rose. About thirty minutes after Virginia and her friends arrived, two showgirls, Alice Blake and Zey Prevon, joined the gathering. The boys phoned down for a Victrola and some records, and the party began to hum.

The fourth man at the party was Ira Fortlouis. Although unconnected with the movies and therefore not in a position to offer any of the girls 'a part in my next major production', he was in a line of business that was close to their hearts. He was a gown salesman.

The suite consisted of three large rooms and a couple of bathrooms. The rooms – 1219, 1220 and 1221 – had magnificent views of the city, and the girls oohed and ahed as they pointed out various landmarks. Maude Delmont turned from one of the windows to see Virginia emerging from the bathroom adjacent to 1219. The pretty young actress joined Maude at the window and confided to her friend that Roscoe had got hold of her in the bathroom. Maude, intent on having a good time, shrugged the incident off. The next thing she knew, Roscoe was back in the bathroom again with Virginia. Then, moving from the bathroom, Roscoe locked the door to 1219, shielding it from the view of Maude and the rest of the guests in 1220. Maude again shrugged it off, since Virginia had had only three drinks. Maude had noticed earlier when Roscoe had pulled up a chair and sat next to Virginia that he appeared to be more intoxicated than the other men – he showed it in his eyes and his general manner – but Virginia was a big girl and could take care of herself.

Maude got up and began to dance with Lowell Sherman. As time passed, she was conscious of the fact that neither Roscoe nor Virginia had rejoined the main party, and she wondered why her young friend had not re-emerged from Room 1219. She didn't like the idea of Virginia's being in there alone with Roscoe. It didn't look nice.

The Victrola was playing a current hit of the period, 'I've Got the Wonder-Where-He-Went-and-When-He's-Coming-Back Blues'. As vocalist Marion Harris wailed the words, Maude swayed in time to the music. Giggling, she remarked to Lowell Sherman, 'I'm so warm. I wish I could take this dress off and slip into something cool. Do you mind if I slip on a pair of pyjamas?' Lowell offered her a pair of his. They went into 1221, where Lowell opened a dresser drawer, pulled out a pair of yellow silk pyjamas, and handed them to her. Then to show how much of a gentleman he was, he left the room while Maude disrobed. She was certainly taking up Sherman's offer to make herself at home. Maude emerged resplendent in pyjamas. She continued dancing and, as she later expressed it, 'having my pleasure'.

As the party progressed, Maude became obsessed with the thought that Arbuckle and Virginia were together behind a locked door. From time to time she moved to the door and called out to her friend, but there was no reply. She turned to Al Semnacher about the situation, but he and Ira Fortlouis had left to take a car ride around town.

Time passed, and Maude became more and more concerned at the continued absence of Roscoe and Virginia. She called out again. After getting no response, she took off her shoe and began hammering on the door with the heel. The others, presuming this was a party trick of Maude's, took no notice. But after an hour had elapsed, something occurred that made them all take notice. From behind the locked door they heard Virginia screaming. The sounds were those of a woman in agony. Maude repeatedly hammered on the door, but there was no response. Grabbing the phone, Maude screamed, 'Send someone up, please, right away. There is someone here in trouble.' After replacing the receiver, Maude began kicking on the locked door.

'You'd better get changed, Maude,' Zey Prevon exclaimed. 'The manager is coming up. Go in and slip your dress on, quick!'

Hurrying back to Sherman's room, Maude Delmont quickly slipped out of the pyjamas and into her dress. Mr Boyle, the assistant manager of the St Francis, appeared and called out for Arbuckle to open the door. The door opened. There stood Roscoe, minus his bathrobe, his pyjamas wringing wet and clinging to his body. On his face was the famous Arbuckle foolish grin; on his head, Virginia Rappe's Panama hat. 'She's in here,' he said.

With Mr Boyle leading, the entire party rushed into Room 1219. Virginia was lying on the twin bed nearest the wall; screaming and tearing at her clothes. She was fully dressed. As she tore the clothes from her body, everyone present heard her yell, 'I am hurt, I am dying. He did it, Maudie.' One moment she was conscious and hysterical, the next semiconscious.

Maude, who had been a nurse, concluded that a cold

bath would 'brace her up'. They removed her green dress, shirtwaist, brassiere, panties and stockings.

Virginia clutched at her stomach and screamed, 'I am hurt.'

Maude asked her, 'What happened to you, Virginia?' and the young girl replied simply, 'I don't know.'

Roscoe moved indifferently in and out of the room as the others fussed around the distressed girl. Fred Fischbach picked her up like a baby doll, carried her to the full bathtub, dropped her in it and then pulled her out. He carried her back and placed her on the bed. Maude was too excited to organize the drying, so the others rubbed Virginia thoroughly. After she had been wrapped in a sheet, Fred Fischbach, at Mr Boyle's suggestion, went down to the reception desk and registered the sick girl in Room 1227.

Picking her up, Roscoe walked out of the suite and made his way along the corridor towards 1227, accompanied by the assistant hotel manager and Maude. Fearing that Roscoe was about to let her slip, Mr Boyle took the girl from him and carried her the rest of the way.

When she was settled, the hotel doctor was called. The house detective had already arrived, and the party was virtually over. Everyone but Roscoe Arbuckle was worried about Virginia Rappe's condition. Alice Blake, Zey Prevon, and Fred Fischbach all came to see if they could help. Roscoe Arbuckle didn't come near her again.

While they waited for the hotel doctor, Virginia continued to writhe, crying and complaining of terrible pain. 'Maudie, what has happened to me?' she asked. 'What could he have done to me?'

Puzzled, Maude asked in return, 'Virginia, don't you remember anything at all?'

'Not one thing,' the girl replied. 'I do not, no.'

At this point the hotel physician, Dr Beardslee, arrived. After listening to the garbled accounts of the partygoers, Dr Beardslee concluded that Virginia was hysterical because she was drunk. His examination was slight. He felt her abdomen, and as he did so she screamed, 'Don't touch me! I can't stand it!' He gave her a morphine injection to calm her, but she continued to cry aloud, complaining of pain. Nevertheless, he held to his opinion that her only problem was having drunk too much. Maude Delmont did not agree. She knew that the girl had had only three drinks and must be seriously hurt.

The doctor gave Virginia a second injection of morphine, which quieted her a little. Satisfied that the situation was under control and that his patient would soon be suffering only a hangover, the doctor left.

Maude undressed and got into bed beside the now-sleeping girl. Although the party guests had left the room, the hotel detective stayed to keep her company. Some two and a half hours later, Maude woke up. Virginia was still sleeping. Maude and the house detective went to the party suite, collected the last of the liquor, brought it back to Virginia's room, and finished it off. At about three o'clock in the morning the detective left.

At six-thirty in the morning Maude was awakened by Virginia's crying out in pain. Dr Beardslee was summoned and quickly gave Virginia a morphine injection. As Virginia had been unable to urinate all night, Maude asked the doctor to catheterize her. He used a glass catheter, the biggest that Maude had ever seen. The urine came out thick with blood, filling about two-thirds of the glass that Maude was holding. To Maude's startled 'What in heaven is that, Doctor?', he replied, 'Blood.' At this point Maude realized the seriousness of Virginia's condition, that she was probably suffering from an internal injury. Saying no more to Dr Beardslee, she resolved to dismiss him from the case. She did not care for his attitude or his appearance.

After the doctor had left, Maude, persuaded of the extreme urgency of the situation, telephoned a Dr Rumwell, who had been a friend of hers for nine years.

When Rumwell learned that there was already a doctor on the case, he was reluctant to come to the hotel. 'You understand, Maudie,' he told her, 'that I cannot take the case until you have dismissed the hotel physician.' Maude said that she understood, but that she still wanted him to come over. He obliged her, but when Maude asked him to give the young woman a thorough examination, he demurred, saying that he had come merely as a friend.

Desperately, Maude told him of what had taken place at the party, how Virginia had complained of being injured, and how Dr Beardslee had catheterized her. She declared that Arbuckle had lain on Virginia and crushed her. Virginia confirmed this herself, saying she thought her body had been crushed by the weight of the 266-pound comedian. The bed on which the partygoers had found Virginia had been soaking wet, just as Arbuckle's pyjamas had been, and to Virginia this was evidence that Arbuckle had assaulted her.

Maude then told the doctor of the blood that had been passed, but Rumwell only repeated, 'I cannot take the case until Dr Beardslee has been dismissed. You understand that, Maudie. Dr Beardslee and I have worked together. I cannot afford any mix-up with him.' Maude said that she understood, and the doctor left without examining Virginia Rappe.

At about noon that day, Tuesday, he returned; this time he did examine the girl. He checked her lungs with a stethoscope, then looked at the little marks on her neck, her arm, and her leg. He felt her abdomen, but when he lay his head on her stomach, she exclaimed, 'Oh, please, Doctor! I cannot bear the weight of your head. It hurts so.'

Soothingly the doctor reassured her: 'I'm not going to hurt you. I'll be just as easy as I can be.' He made no attempt to examine her internally.

When he had finished, the doctor did not offer his diagnosis to either woman. He simply told Maude

Delmont that he would order a hot-water bottle and some medicine from the store. He did this, and left.

By Tuesday evening an exhausted Maude telephoned Dr Rumwell, requesting assistance. He sent a nurse, Miss Jameson, and the two women kept vigil through the night by the sick girl's bedside.

By Wednesday morning Virginia was still unable to urinate normally. Nurse Jameson telephoned Rumwell, who advised her to catheterize the patient. The waste fluid resembled that of the first catheterization.

Throughout this period Virginia asked a number of times what had happened to her.

At about noon on Thursday, Virginia Rappe was moved to the Wakefield Sanatorium.

Shortly after noon on Friday she died.

The foregoing account of what happened at that fateful Labor Day party and in the days that followed is based entirely on a verbatim record of the testimony that was given by Maude Delmont at the coroner's inquest into the death of Virginia Rappe. Before the inquest, a post-mortem examination of the young woman's body revealed that the cause of death was peritonitis, caused by a rupture of the urinary bladder.

Within twenty-four hours of Virginia Rappe's death, Maude Delmont had sworn out a complaint against Roscoe Arbuckle, accusing him of the murder of Virginia Rappe. Twenty-four hours later, Arbuckle was arrested and officially charged with murder.

The state's star witness, Bambina Maude Delmont, never gave evidence in court. She initiated the charge that Arbuckle had murdered Virginia Rappe, and she told this story at the coroner's inquest. But Maude Delmont was never again allowed to give official testimony. And there was a very good reason for this: Maude Delmont's account was a tissue of lies.

Within twenty-four hours of Roscoe Arbuckle's arrest on the charge of murder, the district attorney, Matthew

Brady, was aware that the testimony of his star witness was riddled with lies. Yet he pursued Arbuckle through the courts of San Francisco for eight months.

Thus was born the myth of Arbuckle the rapist, Arbuckle the murderer, Arbuckle the monster. On that Labor Day there began an American drama, with a cast of thousands, which would ultimately cost, at a conservative estimate, one hundred million dollars. Besides the drama, there is the fantasy: the majority of the people who have heard of Fatty Arbuckle will tell you he is the man who killed a girl with a Coke bottle.

So this book does not deal merely with the events of one party. It is the life story of Hollywood's first comedy star to sign a three-million-dollar contract, a man who in 1921 was one of the best-known, best-loved people on this planet. And it is the story of much more, because the day the laughter stopped for Roscoe Conkling Arbuckle, it did not stop just for him. In the aftermath of that party came censorship, repression, fear, the Hays Office, two generations of an industry running scared before the self-appointed arbiters of morality in America. It is reasonable to say that on one hot September day seventy years ago there occurred a macabre event that is still having an effect on everyone in America today.

To any reader who has previous beliefs about any of the events I am about to record, I offer a suggestion: forget all that you have read or been told. Here, for the first time, is the truth.

PART ONE

BEFORE

The United States in the late nineteenth century was an exciting country to live in. The whole western seaboard was opening up to an invasion of determined pioneers striking out from the East. In the West, it was said, a man could be penniless at breakfast and a millionaire by suppertime, as the result of a gold or silver strike. Thousands, dreaming of easy wealth, literally fell by the wayside in the great trek west. Many others were content to become ranchers or farmers along the way. One of those who settled for the gold of wheat fields in Kansas was William Goodrich Arbuckle.

Born in Indiana in 1849, William Arbuckle settled just outside the town of Smith Center, Kansas, in 1880, when the town was at the precise geographical centre of the United States. The life of a farmer then was not without danger. A man could get an arrow in the back while farming the land – the massacre of the Seventh United States Cavalry, commanded by General Custer, had taken place a mere four years earlier. And with the nation still licking its wounds from the Civil War, a man could also get himself killed just by whistling the wrong song.

Roscoe Arbuckle was later to say, 'My birth and a cyclone blew Smith Center off of the map. The place has not been heard of since.' There was to be a cyclone in Roscoe's life, but not till thirty-four years later. It is perhaps fitting that Roscoe, about whom a million words of myth and lies would eventually be written, should create his own fantasy about his first hour on earth. The fact is that 24 March 1887, was a warm, pleasant day in Smith Center. William Arbuckle and his eldest son Arthur – William had four children – were out early working in the fields that day. From time to time William would leave his son and stroll back to the sod hut that was their home. He would stay a few minutes, then return without comment and resume working. At dusk they returned to the hut. As they entered, William turned to his son and said casually, 'Come on over here and meet your new brother.' Moving to his parents' bed, Arthur saw in his mother's arms a huge, red-faced baby boy with a face so fat that the closed eyes were hidden. Staring in awe at the 14-pound bundle, Arthur said, 'Oh, Christ!'

For some reason, William Arbuckle, who was an ardent Democrat, named his latest son after a notorious right-wing Republican, Roscoe Conkling.

Recalling his early life in Smith Center, Roscoe would later describe an idyllic childhood for the press. Speaking of his earliest Christmas memories, he said,

> Now, let me think, yes. I was only five or six years of age, a good little boy, and it was back in Smith Center, Kansas, the little western town where I was born. Naturally, at that early date, my mind ran to tin soldiers and locomotives, candy, ice-cream cones and popcorn balls. In those days, it was a long, long way to slapstick comedy and the dramatic possibilities of custard pie, and I never worried about either.
>
> It is my earliest recollection that my mother was the best first-aid to Santa Claus in existence, and that my Christmas stocking never lacked anything in depth or in the variety and desirability of its contents. On this occasion, if memory does not fail me, it began with a big red apple and continued down through oranges and nuts and marbles and knives to the most deafening of gaudy tin horns.
>
> If the truth must be told, my innate fondness for custard pies dates back to this epoch of my career. Also

the memory of a big freezer full of chocolate ice cream half-buried under the snow is still fresh in my mind.

My mother always insisted that we all sing Christmas carols together on Christmas night, and even as a very small lad I can remember my father's deep bass and my mother's soprano, singing the quaint old hymns. Our Christmas tree was always larger than any of the neighbours', and it seemed to me to be a never-failing treasure trove.

I've spent many different Christmases in many different parts of the country, but never, even in New York, have I enjoyed the holiday as much as I did back in the old days in Smith Center.

Presumably the truth would have been less palatable to film fans. *The Arbuckle family moved from Kansas when Roscoe was less than two years old. His early life was one of extreme poverty. He was regularly beaten by his father, and the harsh reality of the sod hut was a far remove from freezers full of chocolate ice cream. The most interesting fact about Roscoe's childhood is that he did not have one.*

During the autumn of 1888, William Arbuckle decided that the pioneers who had pushed on to California were smarter than those who had settled in the Midwest. The end of the rainbow, wherever it was, was not to be found in Kansas. He sold his farm and took the Arbuckle family nearly two thousand miles west, to Santa Ana, California, a small town near Los Angeles which would later become famous as the home of Disneyland. After opening a 'small hotel' – really a double house, at 826-828 North Birch Street – he promptly left his wife and children there and went north to Watsonville, California, apparently to look for the elusive pot of gold.

With the senior Arbuckle gone, Roscoe had to help out almost as soon as he could walk. He'd never lost his early fatness, and his playmates quickly gave him the nickname 'Fatty', which would stay with him throughout his life. The fat was in fact mainly muscle. He seemed to thrive on all work and little play, and even the thrashings his father gave him each time he returned to the North Birch Street house could not keep the youth down for long. (The antagonism William Arbuckle showed towards his youngest child is something of a mystery. One member of the Arbuckle clan suggested to me that the reason for it was William's suspicion that he was not Roscoe's father. Since Mrs Arbuckle was a devout, hard-working Baptist, this would be surprising.)

Roscoe was seldom in school. If he wasn't helping out around the house, he could invariably be found at the local theatre, the Grand Opera House. At a time when the phrase 'live entertainment' still had some meaning, Roscoe's idea of bliss was to creep in the stage door and watch the visiting company rehearse. One such company gave Roscoe Arbuckle his first stage experience.

The Frank Bacon Stock Company came to Santa Ana during the summer of 1895 with a revue called 'Turned Up'. One of the sketches involved a small black boy, and when the touring company began to rehearse, they realized that they had lost their resident boy. The rehearsal ground to a halt. Telling the cast to take ten minutes' rest, Bacon strode towards the stage door in search of a large whisky and a small boy. He found eight-year-old Roscoe standing barefoot at the door, gazing wistfully at the actors. Bacon asked him if he would like to play the part of the black boy, and Roscoe, delighted, said yes. Bacon told him to go home and get his socks and shoes, explaining, 'If you are going to play the part of a pickaninny, your white legs must not show.' The boy began to cry. 'If I go home, my mother won't let me come back.' Bacon solved the problem by blacking Roscoe's legs and feet as well as his face. Roscoe's fee for his first week's work was fifty cents.

Between 1895 and 1899 he took every opportunity to get involved in the theatre's productions. One week he was assistant to Marvo the hypnotist, the next a demure little girl in a melodrama. His schoolteachers often lectured his harassed, overworked mother about his constant absence from the classroom, saying Roscoe would never amount to anything unless he learned his multiplication tables and what Julius Caesar had said when he landed in Britain. But if he was missing a traditional education, he was learning a great deal about the stage, which he had decided to make his career.

He was by now the only child remaining in the Santa Ana home. Some had gone out to seek their fortunes, others had joined their father in Watsonville. Suddenly the young boy had to cope with the most devastating of situations: his mother died. His oldest sister Nora, by now married to Walter St John, helped Roscoe through the traumatic period that immediately followed the death of their mother, then packed his bags and put him on a train for Watsonville and William Arbuckle.

Robert Louis Stevenson's remark that 'To travel hopefully is a better thing than to arrive' certainly applied to Roscoe. The twelve-year-old alighted at Watsonville only to find that his father had moved on. As he sat in the station clutching his cardboard suitcase and sobbing, a man named Sam Booker walked up to him. Booker had purchased William Arbuckle's hotel, and Arbuckle had then left town without leaving a forwarding address, despite the fact – or perhaps because of it – that he knew Roscoe was coming to join him.

Booker took Roscoe to his small railroad hotel and gave him a bed for the night. They agreed that Roscoe would help out in the hotel in return for free bed and board. Sam Booker, meanwhile, began trying to trace William Arbuckle – buying the man's hotel was one thing; a twelve-year-old boy was not part of the deal.

Between washing plates and setting tables, the youth was given lessons by the local teacher, a young woman named Pansy Jones. Pansy Jones quickly discovered what Roscoe's teachers in Santa Ana already knew – that his only interest was in the stage – but, unlike his previous teachers, she did not regard the stage as the invention of the devil. She actually encouraged Roscoe's musical talent.

The local theatre, the Victory, regularly held amateur-talent nights, with a top prize of five dollars. Pansy persuaded Roscoe to enter. It was traditional at that time in the theatre for the management to literally hook off the stage any act that it felt was going badly or running over. The night that Roscoe sang his songs, he was warmly received. Inspired by his success, he announced to the packed theatre that he would sing some more. The stage manager thought otherwise, and the hook shot out from the wings. Still singing, Roscoe danced nimbly about the stage, avoiding the hook, to the huge delight of the audience. While finishing his encores, he bowed to acknowledge the applause. The hook crept out again and was about to pull him off when he somersaulted and did a pratfall right into the orchestra pit. It brought the house down. He won the five dollars and became a popular regular Friday-night act.

Besides having Roscoe help out in the hotel, Sam Booker gave him the job of delivering meat around town in a horse-drawn wagon. Roscoe soon became a familiar feature of Watsonville, singing his head off as he came hurtling down Main Street. On one occasion he took a corner too fast, and the wagon toppled over. When Roscoe got back to the hotel, Booker surveyed the wrecked truck and the dusty meat, turned to Roscoe and drawled, 'You know, boy, I think you'd better move on. There's another world to live in.' The same day word arrived that William Arbuckle had been located in San Jose.

In San Jose, Roscoe discovered that his father, who was working a small farm, had married again, a homely woman by the name of Mary Ellen Gordan. It was a second marriage for both, and together they already had twelve children. Undeterred, they went on to produce two more.

The lifestyle Roscoe had established in Santa Ana and

Watsonville continued. At every opportunity he played hooky from Santa Clara High School; his father regularly thrashed him. By the time Roscoe was thirteen, his father bowed to the fact that Roscoe would not stay in school, and the boy was put to work on the farm. In later years Roscoe wryly recalled, 'I went to Santa Clara High, where I graduated in football, baseball and avoirdupois.'

He treated farm work much the same as he had schoolwork. The hay press held little excitement for him. He knew what he wanted to be, and it was not one of America's great farmers. At the slightest opportunity he would dance, sing and fool around. Fortunately, his stepmother was a kindly woman, and though she and Roscoe never developed a true mother-son relationship, she prevailed upon her husband to show greater tolerance towards his son. Of Scottish descent, she was more than a match for her second husband. Her youngest son, Clyde, said to me, 'Mother had two driving urges. One, to keep out of debt. Two, to keep her children out of San Quentin.'

Even at this age Roscoe was showing signs of the Pied Piper quality that would bring him worldwide popularity. He was in constant demand at socials and concerts, and achieved real fame among his peers when he became champion pie-eater of the county. (His weight at the time was 215 pounds. It was all muscle, but the nickname 'Fatty' had stuck, though it didn't hurt him at thirteen the way it would in later years.)

In 1902 William Arbuckle moved again. This time he acquired a restaurant in Santa Clara. Roscoe was employed in the restaurant on a fixed wage – although the wage usually remained fixed in William Arbuckle's pocket.

Roscoe's stepbrother, Clyde Arbuckle, recalled that time for me:

> I tell you, Roscoe worked like a dog in that restaurant. He hardly ever got paid. One particular night [the

restaurant was open twenty-four hours a day] Roscoe is trying unsuccessfully to get the money he is owed out of his father. The hassle is going on all night, with Dad in the kitchen and Roscoe and Charlie [another brother] waiting on tables. Just before dawn in comes the local shoemaker, a German by the name of Friedrich Zipelheim. Now this Zipelheim has a reputation in town for salty language. He throws himself into a chair and shouts at Roscoe, 'Hey, fat boy, I want ham and eggs. Move that fat ass and get them here damn quick.' Now, it's been a long night for Roscoe, what with one thing and another. He takes one look at Zipelheim and then he bursts into beautiful song that can be heard blocks away: 'Hey, Pa, this son of a bitch wants ham and eggs.'

Roscoe supplemented his nonexistent salary in a number of ways. He worked at the Pabst beer café, serving beer. On amateur nights at the Unique Theatre he would either entertain the audience with his rendition of 'The Holy City', or he would sell ten-, twenty- and thirty-cent tickets for the theatre, for pocket money.

Living in San Jose at this time were two men who were destined to make significant contributions to the motion picture industry: Jesse Lasky and Sid Grauman, Jr. Grauman's father, impressed with the quality of Arbuckle's singing, gave him a permanent job singing illustrated songs at the Unique Theatre, which he owned. Roscoe would sing about the moonlight, the river, the girl – real moon-June-spoon material. He would warble 'Tell Mother That You Saw Me' while gorgeously-coloured slides with the lyrics were projected on a screen to his left, thereby 'illustrating' the song. Sometimes the slides got behind the song, but when the singer and the slides did not finish together, Roscoe merely improvised an extra verse. He received a salary of $17.50 a week.

One night in 1904 Sid Grauman, Sr, entered the restaurant with a stranger and said, 'Roscoe, I wonder if you would oblige my friend with a song?' Roscoe launched into song, and Grauman's friend was very impressed. He immediately offered seventeen-year-old Roscoe a job for one month at the Portola Café in San Francisco. The stranger was Alexander Pantages, a man with a whole circuit of theatres, clubs and cafés.

San Francisco in 1904 was, as it is today, unique, a city for all seasons. Rudyard Kipling said of it, 'This San Francisco, it is a mad city inhabited for the most part by perfectly insane people whose women own remarkable beauty. It has only one drawback, 'tis almost impossible to leave.' An anonymous poet was more caustic:

> The pioneers came in '49, the whores in '51.
> Between the two they then begat the Native Son.

One of San Francisco's native daughters, prostitute Iodoform Kate, made an international symbol of the red lamp; Kate's red lamp ensured that her customers found their way to her through the city's fogs. One of San Francisco's native sons was publisher William Randolph Hearst, who was largely responsible for creating yellow journalism. (I asked one former Hearst editor what the editorial policy had been during the twenties. He looked at me, amazed, and remarked, 'You mean to say he had an editorial policy?' With one particular editorial policy, Citizen Hearst was later destined to play a crucial role in the destruction of Roscoe Arbuckle.)

During the early years of this century San Francisco attracted an extraordinary variety of people. Heavy-weight champion of the world, black Jack Johnson, in a pearl-grey cutaway and top hat, strolled with a white woman on either arm. And Johnson wasn't the only boxer around town: Joe Gans, Jimmy Britt and Stanley Ketchel were only a few of those who trained and ran riot through the town. Writer Jack London, lawyer Earl Rogers, and boxer Jack Sharkey were once arrested twice on the same night for brawling on the Embarcadero. When the police realized who they had arrested, they apologized and released them. The men refused to leave jail and finally departed only when the police chief threatened to charge them rent.

A thousand strange accents floated on the cool summer breeze: Chinese, Italian, Greek, Hawaiian, Irish, French, Japanese and Scandinavian. Sailors of every size and shape arrived from sixty different countries, bringing with them the food, songs and costumes of their native lands. Tetrazzini, one of the world's great coloraturas, would stop on street corners and sing arias. Blossom Seeley could be heard singing the blues on the beach. The town's high society would leave Nob Hill and gather at the opera to hear Melba or Caruso. Low society contented itself with the jazz clubs imported directly from New Orleans. Those who fancied neither opera nor jazz could listen to performers like Roscoe Arbuckle at the Portola Café.

Roscoe was such a success at the Portola that his one-month contract was extended again and again, until he realized with surprise that he had been singing there for over a year. Then he went on a tour of the Pantages circuit, travelling to theatres and cafés all over the West Coast. During 1905 another western exhibitor, Chris Brown, booked him into the Star Theater in Portland, Oregon – and he became a favourite of visitors to the 1905 Portland Fair. By now his salary had risen to $50.00 a week. Another tour of the Pantages circuit followed, with Arbuckle playing a hundred theatres between Spokane, Washington, and Tucson, Arizona. By April 1906 he was back in San Francisco – in time to witness one of the world's greatest natural disasters.

On the morning of 19 April 1906, emergency editions of the city's newspapers carried headlines like this:

EARTHQUAKE AND FIRE: SAN FRANCISCO IN RUINS

Mayor Eugene Schmidt declared, 'I have ordered my

men to KILL anyone caught looting or taking advantage of any other man or woman in this time.' A number of looters were later shot. (Mayor Schmidt had taken advantage of a number of people in his own time. A fiddler in a dance band before he was elected, he was later found guilty of graft, corruption, bribery, vice and embezzlement. Gavin McNab, one of San Francisco's most famous lawyers and someone who would play a key role in Arbuckle's life many years later, was asked if he thought Schmidt an honest man. He replied, 'Well, I think you should work it out for yourself. I'll give you a clue, though. The night Schmidt was elected mayor every burglar alarm in San Francisco went off automatically.')

Meanwhile, Roscoe found himself being forced at gunpoint to clear debris. He was not the only member of his profession to find himself employed in this manner; John Barrymore was another. Barrymore had been sleeping in the city's finest hotel, the St Francis (which would also figure in Roscoe's life), when he was thrown from his bed by the earthquake. Dazed, he wandered into the street, where an army sergeant put a shovel in his hands and forced him to work among the ruins of the city for twenty-four hours. His family in New York received this news with some scepticism. Ethel Barrymore read her brother's cable to their uncle, Jack Drew, and asked him if he believed it. Drew replied, 'Every word. It took an act of God to get him out of bed, and the United States Army to put him to work.'

Roscoe Arbuckle must have undertaken his next professional engagement, with the makers of Murads cigarettes, with a sense of wry amusement. People opened their newspapers and read the first cigarette testimonial: 'Roscoe Arbuckle enjoys a good smoke, provided it's Murads.'

In the summer of 1906, Roscoe returned to Portland. He was singing his illustrated songs at the Star Theater when an Australian with an accent a mile wide called back stage with an offer. The Australian, comedian and theatre manager Leon Errol, told Arbuckle to 'come on down to the Orpheum [also in Portland] and I'll teach you show business.'

Arbuckle went down in more ways than one. He gave up a job that was paying him $50.00 a week and began working for Errol for half that amount. It was a transaction that indicated foresight and a keen business sense. Roscoe realized that the day of the illustrated song was nearing its end. By taking a fifty per cent cut in salary, he was able to get in on the ground floor of a new field. What he learned from Leon Errol and those around him was worth more than a few dollars: comedy timing, how to tumble and fall, how to apply stage make-up – the tricks of the trade. Arbuckle's range increased enormously: he did burlesque comedy, black-faced monologues, songs. He was becoming an all-round entertainer.

Using the Orpheum as his base, Leon Errol took his company of performers all over the country. On a trip to Butte, Montana, Roscoe added yet another string to his artistic bow.

They were booked to appear at the Last Chance Saloon, where a regular feature was the resident singer, Lilly, a big blonde with large breasts, who had been the uncrowned queen of Butte for some time. The miners would leave their gold dust and guns at the saloon door. Lilly's appearance was invariably the cue for the clientele to roar with delight; they gave each of her songs a ten-minute ovation. It was rumoured that Lilly's popularity owed as much to her horizontal performances as to her vertical ones, but, whatever the reason, Lilly was clearly a big favourite with the men. The only difficulty was that Lilly had a drinking problem, and one night the inevitable happened. Lilly, who always opened the show, didn't show up.

In a panic Errol pushed Roscoe on stage. Now the miners had grown to like Roscoe, but he wasn't Lilly. He began to get the bird as soon as he walked on. By the time he finished, the miners were threatening to rip the place apart if Lilly did not appear immediately. While Leon Errol quietly began to tear his hair out and wish he were back in Sydney, Roscoe walked into Lilly's dressing room and closed the door. The next thing Errol knew, he was confronted by an enormous woman dressed in Lilly's clothes, which looked better on this stranger than they did on Lilly. The woman demurely requested that Errol introduce her as his next artiste. Errol stammered, 'I'm sorry, madam, I'm not auditioning tonight,' and stopped dead. The woman lifted her wig to reveal Roscoe's short blond hair. Roscoe muttered, 'If you don't get me on quick, we'll all be on Boot Hill.' Errol needed no more bidding; the 'surprise artiste' was brought on.

The audience of miners fell silent. It wasn't Lilly, though the clothes were hers. It wasn't Lilly, though the songs were hers. It wasn't Lilly – because this woman sang better. A beautiful soprano voice filled the saloon, and the miners were entranced. They gave 'her' a standing ovation. The fact that Roscoe's body was entirely hairless helped. A star had been born.

Word spread through the town: 'Get down to the Last Chance and hear the new singer.' The charade continued on the second night and then the third. By this time word had reached even Lilly. She staggered into the saloon on the third night, just in time to see Roscoe, who was dressed in her clothes, finishing his third encore of her songs. With a scream of rage she leaped on the stage and tore her wig from his head. Playing the situation for all it was worth, Roscoe affected fear and scrambled among the chairs and tables, followed by the furious Lilly. The miners, convinced that the whole thing was a superbly-rehearsed piece of comedy, howled with laughter as Roscoe, with Lilly in hot pursuit, jumped over tables, swung on lamps, did cartwheels and pratfalls, and finally vanished into the street. The next morning Lilly showed just who was Queen of Butte, and Errol's company left town.

The troupe moved on to Boise, Idaho, and played in a theatre that had once been a church. While Errol packed his bags and headed for the friendlier pastures of New York, Roscoe returned temporarily to the relatively safe pastures of illustrated songs. He secured an engagement in Boise, but it was cut short by his second encounter with natural disaster: the theatre was burned to the ground.

Moving further northwest, he extended his range by working in a number of musical comedies. One of the men he worked with in Seattle was Mack Swain; in a few years' time they would both be working in a lunatic asylum called Keystone.

During the winter of 1907, at the age of twenty, Roscoe was on the move again – this time north to Canada with John Burke's burlesque show, which played first in Vancouver. When the company moved on to Winnipeg and subzero temperatures, the show folded, and Arbuckle was out of work again. He bought a ticket for San Francisco and counted his wealth, $2.00. Roscoe shivered, remembered that the last time he had been in San Francisco quite a good fire had been raging, and went south.

Back in San Francisco he did the round of burlesque theatres, working where he could. Then early in 1908 he signed with the Elwood Tabloid Musical Company, for an engagement that opened in San Francisco and moved on to southern California. They began rehearsals at the Byde A Wyle Theatre on the Pike in Long Beach. As a seasoned performer once again singing illustrated songs, Roscoe was not needed for rehearsals. There were several weeks to kill before opening night, so he had a chance to explore a strange new world, the movies – or, as they were popularly known in 1908, 'canned melodrama'.

At that time films were regarded with suspicion or contempt by people in 'legitimate' theatre, so Roscoe was secretive when he went to the Los Angeles studio of film pioneer Colonel William Selig. (He was so successful in covering his tracks that although at the time he was courting the woman who would become his first wife, Minta Durfee, she had no knowledge of his film-making experience with Selig.)

Roscoe was not alone in approaching the film industry with caution. D. W. Griffith – who more than any other American lifted the flickering pictures on the screen to a new art form – directed under a pseudonym at first, for fear that his colleagues in the theatre might learn what he was doing. Film historians credit Griffith with great vision, suggesting that he realized from the beginning the enormous potential of the cinema; but, far from being keen to mould this stepchild of the stage into a serious art, Griffith was reluctant at first to be associated with it – except that it guaranteed actors $5.00 a day. He considered himself primarily an actor, and though in those days people were asked rather casually to direct, he said to his wife, Linda Arvidson, 'Now, if I take this picture-directing job over and fall down, then, you see, I'll be out of an acting job.' Commenting on the future of film during his early days at the Biograph Company, he said, 'They can't last, I give them a few years . . . Nobody is going to know I ever did this sort of thing when I am a famous playwright.'

The secrecy with which men like Arbuckle and Griffith cloaked their initial involvement in the movies was paralleled in the attitude of early film producers. It is hard to believe that an industry that has so celebrated the movie star avoided publicity during the first decade of the century, but by not advertising, even on the film itself, the names of their actors and directors, producers kept salaries down (and other studios couldn't hire them away as easily). Thus the public was obliged to identify Mary Pickford, for example, by the name of the character she played ('Little Mary'). Florence Lawrence was to change all that with the aid of Carl Laemmle in 1910. Until then she was known simply as 'the Biograph Girl', after the company that featured her. Laemmle lured her away to work for him, partially by promising her the chance to be known by her actual name, which he advertised – a move prompted in part by a natural reluctance to give publicity to a bitter rival. Things were never the same after that. The star system had begun – but it wouldn't develop fully until the end of the decade.

Early in the twentieth century, virtually all of the films made in America were made on the East Coast. They were made on shoe-string budgets, and were usually crude and unimaginative. This did little to inhibit the audiences who watched them in the nickelodeons, where a frequent sign was 'Please do not stamp, the floor may cave in'. By 1908 there were nearly ten thousand exhibitors in the United States. 'Picture shows' ran half an hour or an hour, and were shown continuously all day.

The early moviemakers were not afraid to express themselves on the social issues of the day. (For example, a number of them ridiculed the movement for women's rights, in movies like *Why Mr Nation Wants a Divorce*.) Unencumbered by censorship, the film-makers were free to comment on anything. *Escape from the Asylum* argued sympathetically for Harry Thaw, an excitable young man who had murdered Stanford White, his wife's lover. Thaw had been saved from execution by the testimony of a certain Dr Sheils, who declared that Thaw was suffering from 'Dementia Americana'. Film historian Lewis Jacobs said, 'Observers generally believed that this movie converted many people to the belief that Thaw had been sufficiently punished and that he deserved sympathy.'

By 1908 the industry had begun to move geographically as well as artistically. By 1910 a fifth of the world's films were being made in Chicago and surrounding areas. Then Selig led the way further west to California, shooting interior scenes of *The Count of Monte Cristo* with one 'Count' in Chicago and exterior scenes with another 'Count' on the shores of the Pacific – the audiences apparently didn't mind.

The reason for moving to the West Coast was simple: all summer and most of the winter the weather and the natural light were reasonably constant, so most of the time there was no need for expensive electricity. The variation of virgin landscape in California produced an endless supply of locations, and for film-makers using 'bootleg' cameras, the Mexican border was nearby, in case Edison's spies appeared, as they frequently did.

Thomas Edison had come to the conclusion that he alone was responsible for the invention of the film camera, and he was determined that none should be used unless royalties were paid to him. A number of men took exception to this point of view, and the ranks of the West Coast film-makers were further swelled. A legal judgement of 1902 had said in part, 'It is obvious that Mr Edison was not a pioneer. It is equally obvious that he did not invent the film camera.' Indeed, had he not 'economized' some years earlier by refusing to pay a $150 international patent fee on inventions that made the movie camera more likely to be developed, he might have had stronger claims to royalties later. But he did economize, and thus the 'flickers' were invented almost simultaneously in four different countries. In fact, America at first lagged behind England, France and Italy in the development of its film industry. In 1912, while Griffith was still making one- and two-reel films, Italy produced an eight-reel *Quo Vadis*? It wasn't until 1915 that Griffith (working for Mutual by now) was to establish American domination of the film industry with the production of *The Birth of a Nation*, an epic movie that ended the period of the nickelodeon and brought about the era of the movie palace.

In the meantime, it became apparent to some that the new gold rush was in southern California, because the mushrooming nickelodeons were producing a fortune. Optimistic adventurers jumped on the bandwagon west.

Some got their film and their fingers burned, others plotted, connived, had good luck – and made a fortune. One of these was former jeweller Lewis J. Selznick, who joined Universal Pictures, which was rife with internal politics, found there was no general manager, got himself that position, and eventually became a powerful force in the industry. His success story was fairly typical, involving a sharp business sense and con as much as anything else.

Pirating and plagiarism were common. Films were not rented, but were sold outright, and it was easy for pirates to make cheap multiple prints. (Not until later would a system of film rentals evolve.) And there were other kinds of stealing. An enterprising gentleman by the name of Albert Smith gave new meaning to the word 'opportunist'. Biograph had bought exclusive rights to the Jim Jeffries-Tom Sharkey fight, but Smith had other ideas. On the night of the fight he smuggled a camera into the stadium and, sitting a few rows from ringside, cranked away, courtesy of Biograph's lights. Fight promoter Bill Brady spotted the camera and ordered a phalanx of private detectives to snatch it. The sporting crowd, feeling that odds of twenty to one were unsporting, set upon the detectives with a vengeance, and Smith escaped from the area with his camera and bootleg film intact. Jeffries and Brady gave chase, but he eluded them and developed the film – which was in turn stolen from him.

Bill Brady had good reason to watch for pirates: another of his promotions had launched a man who was to become a significant force in the movies, Sigmund Lubin. Brady, who had the film rights to the Corbett-Fitzsimmons fight, found that the film was popular everywhere but in Philadelphia. He dropped in at one of that city's nickelodeons and learned the reason. Lubin had hired two muscular 'actors' to re-enact the fight, based on press accounts, and Lubin had filmed them. Lubin did not corner the market in Celluloid fakery.

Arbuckle's first film employer, Colonel Selig, had arrived at an agreement with President Teddy Roosevelt to film the man from the White House in darkest Africa. Film of the brave Roosevelt standing triumphant on the carcass of a dead lion was guaranteed to be a box-office sellout. To Selig's chagrin, the President not only forgot their agreement, but had the audacity to take an English cameraman on safari. The thought of all those lost nickels was too much for Selig. He acquired a secondhand lion and a starving third-rate actor who bore a remarkable resemblance to the President. When a cable reached the United States with news that Roosevelt had actually killed a lion, the picture-going public was astonished and delighted the same week to see *Hunting Big Game in Africa*.

After making *The 'Counts' of Monte Cristo*, Colonel Selig filmed *In the Sultan's Palace*, the first film to be made entirely in California. Shortly after this, Roscoe glided his 266 pounds on to the Selig lot, which was behind a Chinese laundry at Eighth and Hill streets. There he was to meet and work with the victim of filmland's first murder.

One of Roscoe's first films at the Selig studios was *Ben's Kid*, starring Tom Santschi and directed by Francis Boggs. Some feel that if Boggs had lived long enough, he would have proved a serious rival to Griffith – that in fact some of the innovations attributed to Griffith should have been credited to Boggs. Arbuckle hardly set the screen afire with his first performance. *Ben's Kid* was followed by a half-reeler called *Mrs Jones' Birthday*. The *New York Dramatic Mirror* of 11 September 1909, said of Roscoe's performance, 'The Jones of the picture is a fat fellow, a new face in picture pantomime, and the earnestness of his work adds greatly to its value. There are times when he plays to the camera, but there are other actors more experienced than he is in this line of work, who do the same thing . . .'

Roscoe made several movies for Selig under the

direction of Boggs. How many is uncertain; beyond any doubt, however, the last of them was made in 1913 without the benefit of Mr Boggs' direction.

In early November, 1911, the Selig actors assembled on the small set awaiting the arrival of Boggs heard the sound of gunfire. They rushed outside to find that a demented Japanese gardener had shot and killed Francis Boggs, and had put a bullet in the arm of Colonel Selig. Tom Santschi, hero of a hundred gunfights, started running in the direction of Mexico. The gardener was apprehended and brought before Selig, who demanded an explanation. He pointed towards the film set and said, 'Too damn much shooting all the time. Boom! Boom! All day, boom! Boom! It make me crazy.'

If Los Angeles attracted eccentric characters, there were others there who led quite normal lives – families like the Durfees. Railroad engineer Charles Warren Durfee and his wife lived with their four children in one of the better areas of the city, near churches that served all denominations and brothels that served all manner of clientele. The Durfees were of French, Welsh and Dutch extraction. Their youngest child, Araminta Estelle, was seventeen in 1908 and was still attending school. She would have been the last to believe that in a few months she would be Roscoe Arbuckle's wife, and within a few years the leading lady in ten of Charlie Chaplin's first films (not that she knew who either man was). Boardinghouses in the city displayed the sign 'No Dogs or Actors', which summed up the typical attitude of families like the Durfees towards the stage and the movies.

Minta stood less than five feet tall and weighed just over one hundred pounds. Her auburn hair when unpinned cascaded to her waist. Though diminutive, she was elegant and beautiful, with a grace that ensured that she was always noticed. One man to notice her was theatre owner Walter Morosco.

At that time there were two stock companies in Los

Angeles, the Belasco and the Morosco. Both were part of theatre circuits that stretched across the US. Oliver Morosco had placed his son Walter in charge of his Los Angeles theatre, The Burbank. As regular theatregoers, the Durfees were well known to Walter. One day after a matinee he stopped Minta and, after exchanging pleasantries, asked her suddenly if she would like to be on the stage. Minta, who had never considered the possibility, answered, 'Sure I would, but I couldn't do that. I wouldn't know what to do.' Walter explained, 'Kolb and Dill have a problem' – which meant that he had a problem. Kolb and Dill were a famous comedy team of the period. They worked their act with a group of girls, a 'pony chorus', and they had married the two end girls, but when the honeymoon was over, the two girls wouldn't go back on the boards – hence the problem. Morosco's new show was to open in two weeks, and he needed to find one more end girl.

Excited, Minta decided that this was for her. She confided to me recently, 'I didn't know what an "end girl" was any more than I knew how to fly a plane. I knew how to get on and off a stage – I had learned that during school productions – but that was the limit of my experience.'

Her parents, although more liberal than most, were reluctant to expose their youngest daughter to the stage-door Johnnies who, they felt, waited nightly to ravish young women of the theatre; but since the streetcar ran directly from the theatre to their home, they finally said yes, reasoning that Minta could scarcely come to harm on a trolley. (Her eldest brother, doubtless encouraged by his parents' modern thinking, asked permission to become a prize-fighter. They flatly refused. One bizarre profession was quite enough to cope with.)

So, in the early summer of 1908, Minta Durfee gaily tripped down to The Burbank to take part in *The Milk-White Flag*, the first musical ever staged there. Immediately after each night's performance, Minta caught the trolley home; at her stop, she would be snatched up by her mother and hurried away before the wolves of Los Angeles could catch so much as a glimpse of her pretty ankles.

Minta wryly recalled to me how popular she was:

> I had finished rehearsals one day and remarked that I was going home for dinner. Two tall showgirls, upon hearing this, looked at me wistfully and sighed, 'Oh, it's been years since we had a home-cooked dinner.'
>
> Well, I've never been one to keep the good things of life to myself. I believe there are so few of them, they should be shared among the greatest possible number. I telephoned home. 'Momma,' I said, 'I can't leave these poor starving girls here while I enjoy a good dinner. Can I bring my friends home with me?' Mother of course said yes. A little while later I appeared home with ten show-girls. Yes, you make friends quickly in the theatre.

After Minta's two-week engagement at The Burbank, she was offered a summer engagement at the Byde A Wyle Theatre in Long Beach, a theatre which was as elegant as the Virginia Hotel, which owned it. Excited, Minta and some of her new friends caught a trolley to Long Beach. Minta recalled that trolley ride for me:

> Sitting opposite me was this great big blond boy. As smart as a new pin. Brown suit. Blue bow tie. Blue eyes. When he took off his hat, his hair was pure gold. I didn't pay any attention to him, just glanced over and thought, 'What a clean-looking young man.' You must remember this was my first time away from home. I was determined to be very proper about everything.
>
> I struggled with my suitcase when we reached our destination. The young man rose and, doffing his hat, said, 'I would be very glad to take your suitcase off for you.' I said, 'I beg your pardon. I don't like blonds and I don't like fat men. I would be very happy if you would keep your hands off of my suitcase.' The young man

blushed bright red to the roots of his hair as I stormed down the stairs of the streetcar.

Having put him in his place, Minta continued on her way. She became engrossed in rehearsals for the show, which was to run for an hour and be performed twice nightly. Full dress rehearsals were unheard of at the Byde A Wyle Theatre, so members of the cast did not really see each other until the first performance.

On opening night the hotel guests sauntered down the steps of the Virginia Hotel, through the tennis courts, and into the theatre. The gentlemen sat in wicker chairs and smoked cigars during the performance. Minta was standing in the wings with the other girls and chatting excitedly, when she became entranced with the voice of the singer on stage. Peeking round the wings, she saw that the singer was the young man she had so effectively scorned on the trolley, Roscoe Arbuckle. She stared at him in amazement. The song, 'When You Were Sweet Sixteen', was a sing-along, but there was not a sound from the audience. His voice was so beautiful and clear that they listened in silence. Without the aid of a microphone his voice filled every corner of the theatre, and when he had finished, he received an ovation.

In a daze, Minta did her routine with the chorus. Then, as the chorus line waited behind the closed curtain, she again heard the voice, this time singing 'Glowworm'. The curtains opened, and the dancing line came forward. There, lying stretched out on the stage and wearing a comic German suit and an extraordinary wig, was Roscoe. Again the audience was enthusiastic.

At the end of the show, when the entire company assembled on stage for a curtain call, Roscoe came and stood next to Minta. With the applause ringing in their ears, he calmly asked, 'Can I walk you home?'

Still bowing, Minta said, 'How dare you!'

'What have I done?' he asked sheepishly.

Stamping her size-two shoe, Minta went on, 'How dare

you be in such a small company as this with such a gorgeous voice and with so much talent! What's the matter with you? I don't want to talk to you or ever speak to you again.'

And so Minta entered Roscoe's life.

As the season progressed, their romance ripened. While it was obvious to Minta that Roscoe had fallen deeply in love with her, she didn't know whether she loved him or not, although she had never met anybody like him – he was 'the most unconceited human being who ever lived'. Roscoe had found in Minta an interest that far exceeded his fondness for swimming, playing pool and drinking buttermilk. They would lunch at a little café on the waterfront, Roscoe nibbling on a piece of bread and gazing into Minta's eyes. He would hire a pony and trap, and they would go for long rides. There was a charming formality about their courtship.

Towards the end of July, as the summer season drew to a close, Roscoe asked Minta what she intended to do when the time came to leave the Byde A Wyle Theatre. Sixty-four years later, in the summer of 1972, Minta recalled for me that conversation.

'I think I ought to go back to school,' she had replied.

Roscoe thought for a moment, then declared, 'You know, I'm very much in love with you.'

Minta blushed and said, 'Well, thank you very much, but I want to say goodbye to you.'

Roscoe stopped walking and, holding her in his arms, spoke quietly. 'Well, you can't say goodbye to me. You're the first person in the world who ever believed in me. What do you mean you're going to say goodbye to me?'

That evening, before the show, they walked by the sea. Roscoe had said little since their earlier conversation, and now he suggested, 'Let's go down by the pier.'

Minta agreed without enthusiasm; she liked swimming, but had a fear of the sea and hated getting her hair wet. As they walked towards the pier, Roscoe said, 'I'm in love with you, and I want to marry you.'

Minta replied shyly, 'Well, thank you very much, but I don't think I should marry. I'm too young.'

Recalling this moment during our interview, Minta observed, 'Sometimes when you are in love, you don't know what to say. I was in love with his ability, his talent.'

They walked to the end of the pier. Roscoe asked intently, 'Are you going to marry me or not?'

Certainty had deserted her. 'Roscoe, I don't know.'

He picked her up in his arms and, standing at the edge of the pier, holding her out over the water, said, 'You are either going to say yes or no, or I'll drop you in the water. Do you love me or don't you love me? I love you and adore you.'

Minta looked down at the waves below and then at the determined face of Roscoe. 'Thank you,' she said, 'I love you too, you're a lovely person.'

Still holding her at arm's length above the water, he asked, 'Are you going to marry me?'

Again she looked down at the waves. 'Yes, of course I am, dear,' she replied. She intended to change her answer when back on dry land and in the bosom of her family, but somehow she never did.

Their friends were delighted at the news, none more so than the manager of the Byde A Wyle Theatre, Charles E. Moore. He got official permission to have the wedding ceremony performed on the stage of his theatre. The date was fixed for 5 August. Two weeks before, every seat in the house had been reserved at escalated prices – there's no business like show business.

Soon twenty-one-year-old Roscoe and his seventeen-year-old bride-to-be got their first taste of the ballyhoo that in later years would be a daily part of their lives. The theatre was transformed into a chapel, and there on stage – after the two evening shows – they were married by the mayor of Long Beach. Among the guests was Minta's cousin Marjorie Rambeau, one of America's foremost dramatic actresses. Roscoe, the $50.00-a-week singer-comedian and Minta the $18.00-a-week dancer gazed in awe at the mountain of presents, many of them from people they had never met. (A big local store, Buffum's, displayed the wedding gifts in its windows.)

During the wedding reception at the Virginia Hotel, Roscoe heard the showgirls teasing Minta. 'Wait until we see you tomorrow,' one said. 'You'll sure look different.'

When they retired for the night, Roscoe emerged from the bathroom in a tan pyjama suit of Chinese shantung, topped by a robe of the same material, a wedding gift from the mayor. He sat on the bed and watched Minta change from a white chiffon nightgown to a pink gown, then asked her why she had changed. She told him that the pink gown was more appropriate for love-making. He brought up the teasing at the reception, which had obviously appalled him, although it had meant little to Minta. 'Those girls have made up their minds that they are going to be able to tell we have made love,' he said. 'I've made up my mind that they will not be able to tell.' The pink nightgown remained uncrumpled that night. It was ten days before they made love.

Minta told me that although he was affectionate, Roscoe was shy and experienced difficulty expressing love either verbally or physically. He told her that before his marriage his only sexual experience had been a brief encounter with a showgirl in Spokane, and as he told it, 'She knew more than I did. Well, let's face it, she couldn't have known less.'

They honeymooned in San Bernardino. It was a working honeymoon, the only kind they could afford. Arbuckle had formed a touring company with Irish comedian Walter Reed, and they toured the state from Eureka in the north to San Diego in the south. Like Roscoe, Reed was a versatile performer: he choreographed the dances, did a Dutch comedy routine, and sang ditties like 'When You and I Were Young, Honey'. Under Roscoe's guidance Minta left the chorus line and began singing. The chorus accompanied her on songs like 'By the Light of the Silvery Moon', which

Minta performed sitting on a cardboard cutout of the moon that was 'flown in' on stage wires. Her salary had increased to $30.00 a week. Roscoe was getting $50.00.

After a three-month tour of California the Arbuckles faced their first marital crisis. Roscoe and his partner, Walter Reed, decided to take their Musical Tabloid Company to Arizona. Minta refused to go to a place populated by snakes and outlaws, and went home to Mother. Mother Durfee told her daughter that her place was with her husband – outlaws, snakes and all – and Minta was put on the next train to Bisbee, Arizona.

She was met at Bisbee by a delighted Roscoe, the rest of the company, and a platform full of prostitutes, who in late 1908 were still called 'sporting girls'. The sporting girls of Bisbee had come to meet the train and look over potential clients.

In Bisbee the company performed at the Orpheum Theatre at Brewery Gulch. There were three classes of patrons: the mining executives, the miners, and the sporting girls.

Minta's song on the cardboard moon had by now become a regular part of the show. On opening night, after 'By the Light of the Silvery Moon', and halfway through 'The Moon Has His Eyes on You', the wires that suspended the moon about ten feet above the stage began to slip. With Minta clinging to it, the moon sank towards the stage. The tinsel on her yellow chiffon dress fluttering madly and her picture hat flying, Minta and the moon hit the stage with a thud. Walter Reed rushed on stage, picked Minta up and announced, 'I'm one of the little stars, helping the moon out.' It became a regular part of the show.

The company moved on from Bisbee (where they had shared the hotel with baseball's Ty Cobb) and toured all over the state. At Tombstone, the proud sheriff showed the company the site of Wyatt Earp's battle, the O. K. Corral. Roscoe asked him if things were quiet now. 'Sure are,' said the sheriff. 'Nobody's died of a sore throat for nigh on a month.' (Dying of a sore throat meant death by hanging.)

Summer 1909 found the company in El Paso, Texas, where their show was such a success that the theatre owner announced at the end of the first week that he was taking the entire cast on a picnic. They all piled into and on top of a stagecoach and set out for the banks of the Rio Grande, the river that separates the United States from Mexico. Most of them lay on the grassy bank, eating and drinking; some splashed in the river.

Suddenly on the Mexican side of the river a row of large Mexican hats popped up, under each hat a swarthy gentleman – the famous (or infamous) Uralees, Pancho Villa's guerrilla army. They had obviously decided that Roscoe's company was no threat to the Revolution, for they waved and smiled at the comedian and his friends. Despite the army's apparent friendliness, most of the picnickers were glad that the river stood between them and the guerrillas.

Roscoe, ever a man to share his good fortune, decided that the revolutionaries should join the picnic. He beckoned them over, but they shook their heads vigorously. Then Roscoe had a brainwave. He would become famous in later years for the unerring, almost uncanny accuracy with which he could toss a custard pie into a surprised face. That day on the banks of the Rio Grande he got in a little practice. Saying, 'Well, if the war won't come to the picnic, I guess the picnic had better go to the war,' he picked up a large bunch of bananas and, adopting a pitching stance, hurled them across the Rio Grande. The bananas caught one of the Mexicans full in the stomach, sending him flying. His compatriots howled with laughter and began eating the bananas.

Now Roscoe sent a hail of oranges, fruit pies, and assorted goodies across the river. Each morsel went directly to one of the revolutionaries. The Mexicans became very excited; more and more of them appeared as if from nowhere. Each hit by Roscoe was accompanied by loud cries of '*Bravo*' and '*Olé*'!

Suddenly a man on horseback appeared on the Mexican side, dismounted, came to the riverbank and called out to Roscoe, asking his name. Roscoe told him and added, 'And may I enquire, sir, who you are?'

The answer came out loud and clear across the river. 'I am Panchito Villa.'

Excitement on the American side of the river was by now intense. There stood the most hunted man in Mexico, a man with a price on his head, and he chatted with Roscoe as if they were at a party, Villa speaking in broken English and Roscoe in fractured Spanish. At one point Roscoe threw a pie, which Villa neatly caught single-handed.

The picnickers did not hear a horse approach from behind, but they heard the voice that called out, 'Big boy!' and they all turned. It was the sheriff of El Paso, with one of his hands dangerously near a Colt .45. Looking at Roscoe, he said, 'What are you doing with all that fruit and stuff, big boy?' Roscoe's face broke into that famous foolish grin that was soon to delight millions. 'Oh, nothing, Sheriff. Just tidying up after the picnic, you know.' The sheriff laughed, dismounted, and joined the party. When the group turned back towards the Mexican side of the river, there was no-one in sight. Pancho Villa, his men, and their horses had vanished as silently as they had appeared.

There is an amazing sequel to this story. In late 1913 Roscoe Arbuckle's face was appearing on cinema screens around the world – including those in Mexico. Although the Revolution continued, in Mexico everything – even a war – stopped for siesta and cinema, and one day Villa was sitting in the ten-peso section when Roscoe came on the screen. With a start, Panchito recognized the fat gringo he had broken bread with in 1909, and he became curious about the financial rewards of being a motion picture star. A short while later in El Paso, the agents of

Pancho Villa let it be known that their client was available. *On 3 January 1914, the Mutual Film Corporation of New York bought the motion picture rights to the Mexican Civil War from Villa.* He was obviously a negotiator as well as a fighter. Besides a percentage of the box-office takings, he got an advance of $25,000. One of Mutual's conditions was that as far as possible all battles would be fought in daylight, because beyond the high cost of transporting expensive electrical equipment to Mexico, there was the problem of finding a place to plug it in at a battle site. When Villa had the city of Ojinaga under siege, he delayed his final attack until Mutual had its cameras in position. The city fell, and *The Life of Villa* had a true-to-life dramatic opening. The problem was that Villa hogged the camera, so that Mutual shot hundreds of feet of Villa smiling, shouting, firing – Villa triumphant, Villa magnificent. Of the war itself, though, there was very little. In despair, Mutual negotiated a new contract. The company had learned a lesson that would be handed down to posterity and Errol Flynn: if you are going to fight a Celluloid war, fight it in Hollywood.

By early 1910 the Arbuckle-Reed touring company had disbanded. As Roscoe and Minta worked the vaudeville circuits from California to New York, Roscoe's versatility increased constantly, although he seemed unaware of the extent of his talent. He had a superb voice, and was a first-rate acrobat and a naturally funny man. Now Minta was surprised to hear him speaking in French, German, Italian, Dutch and Spanish. Because he had a good ear, the man who had left school at the age of 13 was quickly becoming multilingual.

More astonishing was his dancing ability. At the time he never weighed less than 266 pounds, yet when he danced he floated. (Any man who could partner the legendary Bill 'Bojangles' Robinson and not suffer by comparison must have been good – and it has been said by some that Bojangles taught Fred Astaire how to dance.) Roscoe would sometimes mutter, 'Hell, I'm fat,' but he manipulated his body so skilfully that he seemed unaware of being built different from most men. He was a fat man, but he moved as if he were thin.

Show business history can be distorted; during this period (early 1910) *Variety*, widely regarded as the bible of show business, proved it by publishing a list of the highest weekly salaries in show business. Heading the list was Gertrude Hoffman with $3,000, followed by Eva Tanguay ($2,000), Annette Kellerman (the 1910 version of Esther Williams) and the Gus Edwards (*School Days*) Song Revue ($1,500 each). Eighth on the list, ahead of people like Lionel Barrymore and Pat Rooney, was Roscoe Arbuckle, who, according to *Variety*, was earning $1,250 a week. He was actually earning $50.00, and some weeks he couldn't get work, but with the *Variety* news to inspire him, he redoubled his efforts to find a job.

Eventually he and Minta were engaged by the Ferris Hartman Musical Comedy and Opera Company. They toured successfully along the West Coast, and at the old Grand Opera House in Los Angeles the company's version of the musical *The Campus* had a record-breaking run. Encouraged by his Western success, Hartman decided to take the show to Chicago, but the citizens of the Windy City were not delighted. The show laid an egg, and the company was obliged to disband. Roscoe and Minta worked their way across country until they were back in San Francisco.

In 1911 the irrepressible Hartman bobbed up again in Los Angeles, reassembled his company and took them to the Hawaiian Islands. Roscoe had seen the daughters of Liliuokalani, the last queen of Hawaii, in San Francisco in 1905, little dreaming that in 1911 he would give a Royal Command Performance before their mother. On 30 August 1911, at the Royal Hawaiian Opera House, in Honolulu, the Ferris Hartman Company performed for the Queen and her court *The Girl and the Boy*, a musical written by Walter De Leon. Roscoe played the part of Slats, the comedy lead; and Minta the part of Edith Rocksley, a millionaire's daughter. After a successful season in Honolulu, they went on to Japan, where audiences saw the usual company musicals, but more astonishingly, *The Mikado* as well. It is one thing to satirize the Orient on Broadway or Shaftesbury Avenue. To do so in Tokyo in 1911 required a bland indifference to one's own safety, but the Japanese audiences somehow loved it.

From Japan the company moved to China, where they performed before the Chinese Royal Family. Drunk with success, Ferris Hartman contemplated a tour of the crowned heads of Europe, but, dissuaded by his colleagues, he settled for the Philippine Islands. They took Manila by storm, and then returned triumphantly to the United States on the last day of February 1913. Roscoe and Minta travelled down from San Francisco, distributed shantung to all of Minta's relatives, then looked around for work.

Minta's father knew the owner of Quinn's Theatre, and before long she was singing selections from the musicals they had performed on the Far Eastern tour. But for Roscoe there was little work, which disturbed him. He made at least one more movie for Selig during this period, *Alas! Poor Yorick*, during the filming of which he met Robert Leonard, a friend and a fellow actor from Roscoe's earlier days at Selig. Leonard told him that there was an opening at Universal, and urged Roscoe to go and see director Al E. Christie there. Roscoe's stay at Universal was short. One month later he was out of work again. Then, as Minta recalls, 'It was at this time that he was advised that there was some kind of shindig going on out on Effie Street.'

Many weird and wonderful tales have been told of how Roscoe Arbuckle first joined Mack Sennett's Keystone

Film Company. Sennett himself in his autobiography, *King of Comedy*, says that Arbuckle came into his office while he was in conference with Mabel Normand. He recalls,

> A tremendous man skipped up the steps as lightly as Fred Astaire. He was tremendous, obese – just plain fat. 'Name's Arbuckle,' he said, 'Roscoe Arbuckle. Call me "Fatty". I'm with a stock company. I'm a funnyman and acrobat. Bet I could do good in pictures. Watcha think?' With no warning, he went into a feather-light step, clapped his hands, and did a backward somersault as gracefully as a girl tumbler. And that was how the famous and later infamous Roscoe (Fatty) Arbuckle introduced himself to motion pictures.

Sennett doesn't mention the three films at Selig's studios or the month at Universal, but in the overall picture they were probably insignificant.

The following is Minta Durfee's account of how Roscoe really joined Keystone. When he heard about the 'shindig' on Effie Street, Roscoe decided to investigate and caught the trolley out there. As always, he was dressed immaculately: white pumps, white trousers, white shirt, blue bow tie, blue coat, and, above his glowing face, a straw hat. He got off the trolley and was directed to a high building. The dust from the unpaved road speckled his white trousers as he tried to peer over the fence. Finding a large wooden gate, he walked in and saw something resembling a stage with an odd assortment of props lying around, bits of camera equipment and many strange-looking objects. But of people, there was no sign. He walked around looking for someone, and as he walked he hummed and sang. Suddenly a door opened, and there stood a man with a shock of grey hair and a mouthful of tobacco. With a grunt he spat a stream of tobacco juice in the general direction of Roscoe, who moved to avoid it, and shouted, 'You! Be here tomorrow morning at eight o'clock.' With that, he moved back into his room and slammed the door.

Assuming that the man was a passing idiot, Roscoe clutched his portfolio of photographs and walked around the deserted lot, then decided to call it a day. He was back at the gate when a door opened and the same grey-haired lunatic, spitting another stream of tobacco juice, shouted at Roscoe, 'Listen to me, young fellow. You be here tomorrow at eight o'clock. How in the hell do you know, you might be a star someday.' Again the man, who resembled a gorilla, vanished. Again a door slammed. The grey-haired gorilla was Mack Sennett. And thus Roscoe Arbuckle joined the maddest funny farm the world has ever known, the Keystone Film Company.

Learned men have waxed long and lyrical about Keystone. Its films have been compared with the *commedia dell'arte* scenarios of the seventeenth century. They have been called balletic, symbolic and ingenious. Few of the filmgoers who laughed themselves hoarse at the Keystone films knew about *commedia dell'arte*, but they knew a funny thing when they saw it. Despite a lot of rubbish that has been written about silent films, I believe the number of silent *dramatic* films that could stand close scrutiny and not be laughed off the screen is fewer than thirty. But the silent *comedy* films made over seventy years ago are increasingly popular; they have stood the test of time. Not that the primary purpose of Keystone films was to achieve a place in history. Mixing slapstick comedy and pretty girls, they worked on a formula: police, pies, pulchritude, pace and pursuit – all of which produced pandemonium. And profits. Keystone made films to make money, and make it Keystone did, barrels of it.

When Roscoe Arbuckle joined Keystone in April 1913, the film company was less than eight months old. It was a subsidiary of the New York Motion Picture Company and the brainchild of three men, former bookmakers Adam Kessel and Charles Baumann and former iron-worker, Mack Sennett, born Michael Sinnott. Each man owned a third of Keystone. Sennett gained his early knowledge of film technique working for the Biograph Film Company in New York. He quickly evolved a philosophy that he would frequently air to Biograph's David Wark ('I see no future in films') Griffith, who, Sennett said later, was 'my day school, my night school, my university'. Griffith dismissed Sennett's ideas with the comment, 'You want to film cops chasing people, Sennett? Forget it, nothing funny in that.'

In August 1912, Mack Sennett had a chance to test the value of his comic theory. Having shot Keystone's first film at Fort Lee, New Jersey (a one-reeler called *Cohen at Coney Island*), Sennett, director Henry 'Pathé' Lehrman, and film comedians Mabel Normand and Ford Sterling travelled to Los Angeles, where they were met by comedian Fred Mace. This was the nucleus of a company that by 1916 would have many hundreds on its payroll.

As one story goes, the group left the train station, heard a brass band and saw crowds of people everywhere. Sennett smiled. His ideas might count for nothing with Griffith, but people on the West Coast were obviously discerning. Sennett started a speech of thanks, only to be told by Mabel Normand that the crowds and band were for an army parade. Sennett paused. He wanted to kick off his production in Los Angeles with a big film, one that would really impress his backers, Kessel and Baumann. He sent Pathé Lehrman to a nearby shop to purchase a doll and a shawl. Before you could say 'epic', Mabel Normand had been transformed into an abandoned young mother, complete with baby. She moved among the marching soldiers searching vainly for her ne'er-do-well lover. The reactions she got from the soldiers were superb. One even stopped marching to help her in her search. At this point Ford Sterling entered the parade and engaged the good Samaritan in a ferocious argument. All hell broke loose. Meanwhile Pathé Lehrman cranked away behind the camera. The Los Angeles Police Department joined the fracas, and Mabel and Ford shot down the centre of the road with the police in pursuit. The Keystone Kops and the classic chase had been born. (As often happens with Keystone films, this one had a variety of titles: *Stolen Glory, The Shriners Parade,* and *The Grand Army of the Republic.*)

The technique of 'borrowing' from public events was frequently employed at Keystone. Sennett must have had nearly every local councillor on his payroll at one time. If a lake was being drained or a dangerous chimney stack blown up, his cameras were always there, filming the event with Keystone actors involved in the situation. A story would then be built around that basic situation. Although he had a studio lot at Allesandro and Effie streets, the cameras were more out than in. Women hanging out their washing might find Mabel Normand hurtling through their gardens pursued by a chimpanzee. If the owner of the property thought of complaining, he was paid – $10.00 for having his lawn filmed, $15.00 for having his porch filmed, $20.00 for having the interior of the house wrecked. (In 1915, at the San Diego Exposition, Sennett set up a demonstration of how movies were made. Roscoe and Mabel Normand drew huge crowds as they mugged it up for an unloaded camera, while other cameras, fully loaded, shot every inch of the exposition. Sennett got invaluable stock film to be dropped into dozens of stories. He did the same thing at the 1915 San Francisco World's Fair.)

Sennett was definitely eccentric. He could hit a spittoon at thirteen paces with his tobacco juice, and he wore a Panama hat with the crown cut out, claiming that the California sun shining on his locks prevented baldness. On one occasion he had his hair dyed black, but it came out green. His first driving ambition was a fairly simple one: he wanted a large bath installed in his office. Within a year he had his bath. He also acquired the services of an ex-wrestler, a Turk named Abdul Maljan, and a large marble slab. When Sennett emerged from his bath, Abdul would massage away the tensions of film-making as Mack lay on the slab. Nothing was allowed to interrupt this ritual. If one of his employees chanced to enter while Sennett was in the bath, Mack would invite him into the water while they sorted out the problem. Only an act of God could have got Sennett out of his bath prematurely, and only an act of God did, once: an earthquake. Passers-by in the street were treated to the sight of a naked Mack Sennett pursued by an equally naked Turk.

Minta Durfee reminisced with me about Sennett:

> Sennett certainly was an oddball. His office with the bath was on the second storey. He had it put there so that he could watch everybody, to make sure they weren't slacking. For breakfast he ate green onions, lettuce and radishes, washed down with whisky. He'd stroll down, watch us make a scene, laugh like hell. We'd think it was great, then he'd say, 'Do it again.' Sometimes when his office got crowded with Abdul taking care of the boys who were getting slaughtered below, Sennett would walk on to the set, ask what we were doing, then he'd make up a part for himself, do a little bit, then go back upstairs. His comedy ideas included contrasts. Big woman, small man. A moustache or a suit that were too big or too small.

During a script conference in his office one day, three of his writers noticed that Sennett seemed unduly preoccupied. He was having a foundation built for a dynamo in the lot below, and no matter how the three men tried, they could not get him interested in their ideas. He remained rooted, staring moodily at the work in progress below. The conference went on all day, the atmosphere grim. As five o'clock approached, the three writers were convinced that they were about to be fired, that Sennett had been working up to it. Suddenly he turned to Abdul and said, 'Abdul, that phoney bricklayer walking through the gate. Catch him, tell him he's fired. I'm told that a bricklayer should get twelve hundred bricks laid in a day on a foundation. That guy's only laid 862 the whole damned day. I've counted them.' Brightening, he turned to his writers and said, 'I think it's a great story. Let's make it.'

There are many myths about Keystone, and one of them is that there were no writers. One old star after another has said that the films were created in a marvellous mystical way, that they 'evolved'. Somebody would have an idea, they would all throw in suggestions, and bingo: a film was born. In fact, Keystone employed script editors and writers from the start. One of the first things that Sennett did on reaching the West Coast was to engage Karl Coolidge as script editor. Some old-timers who admit that Coolidge and other writers were around, insist that there were never scripts, that the writers didn't write, that they merely suggested story ideas. But I have in my possession a number of those Keystone scripts. They include not only highly comprehensive story outlines, but detailed shot breakdowns that reveal a high degree of professionalism. Mad they certainly were at Keystone, but there was method in their madness.

Other writers who followed Coolidge were Craig Hutchinson, Hampton Del Ruth, Robert Wagner, Ray Griffith, Johnny Grey and Albert Glassmyer. The last three were more than a match for Sennett's eccentricities. When Sennett installed them in a penthouse above his office, it was not so they could enjoy the view. Before this they had worked in a bungalow on the Keystone lot, but bungalows are easy to escape from. With the writers above Sennett, they were obliged to pass his open office door every time they came or left, and he could creep up to see if they were working. The three men countered this by bribing a carpenter to fix an extra piece of wood on the top stair so that for a few weeks every time Sennett crept up he fell over it. Recovering, he would enter a hive of industry.

Sennett constructed a restaurant on the lot. Everyone was allowed in but the writers. It was the King of Comedy's theory that food would make them sleepy, and sleeping writers don't write. The writers took to crawling over the rooftops in search of food. No telephones, newspapers, books or cards were allowed in the writing room. They were considered distractions.

Sennett was a great 'borrower' of material. One early attempt at plagiarism ended in disaster. He tried to sell Biograph three stories he had 'written', and it turned out that identical stories had already been written by a man named O. Henry. Sennett obviously concluded that it was better to take material from foreigners, because by the time they heard about it, it would be too late to take action. Many Keystone films bear a remarkable resemblance to earlier films made by the Pathé film company of France. When Sennett admitted this deception in his autobiography, it was some fifty years (and several hundred million dollars of profit) later. Of course, Sennett was not alone in using other people's material; copying was the order of the day.

The man who took the world's flotsam and jetsam and made great comic films of them, was not without his detractors. Many considered his films vulgar, and some still do. Others considered the man himself coarse and vulgar. Film comedienne Babe London, for example, told me, 'I didn't like Sennett. He wasn't my dish of peas. He was crude. He made uncouth remarks. I've known a lot of people that worked for him. They all said the same.' Screen writer and film historian De Witt Bodeen was equally frank: 'I must say I have never heard of a man being so disliked by the people who worked for him as Sennett was. He was a common, vulgar man. People could just not understand how Mabel Normand fell in love with him, but she certainly did.' Linda Arvidson, D. W. Griffith's wife during the Biograph period, thought that Sennett was hypercritical of everybody at Biograph.

But Adela Rogers St Johns, Hollywood's first gossip columnist (writing originally as Adela Rogers), declared,

> Sennett was a big, rough, tough Irish plumber, but he had an abundance of talent, which was just as well, because most of the other people making comedies during that period were stealing from him. They were all as mad as hatters at Keystone. I remember one day being in his office when Raymond Griffith came roaring in shouting, 'How did the bass get into the cellar?' Sennett said, 'Why should you care how it got there? Just photograph it.'

Minta Durfee Arbuckle said simply that Sennett was a 'divine man'.

Whenever Sennett lost one of his stars – and towards the end of the decade he lost most of them – he never considered that perhaps he had done something to bring their departure about. His attitude was that they were traitors, people to be ostracized. Gene Fowler, a devout Sennett partisan, comments in *Father Goose*: 'Desertion from Keystone was an act of treachery in Sennett's eyes. Even when he boasted that he would stand in no-one's way, a change of allegiance by his actors rankled in the King's bosom. He was a tenacious and forthright hater. Loyalty, however, won from him a never-failing friendship and affection.'

For all Sennett's faults, real and imagined, by 1913 something remarkable had begun to happen at Keystone. What Griffith was doing for dramatic films, Sennett was doing for comedy. Techniques he borrowed from the Pathé film company in France became unique when reworked through his fertile imagination. His sense of comedy timing and his editing were superb. Most pre-Keystone comedy films look funereal in comparison. Pace, always pace. 'The gag must follow the plant as quickly as possible,' was one of Arbuckle's most frequent comments at Keystone, and Sennett endorsed it fully. More basically, his philosophy of moviemaking was summed up in a saying that hung on his wall: 'The extent of the intelligence of the average public mind is eleven years. Moving pictures should be made accordingly.'

The company made a net profit of over a million dollars in its first full year of business, and Sennett was determined to do better thereafter.

The first film Roscoe made for Sennett, a one-reeler called *The Gangsters*, was directed by Henry Lehrman and featured Ford Sterling, Fred Mace, Hank Mann and a young man named Al St John, who was Roscoe's nephew. Al had followed Roscoe to Keystone from vaudeville, where they had worked together, and he was to serve often as comic foil to his uncle.

When Roscoe began at Keystone, his salary was $5.00 a day. After observing his newest actor's work in *The Gangsters,* Sennett was not inclined to offer him an increase. At first Sennett was not at all impressed with Arbuckle. It was Mabel Normand's insistence that Roscoe was not only fat but also very funny that persuaded Sennett to keep him on. This inability to spot talent quickly was a Sennett trait that persisted through the history of Keystone. Within twelve months Roscoe would be writing and directing all of his own films, and he and Mabel Normand would create the most successful comedy duo to emerge from Keystone.

A Noise from the Deep, a one-reel comedy released on 17 July 1913, recorded film's first custard pie-throwing. Mabel Normand threw and Roscoe Arbuckle caught the pie squarely in the face. Many pies have been thrown since, but the master of the art was Roscoe. His technique drew gasps of astonishment from both moviegoers and those in the business. Gene Fowler observed that 'all of these pie-tossers were mere *petits-fours* twiddlers when compared with that greatest pie-slinger of all time, the mightiest triple-threat man that ever stepped on the waffle-iron, the All-American of All-Americans, the supreme grand lama of the meringue, the Hercules of the winged dessert, the Ajax of the hurtling fritter, the paragon of the patty-casters, the unconquerable and valiant flinger of open and closed mince models, the monarch of the zooming *rissoles*, Roscoe "Fatty" Arbuckle!'

Arbuckle's physical dexterity, extraordinary considering his size, was fully utilized when it came to throwing pies. Ambidextrous, he threw with such deadly accuracy that he could hit any target up to ten feet away with ease, and in a number of the Keystone films he hurled two pies at once – in opposite directions!

A Keystone pie occasionally performed a figure-eight before landing on target. This effect was achieved by setting an expert fly-caster on top of a step-ladder out of camera range. The owner of a small local bakery grew rich coping with the studio's demands. It was soon apparent that real custard pies were inclined to break up in flight. The enterprising baker, named Greenberg, concocted a pie of blackberries and whipped cream or paste. (If there is a renaissance of this lost art, a second Greenberg will have to emerge to overcome the problem of colour film.)

It has been said many times that retakes were rare at Keystone, that virtually everything was shot in one take. It is not true. For example, Roscoe was assigned a visual gag in *Fickle Fatty's Fall*: having cooked an omelette, he had to flip it up in the air and catch it behind his back in the frying pan. At eight o'clock in the morning the gag was rehearsed, and it worked beautifully. Roscoe directed the cameraman to start cranking. At four in the afternoon the cameraman was still cranking and Roscoe was still tossing omelettes. After nearly nine hours' shooting, an omelette dropped into the pan. Although this was a particularly slow take, it does illustrate Sennett's attitude. He would lose star after star because he stubbornly refused to pay them what they were worth, and he would raise hell if the swimming pool was filled merely so his staff could use it during the lunch break (filling the pool cost $12.00), but he would spend $10,000 getting a single gag perfect.

Like all male actors on the lot, Arbuckle served for a time as a Keystone Kop. Ford Sterling portrayed the officer who was theoretically in charge of a group of men no right-thinking citizen would call to his aid. The Kops serving under Sterling changed with every film, for two reasons: because of the number of injuries sustained, or because while an actor was going through his paces as a Kop, Sennett was watching to see if the man justified promotion to safer film pastures. There were two kinds of Kop: the quick, brave and successful; and the slow, cowardly, and retired (usually through injury). Sennett had a particularly callous attitude about the safety of his Kops. In the pursuit of laughter these men entered burning buildings and left dangerously late, threw themselves over cliffs or off high buildings, crashing on to the concrete below. They leaped under trains, drove through hotels. No price was too high for a gag that worked. Their anarchic comedy spread before them like a tidal wave, and in an age of materialism they destroyed everything that stood in their path. Cars were smashed, houses wrecked, towns devastated. Those policemen with English hats and American uniforms deflated the pomposity of authority and destroyed respect for the law at a breathtaking speed.

Arbuckle was one of the few men to portray a Kop without sustaining injury. His ability to fall from heights of up to twenty feet, get up and walk away, astonished Sennett and many others. However, it was not his indestructibility that gained him promotion from the ranks. Despite Sennett's misgivings, Roscoe's talent was obvious to Mabel Normand and the other stars at Keystone, and he graduated quickly to feature roles.

By modern standards the story lines of those Keystone

features seem naive. *Mabel's New Hero,* released in August 1913, was described this way in a review: 'Starring Fatty and the bathing beauties with Mabel Normand. At the beach with Fatty, Mabel catches Harry's villainous eye. Hearty competition between Fatty and Harry involves a bust on the nose for Fatty and a free ride for Mabel, in Harry's balloon. The result: Fatty calls on the Keystone Kops for a rousing climax, Keystone style.'

In his first year at Keystone, Roscoe made at least fifty comedies.[1] *Mabel's New Hero* and others like it rocketed Arbuckle to international popularity. He was enormously popular not only in his own country, but also in Great Britain, France, Italy and elsewhere; in Germany he became the top film comedian virtually overnight. Arbuckle knew nothing of his foreign success. Sennett took care that his artists did not know their commercial worth; if they had known, they might have demanded salary increases. Within a few months Roscoe Arbuckle's face, the face of a cynical baby, had become better known than that of the President. He had about him a boy-man quality – sometimes almost androgynous – that audiences loved. Forever countering the slings and arrows of misfortune with an ingenuity that ensured his triumph, he touched a receptive chord in millions. Even members of the Puritanical Society, which in 1913 considered films the invention of the devil, allowed themselves and their children to laugh at Arbuckle.

By the end of that first year Roscoe was not only starring in films, he was also directing them – his own and those of other Keystone stars – since at that time directing was work accessible to an actor. He was also

---

[1] He may have made between fifty and one hundred movies that first year. The precise number cannot be ascertained because many of them no longer exist. Details of forty of these films will be found in the filmography at the end of this book.

frequently responsible for the scripts of the films in which he appeared.

The year 1913 ended with a bang for everybody at Keystone. Sennett was tipped off by a friendly district attorney that a young woman was in his office complaining that someone at Keystone had had his way with her. She was known to have bestowed her favours freely among the Keystone staff, and since she was under the age of consent, they had all committed criminal acts. Sennett, known now to most of the Keystone people as Napoleon, considered that he was about to meet his Waterloo. He ordered everybody to pack, fast. A convoy of cars screamed out of the lot and did not stop until it had reached Mexico. After a few weeks, word reached the intrepid film-makers that the guilty party was not a Keystone employee but the owner of a grocery store. A story appeared later in a movie magazine extolling the virtues of Sennett and his merry band for braving the wilds of Mexico merely to get authentic location shots.

The collection of people and animals that at one time or another worked for Mack Sennett was bizarre in the extreme: the people included wrestlers, cops, old women, babes in arms, acrobats, and prizefighters; the animals ranged from fleas to elephants. A good many of the people became famous: Charles Chaplin, Gloria Swanson, Ben Turpin, Harry Langdon, Harold Lloyd, Carole Lombard, Bing Crosby, Chester Conklin and W. C. Fields.

Shortly after Roscoe joined Keystone, his wife Minta was put on the payroll. With his nephew Al St John there too, it began to look like a takeover bid. Old friends such as Mack Swain left vaudeville and swelled the ever-growing ranks of comedians. The vaudeville situation was heaven-made for the West Coast film-makers, as Jackie Coogan explained to me:

> You would sign for a fifty-week tour of the circuits, right across the country. You'd start in New York and wind up in San Diego. The forty-ninth week would be in

Los Angeles. The motion picture industry started to get important around 1912. It really started to grow on the West Coast. Now where were they going to get all the people from? They got them from vaudeville. The film-makers would go to the Orpheum and other theatres in LA. Having viewed the assembled talent, they would contract anyone that caught their eye. When the artiste finished his tour the following week, he or she would return to LA to work in films. They had a deal, usually at a much higher salary than they were accustomed to. The vast majority broke into the film business that way.

This was how Charles Chaplin got into the movies.

Mack Sennett says in *King of Comedy* that Roscoe Arbuckle was engaged at Keystone to replace Chaplin. But Arbuckle joined Keystone in 1913 and left at the end of 1916. Chaplin joined in 1914 and left in 1915. Abel Green and Joe Laurie Jr in *Show Biz: from Vaude to Video* say, 'Chaplin walked into Sennett's office unannounced and asked for a tryout in Keystone comedies.' But when Chaplin walked on to the Sennett lot, he was far from being unannounced: he had in his pocket a contract with the company for a year's work, his salary for the first three months to be $150 a week, and for the remaining nine, $175. *For this Chaplin agreed to make three films a week.* The salary was large by Keystone standards, but Arbuckle was earning more. From a starting salary of $25.00 a week in March 1913 he had risen by early 1914 to over $200.

Sennett had misgivings about Chaplin, a doubt shared this time by Mabel Normand. Mabel was due to play opposite Chaplin in his first film, *Making a Living*, but after watching him rehearse, she withdrew and her place was taken by Roscoe's wife, Minta Durfee, who went on to make eleven films with Chaplin. The small Englishman was destined to make not merely a living, but a fortune from his work in the film industry, though none thought so after watching his initial efforts. Chaplin's comedy style, largely based on the techniques of French comedian Max Linder, was not particularly suited to the Keystone formula, was in fact diametrically opposed to it. The Keystone comedians relied on pace, Chaplin on the slow build. Nor were matters helped when Chaplin clashed with his director, Henry 'Pathé' Lehrman. When Chaplin made suggestions for improving the comedy, Lehrman flared up. *Making a Living*, their first joint effort, was made in three days. Chaplin packed into it every conceivable gag, only to find when he watched the edited film that Lehrman had deliberately butchered it, cutting the comedy business to shreds. In Chaplin's autobiography he says that years later Lehrman confessed that he had done this deliberately because he thought Chaplin knew too much.

Lehrman, who had been a tram conductor and a cinema usher, had conned his way into films in 1910. He walked into the Biograph studio in New York, said he had been working for the Pathé film company in France and was prepared to share his knowledge with Biograph. Griffith realized Lehrman was a phoney and dubbed him 'Pathé', a nickname that was to stick for life. But Griffith also seems to have felt that Lehrman had novelty value, because he hired him as an extra. And it was as an extra that Lehrman became friendly with Sennett, who was telling everyone who would listen about his idea of making films with cops. Lehrman listened. And, surprisingly, when his chance came, he proved a highly capable director. Chaplin said that what success Lehrman achieved was of a mechanical nature, but whether this was so or not, Lehrman learned his craft well – and from a master, D. W. Griffith. Unfortunately his talent was surpassed by his vanity and arrogance. He antagonized many people in the industry, among them Mack Sennett; and his tendency to date Mabel Normand, Sennett's mistress, was hardly likely to endear him to the King of Comedy.

Hostilities at Keystone reached a climax when Chaplin

clashed with Lehrman. Pathé directed four of Chaplin's films, which for both men was four too many. After a series of furious arguments between Lehrman, Chaplin and Sennett, Pathé left to form his own company. He had not disappeared from Roscoe Arbuckle's life, but no-one could know this yet. For Chaplin, there remained the problem of beating the one-eyed monster that mercilessly photographed his every action.

Chaplin shared the star dressing room with Ford Sterling, Mack Swain and Roscoe Arbuckle, among others. Keystone comedian Chester Conklin later recalled that Chaplin was in such awe of Arbuckle and the others that for weeks he was frightened to change his clothes in their presence, but one day he plucked up courage to do so, having just been told by Sennett to dress like a bumbling photographer, because they would shoot film that day at the kid auto races in Venice. He didn't know it then, but that dress change put him on the road to greatness. From Roscoe he borrowed a pair of balloon-like trousers, which he tied round his waist, a small hat (one of Arbuckle's trademarks), and a pair of outsize shoes. He slipped the shoes on the wrong feet, merely to keep them on. He borrowed a cutaway coat from Chester Conklin, and a moustache from Mack Swain. Amused, Arbuckle and the others watched, and Chaplin, encouraged, proceeded to put together the basic costume for what was to become one of the screen's greatest characters, the Tramp.

The proto-Tramp was first seen in *Kid Auto Races at Venice*. There were no shafts of lightning, no rolls of drums; the character was thought funny enough to persist, but no more. Indeed, Sennett still had grave misgivings about Chaplin and confided to Roscoe Arbuckle, who by mid-1914 was his most trusted employee, 'I'm going to let Chaplin go. He's not for us.' Much has been written about how ambitious the comedians at Keystone were, how they stole scenes from each other to further their careers – and this is probably true.

But Roscoe at this point had a perfect opportunity to get rid of Chaplin, a man who was in competition with him for laughs, and he didn't. Minta Durfee recalls that exchange:

> When Sennett made this announcement, about getting rid of Chaplin, Roscoe was silent for a while. Then he said, 'Boss, don't let him go, he's a very funny man.' Sennett replied, 'Listen, Big Boy, he's so damn slow.' Sennett was not merely referring to Chaplin's technique. He was more concerned with making his delivery dates to the exhibitors, and [by Keystone standards] Chaplin's films took a long time to make. Roscoe was not prepared to let it go at that; when he made up his mind he could be just as determined about something as Mack. He turned to Mack and said, 'Listen, he's doing beautiful things. Don't worry about the shipping dates. We'll make them. I guarantee it.'

Mollified, Sennett agreed to keep Chaplin on, knowing that if anyone could keep the delivery dates, Roscoe could. Arbuckle was by then the fastest director on the lot.

While Arbuckle went from strength to strength, Chaplin still struggled. In September 1914, one film critic reviewing *His New Profession* referred to him as Chaplain, and another, reviewing *The Rounders*, referred to him as Chapman. If Sennett was dissatisfied, so was Chaplin. Despondent, he thought of returning to vaudeville. He could not adjust to the pace and style of his fellow cast members in the first six films he made. In three of those films he played opposite Arbuckle. Chester Conklin recalls,

> He [Chaplin] had told me the day before that he was going to quit the motion pictures as soon as he could. 'I'm going to get out of this business. It's too much for me. I'll never catch on. It's too fast. I can't tell what I'm doing or what anybody wants me to do,' Charlie said. 'At any

rate, I figure the cinema is little more than a fad. It's canned melodrama. What audiences want to see is flesh and blood on the stage. I'm not sure any real actor should get caught posing for the flickahs.'

Certainly some actors might have been exhausted by the pranks played at the Keystone madhouse. On one occasion during his Keystone days, Charlie and Arbuckle were being filmed in a small rowingboat. Roscoe, knowing that Chaplin had a deep aversion to water, pulled out the bung. There was nothing Chaplin could do but keep acting as the boat sank beneath them. On another occasion when Charlie was using the toilet, the other actors 'forgot' to tell him that the seat had been electrified. There are those who believe that was the day he first performed his famous funny walk.

Meanwhile the Arbuckles, enjoying their rising standard of living, had rented a house by the beach. For six years Minta had been married to a man who could not afford to buy her jewels; now that he could, he showered her with them, or with anything else that she wanted. About the only thing he bought for himself that year (1914) was his first car, an Alco. They also had a Japanese servant by the name of Okie.

At every opportunity Roscoe took to the sea for a swim, invariably with Mabel Normand, who had become a close friend of the Arbuckles. One Sunday morning a dolphin swam with them from Santa Monica Beach to Venice and back again. The story is that this strange ritual occurred regularly on Sunday mornings for over a year. Roscoe, always quick to learn a new trick, swam alongside the dolphin and watched closely as it rose and fell in the water. He then imitated it to hilarious effect in a number of pictures, including *Fatty at Coney Island*.

The swimming was preparation also for the hard physical work he did in his films. While filming *Fatty's Jonah Day*, he dived seventy feet from the top of an electric mast above the bridge in Hollenbeck Park, into twelve feet of water. The effect was spectacular, not least on his teeth: all those in front were jarred. While on location with Mabel Normand at Santa Monica for another film, he made over fifty dives into the water during one day's filming; his skin was so battered from the water's friction that a doctor ordered him to bed.

Few men could suffer the pounding that Arbuckle's body took day after day in the cause of 'fun'. And his body was still solid muscle, as he proved to a group of bullfighters while on location one day. They mocked him for his fatness, and he challenged them to run one hundred yards in the arena before the crowd. He won the race with ease. Sennett had a preservation harness made for Roscoe; made of the same material as a horse's girth, it gave the comic's body a measure of protection.

There were times at Keystone when the lot resembled a casualty clearing station: Nick Cogley on crutches after a compound fracture of the leg, Charlie Murray suffering from temporary deafness after being hit with a bomb, and Chester Conklin still twitching after being prematurely fired from a cannon and landing on concrete. There is a popular saying, 'You don't have to be crazy to work here, but it helps.' At Keystone it was essential. By 1915 the most frequently-used product on the lot was not film but plaster to set broken limbs.

One of the myths handed down to us from Keystone days is that there were no stunt men, that everybody did his own stunt, no matter how dangerous. Film companies had used stunt men and women virtually from the beginning. Pearl White, for example, who was featured in a popular serial, used them often, and in one episode the stunt man who substituted for her in a daring leap from an elevator to a moving car was killed in the process. Even Douglas Fairbanks, famed for his athletic prowess, used a stunt man if the odds seemed to be against survival. The situation at Keystone was somewhat different. Although stunt men and women were employed, the stars were also expected to perform any reasonable stunts. But Sennett, who remarked in 1915 that the 'people who make Keystone comedies do not repose on sofa pillows until work is done', gave unusual latitude to the word 'reasonable'.

In one sequence of *Love, Speed and Thrills*, released in 1915, Minta Durfee hangs from the root of a tree, below her a three-hundred-foot drop. The only thing that prevented her early death was a length of piano wire. She had been induced to do this by director Wilfred Lucas, on the promise of a bonus, which turned out to be a puppy. Roscoe and Minta named the dog Luke, after her benefactor.

Fatty's Tintype Tangle (1915) contains a sequence in which Roscoe walks along telephone wires thirty feet above the ground, drops from the wires when he is over a housetop, crashes through a skylight and lands on a bed eighteen feet below. A series of stills shows that the stunt was performed by a well-padded stunt man. Having probably concluded by then that it was only a matter of time before Roscoe killed himself, Sennett took precautions.

Minta recalled for me what it was like on the Keystone lot during 1914:

> There was very little scenery on the lot at that time. We worked out on the streets, the fields, the lakes, everywhere. I don't recall that anybody paid too much attention to the script. Improvisation was the key. One-camera setups. I remember before Charlie got on to the beginnings of what was to become his Tramp character, he tried a whole range of ideas. One of them was a fat man. Sennett figured that Roscoe was handling that role OK and didn't need any help. He told Charlie to forget it. Roscoe would go out with a crew at eight in the morning, come back at six in the evening with a thousand feet of film shot. It was at this time when Sennett gave him a thousand-dollar bonus for ensuring that our

shipping dates under the Mutual contract were maintained. We had to have three films a week in New York.

During 1914, Sennett with great daring embarked on a six-reel comedy. At the time a two-reeler was considered the maximum for comedy, and he encountered tremendous opposition from his partners, who thought he was throwing money away. The film, *Tilli's Punctured Romance*, starring Mabel Normand, Charles Chaplin, Marie Dressler, Minta Durfee, Mack Swain and many other Keystone regulars, was a big success. If the risks were high, so were the profits at the end of the year. And the official census figures showed that in 1914 at least ten million people were going to the movies in the United States *every day*.

Sennett's biggest problem was that he was beginning to lose his stars. Lillian Gish has said that part of Sennett's success came from his following a piece of advice he had been given by D. W. Griffith: always pay generously, particularly when on location. Griffith was referring specifically to 'the policeman who helps you, the man whose front yard you use, the caterer who provides the cast with lunches'. According to Miss Gish, Sennett followed this advice throughout his movie career and found it profitable. Perhaps if he had applied the same principle to his stars, he might have kept them. (But then, if Griffith had done the same, he might have kept his stars too.)

By the end of 1914 Chaplin's Tramp character was clearly defined and firmly established with the public. So were the little Englishman's ambitions. He wanted money, lots of it, more than Sennett would pay. Sennett said later that Chaplin wanted more than he *could* pay, that he had offered the comedian half of his Keystone empire in an attempt to keep him. (Half of a third of the company would have meant an income of at least half a million dollars a year for Chaplin.) Chaplin on the other hand says that Sennett offered him a three-year contract, at $500 a week the first year, $700 the second, and $1,500 the third. Chaplin wanted to reverse the payments so that the maximum amount was paid the first year and the least in the third, but Sennett wouldn't agree, so they parted company. Most likely Sennett did baulk at paying Chaplin the money he demanded, but the King of Comedy was not prepared to admit that his false thrift in paying salaries was the reason for Chaplin's departure.

Time and time again Sennett lost his stars because he wouldn't meet salary demands that other companies were willing to meet. He refused to pay Ford Sterling more than $700 a week in 1913, when Sterling was the most popular film comedian in the country; Sterling left. Harold Lloyd wanted $40 a week; Sennett fired him. He refused even to discuss an increase with Chester Conklin and lost him, and eventually he would lose Arbuckle, although not only because of money. Meanwhile, in 1915, Chaplin left Keystone for the Essanay Company, where he received $1,250 a week. In 1916 he signed a contract with Mutual Film Corporation that was worth $670,000 a year.

In 1915 Sennett was saying publicly that Arbuckle was his righthand man. He acknowledged his debt to the heavyweight comedian, saying that Arbuckle was 'responsible for the success of many pictures in which he does not appear at all, but has directed'. He continued, 'There is perhaps not a superior combination on earth from the standpoint of good comedy to Miss Normand and Roscoe Arbuckle. Roscoe may act foolish before the camera, but he is one of the most sensible young men in pictures.' Sennett had good reason to be grateful to Roscoe. The King of Comedy was now immersed in the business end of the company, and responsibility for seeing that the films actually got made fell largely on Roscoe's broad shoulders.

Yet Roscoe was chafing at the artistic bit. He had

learned his craft well and was continually urging Sennett to allow him to introduce more subtle dimensions to the Keystone comedies. Sennett would have none of it. What he wanted was broad, fast comedy; so did his partners and so did the American public. Why rock the boat?

As for Mabel Normand, Roscoe's comedy partner and Sennett's lover for many years: it is difficult to penetrate a legend, to grasp its reality, but if only a fraction of the information I have about Mabel Normand is correct, she was the most talented comedienne of the entire silent film period. Again and again during my interviews the word 'genius' was used to describe her. Gene Fowler in his amusing biography of Mack Sennett says that Isadora Duncan was the only woman of the time who possessed beauty, charm, ability and courage to equal Mabel's. Minta Durfee was to tell me, years after Mabel had finally died of tuberculosis, 'If there is anything better in the next life than this, then Mabel Normand is in the dollar seat.' Her career blossomed, but her talent was never fully developed during her years at Keystone, a problem she shared with Arbuckle and Chaplin.

By 1915 her love affair with Mack Sennett had lasted for seven years, extending back to the days when they both worked for Biograph. It was beginning to look as if the unconventional relationship would continue for ever, when she and Sennett announced that they intended to get married. The wedding dress was bought and the date set. Then fate intervened in the form of a 'well-meaning friend'. While Mabel was out driving with Minta Durfee and actress Anne Luther, Anne informed her that if she went home right away she would catch her lover with another woman. Mabel scoffed at the idea, particularly when Anne said the other woman was Mae Busch (who would be famous later as one of the 'angry wives' in the Laurel and Hardy movies). Mabel had befriended Mae in New York; when Mae had come out to California, Mabel had brought her to Keystone and persuaded Mack to contract her. Also, Mae had stayed at Mabel's home – she would be the last person to betray her. But just to make sure . . .

Mabel burst into her own apartment and found Mae Busch naked and the King of Comedy in his long underpants. For once his fertile imagination deserted him; he told Mabel that he was discussing Mae's 'first role'. Mae panicked. She picked up a vase and smashed it over Mabel Normand's head. Stunned in every sense of the word, Mabel staggered out into the night. An hour later the Arbuckles found her – blood pouring from a head wound – on their porch. The film Sennett said he was discussing with Mae went into production the next day – *A One Night Stand*.

One night two weeks later, Mabel Normand jumped off a Los Angeles pier in an attempt to kill herself. Half-dead, she was pulled from the Pacific and was rushed back to the Arbuckles' home. Sennett finally persuaded Roscoe to intervene on his bahalf, and a compromise was reached. Sennett and Mabel stayed together professionally for two more years, but the love affair had ended.

Though the cut on Mabel's head healed, something else seemed to be permanently damaged. Her behaviour had always been eccentric (she had once cartwheeled across a field before a convulsed film crew, revealing that she was not wearing underpants); after she left Sennett, it became even more bizarre.

She signed a five-year contract with Sam Goldwyn in 1917. Goldwyn fell in love with her, but it was a love that she pushed to breaking point. In the middle of a film she was making for him, she suddenly vanished, turning up later in Paris. Even that city, used to unusual people, was startled by Mabel Normand, who threw money around as if it were going out of fashion. She bought a dress for $15,000 and her tip to a waiter who brought coffee was a large diamond.

Having tired of Paris, she caught a boat back to America. On the boat a male passenger, beguiled by the combination of Mabel and the moon, made a pass at her. Outraged, she summoned the captain, and in front of dozens of people, at the captain's command, the passenger stuttered a formal apology. Mabel said, 'I should think so, too. I don't know what made you think I was that kind of girl.' Then she took off all her clothes and dived naked into the ship's swimming pool.

When the boat docked in New York, a group of friends met her and expressed envy at her stay in Paris. Mabel promptly booked passage for all of them and accompanied them back to France. After another blitz on Paris, she returned once more to America where she found yet another group of friends waiting at the pier. Laughing, they said, 'It's our turn to go now.' She agreed, and they all left on the next boat for a Paris whose supply of gowns, jewellery and fine wines was dwindling from this triple onslaught. Finally, Mabel called it a day and returned to America to work. The three trips had cost her nearly half a million dollars.

Now, however, Roscoe and Mabel were making *That Little Band of Gold*, a satire on divorce which was released in 1915. Roscoe had mastered both pantomime and the elemental Keystone style (which comedians like Eddie Foy would not learn nearly so well), but it was evident from the increasingly subtle changes of his facial expression in this new film that he was extending his range. Despite his 266 pounds, Roscoe often played the role of the little man in the big world, although he was also attracted to female disguises and was astonishingly successful in portraying women, projecting a strangely androgynous image when he did so. A film critic who in 1915 had described Charles Chaplin as 'a thin shoe salesman in Roscoe Arbuckle's pants' said that Roscoe reminded her of 'Falstaff in a ladies' waiting room'. Roscoe brought laughter to millions as he raced along the dusty roads of Los Angeles in a dozen guises. Like the roads themselves, there seemed no limit to Roscoe

Arbuckle's potential. He thrived on his work – which would all too soon be brought to a halt.

In the middle of 1915, Sennett, D. W. Griffith and Thomas H. Ince (together with such men as Harry Aitken, Adam Kessel and Charles Baumann) came together to form the Triangle Film Corporation. Thereafter Sennett's films were to be Triangle-Keystone Productions.

Thomas H. Ince had joined the movies as an actor in 1910, but had begun directing almost immediately. By 1914 he had his own well-outfitted studio and ranch in Culver City, 'Inceville'. Many early films were static, slow-paced and sentimental, but Ince's were relatively well-edited, fast-paced and realistic; he was known especially, though not exclusively, for his Westerns. Ince introduced the concept of the producer who oversees all aspects of a picture, and soon he became more involved in producing than in directing pictures. He died in 1924 under mysterious circumstances, after an outing on William Randolph Hearst's yacht. It was rumoured that Hearst, suspicious of Ince's attentions to his mistress, Marion Davies, had shot him, but the official cause of death was listed as 'heart failure as a result of an attack of acute indigestion'. Hearst would also figure in Roscoe Arbuckle's life, but his influence on Arbuckle's fate would be crystal clear.

However, 1915 was still magic time. The newspapers were lavish with praise of the three creative heads of Triangle. Griffith had become the 'Da Vinci of the screen', Ince was cinema's Rodin, and Sennett was 'the Molière of the movies'. (Puzzled, Sennett brought a press clipping to his writers and asked, 'Who is this fellow Moly-something?' Ray Griffith looked at him and said, 'Molière was a smart French plagiarist who hired three men to do his thinking for him.' Sennett left, clutching his press cutting.)

Triangle was headed by the three most creative men

in the business, each successful and talented. If ever an idea deserved to succeed it was this one. The reasons for its eventual failure were complex, but were probably related to one of Triangle's boldest innovations: the double feature. Many people in the film industry believed that it was economic madness to give the public two movies for the price of one, not only because it meant that output doubled while profits didn't, but also because of the danger that the public might react from an overdose. And Triangle was offering not double features but double-features-plus: each programme consisted of two features, one each by Griffith and Ince, and a two-reel comedy by Sennett. For the moment, everything Triangle – and Sennett's Keystone – touched, turned to gold, but one thing was clear: the pressure for more and more movies gave no-one time to relax.

The date for the Sennett/Normand wedding had been set for 4 July 1915. When that blew up in his face, Sennett had real trouble on his hands, not only personally but professionally. Mabel Normand and Roscoe Arbuckle were his biggest assets and their talents, instead of declining, seemed to expand with each new film. Both individually and as a team they accounted for the bulk of Keystone's profits, but within two years he was to lose both of them – a double blow from which Keystone would never recover.

Early January 1916 found Roscoe Arbuckle in New York with a full crew. The visit lasted over six months, during which time Roscoe made at least six films for Keystone. It was the first time in three years that Roscoe had left the West Coast film colony. He had started at Keystone as an obscure vaudevillian, and now he was at the top of his field, a movie comedian with millions of fans all over the world. But until this visit to New York, Arbuckle seems to have been unaware of the impact he had made outside the insular world of film-making. Now he could not ignore the evidence of his popularity. The Fort Lee studios where he was filming in New Jersey were besieged every day by journalists. When he filmed street scenes, the crowds had to be held back. When he walked into a restaurant or a hotel, the public cheered him. At first when this happened, Roscoe would look over his shoulder to see who was behind him but the crowds made it clear that he was the one they wanted to touch, to talk to, to get autographs from.

The privileged few who were allowed to stand near the set and watch the filming in January of *He Did and He Didn't*, gasped at some of the incidents. In one scene an actor broke his jaw; a few moments later Lloyd Peddrick, playing a butler, broke his nose. Before shooting, Roscoe had told the onlookers, 'You'll probably find this rather quiet; there's no rough stuff in this scene.'

The writers who interviewed him wanted to know his opinion on everything from the quality of New York steaks to when the war in Europe would end. Some even asked about film. He made it clear to reporters that he was moving beyond the Keystone philosophy: 'I'm not trying to be highbrow or anything like that, but I'm going to cut an awful lot of the slapstick out hereafter. If anyone gets kicked, or a pie thrown in his face, there's going to be a reason for it.' Asked where he got his ideas, he replied, 'I get a plot in my head, gather up the company, and start out. As we go along, fresh ideas pop out, and we all talk it over. I certainly have a clever crowd working with me. Mabel, alone, is good for a dozen new suggestions in every picture. And the others aren't far behind. I take advice from everyone. It's a wise man who realizes that there are others who know as much, if not more than he does himself. Some of my greatest stuff comes from the supposed-dull brains of "supers" [extras].'

Reporters were fascinated with Arbuckle's size. They invariably gave his weight as 385 pounds, although by this time he had settled at 266. Feature articles such as 'Feeding with Fatty' added to the myth of a huge appetite, although he really ate less than many normal-sized men. His three wives have told me that an average breakfast for Roscoe included fruit juice, toast or hot biscuits, scrambled eggs and a couple of cups of coffee.

From his earliest films, reviewers had referred to him as 'the fat boy', and by 1916 he was 'Fatty' to millions of people around the world. The name would never leave him, though *he had grown to hate it*. While accepting the fact that on screen he was 'Fatty', off camera he winced whenever the name was used. Sometimes he would say gently, 'I've got a name, you know.'

None of his friends or those who worked with him ever referred to him by the name that had become for him an albatross. Mabel Normand called him 'Big Otto'; Fred Mace, 'Crab'; Alice Lake, 'Arbie'. By 1916 many referred to him as 'the Chief', the name by which Buster Keaton would later know him. Comedian Charles Murray, for whom Roscoe had a deep affection, somehow got away with calling Roscoe the oddest name of all, 'My Child the Fat'.

The search for new angles in writing about Roscoe reached absurd proportions during his New York stay; reporters even took to interviewing his dog Luke. In that crazy world of movies, Luke had become a star himself. He was frequently featured in Arbuckle's films and by 1916 was under contract to Sennett at a salary of $150 a week. What the bull terrier himself made of all this is not recorded, despite the interviews he had.

One of the funniest stories about the dog has never been told before. In a sequence being filmed for Keystone in Los Angeles, one scene opened in an animal-shelter wagon parked on a nearby street corner. Two bear cubs emerged from the back of the wagon and started to walk along the sidewalk. At that point Luke, who was not appearing in this film, came roaring out of an alleyway and charged at the bear cubs, who hurtled down the street, with the dog in pursuit. Roscoe, who also had nothing to do with the picture, was walking towards the lot with his arms full of groceries when he saw the two bear cubs moving towards him at high speed. He dropped the groceries and shinnied up the nearest telegraph pole. The bears followed him up the pole, and Luke did his best to follow the bears. Director Del Lord had by now lost control of the scene and his crew, who were hysterical with laughter. Just then, fire sirens were heard and the Edendale fire department (at that time an all-Negro unit) came screeching into view. Paying no attention to anyone, they hooked up their hoses and began playing them on the back of the studios. Needless to say, the pole that Roscoe, the bears and Luke had developed such an interest in was situated at the back of the studios. The pole-climbing menagerie was soaked. Del Lord, on the floor laughing, shouted to the firemen that the fire was at Tom Mix's studio, not Sennett's. The firemen uncoupled their hoses and drove off.

Between filming and interviews, Arbuckle also found a little time to socialize. One of the people he met was Enrico Caruso. Somewhere the world-famous Italian tenor had read that Roscoe could sing; when they met in a restaurant, he ordered him to, and Roscoe obliged. After he finished, Caruso was silent a moment, then remarked, 'You have a superb voice, a magnificent voice. You must give up this nonsense that you do for a living and have your voice trained professionally. With training you could become the second greatest singer in the world.'

Roscoe was receiving daily offers to work with rival film companies. His reception in New York helped to convince him to leave Keystone, although a stronger reason was his increasing impatience during the last year with the artistic limitations imposed on him by the King of Comedy – a dissatisfaction he shared with Mabel Normand. Money was another problem. Keystone was paying him less than $500 a week. It was a large salary by 1916 standards, but every film that Roscoe was making for Keystone produced over $200,000 net profit, by conservative estimate. Because Roscoe now knew how profitable his films were to Keystone, his salary suddenly seemed inadequate. Also, Chaplin had left Keystone for considerably more money, and since Arbuckle was at least as popular as Chaplin, he didn't see why he shouldn't be well paid also.

Eventually he signed with the New York agent, Max Hart, who guaranteed Roscoe $200,000 a year – for which Hart got not only Roscoe, but also Minta and Al St John. One of the other film companies that had been eager to sign Arbuckle was Adolph Zukor's Paramount; having heard of Arbuckle's deal with Hart, Paramount moved fast. A man named Lou Anger appeared at the Fort Lee studios and invited Roscoe to take a trip to Atlantic City. Roscoe went. Waiting for him at Atlantic City was one of the most powerful men in the film industry, Joseph Schenck. The deal that Schenck had in mind for Arbuckle was superior to the one he had already agreed on with Max Hart. Arbuckle reviewed his career for Schenck, telling the movie executive that his main concern was not primarily the money, but the degree of artistic control he had over his pictures. Schenck offered him a deal that only one or two people in the history of the film industry have been offered: *complete artistic control of his pictures*. Schenck told Roscoe that he would create a film company, the Comique Film Corporation, whose sole function would be the creation of Roscoe's films. There was to be absolutely no interference from Paramount, which would distribute the pictures through Famous Players-Lasky. Roscoe could make what he liked, how he liked. In 1916 such an offer was unheard of. Not until the late 1930s would Orson Welles get anything approaching such terms again – and then it could be for only one picture, a masterpiece, *Citizen Kane*.

Comique would be financed by Paramount, and money and materials would be requisitioned from them. Lou Anger would be studio manager, to assist Roscoe in the day-to-day running of the company, but at no time would

Anger have authority to veto any of Arbuckle's demands – indeed, Anger would be paid by Arbuckle.

While Roscoe listened, astonished at the breadth of the offer, Schenck moved on to financial matters. At first, Roscoe would receive a salary of $1,000 a day, and a staggering twenty-five per cent of the profits. *This would ensure an annual salary of over one million dollars.* Remember that this was 1916, when money was worth more and when taxes were much lower. The contract Schenck offered was to cover ten years, with periodic reviews to ensure Arbuckle regular increases. Today such a contract would take twenty lawyers and three years to draft. In 1916 it was discussed over a meal and agreed to with a handshake. When Roscoe withdrew his hand he found a car key in it. The key was for what Joe Schenck called 'a little signing-on bonus' – a brand-new Rolls Royce. No formal contract was ever drafted. Each man had given his word, and that was good enough.

For Roscoe there remained the matter of Max Hart. Returning to New York, he told Hart that he wanted to be released from his contract with him. Sadly, Hart agreed. His net personal profit on the deal with Roscoe would have been at least $800,000 a year, and all he had to do was sell Roscoe to the highest bidder, but he bowed out gracefully.

Outraged, Minta urged Hart to hold Roscoe to the agreement that guaranteed work for her and Al St John, but Hart refused, saying, 'If a man does not want to work for you, you can't do anything about it.' The animosity between Roscoe and Minta caused by the Paramount signing did nothing to improve an already deteriorating situation. Minta revealed in an interview in April 1916 some of the pressures on her relationship with Roscoe. The interviewer wrote that Minta was 'trying to figure out whether it were better to remain permanently eclipsed by the bulk of his hilarious personality, or to be separated from his company, both personal and business.'

As for Roscoe, when Minta had remonstrated with him about dropping the contract that assured her of work, he had replied, 'I don't need anybody. I'm a star.' Fame was proving destructive to their marriage.

Arbuckle's deal with Paramount was international news in August 1916. In one of the many interviews he was obliged to give, he made the following remarks, which later events would prove sadly ironic: 'I shall produce nothing that will offend the proprieties, whether applied to children or grownups. My pictures are turned out with clean hands and, therefore, with a clear conscience, which, like virtue, is its own reward. Nothing would grieve me more than to have mothers say, "Let's not go there today. Arbuckle is playing and he isn't fit for the children to see." I want them always to speak otherwise of me, for as long as I can please the kiddies, I don't care who entertains their elders.'

When those remarks were made, Arbuckle and Chaplin were equally popular with adults, but Roscoe was clearly the children's favourite. It is sad that a man who gave so much pleasure to so many people's children was denied giving pleasure to his own. He desperately wanted his own family, but was destined never to have one.

Roscoe had been the biggest money-earner in the history of Keystone, and Sennett must have felt his absence keenly. Within months of Arbuckle's departure, the company ceased to exist. (Sennett continued making movies for several years, but never again with the success he had had at Keystone.)

Roscoe had returned from New York during July 1916 and made two more films for Keystone, *A Reckless Romeo* and *A Creampuff Romance*. At least twelve more scripts had been lined up for him when in early September he developed a carbuncle on his left thigh. Roscoe and Minta were now living on Grand Park Boulevard. Eight years earlier they had had to take a working honeymoon, but now they lived regally, in a house that rented for $200 a month. On one side of them lived actor Lew Stone, on the other actor Hobart Bosworth. By Labor Day 1916, the carbuncle on Roscoe's leg was very painful, so Minta decided to call in a doctor. It was then that their problems began. Their only contact with the medical profession had been at Keystone, whenever either of them had been injured; on their own they had never had a family doctor. Minta got several numbers and called them, but because it was a holiday no-one replied. Eventually she found someone, who later turned out to be an intern, and he, after examining Roscoe, cut open the thigh in the area of the carbuncle and put drains on the leg. He also put Roscoe on a daily dose of heroin.

Reassured that Roscoe was receiving expert medical attention, Minta continued working. Keystone was filming *Mickey*, a film comedy starring Mabel Normand and featuring Minta. There were constant delays on the filming, partially because Mabel was haemorrhaging internally; a consumptive condition that had been dormant for years had flared up again after Mabel's discovery of Sennett in the arms of Mae Busch, and her subsequent suicide attempt. Mabel Normand was seriously ill, but no-one at Keystone seems to have thought of calling a doctor for her.

Meanwhile, Paramount had arranged a 23-city tour of the country which Roscoe was to begin on 17 February. It seemed as if there were plenty of time to get Roscoe fit, but as time passed, his condition did not improve. Racing driver Barney Oldfield, Charles Chaplin, Lew Stone, and many other friends who visited Roscoe became disturbed about what was happening to the man who had appeared indestructible. They found him increasingly vague, bemused and rambling. Hobart Bosworth reported, when Minta returned home from the Keystone lot one day, 'He's not right, Minta. I was sitting there talking to him when suddenly he puts his hands out into space and begins moving them up and down with a funny little jerking action. I asked him what he

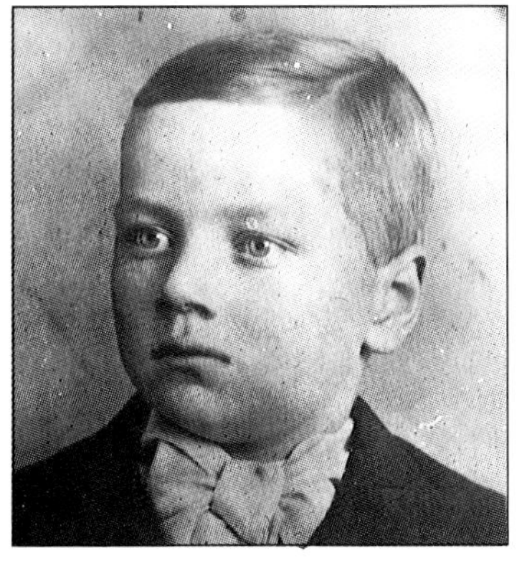

Roscoe Conklin Arbuckle at eight years of age. He had already acquired the nickname by which he would be known throughout the world, 'Fatty'.

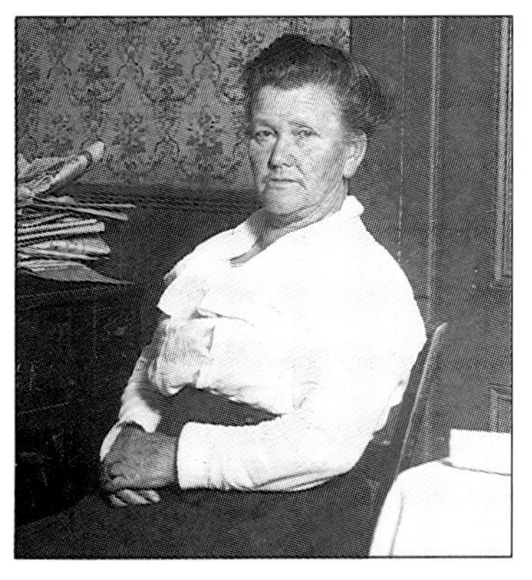

William Goodrich Arbuckle and Roscoe's stepmother, Mary Ellen Arbuckle.

Minta Durfee Arbuckle. Her mother had warned her about talking to strange young men on streetcars.

Roscoe and Minta after they had been married on the stage of the Byde-a-Wyle Theatre, Long Beach.

Minta making her first stage appearance and Roscoe cavorting in front of a film camera for the first time. Both events occurred in 1908.

A madhouse called Keystone. Roscoe's first role was as a five-dollar-a-day 'Kop'.

The photograph below gives a clear indication of the average movie-house, circa 1913. It also shows the eccentric Mack Sennett being attacked by Roscoe in a scene from *Mabel's Dramatic Career.*

Mabel Normand was considered by many, including Charlie Chaplin, to be the supreme film artiste. The top photographs are from two of the many films she made with Roscoe, *He Did And He Didn't* and *Fatty and Mable Adrift*. The lower photograph was taken at the time of her engagement to Mack Sennett in 1915.

The first three photos show a stunt allegedly performed by Roscoe in *Fatty's Tintype Tangle*. A stunt man doubled for the star. The last still from *Their Ups and Downs* made in 1914 catches Roscoe without the benefit of a 'double'.

A Man's Best Friend. By 1916, 'Luke' was under contract to Sennett and earning 150 dollars per week.

The three-million-dollar contract tour that ended with the Boston orgy. L to R: Mrs Zukor, Adolph Zukor, Roscoe, Minta and Marcus Loew. Seated on the car above Loew is Lou Anger.

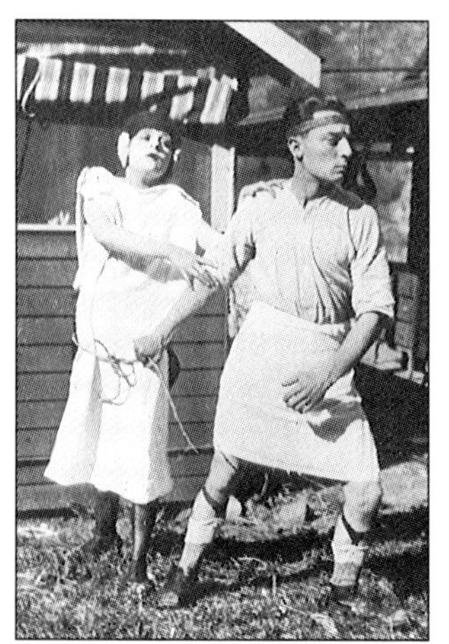

Private photographs taken on location in 1918 during the shooting of *Moonshine.* The inscriptions are by Alice Lake who in the first two is camping it up with Buster Keaton for the benefit of the film crew, and in the bottom one is giving her all for the benefit of the moviegoers.

was doing. "Oh, just milking the pretty butterflies," he replied.'

One day Minta returned from the studios and found the 'doctor' preparing to cut off Roscoe's leg. He had decided that amputation was the only remedy. Appalled, Minta turned for advice to her neighbours, Lew Stone and Hobart Bosworth, who called in not one doctor but three. Gently, the three doctors informed Minta that Roscoe, through the daily injections, had become addicted to heroin. They ordered his immediate removal to a Los Angeles hospital and told Minta that nobody would be allowed to visit Roscoe for several weeks, while Roscoe endured the private hell of being cured of heroin addiction. The infected leg was not improved by being cut open from the knee to the groin, but in his new role as a well-paid comedian Roscoe was not to recover at leisure. Paramount Pictures had announced that Roscoe would begin his nationwide tour on 17 February.

In the early years the film industry had maintained strict anonymity among its actors and actresses, so that the best of them would not be snatched up by rival companies. But by 1917 the 'star system' was fully launched. It would mean fame and fortune to the few who rose to the top, but the price it demanded was high, sometimes tragic. It certainly meant the end of personal privacy; every detail of a star's personal life was of interest to his fans. Roscoe Arbuckle was to become one of the first victims of the new system; for the moment, though, it was simply making a terrible demand. Film stars must not disappoint their public.

As a result of his illness, Arbuckle had lost over eighty pounds. His clothes hung on him like a shroud. A team of tailors worked round the clock to alter his clothes, and a doctor was assigned to accompany him across country. By early February he could walk only with the aid of two sticks and people on either side supporting him; on the trip, the people supporting him would at the same time hide the walking sticks from view, so that his fans would not be able to tell how ill their star really was.

The evening before the macabre tour was to begin, 16 February 1917, a banquet was given in Roscoe's honour. Among the heads of all the big studios and such eminent performers as Charlie Chaplin, Douglas Fairbanks, and Mary Pickford, Roscoe sat at the head of a rose-bedecked table and listened to the city's district attorney, Thomas Woolwine, who served as toastmaster. The former Keystone Kop had arrived.

The next day he set out from San Francisco in a private railway car which had been loaned for the occasion by Mrs Evalyn Walsh McLean, a Washington newspaper publisher who had also loaned it to President Roosevelt's daughter for her honeymoon trip. With him on the trip were Minta; Minta's sister, Marie, and her new husband, Herbert Maclean, who acted at the time as Roscoe's manager; Joe Bordeau, Roscoe's chauffeur and assistant director; Jimmy Bryant, his masseur; and the doctor assigned for the trip. Among studio bigwigs who joined the group for different parts of the junket were Joseph Schenck, Jesse Lasky, Marcus Loew, Lou Anger and even the president of Paramount, Adolph Zukor.

As if the trip itself were not enough of an ordeal for Roscoe, it also marked the beginning of the intrigue that would now plague him constantly: the infighting of the star's entourage. After the train pulled out of San Francisco, Lou Anger announced to the group that he was Roscoe's manager. Roscoe had agreed to this when he discussed his million-dollar deal with Joseph Schenck, but he had not told Minta. His signing a contract that excluded her had cut deep. Now she was learning for the first time that he was also dispensing with the services of her brother-in-law, Herbert Maclean. The gulf between the couple widened.

At every stop, Paramount Pictures had carefully planned official functions honouring Roscoe; these were attended by film exhibitors, producers and various ancillary workers of the movie world. But Adolph Zukor and his business colleagues hadn't counted on the public reaction to the tour. Their eyes must have lit with joy at the acclaim Roscoe received in what became a triumphant trip. When he reached his home state of Kansas, a state notoriously indifferent to the film industry at that time, the train was brought to a standstill by a crowd estimated at a quarter of a million people.

At every function Roscoe was obliged to make a speech of thanks and to be funny. Somehow he succeeded, though in truth his audiences so loved him that he had merely to say in the pouring rain that it 'Looks like being a nice day' to send people into peals of laughter. Few if any realized that he needed his walking sticks and the supporting arms of his sister-in-law Marie and her husband Herbert, to whom he said frequently, 'Stay close to me, I can't walk.' His condition was such that daily throughout the entire journey his physician had to give him painkilling drugs.

The climax of the trip was the arrival in Boston, where Mrs Mclean was given back her railway car. Roscoe and his entourage would make the trip to New York by the regular train, but first there was a final banquet scheduled in Boston. Out of that banquet has grown another of the myths about Roscoe.

At least twenty books, including many listed at the end of this one, mention Roscoe Arbuckle's participation in an orgy in Boston. Fairly typical is the account given by Kenneth Anger in *Hollywood Babylon*, a monument to bad taste and innuendo:

> One of Fatty's parties in 1917 came within a hairs-breadth of public scandal. The roaring, all-night revel in a rented roadhouse to celebrate Fatty's signing with Paramount roused a neighbour, who went to investigate. The elderly lady busybody managed to peek through an open transom at the liquor-soaked festivities, and after observing the host complete a tabletop striptease and a

round-the-table starlet-chase *in naturalis*, decided 'decency' had been outraged and called the cops. Caught with his pants *down* and a starlet's skirt *up*, the famous funnyman was a perfect patsy for blackmail. Lou Anger worked overtime, and reportedly had to cross many official palms with silver, to chill the beef over Fatty's bawdy flight of fancy.[1] [The italics are Kenneth Anger's.]

What follows is the true story of what happened in Boston, based on transcripts of a later trial for corruption in the office of DA Nathan Tufts.

On the evening of 6 March 1917, Roscoe Arbuckle was the guest of honour at a banquet given by Famous Players-Lasky, which by then meant Paramount. The dinner, staged at the Copley Plaza, a staid Back Bay hotel, was attended by 125 Paramount exhibitors from the New England area; Adolph Zukor, Hiram Abrams, and Walter Greene, the three men who owned Paramount and were

---

[1] While this book was being copyedited for the printer, a new edition of *Hollywood Babylon* was published in the United States. The passage quoted above was from a pirated translation of the original French version. Clearly the new version has been toned down, but it is amazing how much misinformation was allowed to remain (including a photo of Minta Durfee captioned 'Witness Maude Delmont'):

'The boozy all-night revel held on 6 March at Mishawn [*sic*] Manor, Boston [*sic*], to celebrate that signing *almost* became a public scandal. It took place at Brownie Kennedy's Roadhouse, where the lavish entertainment laid on in Fatty's honour included twelve 'party girls' who were paid $1,050 for their contribution to the evening's fun. A bluenose busybody peeked through an open transom just as Fatty and the girls were stripping on the table, decided 'decency' had been outraged and called the cops. Attending the festivities were movie magnates Adolph Zukor, Jesse Lasky and Joseph Schenck. They ended up paying $100,000 in hush money to the Boston District Attorney and Mayor James Curley to bury the incident.'

presidents of the company; Jesse Lasky, Paramount vice president; Marcus Loew, who controlled the largest circuit of theatres in the United States; Attorney General Henry Atwill; and members of the mayor's office and the governor's staff. It was a powerful and wealthy group. Marcus Loew and Adolph Zukor alone were worth more than seventy-five million dollars. That year Loew, known as the 'Henry Ford of show business', spent eight million dollars building ten new theatres in eight cities. In 1920, he would pay over three million dollars to gain control of Metro Pictures. Toastmaster Joseph Levenson, a prominent Boston lawyer, introduced the speakers, including Roscoe himself. The Boston society columns the next day observed that Roscoe was 'as great a success as an after-dinner speaker as he is in comedy'.

Arbuckle was still a sick man, and the tour he had just completed would have exhausted most fit men. The strain of public functions in twenty-three cities, in the space of little more than four weeks, had taken a terrible toll. Shortly after eleven o'clock, Roscoe, leaning heavily on the arms of Minta and Lou Anger, bid the assembled company good night and left the banquet hall. After a drink with Anger in a nearby club, the Arbuckles retired for the night.

Some of the other dinner guests still had appetites to satisfy. Hiram Abrams, one of the Paramount presidents, had arranged an intimate chicken-and-champagne party for a favoured few. The main item on the party menu was a sex orgy, to be held at Mishawum Manor in nearby Woburn, Massachusetts. It was delightfully fitting that members of the movie industry should choose Woburn for their orgy. Just four years earlier the fifteen thousand citizens of Woburn had narrowly missed contact with the devil: the guardians of Woburn decency (not wanting to 'expose our citizens to Celluloid debauchery') had decreed that film exhibitors would not be granted licences to show movies. Apparently the top brass at Paramount had decided that if the people of Woburn could not be debauched via Celluloid, they should be treated to the real thing.

And so they were, during the early hours of 7 March 1917.

Mishawum Manor was later to be described by a chief justice as a 'house of ill fame'. The madam had as many names as bedrooms: Brownie Kennedy, alias Lillian Kingston, alias Stella Webber, alias Helen Morse, alias Lillian Dale, alias Stella Kennedy. Sixteen film men arrived at the brothel shortly after midnight. Besides the three Paramount presidents, Zukor, Abrams and Greene, and Vice President Jesse Lasky, the group included the convivial toastmaster, Joseph Levenson, and Famous Players managers Harry Asher and Edward Golden.

Brownie Kennedy's hospitality was designed to suit a variety of palates. After the chicken and champagne, as pianist Theresa Sears tickled the ivories, a huge salver was placed in the centre of the room. The cover was removed to reveal a young woman wearing a few small pieces of parsley and a sprinkling of salad dressing. Fourteen other young women then entered the room, wearing only inviting smiles, and the orgy began. During the night, the group consumed fifty-two bottles of champagne. Came the dawn, and Hiram Abrams paid the bill of $1,050. The party would ultimately cost much more.

Several weeks later, Hiram Abrams received a phone call from Mayor James M. Curley of Boston, advising him of 'a serious matter likely to arise'. Abrams hurried from Portland to Boston and met with his lawyer, Joseph Levenson – toastmaster at the banquet and one of the guests at the chicken-and-champagne affair. They conferred with the mayor and others at the Hotel Touraine.

Mayor Curley advised them that a number of girls at the orgy had talked, and that District Attorney Nathan A. Tufts of Middlesex County was investigating the affair. Some of the young prostitutes at Mishawum Manor had been under the age of consent; and the husbands of some of the others were bringing actions, alleging that the affections of their wives had been alienated as a result of the orgy. The Paramount presidents faced inevitable criminal proceedings. Brownie Kennedy had already been brought to trial. The police had raided her 'house of ill fame' a few days after the film orgy, and Brownie, wearing a pair of flimsy pyjamas, was arrested as she tried to escape through a window. She got away with a $100 fine and a six-month suspended sentence. Brownie had used one of her many aliases in court, but for men like Zukor, Lasky, Greene and Abrams, there could be no hiding behind aliases.

The film men went with their attorneys to see DA Tufts. They told him that they were law-abiding citizens, upright, honourable men. Tufts, referring to the presidents of Paramount as 'licentious Jews' said, 'Practices which might pass unnoticed in a large city could not be permitted in a small place like Woburn.' Prosecution was imminent.

The film men held a series of conferences in Boston, New York and New London, Connecticut, and concluded that the only way of averting disaster was to pay out a large bribe. Boston lawyer Daniel Coakley felt certain he could buy everybody off for $100,000. Adolph Zukor feared that if there were legal action against him, an outraged husband might collect $250,000 through the courts, and that would only be the beginning – the publicity would destroy his career. Still, he baulked at putting up any of the bribe money, arguing that it was Abrams' party and that it was therefore up to Abrams to settle. Eventually they raised the $100,000. Zukor put up $25,000 for himself and $25,000 for Jesse Lasky, and the other two Paramount presidents put up $50,000. Attorney David Stoneman, acting on behalf of Abrams, handed the money over to Coakley to 'use as he saw fit'. Ironically, not all of the money was cash; the payment included five hundred shares of Famous Players stock.

Coakley, a close friend and associate of Tufts, placed the money judiciously. DA Tufts lost all interest in proceeding against the film men. Everyone hoped that there the matter would rest. And there it did – until 12 July 1921. Then the partygoers would hear of the Boston orgy again – and so would Roscoe Arbuckle, who had not attended.

The day after the Boston reception – the official one – the Arbuckle entourage journeyed to New York. Roscoe and his wife booked in at the Cumberland Hotel. Although their marriage was dying, there was still at that time a great deal of love between them. Minta recalled for me that first day in New York:

> Apparently he'd gone into a perfume shop to buy me a little present. He told the assistant that he wanted a bottle of the best perfume in the place. They showed him a bottle of *Quelques Fleurs*. I don't remember what the exact price was, but it was terribly expensive. Well, Roscoe looked at this little bottle containing a half-ounce of perfume and remarked, 'There's not enough in there for one ear.' He persuaded them to get a huge display out of the window. It was one of those mock bottles. Stood about five feet high and was filled with coloured water. They emptied out the coloured water and began to fill the display bottle with *Quelques Fleurs*, opening up all their half-ounce and one-ounce bottles and pouring them in. They used up their entire stock and had to send out for fresh supplies to get the bottle filled. All this was causing complete havoc in the shop. Assistants running about, emptying hundreds of little perfume bottles. The first I knew of all this was when I opened the door to our hotel suite, and Roscoe hobbled in. He was followed by two men, who staggered in with this huge bottle of perfume. Roscoe gave me a smile, and said, 'Thought you might like a little present, Minty.'

Minta's account of the first day after the Boston reception continued with her description of what happened when they retired for the night:

When we got into bed, Roscoe took me into his arms and said, 'You know, Minty, I would love to make love to you. But I just don't know whether I'll be able to or not. I haven't for so long.' I said, 'Well, if you can, that would be very nice. If you can't, it'll be nice just to cuddle.' He fondled me, then tried to make love. He couldn't. His leg gave way, and he fell back on his side of the bed. He cried like a baby.

Then and later, Roscoe was hardly the kind of man to take part in an orgy.

In New York, under the best medical care available, Roscoe's condition improved rapidly. Just as rapidly, his marriage deteriorated. Because of events that were later to change the course of his life, it is important to emphasize here that the marriage was not breaking up because Roscoe was unfaithful. Adela Rogers St Johns, for many years a shrewd film columnist, became friendly with the Arbuckles through Mabel Normand, her closest friend. Commenting on their marriage, she said to me, 'I was very fond of Roscoe, everybody was. He was a pleasant, big man. I thought their marriage was a very good one. Roscoe never played around. It was inconceivable to think of Roscoe having a sex life. He was never crude. I remember one occasion. There had been rumours that Roscoe was seeing one of the Sennett bathing beauties. Mabel and I mentioned it to Minta. She roared with laughter and told Roscoe, who joined in the laughter.'

Minta herself said that there was never the slightest suggestion that Roscoe was 'playing around'; he was shy and never familiar with women. 'No woman ever came between us. It was a man. Lou Anger.' Minta has always believed that Anger had a Svengali-like influence on her husband. If so, Arbuckle was a willing subject. For nine years Minta, on her own admission, had been pushing her husband to a realization of his talent. She had succeeded, but at a cost: Roscoe had grown tired of the pushing. Minta had appeared in over two hundred films at Keystone, and would have made an excellent foil for her husband in the films he was to make for Paramount, but she never appeared in one. By early 1917 Roscoe was at the top of his profession, and he was determined to be on his own.

His parting from Minta occurred slowly. For his birthday, on 24 March, Minta had bought him membership in the Friars and the Lambs clubs. He moved into the Friars, a show business club, telling Minta that he did not feel well and would be able to get constant baths and massages at the club. A few days later Norma Talmadge and her mother called on Minta: Norma, the wife of Joseph Schenck, told Minta that Lou Anger would be on the phone soon suggesting that all of Roscoe's clothes be sent to the Friars Club, but that Minta should refuse because this was a device to make it seem that Minta was refusing to live with her husband. They reasoned that if Minta could establish that she was the innocent party in every way, she would be entitled to more alimony. The phone call came a few hours later, and Minta told her husband's new manager that if Roscoe wanted his clothes, he could come and get them. This he did, moving a few at a time over a period of six weeks. Roscoe continued to phone her and take her out socially, and he saw to her material needs. Without going to court, Arbuckle offered to pay his wife $3,000 a month, far more than she expected to receive.

Minta was only one of Roscoe's problems in 1917. He was also getting his film company into production. In late March he began work on his first production, *The Butcher Boy*, which he wrote, directed, and starred in. Production was well under way at Norma Talmadge's Colony Studio when Lou Anger brought a quiet young man on to the set and introduced him to Roscoe. The young man knew a lot about vaudeville but nothing at all about the movies, though he was destined to learn a great deal – most of it from Roscoe. His name was Buster Keaton; he would later become one of the world's greatest film comedians and directors. Rudi Blesh's superb biography of Keaton is one of the only books that in any way attempts to do justice to Arbuckle's role in Keaton's career, though even Blesh doesn't reveal the full debt that the comedian of the sad countenance owed to Roscoe. But Keaton himself was quick to acknowledge it:

> Roscoe took the camera apart for me so I would understand how it worked and what it could do. He showed me how film was developed, cut and then spliced together . . . the longer I worked with Roscoe the more I liked him. I respected, without reservation, his work both as an actor and a comedy director. He took falls no other man of his weight ever attempted, had a wonderful mind for action gags, which he could devise on the spot. Roscoe loved all the world, and the whole world loved him in those days. His popularity as a performer was increasing so rapidly that soon he ranked second only to Charlie Chaplin.
>
> Arbuckle was that rarity, a truly jolly fat man. He had no meanness or malice or jealousy in him. Everything seemed to amuse and delight him. He was free with his advice and too free in spending and lending money. I could not have found a better-natured man to teach me the movie business, or a more knowledgeable one.

During an interview with film historian Kevin Brownlow, Keaton put it in a line: 'I learned it all from him.'

Arbuckle had said to Minta after the million-dollar deal with Joseph Schenck, 'I don't need anybody, I'm a star', but on the set he knew that he needed the help of others. Free both in giving and taking advice, he encouraged in his staff an exchange of ideas unique in the film industry. Unfettered by 'front office' interference, Arbuckle and the people he had gathered around him at Comique achieved staggering success. Before Comique was formed, Paramount had found that seventy-five prints of their comedies more than filled the exhibitors' needs. When Arbuckle's two-reelers began emerging from the New York studios, exhibitors all over the country wanted them, and Paramount found it necessary to increase the number of prints first to 100, then to 150, then to 200. No matter how much they increased the supply, the demand always exceeded it.

Arbuckle had gathered together the best comedy team in the business. His writers included Herbert Warren, Clyde Bruckman, Jean Havez and Mario Bianchi. Bianchi later became a comedy star under the name of Monte Banks, and later still he married Gracie Fields. Long before working for Roscoe, Jean Havez wrote for Kolb and Dill, the comedy team that had introduced Minta Durfee to the stage. Arbuckle used cameramen like Elgin Lessley and George Peters. Under Roscoe's guidance, his chauffeur, Joe Bordeau, and his masseur, Jimmy Bryant, both ex-Keystone Kops, became highly competent stock players, and Bordeau also became a director. These names probably mean nothing to the average reader, but the film world knew how much pure talent emerged from Comique; after Arbuckle's destruction in San Francisco, the team he had created was eagerly snapped up by Buster Keaton, Harold Lloyd and W. C. Fields.

When Buster Keaton first visited the Comique studios in late March 1917, he had no intention of deserting the lucrative vaudeville field; in fact he had just signed a contract with Max Hart (the agent Roscoe had signed with briefly) that would pay him $250 a week to appear in a New York show. The day spent in Roscoe's company ended with Keaton's playing a part in *The Butcher Boy*. Buster decided that this was for him. He went to Hart and asked to be released from the contract – a precedent established by Roscoe – explaining that he was going into the movies. The agent asked what Keaton's salary was to be, and Keaton replied, 'I didn't ask.' He got $40.00 a week, and Hart's blessing.

In *The Butcher Boy* Keaton discovered that custard pies were not the only thing that Arbuckle threw with unerring accuracy. One scene called for Keaton to be hit in the face with a sack of flour. In Rudi Blesh's *Keaton*, Buster recalls how after they had completed the film he sneaked into a New York cinema alone to see the film quietly from an aisle seat: 'Comes that scene, the sack is in the air; I half stand up in my excitement and suddenly – pow! – I – that's me *myself*, not me on the screen – I'm flat on my neck in the theatre aisle. Now hear this; I got up and sat down in my seat again, *honestly*, without realizing what had happened. Then I heard Arbuckle laugh. The bastard had slipped in the theatre and sat down behind me. He waited for that scene. At the very second that sack landed on the screen, he bopped me in the back of the neck.'

There were some things Arbuckle didn't find amusing. A voluptuous young blonde was playing a part in the final Comique production to be filmed in New York, *Fatty at Coney Island.* She came into Roscoe's dressing room holding two bathing costumes in front of her, and asked Roscoe which she should wear. She dropped the first, then the second, revealing that she was nude. Roscoe ran from the room and instructed Lou Anger to fire her immediately, even though they had already shot two days of film with scenes including the ambitious girl. She was replaced, and the two days shot over again.

After six months in New York and with at least six comedies in the can, Roscoe moved the entire unit to California. But before leaving for the West Coast, Roscoe found time to get involved in one more escapade. Actor Lew Cody had come to town, and they decided to paint it red. After visiting several bars they breezed into Reisenweber's, a nightclub on Eighth Avenue where trumpeter Nick la Rocca and his band were ripping the place apart with Dixieland 'jass', as it was then called. Arbuckle and Cody were given the best table in the club and settled back to enjoy the music. Glancing at the next table, Roscoe said, 'I think you know that woman.' Cody certainly did. The woman was Dorothy Dalton, and they had been married, divorced, remarried and redivorced. That evening Cody, evidently a man who did not know when to call it a day, proposed to Dorothy again. Miss Dalton, obviously made of the same stuff as Cody, agreed. They arranged to marry for the third time the next day at noon, and Miss Dalton retired for the night. Roscoe and Cody got down to the serious business of celebrating the wedding. Early in the morning they retired to the Friars Club for a little nap before the wedding. Cody, the first to wake up, looked at his watch and saw that it was nearly noon. He rang Miss Dalton, saying that he would be grateful for a thirty-minute postponement, and she told him that he had been granted a lifetime delay. It seemed a harsh reaction until she asked, 'Where were you *yesterday* at noon?'

The Comique Company moved into the Horkheimer Brothers' Balboa Amusement Producing Company studios on Sixth and Alamitos streets in Long Beach, California, in October 1917. Comique never had its own studios, but rented or leased space at existing studios. The philosophy was sound. Instead of tying up millions of dollars of capital in a huge studio complex, Arbuckle improvised with facilities available at relatively low rents. His view was that the quality of the finished product was not enhanced by wall-to-wall carpeting in the dressing rooms.

If he was frugal about nonessentials, he certainly didn't spare the dollar when it came to actual production. Some observers considered it scandalous the way custard and eggs were wasted at the studios, particularly since many of the studio extras couldn't afford to buy the food being thrown at them. The cost of the foodstuffs was minor, however, compared with other props. One scene in *A Country Hero* – the first California production – involved the wrecking of two Ford cars by a locomotive. The cost of that sequence was over $20,000 because it took many retakes to satisfy Arbuckle, and this was not a feature-length film, merely a two-reeler, running about twenty minutes. At least that costly sequence was used; some never were. For example, when he had filmed *A Reckless Romeo,* Roscoe had imported an entire Broadway cabaret. The story involved Roscoe's performing as a Hawaiian dancer with the cabaret, which consisted of twenty chorus members, eight featured artists, the full restaurant orchestra, a large staff of waiters, and three dozen extras. The total cost of the scene was over $10,000, but, after viewing the filmed sequence, Roscoe scrapped it.

Curiously, he often assumed the role of a woman in his films. His success with female impersonation was a fascinating aspect of his comic abilities. In *His Wedding Night* Roscoe appeared as a female Spanish dancer, Al St John as a Scottish highlander, and Buster Keaton as a blushing bride. The clothes they wore were masterpieces. So was the comedy.

The second film the company made in California was *Out West*, a large part of which was filmed on location. Roscoe had a Western mining camp, 'Mad Dog Gulch', built among the cactus plants in the San Gabriel Canyon near Los Angeles. What the sight of 270 pounds of humanity being pursued by Indians did to the sensibilities of the local citizens is not recorded. What it did to Paramount's profits is a matter of record: they continued to soar.

Estranged from Minta, who continued to live in New York, Roscoe lived like a gypsy on the West Coast, moving from friend to friend – a week at Buster Keaton's, a fortnight at Lew Stone's. He stayed for a while at the Hollywood Hotel, a fact which at least one of the residents viewed with dismay. Anita Loos wrote in her autobiography: 'Off screen and on, Fatty was a clown and not a very good one, his comedy being the type which relies on fat, in itself, being funny. He invented one gag which all but drove poor old Miss Hershey [the hotel owner] mad. Fatty would fold his napkin into a long narrow strip, place a pat of butter in the centre of it, and then, by bringing the two ends together and abruptly jerking them apart, he would flip the butter clear up to the ceiling, where it would cling until the heat caused it to melt and drip on the diners below.'

On 6 April 1917, the United States had declared war on Germany. President Wilson had been re-elected because 'he kept us out of the war', but now, to the nation's surprise, voters found themselves in it. Men began to enlist to fight on the front. Buster was to serve eleven months in the infantry, seven of them in France. The army refused to accept Roscoe because he was one hundred pounds overweight.

Roscoe went down to the Marine training centre on Mare Island to boost the morale of the troops who were about to be sent out. During the course of the day Roscoe engaged in a game of pushball, using a huge man-sized ball. He stood with his back against it while twenty-five Marines heaved from the other side. They couldn't budge Roscoe. Next they played baseball, and Roscoe hit three homers. Then he took part in a battle exercise, and for a finale treated the Marines to a 'freak' gymnastic exhibition including pratfalls and 108's (standing somersaults). The men were impressed, but the authorities still said for a man standing under five feet ten inches tall, Roscoe was one hundred pounds overweight. He quietly purchased a trainload of Bull Durham tobacco, arranged for it to be given anonymously to the troops, and returned to film-making.

Arbuckle's next film, *The Bell Boy*, went into production in February 1918. Buster Keaton, not yet a soldier, must have yearned for the quiet of war-torn France. The climax of the film involves a bank robbery in which the robbers make their getaway by jumping on a horsecar that is ascending a very steep cobblestone street. They force the driver to whip his horse into a gallop. Near the top of the hill the traces break, jerking the driver through the air so that he lands on the back of the horse. Meanwhile the horsecar, with the robbers still on board, rolls straight back down the hill into the bank they have just robbed. On the first take of this sequence, the driver flew through the air with the greatest of unease, missed the horse, and crashed on to the cobblestones. He showed a marked reluctance to try it again. Buster volunteered to stand in. The distance between carriage and horse was nearly five feet. To ensure that the horse did not break free at the moment of separation from the carriage, Buster wound the reins tightly around his wrists. At the precise moment of separation Buster leaped for the horse, but as Buster sailed through the air, the horse elegantly stepped to one side and began galloping for dear life. Buster crashed on to the cobblestones and, unable to free the reins from his wrists, was dragged half a block.

Another sequence in the film involved Alice Lake and Al St John. They were ascending in a hotel elevator when the elevator suddenly collapsed and began to hurtle to the ground. Al St John was dug out, miraculously uninjured, from the debris below. Alice was left some forty feet up, clinging to a rope. Looking up at her, Roscoe remarked, 'Don't go away, Alice. I might want to shoot that again.'

Yet another sequence from the same film, shot this time without mishap, demonstrates Arbuckle's comic inventiveness. Actor Charles Dudley, playing a hotel guest, enters the hotel's barber shop and demands immediate attention; bellboy Arbuckle becomes barber Arbuckle and goes to work with his scissors. In a trice the heavily-bearded Dudley, who begins the scene looking like Rasputin, is transformed into an astonishing duplicate of President Lincoln. Arbuckle eyes his handiwork for a moment, then recommences snipping. A moment later President Lincoln has been transformed into General Grant.

During this period, Arbuckle's nomadic life continued.

He lived for a while with his scenario editor, Herbert Warren, and Warren's wife in a small bungalow near the film studios. Schenck urged him to live in a manner befitting his position, but, apart from acquiring motor cars with an alarming frequency, Roscoe refused to play the game of keeping up with the Mary Pickfords.

Roscoe wasn't always successful in his attempts to get away from the slapstick comedy of Keystone days, but he was learning. He filmed *Moonshine* with Keaton, again in the San Gabriel Canyon, and about a year after it was released he had this to say: 'An illustration of satire that didn't "get over" with the masses is furnished by the scene in *Moonshine* of the elaborately furnished underground retreat of the moonshiners. The travesty was carried a little too far. Take again the scene of the moonshiners donning evening clothes for dinner. It "went" great with those who are familiar with social customs and slipped completely over the heads of those who were not. Yet the kids invariably "got" it for they immediately sensed the incongruity of the roughneck mountaineers putting on "soup and fish". But as a piece of business it scored a failure on the whole because it required thought to grasp the satire; somehow it was out of rhythm.'

Sennett had put the average mental age of the public at eleven and had geared his movies to that level. While Roscoe had felt restrained by the Keystone philosophy, he also had been clearly influenced by it: 'I endeavour to cater to the masses as well as the classes, not forgetting the kids. Children like the purely physical comedy – the fall and the knockdown – and the more exaggerated the action, the more they laugh. The average person watching a comedy on the screen does not want to be compelled to think – to figure out a piece of business – so that there is always a little hesitancy in dealing with satire and the little subtleties that are enjoyed by the clever people.'

Whether Roscoe changed his views, or was simply

more successful in subsequent films, or whether after the war audiences were in fact becoming more sophisticated, the time would come when Roscoe felt there were enough 'clever people' to justify subtlety in his films.

At about this time (early 1918) the name 'Hollywood' came into popular use to describe America's film town. Inasmuch as it suggests a vast conglomerate of film studios in a small area, Hollywood is and was a myth – the studios have always been widely scattered. Hollywood is a state of mind surrounded by Los Angeles. It is an illusion, but an illusion with some tangible assets. Movie-goers were given not merely Celluloid fantasy; what they read about the stars was largely fantasy too, and Hollywood, once a sleepy suburb of Los Angeles, became Dreamland for millions.

Again and again, members of the film industry recalling Hollywood as the 1920s approached, remarked to me, 'It was like a village.' You could walk down Hollywood Boulevard in 1918 and see half a dozen movie stars. Louis Blondeau had been the top barber, but he had realized more quickly than most the implications of the film immigration to the West Coast; pocketing his comb and scissors, he went into real estate, reselling sites to movie companies at huge profits. Now the main barber shop was Helmens, and there on a good day one could reasonably expect to find leading men Wally Reid, Douglas Fairbanks, Charlie Chaplin and Roscoe Arbuckle, waiting for a trim. Rudolph Valentino's engagement to Natacha Rambova was announced in a monthly magazine; a similar event would be front-page news around the world today. Louella Parsons was still waiting for William Randolph Hearst to tell her that she was a gossip columnist, and Hedda Hopper was, to use Adela Rogers St Johns' phrase, 'still a bad actress running around'. The national newspapers weren't geared yet to cope with a phenomenon like Hollywood, nor did they realize what the film industry and its products were coming to mean to millions of people around the world. By the end of the First World War, Hollywood was the centre of the world's film industry.

Wally Reid, America's number-one screen heart throb for years, was learning what it meant to be a leading man: he was plagued by women, who didn't seem to mind that he was married. Driving his car out of his garage one morning, he was surrounded by six girls who had hidden all night in the inspection pit beneath the car. Another girl travelled three thousand miles from New York and offered Reid's dresser a $10,000 bribe to hide her in the star's dressing room. The dresser took the bribe. The time would come when Reid would shock the nation with his drug addiction; Reid would be past caring about his image then, although the news would contribute to destroying his good friend Roscoe Arbuckle.

But now Hollywood was not only young, but also strangely innocent. The glamourous film set was in many ways unsophisticated. A wild night for Bebe Daniels and Adela Rogers St Johns meant stealing a couple of bicycles from Western Union and riding them home. Charles Chaplin gives the impression in his autobiography that when he was not making superb pictures, which he unquestioningly did, he spent all of his spare time in conversation with the likes of Melba, Godowsky, Paderewski and Nijinsky. But his recreation was often less elevated. The Western Athletic Club held weekly boxing promotions in which Chaplin often acted as second for one fight, with Roscoe Arbuckle doing the same in the opponent's corner. (On one occasion Roscoe advised his man: 'Hit him where he is, not where he was.')

Night spots like the Sunset Inn, Al Levy's café, and Baron Long's were favourites of the period, and there was a time when a night out meant nothing more than going to the Vernon Country Club and dancing the turkey trot, the grizzly bear and the black bottom. There was a time when Hollywood did not have a 'society', when an invitation to eat at the home of Tom Mix meant helping to cook the meal and wash up afterwards. Even when the stars felt obliged to hire large domestic staffs, they did so with disarming innocence; a star might insist on cooking the meal if he thought the cook looked tired. As late as 1924 Elinor Glyn, who was into the 'U' and 'non-U' scene a generation before Nancy Mitford, was driven to complain, 'Where else in the world will you find a coloured cook bursting into a drawing room to say, "You folks better hustle to dinner if you don't want the stuff to get cold."' In 1918 few gave dinner parties because few knew how to give them. At that time the candle that an entire generation would burn at both ends had only just been taken from the box. They were still looking for the matches.

Hollywood the film village would quickly be no more than a memory. Already an extraordinary situation was making the innocence unlikely to continue: huge wealth was suddenly placed in the hands of people who a few years before had had barely the price of a dinner. Adela Rogers St Johns talked of this to me:

> None of us had any idea what we were doing. There was no-one to handle our money. The exception was Mary Pickford. She was smart enough to have for a mother a woman who knew more about money than the Secretary of the Treasury. Jack Pickford [Mary's brother] used to say of her, 'Charlotte never buys anything but corners' [a reference to her real estate acumen]. Another exception was Harold Lloyd. His father had been in banking. Most of us, however, spent as fast as we could. We bought houses, automobiles, gold-plated baths, grass lawns imported from England. You name it, we bought it.

If they didn't know what to do with their new wealth in 1918, they certainly knew how to make movies – and they made hundreds of them. Comique was a scene of ceaseless activity. The last film Buster Keaton worked in before he went to war was *The Cook*, a two-reeler that few today have been able to see – a film from which Chaplin in 1925 would lift a whole comic sequence of Arbuckle's to use in *The Gold Rush*.

Comedy routines were not all Chaplin took from his contemporaries. Jackie Coogan recalled for me recently how he came to work with Chaplin in *The Kid*:

> My dad knew all the people in LA. It was like a great club. He was captain of the actors' golf team. He was also captain of the crap-shooting team. He got to LA with the act after a fifty-week tour and Chaplin saw me. Roscoe came down and asked Father if he wanted to go to work in the movies. Meanwhile I had met Chaplin. He was anxious to get into *The Kid*; it was to be his first feature. He was giving a lot of thought to it, but he does not at this stage relate me to it, he doesn't tie me up or anything. So my dad goes down to San Diego to finish his tour, then it's announced in the newspaper that Jack Coogan has been signed by Roscoe Arbuckle. For Charlie the penny drops, he goes nuts, he says, 'I can see that fat son of a bitch with the little boy. God, why didn't I think of that?' Chaplin became determined to buy Roscoe out. He sends people down to discuss a deal with my father. This is done with complete secrecy. My father tells him, 'No, it isn't little Jackie who Roscoe's signed, it's me.' Chaplin gets me contracted, fast.

Later Chaplin signed Coogan Sr up, too, realizing that the boy would feel more at ease with his father on the set.

Coogan continues the story:

> When Dad came over to join us from Roscoe's company, he got more money than I did. He wound up playing six parts in *The Kid*. He also wound up as Chaplin's assistant. I was making $75.00 per week. By the time the picture was finished, Dad was at $150.00 per week. To me, working with Chaplin was like working with a big

kid. He wasn't as physically big as most grown-ups, and we'd play games together; he knew how to entertain a child. There was no script, sometimes we would go a week without shooting. Having established a given situation, Chaplin would work out the business as to exactly what we were going to do. After I got the feel of it, I started to come up with ideas, and I got a dollar for each one that was used. When I realized that, I came up with lots of ideas. I insisted on being paid in gold – that was real, the other stuff was tin money. As for paper money, to my mind that was to hang in the bathroom.

The Kid was destined to make a great deal of paper money. Coogan told me that the film on which he earned a mere $75.00 a week ultimately grossed thirty-five million dollars – at a time when the price of admission was a nickel!

When Roscoe Arbuckle learned how Jackie Coogan had been stolen from under his nose by Chaplin, he laughed and wished Chaplin every success. Arbuckle was a close friend of the Coogan family. Talking of him, Jackie said to me, 'Roscoe used to come over to our house. I loved him, he was always clowning. He used to play and make me laugh. There was no affectation about him. In other words, there were no chinks in his armour as far as a child was concerned. I think that's more important than the opinions of any sixty-year-old bluenose.'

That last remark had to do with Roscoe after his San Francisco trials.

The most significant film Arbuckle made for Comique in 1918 was *The Sheriff*. At the time, Douglas Fairbanks was the action hero of the silver screen. He appeared to spend his entire film life leaping from balconies, diving into raging rivers, or jumping from rooftop to rooftop. I was told in Hollywood that he once refused to make a movie because the plot didn't provide a balcony for him to jump from. Roscoe, although a close friend of Fairbanks, decided the time was ripe for a burlesque.

In *The Sheriff* Roscoe climbs church spires at record speed, leaps on to the balconies of fair *señoritas*, and listens as bandits beg for mercy. One reviewer wrote, 'The most amazing thing about "Fatty Fairbanks" was the downright frankness with which he impersonated the great athletic star. It was the most apparent piece of imitation ever seen on stage or screen, and that is why it proves one of Arbuckle's greatest mirth-provokers. He is a perfect artist in burlesque.' The film was a hit with the general public as well as Hollywood. Even Fairbanks considered the impersonation better than the original.

In *The Sheriff* Arbuckle also introduced macabre humour to the screen. During one sequence in the film he rides into a Western town as the newly-appointed sheriff. Passing a graveyard on the outskirts of town, he sees tombstones almost filling the landscape, and the locals tell him it is the cemetery for sheriffs. Riding closer to town, he passes a large house, in each window of which sits a weeping woman, and the locals tell him that it is the home for the widows of sheriffs.

(Arbuckle's mordant comedy style was evident in a number of movies. In one film a rival suitor for the hand of the heroine lies in ambush for Arbuckle behind a curtain. Arbuckle embraces the girl and empties his revolver into the curtain without taking his lips from the girl's.)

After finishing *The Sheriff*, Arbuckle took time off from making money for himself and Paramount to raise funds for his country. The Germans had surrendered in November, but although the war machine had stopped, somebody had to pick up the bills. In America as in every other country, the bills were to be paid by the people. The government initiated a series of loan drives. One money-raising activity was an all-star Hollywood movie in which the gods and goddesses of the silver screen exhorted their fellow citizens to give. Appearing in the film with Roscoe were, among others, Mary Pickford, Douglas Fairbanks, Lillian Gish and Wallace Reid. The million-dollar cast raised millions of dollars, then did the same for the Canadian government with another film. It was one of Hollywood's finer hours.

Paramount's rivals in the industry were paying close attention to Roscoe; his popularity had soared in his two years with Paramount. When Adolph Zukor heard that a number of rival companies were making overtures to his biggest star, he quickly left New York for the West Coast. A handshake might be good enough between Joe Schenck and Roscoe, but Zukor desired more tangible evidence of commitment. He had not become one of the most powerful men in the film industry through gentlemen's agreements. (Ironically, it was a gentleman's agreement with Schenck that had superseded a written agreement with Max Hart.)

Arriving on the West Coast, Zukor went straight into conference, first with Joseph Schenck, then with Jesse Lasky, and finally with Roscoe Arbuckle. He made Arbuckle an offer that remains unique in the history of cinema: Zukor asked to buy the exclusive rights not to the next two or three of Roscoe's films, but *to the next twenty-two*. Roscoe would retain total artistic control, and the films would be made by his own company. The films for 1919 were already scheduled as two-reelers, but from then on *all were to be feature-length films*. This was unheard of in the industry. No comedian, including Chaplin, had ever been thought good enough to risk in more than an occasional feature film. Chaplin would still be making two-reel comedies in 1922, Harold Lloyd until 1922, Keaton until 1923, and Harry Langdon until 1926. These four men are generally considered to be the major comedians of the silent period. It is possible that Roscoe Arbuckle is not now considered one of the greatest silent film comedians because most experts have never had the chance to see the best of his work. But in 1919 the general public and men like Zukor and Lasky had no doubt who the top film comedian was, and Paramount was prepared to put a fair amount of money down to prove its point. *Paramount offered Roscoe three million dollars over a three-year period.* In precisely six years Arbuckle had risen from a $5.00-a-day extra at Keystone to become the highest-paid star in the world, making nearly $3,000 a day – at a time when taxes were low. As one writer at the time observed, 'Roscoe's income makes that of the President of the United States look like a sick nickel.'

With the new contract signed, Joseph Schenck again urged Roscoe to live in a manner consistent with his astronomical earnings. It was all right for a film extra to stay the odd week here and there, but it was not good enough for a star. Roscoe was disinclined to play the Hollywood game, but under pressure from Schenck he gave way. And when he did, he played a big game.

He bought a house on West Adams Boulevard in Los Angeles. The previous tenant had been Hollywood's first vamp, Theda Bara, and Alla Nazimova had also rented the house for a while. Arbuckle did not waste time renting. He bought the house from Randolph Huntington-Miner for $250,000.

The front door, imported from Spain, had cost $15,000. The drawing room could seat nearly two hundred. A chandelier with a thousand candles hung in the large hall, and each room was decorated and furnished in the style of a different country. The gardens contained plants from all over the world, with other international touches as well, such as a Japanese bridge in one garden and a Mexican love seat in another. Roscoe spent another $33,000 'doing little things to it', and later he would spend even more, buying such things as a $75,000 Chinese rug.

It was a long way from the sod hut in Kansas where he had been born.

Roscoe had always had a passion for automobiles. His West Adams house had a garage big enough to hold six cars; by the end of 1919 it contained a Rolls Royce, a Stevens-Duryea, a white Cadillac, a Renault, and one of the most extraordinary cars ever made, a Pierce Arrow worth $25,000. Among the extras in the Pierce Arrow were a cocktail bar and a toilet. The chauffeur usually rode in the back while Arbuckle drove.

In 1919 he also invested in a baseball club, the Vernon Tigers, 'to please Lou Anger', who was a baseball fanatic. Roscoe had a golden touch that year: in their first season under Roscoe, the Tigers won the Coast League pennant and showed a profit of over $30,000 – after several years of running at a loss.

On 24 March 1919, Roscoe celebrated his thirty-second birthday with plenty of company. The notables of Hollywood dropped in, but they did this even without a birthday to celebrate. It was amazing what news of Roscoe's contract did to Hollywood's social life. He had always been popular, but now he was the wonder boy. Free with both money and advice, he was surrounded by people who seemed to hope his genius, his originality – his success – would rub off on them.

Although his marriage with Minta was shattered, every time he went to New York he would stay with her, and for a while it would be like the old days. Minta told me they would laugh together and make love, but all too soon Roscoe would have to return to the West Coast. He didn't have a sexually active life outside his marriage partially, at least, because self-consciousness about his weight made him shy with women. The only woman with whom he formed a serious friendship during this period was his co-star Alice Lake, and there is no evidence to suggest that he had an affair with her. In fact, Arbuckle may have been the most chaste man in Hollywood.

One day, more than ten years after their last meeting, Roscoe's father turned up. Brushing aside bitter memories of his youth, Roscoe welcomed his father. The obvious pleasure that William Goodrich Arbuckle felt in his son's success was short-lived. He developed cancer of the mouth, and though Roscoe spent large sums of money to save him, he died in November 1920.

Roscoe's stepmother still lived in San Jose, but there was no contact between them. A neighbour of hers who suggested that Roscoe should share his wealth with Mrs William Goodrich Arbuckle was sent packing. Because Roscoe had achieved his success without any help from his family, his stepmother would have considered it immoral to take his money. For his part, Roscoe never regarded his stepmother or her children as his 'family'.

If Mrs William Goodrich Arbuckle had scruples, others did not. Roscoe was approached daily by people begging for loans of 'just a few dollars until I get my next part', and few went away empty-handed. If most of the other stars didn't know what to do with their new-found wealth, Roscoe did: he gave his away.

Redistributing his wealth voluntarily was one thing, though. Having it taken forcibly was another. Roscoe was plagued by robbers. He couldn't walk around the block without being held up. Eventually he presented himself at the office of Sheriff Cline and asked for a sheriff's star and a gun; he wanted the star so he could carry the gun. The delighted sheriff swore him in as a deputy, and the hold-ups stopped immediately.

The pace was quickening, the merry-go-round moving into top gear. If Arbuckle worked hard and worried enough, the three-million-dollar minimum could be doubled. He pushed his mind and body to the limits, staying up till two, three and four in the morning to create new funny situations, driven to make the next film funnier than the last, to improve the timing, polish the techniques. He was making some of his greatest films, but some of his remarks in 1919 indicate the pressure he felt: 'Many a night, I've laid awake for hours chewing over some gag that had to be done on the morrow. And sometimes it wouldn't come, and it took a lot of energy to keep up this sort of thing year in and year out. But the results seem to have justified the effort.'

Irving Thalberg credited Harold Lloyd with being the first star to preview his work publicly, but Lloyd began previewing his work in the early '20s; Arbuckle had been doing it since 1917. The sneak preview allowed the silent-film-maker to size up the finished product before it was released. The film could then be reshot and re-edited, depending on how the audience at the sneak preview had reacted. (Such extensive changes would not be possible under today's system.)

Arbuckle analysed audience reaction to every gag, every foot of film. On one occasion he explained:

> The existence of the comedy-producer is a life of doubt. He never knows anything for sure. The director of dramatic pictures knows when he has made a good photoplay because good drama has a universal appeal. The comedy director, however, has no standard of weights and measures to guide him, because what will make one person laugh may bore another, and completely pass over the head of a third. Of course there are the usual sure-fire gags that can be resorted to in a pinch – the chase, or the exaggerated mechanical tricks – but no miner ever dug further or deeper for the elusive gold than does the comedy-maker delve into real life for the little things that will evoke laughter.

Buster Keaton returned from France in March 1919. The village quality of the Hollywood he had left just a year before was already beginning to vanish. Keaton went back to work with Arbuckle, who was completing the 1919 schedule of two-reelers, before starting his feature films. Besides making a number of superb comedies, the two men found time to engage in a series of practical jokes that are still talked about in Hollywood.

It was appropriate that their first and perhaps their best practical joke had as its victim Roscoe's boss, one of the most powerful men in the industry, Adolph Zukor. He was not an easy man to fool, as others had learned. William S. Hart, the movie cowboy, and Sid Grauman, Sr, who owned 'Chinese' and 'Egyptian' movie theatres in Hollywood, had once held up a Los Angeles train bound for San Francisco, with the object of robbing Adolph Zukor. Nobody ever got Zukor to part with money easily. While the other passengers panicked, Zukor had stared hard at the masked giant standing before him with a gun in either hand, and remarked, 'It's a great idea, Bill; be sure you use it in your next movie.'

On hearing that Zukor was coming out to the West Coast on his annual profit-counting trip, Roscoe invited the great man to dinner.

The dining room at the West Adams house comfortably held twenty-four. Among the guests on this particular occasion were Sid Grauman; Frank Newman, a Kansas City film exhibitor; Bebe Daniels; Anna Q. Nilsson; and the two women Roscoe and Buster were squiring around town, Alice Lake and Viola Dana.

Everything was planned with precision. The guests, who were all in on the joke, were briefed by Roscoe. It was classically simple: Buster Keaton was going to be the butler and wait on table. Keaton had yet to star in his own films and therefore would not be too easily spotted. To be safe, Roscoe dimmed all the lights in the downstairs rooms.

After several rounds of cocktails the guests seated themselves at the table. In through the swinging kitchen doors came butler Keaton, with the first course, shrimp cocktails. Ignoring Roscoe's indication to serve the ladies first, Keaton marched to the head of the table and, commencing with Zukor, served all the men. The men promptly attacked the shrimps. Deadpan, Keaton returned with another tray of shrimp cocktails, served the women, then went back to the kitchen. Roscoe muttered an apology to his guests and strode out to the kitchen. There, loud enough for the assembled guests to hear, he yelled, 'You stupid numskull! Don't you know better than to serve the men first?' With a look of triumph, Roscoe returned to the dinner table. He was followed by Keaton, who then transferred, sometimes in mid-spoonful, the men's shrimps to the ladies, and the ladies' to the men.

Keaton then laid out soup plates for the diners and, returning to the kitchen, created a tremendous noise. He crashed knives and forks about, doused himself with water to create the impression that the soup had spilled all over him, then crashed a tin washtub on the floor. Squelching back into the dining room, he removed the empty soup plates and ladle without a word of explanation.

Roscoe was by now affecting a tremendous rage. Zukor leaned forward from the head of the table and reassuringly cooed, 'That's all right, Roscoe. I never eat soup anyway.' Refusing to be comforted, Arbuckle complained bitterly about the terrible servant problem in Los Angeles. Sympathetically, Zukor advised him that they had the same problem back East. 'You just can't get intelligent servants any more.'

On cue Buster reappeared, this time with ice water in a silver pitcher. He moved around the table, filling the glasses, until he got to Bebe Daniels. Ignoring her glass, he moved on to Roscoe. Proffering her glass, Bebe remarked, 'Could I have some please?' Buster, suddenly struck by Bebe's beauty, stared raptly into her eyes as he poured. He missed the glass and poured the water all over Roscoe. Enraged, Roscoe leaped to his feet and, grabbing Buster by the neck and the seat of his pants, rushed towards the kitchen. In a panic Zukor hurried from the table. Fearing that his superstar was about to commit murder or have a stroke or both, Zukor pleaded with him to release Keaton. Allowing himself to be pacified, Roscoe contented himself with throwing Keaton through the swinging doors.

Back at the table he began building up his mock rage

again. Eventually he told his guests that he intended to quit the house and that if this was what being a film star was all about, he would quit the business as well.

Zukor looked at his three-million-dollar star and went white. He had already aged many years since the dinner began. He listened aghast as Roscoe warmed to his theme.

Roscoe told his listeners that he had never wanted to live in this style in the first place, that it was all Joe Schenck's doing.

Zukor sputtered, 'But, Roscoe, if you left the business, what would you do?'

Roscoe looked at him, then said, 'Seems to me there's plenty of potential in opening a catering agency. Supplying trustworthy staff. I'm definitely going to quit this house and go live in a hotel.'

By now Zukor did not know whether he was coming or going. To pacify Roscoe, he exclaimed, 'I tell you what, Roscoe. I'll go and live in a hotel, too.'

The assembled guests were having a terrible time trying to keep straight faces. There was a great deal of coughing and choking. Sid Grauman offered an explanation for the butler's bizarre behaviour. 'When we were having cocktails, I noticed him helping himself to a couple of large ones. Perhaps he's heard about the Prohibition law?'

Clutching at straws, Zukor declared that that was obviously the explanation. The butler was merely trying to get into the spirit of things and be sociable.

The next course on the mis-menu was a twenty-four-pound turkey. Buster showed it to his master, who smiled his approval and said quietly, 'That's fine. Carve it in the pantry.'

Buster, carrying the turkey, moved towards the swinging doors. As he reached the doors, he stooped to pick up a napkin. This was the prearranged signal for actor Jimmy Bryant, hidden on the other side of the doors. He pushed the door hard, hitting Buster in the backside and propelling him across the turkey. Buster hurtled back towards the dinner table, literally riding the turkey, and smashed into the table before collapsing on the floor. Kneeling on the floor, he began brushing the dirt and dust from the turkey and, pulling pieces from it, threw them on to the guests' plates.

Screaming with rage, Roscoe picked him up one-handed and headed for the kitchen. Keaton, still clutching the turkey as he hung suspended in mid-air, continued throwing pieces of the bird to the guests. Once inside the kitchen, Roscoe and Buster began throwing dishpans and pots and cutlery all over the place. To the listening guests it sounded as if the two men were locked in mortal combat. Roscoe screamed, 'I'll kill you, you damned dumb bastard!'

Zukor, by now quaking, urged Bebe Daniels to try to calm their host. As Bebe reached the swinging doors, Roscoe pushed one of them open. This was to provide the guests, particularly Zukor, with a good view of their host hitting his butler over the head with a full bottle of brandy (a breakaway bottle filled with tea). The bottle was duly smashed over Keaton's head. What followed was not in the script. Some of the pieces and a fair amount of the cold tea fell on Bebe's bosom. Not knowing what had hit her and fearing it was blood, she began to scream. Buster took off in the direction of the garden, with Roscoe in pursuit. As Buster leaped over the Japanese bridge and vanished through the Malayan shrubbery, Roscoe allowed Zukor to catch him and gently lead him back into the house.

Keaton, meanwhile, had slipped around to the front, quietly re-entered the house and made his way upstairs. There he changed his clothes, restyled his hair, sat on a bed, and waited.

Roscoe introduced his real butler as his chef, and a second turkey was served. During the dinner Buster telephoned, ostensibly ringing from his own house. Roscoe told him to come around and join them for dessert and coffee. He told the guests who was coming and

Zukor remarked, 'Oh, I know him well. A wonderful performer.'

Sid Grauman, struggling to suppress his laughter, said, 'He's a very rare kind of actor. The unforgettable type.'

Keaton, having crept downstairs and rung the front-door bell, joined the guests. Sitting next to him was Frank Newman, who said excitedly, 'You should have been here earlier, Keaton. We had the damnedest waiter you ever saw.' Then, pausing for a moment, he wickedly added, 'The odd part is that he looked just like you.'

Zukor reacted. He stared long and hard at Keaton. His eyes moved from Keaton to Arbuckle and back again. Grauman pointed his finger at Zukor and said, 'Came the dawn.'

Zukor did not smile. He just said very quietly, 'Very clever, boys. Very clever.' Later in the evening, when he had recovered from the traumatic dinner, he also thought it was very funny. And the following day he gave the story to the press, thereby proving not only that he was a good judge of comedians, but that he also had a rare sense of humour – and, of course, an eye for publicity.

Contrary to popular opinion, Buster Keaton did smile, at least when he worked with Roscoe. And at the end of 1919 both men had a great deal to smile about. Roscoe was moving into features, and Buster was to inherit the two-reeler Comique Company. The sky seemed the limit for both men.

At the end of 1919, Roscoe went on a European holiday, expecting to travel quietly as a regular tourist. What happened was New York 1916 over again, but more spectacular. In London he was besieged by the press and public. He stayed at Claridges, where there were four press agents and two managers to protect him, but at every meal they were swept away by a rush of reporters. Wherever he went in London, he was followed by cheering crowds. He sailed for France and was greeted so enthusiastically that he was injured: several men in the crowd tried to carry 'their hero' on their shoulders; but they miscalculated his weight, and he fell to the pavement. His reception in Paris was a personal triumph. Roscoe placed a wreath on the Tomb of the Unknown Soldier, and the city rose in salute. The public loved this man, and they let him know it. Dazed but happy, Roscoe returned to the West Coast to do his first feature film.

The Round Up was a seven-reel western romance based on Edmund Day's successful Broadway play of the same name, in which the lead had been played by Roscoe's namesake, Maclyn Arbuckle. *The Round Up* gives a clear indication of the distance Arbuckle had travelled artistically since his Keystone days. It is deliberately paced, with far greater emphasis on characterization, and it gave Arbuckle his first opportunity to show himself an actor as well as a comedian. He played a sheriff, Slim Hoover, and was joined briefly by Buster Keaton, who played an uncredited part for fun – and for an extra's fee of $7.50. (If you see the movie, watch for an Indian biting the dust in a spectacular way.) It was the last film the two men worked on together officially. The public rushed to see *The Round Up*; it was a box-office success. Some critics lamented Roscoe's departure from the Keystone format, but admitted grudgingly that perhaps the man had some acting ability.

Buoyed by the success of *The Round Up*, Arbuckle quickly began work on his second feature, *The Life of the Party*. Again he used material that had already proved successful in another medium, in this case as a story written by Irvin S. Cobb for *The Saturday Evening Post*. Roscoe and Walter Woods rewrote it for the screen, and Roscoe chose Joseph Henabery (who was trained by Griffith) to direct. The result was an even bigger hit. The reviewer in *Kinematograph Weekly* observed, 'Fatty Arbuckle, unlike most comedians, is an artist, and his artistry is manifested with pleasing frequency.' It seemed that Arbuckle could do no wrong.

The Life of the Party was released in November 1920.

The owner of a string of Paramount cinemas in Colorado took out ads that boosted Paramount for its quality and decency, saying, in part: 'The management of the Princess Theatre makes it a personal business to see that every photoplay shown in its house is irreproachable both in morals and good taste. It shows Paramount pictures because Paramount stands first in the motion picture industry for its insistence upon decency. When you see the trademark of Paramount pictures, you need never hesitate about taking your family.'

The ad campaign was quoted in trade magazines in April 1921, as showing patrons not only that Paramount was decent, but that Paramount's actors were, too. Both Paramount and Arbuckle were riding the crest of a tremendous wave, and they eagerly publicized their success, a success that would work against them in the days to come.

To many, it was far from clear that decency was the message Hollywood was sending out to the nation through its films. The film industry had come a long way from the innocent days when the heroine of Sigmund Lubin's *Her Secret* could boldly admit in a screen title, 'Jack, I will be equally frank with you. When we were married, I thought my little vice would shock you. You had placed me on a pedestal. Perhaps I was wrong, but I concealed the little puffs from you, and you, silly boy, suspected a conflagration.' (Her secret vice was cigarette smoking.)

Morc recently Paramount had released ads like that for the movie *The Sheik*, starring an Italian gardener named Rodolfo Alfonzo Rafaelo Pierre Filibert Guglielmi di Valentina d'Antonguolla, better known as Rudolph Valentino:

> SEE:
> The auction of beautiful girls to the lords of Algerian harems. The barbaric gambling fete in the glittering Casino of Biskra. The heroine, disguised, invade the

Bedouin's secret slave rites. Sheik Ahmed raid her caravan and carry her off to his tent. Her stampede his Arabian horses and dash away to freedom. Her captured by bandit tribesmen and enslaved by their chief in his stronghold. The fierce battle of Ahmed's clans to rescue the girl from his foes. The Sheik's vengeance. The storm in the desert. A proud girl's heart surrendered.

By today's standards the films of the early 1920s seem tame, but the studios made them sound naughty. To civic groups and reformers who had been suspicious of the movies all along, ads like that for *The Sheik* were powerful evidence of the evil influence of films. Standards of behaviour were changing all over the country, and many Americans found it easy to believe that Hollywood was leading the country into a state of moral decay with its focus on sex and crime – by its Celluloid portrayal of such things as sophisticated sex and divorce as part of the glamorous life. Whether Hollywood simply reflected changing mores, or whether it speeded a change in attitudes, or both, to those who were dismayed at the course things were taking, it was handy to have the motion picture to blame.

It didn't help matters any that on 2 March 1920, Mary Pickford finally did what most of Hollywood knew she had been planning to do for years: she divorced her husband, Owen Moore, reassuring her fans that she did not intend to marry again. ('Do you think my people will ever forgive me if I divorce Owen?' she asked Adela Rogers St Johns.) Twenty-five days later she married Douglas Fairbanks. On 16 April the attorney general of Nevada, Leonard Fowler, asserted that there had been 'collusion' in the Pickford divorce, and for a while America's sweetheart (and Nevada's divorce industry) was in trouble. The situation was saved by a smart lawyer named Gavin McNab, a lawyer who was soon to play a role in Roscoe Arbuckle's life too.

Beginning in 1921, a series of scandals would rock

Hollywood and the nation, diverting the attention of reformers from the contents of films to the highly-publicized off-screen behaviour of Hollywood's stars:

Paramount's biggest comedy star, Roscoe Arbuckle, would be accused of raping and murdering a young woman.

Paramount's most respected director, William Desmond Taylor, would be murdered and posthumously accused of crimes ranging from witchcraft and drug-trafficking to sexual perversion and adultery with at least four different women.

Paramount's top actress, Mary Miles Minter, would have her career shattered because of her alleged involvement with the murdered Taylor. (Another actress whose career would be ruined for the same reason: Mabel Normand, who would die of tuberculosis in 1930 at the age of 36.)

Paramount's writer Zelda Crosby, one of the women linked with Taylor, would commit suicide.

Paramount's biggest matinee idol, Wallace Reid, would die in an asylum after fighting a losing battle against heroin addiction.

On 16 January 1920, the Eighteenth Amendment to the Constitution outlawed liquor. In Norfolk, Virginia, evangelist Billy Sunday (later immortalized in song as the man who could not shut down Chicago) exulted: 'The slums will soon be a memory. We will turn our prisons into factories and our jails into storehouses and corncribs. Men will walk upright now, women will smile, and the children will laugh. Hell will be forever to rent.' The Temperance Society of America's 'Thou shalt not drink' was no longer a vain plea. The reform movement had achieved a stunning victory with Prohibition. No doubt teetotallers all over the country expected the angel Gabriel to deliver them the keys to heaven. They were met instead by Al Capone bearing a tommy gun and a bottle of bootleg liquor.

Though there was a powerful movement by some people to clean the country up, to curtail liberty – if that's what it took to keep America moral – there was at the same time a strong movement in the other direction, and Hollywood seemed to be taking the lead in that loosening of moral standards.

A pretty actress, Colleen Moore, cut her hair, shortened her dress, and created 'the flapper'. Nothing was quite the same after that. A whole range of apparently unconnected changes began to coalesce as the 1920s began. Not only had women won suffrage in 1920, they had won a great deal more. The First World War had created jobs for women, and they had tasted independence, even if the jobs were now going back to the men; as a result, though, there was a large-scale revolution in domestic life. The old order fought a bitter rearguard action, but girls all over America were emulating their screen idols: they smoked, drank, petted, used make-up, rolled their stockings, cut their hair, abandoned their corsets and petticoats and with them a large amount of Victorian hypocrisy – or so it seemed at the time.

As the skirts got shorter, so did the temper of authority. Bathing beauties were arrested for wearing considerably more than Mack Sennett's lovelies; in New York, women were arrested for smoking in public. The president of the American Society of Dance Teachers demanded government control of ballroom dancing, saying, 'I believe if someone would write some good dance music, the degrading type of music would give way. Jazz music impels body motion, one cannot dance anything but suggestive movement to it. So the modern dance, bred of jazz, has prostituted all dancing. Censors will have to be appointed, as they are to control movies.'

The self-appointed custodians of the country's morals particularly lamented the evil influence of the movies; by pointing to Hollywood, 'sin city', they justified their contention that not only the films were evil, but that the film-makers were in league with the devil.

Just as the whores had once followed the gold miners to San Francisco, so now they followed the film stars, and the money, to Hollywood. Los Angeles was full of good-time girls prepared to give a good time to any client with the right fee. (Whenever one of the prostitutes was arrested, she would give as her profession 'actress', which fed the myth that every actress is a whore. As Minta Durfee said to me, 'I'm a whore, of course – at least in some people's eyes. After all, any woman that spends her life in the movies must be a whore.') And it is said that part of the reason Will Hays later established the Central Casting Agency for the hiring of extras was to screen out would-be starlets who had turned to prostituton.

At the same time, many Hollywood people suddenly had more money than they were used to having, and if they spent it lavishly on fancy cars and fancy women, the studio publicity departments were quick to let the world know how much fun they had leading their glamourous lives. Roscoe Arbuckle wasn't the only Hollywood star giving parties. There was always a party to be found, always a source of bootleg liquor, and more and more often, a source of drugs. Much of this found its way into the movies, and by now the press ate it up. Hollywood was news.

American reformers in 1921 were not to be underrated. Having brought about Prohibition, they now were closing in on the film industry. Since the turn of the century there had been attempts, largely disorganized, to establish national censorship of the movies. Now, inspired by the apparent reality of a dry America, reformers took heart. Motion picture executives had reason to be nervous: censorship of the movies was a serious threat. Several states had adopted state censorship. In 1921, according to Richard S. Randall, author of *Censorship of the Movies*, thirty-seven states introduced one hundred censorship bills. In August 1921, the State of New York established a licencing system for movies. The

International Reform Federation and the Lord's Day Alliance agitated for federal legislation to control the industry.

The General Federation of Women's Clubs undertook a survey of 1,765 films, and concluded that twenty-one per cent of the films were 'bad' and another fifty-nine per cent were 'not morally worthwhile'. Few who read the results of the survey bothered to ask precisely what the surveyors meant or how they arrived at so definite a morality count.

For once the religious leaders of all denominations were united on an issue: they wanted stringent control of the film industry in the form of censorship – or better yet, the closing down of the industry. From pulpits all over the country issued sermons on 'the evils of the movie'. The Central Conference of American Rabbis lamented the 'demoralization of the drama and the motion picture'. The New York Christian Endeavor pleaded at its 1920 convention for greater tolerance to all mankind – except the film industry, which was condemned for, among other things, its film portrayal of ministers. Pamphleteers and periodicals as diverse as *Harpers Weekly, Literary Digest, Outlook* and *Current Opinion* joined in the attack on the industry.

Freedom of speech was one thing; when it came to movies, the Bill of Rights did not apply. (For years, the movies were legally considered strictly 'business' and 'entertainment'. It wasn't until after the Second World War that Supreme Court rulings held that motion pictures were a medium of speech and therefore entitled to First Amendment protection.)

Many elements combined to make would-be reformers of the film industry a powerful force in the early 1920s; some of these elements had nothing to do with the film industry. To begin with, six million people were unemployed in the United States. When these people read of Roscoe Arbuckle's $25,000 Pierce Arrow or of film star Charles Ray's $60,000 cut-glass bath, they were not amused. When the film industry announced in 1921 that it expected its most profitable year, men were being auctioned in Boston; unemployed, they promised to work for the highest bidder. (The film moguls had feared the war would cut into foreign sales, but they were wrong. As a result of the war to end all wars, the American film industry achieved for the first time an international dominance.)

Scott Fitzgerald was to label the decade 'the Jazz Age', but a good many people were dancing not to the syncopated beat of jazz, but to the staccato rhythm of guns. In Charleston, West Virginia, for example, coal miners on strike in September 1921 found themselves being fired on by government planes, which also dropped dynamite on the miners. Meanwhile, President Harding had gone for a weekend cruise on the Potomac in his yacht, the 'Mayflower'.

Harding had struck a responsive chord with his appeal for a 'return to normalcy'. After the war, Americans, who had been united in the struggle for victory and peace, reacted by withdrawing into isolation. Fear and hatred of everything foreign began, ironically, in the administration of liberal Woodrow Wilson.

It is not easy for a generation raised on protest to realize that after the First World War the habit of not criticizing the government was still strong in America. The Sedition Act of 1918 had made it a crime to say anything critical about the war effort of President Wilson's administration; as a result of that act many thousands went to prison. Late in 1919 United States Attorney General A. Mitchell Palmer decided that this was not enough. During the first two days of January 1920, over two thousand people were arrested in thirty-three cities. Their crime: they had not been born in America. Worse still, many of them had been born in Russia. They were promptly deported, without court hearings. The Great Red Raid had begun.

America had watched with fear the revolution in

Russia, and many Americans assumed that 'democracy' would vanish overnight in America unless all potential Bolsheviks were under lock and key. Not one 'German spy' or 'revolutionary workman' or 'Bolshevik' was caught and convicted of an overt act designed to give direct aid and comfort to 'the enemy', though this was the ostensible reason for the wave of arrests.

In 1920, a jury in Hammond, Indiana (the birthplace of Roscoe Arbuckle's father), acquitted a man who had killed an alien for saying, 'To hell with the United States.'

In Massachusetts two anarchists were arrested and charged with a payroll robbery. It was, by the standards of the day, a run-of-the-mill affair. Seven years later, despite protests from millions of people around the world, the two men, Sacco and Vanzetti, were officially executed.

'Reds' were only one minority to feel the sting of prejudice. The Ku Klux Klan resumed branding and lynching Negroes. They also showed a deep hatred for Catholics, Jews and all foreigners. (Meanwhile the Los Angeles Athletic Club had rejected the application of Darryl F. Zanuck, because he was Jewish.) Henry Ford's newspaper published so much anti-Jewish propaganda that Ford was later praised by Adolf Hitler for his anti-Semitism.

Intolerance, bigotry, and hysteria – passing as patriotism and morality – swept the country. To some extent the pressure for film censorship was only part of a larger reaction in the United States. The world was changing too fast for many people.

Oblivious to any potential danger to itself, the film industry assumed that all these events had nothing to do with the movies, and went on with the engrossing business of grossing millions of dollars.

The movement to close the film industry received a shot in the arm in July 1921. Attorney general Allen of Massachusetts took time off from prosecuting Sacco and

Vanzetti to bring a court action for the removal from office of Nathan A. Tufts, the district attorney of Middlesex County, to whom the Paramount executives had indirectly given a $100,000 bribe to keep secret their participation in the orgy at Brownie Kennedy's in 1917. Too many film historians commenting on this incident have said that Arbuckle was not only present, but was the host at the orgy. The Tufts trial transcripts show clearly that Arbuckle was not there, although Paramount was well represented by Adolph Zukor, Jesse Lasky, Walter Greene and Hiram Abrams. Scenting that the Boston orgy involved Hollywood, reporters from every national newspaper dug deep. William H. A. Carr says in *Hollywood Tragedy* that the press was kind to Arbuckle and played down his part in the affair. The American press of the 1920s was not noted for compassion. If reporters played down Arbuckle's part, it was because he had none. It can't have helped him in the days to come, though, that the affair took place on *his* cross-country tour. As Roscoe would learn, there are different ways of being found guilty.

Through all this, Roscoe worked on – worked on and played. His energy appeared limitless, both on and off the set. His philosophy of life (at least after hours) was 'the party's the thing', and – at the drop of his famous brown derby hat – he staged parties at clubs, hotels, inns along the road and particularly at his palatial West Adams residence. All kinds of parties: banquets, teas, breakfasts, dinners, motor parties, weekend parties, house parties, lawn parties – for one party he arranged a dog wedding, in which Luke served as best man (Luke by now was earning $300 a month). He told one reporter how one night at eleven, home alone with Luke, he decided to have a party; by midnight more than forty people were whooping it up in the West Adams house, with a six-piece band pouring out ragtime until dawn. Without pausing for sleep, he drove straight to the studio.

It was almost as if he knew that he was running out of time, that his days as a superstar were numbered, and the number was getting low.

Roscoe often ate at the Sunset Inn, which served 'Mammoth Olives à la Roscoe Arbuckle', 'Chicken à la Fanny Ward', and 'Shrimp Cocktail à la Buster Keaton'. After dinner came the fun, usually in the form of impromptu cabaret acts by Roscoe and his friends. One night Charles Chaplin announced to the diners that there would be a benefit ballet for Mack Sennett. With Sennett scowling, the orchestra struck up 'The Rustle of Spring', and on glided the ensemble: Arbuckle, Chaplin, Charlie Murray, Ford Sterling, Chester Conklin, Al St John, Ben Turpin, Mack Swain, and, guesting in this array of ex-Keystone talent, Buster Keaton. Wrapped in table-cloths, the group performed an outrageous travesty on the 'dance à la Isadora Duncan'.

This was the golden period for the stars of Hollywood. They were charming people leading charmed lives; and everything they said and did was watched intently by millions. The most ordinary events were treated like news. Roscoe was continually being fined for speeding, for example, and his court appearances were always covered by a battery of photographers and reporters. After fining him a few dollars, the judge would then proudly pose with Arbuckle for the photographers.

One traffic accident in 1920 involved another young star, and is reminiscent of the hullabaloo that surrounded Roscoe's wedding in Long Beach. Ben Lyon told me the story, as it concerned his late wife, Bebe Daniels:

> Bebe was driving her car at 72 miles per hour. Her mother is in the car and so is Jack Dempsey. They were on their way to a film preview. Well, they are driving through the little town of Santa Ana when they are picked up by a motorcycle cop and summoned. So, all right, 72 miles per hour, you expect a fine. They had to appear in court before Judge Cox. Apparently his daughter had

been killed by a truck some time before and understandably he is intolerant of speeding. This was before the days of air conditioning. The courtroom was very hot. The judge sat up on his bench. By the side of him he has an earthen jug and an earthen glass. All during the trial he kept pouring himself liberal helpings of what everybody thought was water. But this man was a drunk. This was liquor.

She had to plead guilty, there was nothing else to do but plead guilty. Bebe stands up expecting a small fine. The judge sits there rocking on his bench. Then he says, 'Ten days in jail.'

Paramount had gone down with a thousand dollars cash; they were ready to pay any fine. The man from Paramount stood up and said, 'I've got a thousand dollars right here in my hand. Don't jail her. We'll pay any fine you care to name.'

'No,' said Judge Cox, 'she goes to jail.'

When Bebe had been arrested it had been big news. Now it became a sensation. Headlines all over the country: 'Bebe Daniels jailed for speeding'. Now, God damn it, she goes to jail. Barker Brothers [a large department store] furnish the cell. They bring in a divan, wardrobes, carpets – they even put up curtains over the barred window. Restaurants in Santa Ana bid to send in her meals, free of charge. The one that Bebe selected then had a large sign printed up outside which read, 'We are feeding Bebe Daniels'. Abe Lyman and his orchestra came out from Los Angeles and serenaded her with a concert on the prison lawn twice a week.

Now in theory, Bebe is supposed to be in jail. Of course, she is hardly ever in the cell. Most of the time she is sitting with the prison governor's wife having tea. In fact the only time she goes into the cell is to have her photograph taken for the press, mopping the cell out, and all that kind of thing. But she got out in nine days. Got a day off for good behaviour.

Now all of this was entirely genuine. It had not been done for publicity. But Paramount had got a million dollars worth of free publicity out of it. They had really got something going for themselves. They decide to star Bebe in a movie called *Speed Girl*.

When she was in jail the newspapers besieged the place. They were there in the hundreds. Bebe got very tired. There wasn't a minute's peace. Finally the warden came in one day to tell her that yet another reporter wanted to interview her. Bebe says, 'Oh, I can't see him. Tell him I'm out.'

It was unreal. It was life in a goldfish bowl. And Roscoe Arbuckle would live to regret the attention America was willing to pay to the foibles of its movie stars. But, for now, Roscoe's merry-go-round was still going full speed.

Feature film followed feature film, each one better than the last. *Brewster's Millions* was the first he completed in 1921; it was quickly followed by another five full-length features. *All six features were made in seven months.* Paramount, astounded at the millions pouring in from Arbuckle's feature films, wanted even more. They asked him what Vice President Jesse Lasky later freely admitted was the impossible: *three feature films to be made concurrently*.

The plan was that Roscoe jump from scene to scene. As soon as the set was ready on one film, he would change to the appropriate costume and shoot the scene, then move immediately to another set, change, and shoot that scene. In this way three films could be made in the time normally allotted to one.

Speaking of the extraordinary demands being made on Roscoe, Jesse Lasky later said:

> Arbuckle was conscientious, hard-working, intelligent, always agreeable and anxious to please. He would invent priceless routines and also had a well-developed directorial sense.

I don't know of another star who would have submitted to such extortionate demands on his energy. But Fatty Arbuckle was not one to grumble. There were no temperamental displays in his repertoire. He went through the triple assignment like a whirling dervish, in his top form. They were the funniest pictures he ever made. We were sure we would reap a fortune.

Indeed, if the films had ever been shown, Paramount would probably have reaped a fortune. But fate was about to intervene. With the three films in the can, Roscoe felt entitled to some fun. 'Think I'll take a little trip to the city,' he said, which meant San Francisco, since no-one in 1921 thought of Los Angeles as a city. Labor Day was near, the perfect time for fun and games. He planned to drive to San Francisco one Saturday, 3 September, and invited along two friends, director Fred Fischbach and actor Lowell Sherman.

Shortly before Roscoe left, Buster Keaton called. He had rented a yacht and planned to spend the Labor Day weekend on board with his wife Natalie Talmadge. He wanted Roscoe and Alice Lake to accompany them on a pleasant sail to Catalina Island, where they would 'just swim, fish and take it easy'. Roscoe said he would love to come, but 'I've promised to drive up to San Francisco with Freddie Fischbach and Lowell Sherman.' Buster urged him to break his promise, feeling sure that his friend would have more fun on the yacht, but Roscoe, after hesitating a moment, said, 'I can't. A promise is a promise.'

He and his two companions set out from Los Angeles in the Pierce Arrow. As they zoomed through Fresno on their way north, they were seen by two men working in the fields, Clyde and Harry Arbuckle, Roscoe's step-brothers. Clyde straightened up from his labour and, seeing the Pierce Arrow, the only one of its kind, speeding by, shouted, 'There goes Roscoe!'

Intolerance and hysteria stalked the land. The virtuous

citizens of America were watching Hollywood like a pack of jackals, about to claim a victim.

Roscoe put his foot down hard on the gas pedal and roared on to San Francisco. He was on the road to whoopee . . . and a whole lot more.

PART TWO

DURING THE PARTY AND THE TRIALS

It was late afternoon when they reached San Francisco, and they headed for the best hotel in town, the St Francis. At that time, the St Francis was to San Francisco what the Savoy once was to London. Visiting royalty, presidents, people like Melba and Paderewski stayed there. Among its more eccentric guests had been vaudeville's Anne Held – wife of Flo Ziegfeld and creator of the 'beauty spot' and the 'red carpet' – who insisted on bathing daily in thirty gallons of milk. It was from a bed in the St Francis that actor John Barrymore tumbled on the morning of the earthquake. Now the hotel, which had survived the earthquake and the fire, was about to be shaken to its foundations.

Tired after their five-hundred-mile drive, Roscoe, Fred Fischbach and Lowell Sherman had an early dinner and retired for the night.

Prohibition did not keep Roscoe or most of his countrymen from drinking. Liquor was more freely available in San Francisco during Prohibiton than before or afterwards. It was known as an open town; many of its bars never closed a single day during the entire Prohibition period. Because of his star status, Arbuckle had no need to go to a club for a drink. It came to him. He phoned a nightclub called Gobey's on the morning of Sunday, 4 September. Twenty minutes later a bootlegger by the name of Jack Lawrence tapped gently on one of the doors of Roscoe's twelfth-floor suite. The management of the St Francis later claimed no knowledge of liquor being taken up to Arbuckle, but Jack Lawrence had come in through the main hotel door on Union Square. (The hotel staff who helped Lawrence carry the crates of excellent whisky and gin to the suite doubtless thought that if Anna Held could take her daily bath in thirty gallons of milk, then Roscoe could take his in thirty gallons of whisky.)

Roscoe had a great deal to be happy about. Not only had he finished three feature films simultaneously – an astonishing feat – but also Sunday, 4 September, marked the commencement of the Fourth Annual Paramount Week. By 1921, this Zukor-inspired promotion had become international and very profitable. Backed up by massive studio publicity, cinemas throughout the world showed Paramount films exclusively; in the United States, seventy-five per cent of the cinemas showed Paramount movies. Arbuckle was one of Paramount's most popular stars. He had six different feature films running in Los Angeles that week, and in New York he had six feature films and twenty-seven two-reel films showing.

The LA newspapers that weekend were full of details of the Paramount week. The junketing was to start on Monday afternoon with a parade of the stars through the city, headed by Roscoe Arbuckle in his 'twenty-five-thousand-dollar gasoline palace'. In the event, the parade went on without Roscoe, who was having fun of a more private nature in the St Francis.

The same newspapers also devoted space to the film censorship issue. An editorial in the Los Angeles *Examiner* attacked the city council, which was proposing to introduce film censorship in the city. The editors argued that 'No person on earth is intelligent enough, cultured enough or equipped with the technical ability to pass on the whole output of the world's films. The very suggestion is ridiculous on its face. It is a dangerous folly.'

Within months, certain events, with Roscoe at the centre of them, would ensure film censorship – not by the city council, but by the film industry itself.

The only visitor to the Arbuckle suite on Sunday afternoon was Mae Taube; their mutual friend, Bebe Daniels, had urged Mae to take a ride in Roscoe's gasoline palace. Mae Taube's presence in the liquor-stocked Arbuckle suite was not without irony; she was the daughter-in-law of Billy Sunday, and if any one man was responsible for Prohibition, it was he. The hell-fire evangelist had stumped the country for many years, declaiming the evils of liquor.

The main excitement around the St Francis that Sunday afternoon was provided by a motorcyclist and his female pillion rider. Blindfolded, the motorcyclist had ridden across a wire suspended from the top of the St Francis to an adjoining building. As a publicity stunt, it misfired. Hearing the noise, Roscoe and Mae Taube popped their heads out of a twelfth-floor window. In the days that followed, there were plenty of pictures of Roscoe and 'the mysterious girl' in the papers, but hardly any of the poor aerial motorcyclist.

On Sunday evening, while Roscoe and his entourage enjoyed themselves in a club called Tait's Café, three people booked into the nearby Palace Hotel: screen actress Virginia Rappe; her manager, Al Semnacher; and a friend of Semnacher's, Maude Delmont. The three planned to spend just one night in the City before returning to Los Angeles. At that time neither group knew of the other's presence in the city.

Also staying at the Palace Hotel was a gown salesman named Ira Fortlouis. A mutual friend advised him that Fred Fischbach was in town, so Fortlouis phoned Fischbach on Monday morning and arranged to see him at about 11.00 a.m. Fortlouis unwittingly set in motion a chain of events that would end in the death of Virginia

Rappe and the destruction of Roscoe Arbuckle.

In the months that followed there were varying accounts of what happened that Labor Day weekend. Many details were in conflict, and many were hushed up for one reason or another. Over a three-year period, I have interviewed many of the people who were involved, including some jury members and some of the people who observed the legal proceedings that followed. I have read thousands of pages of transcripts from six proceedings (a coroner's inquest, a grand jury hearing, a police court hearing, and three trials). Some of these transcripts had never before been made public, and all were believed to have been officially destroyed in the early 1930s, ten years after the final verdict. What follows, based on the transcripts I subsequently uncovered (which are now in my possession) and on the testimony of both prosecution and defence witnesses and others intimately involved with the case, is my *reconstruction of what happened that hot September day in 1921*. It is fascinating as a prelude to the real story – about justice and injustice in and out of the courtroom.

It began simply enough. The plan was for Fortlouis to have breakfast with Fischbach. At 10.45 a.m., as Fortlouis was leaving the Palace Hotel, he chanced to see Virginia Rappe, Maude Delmont and Al Semnacher on their way to the lounge for breakfast. Virginia was an attractive girl by 1921 standards, and a very sharp dresser. Fortlouis, always on the lookout for girls to model his dresses, asked a bellboy who she was, and was told, 'Virginia Rappe, the movie actress'. Suitably impressed, Fortlouis left the hotel and a short while later was in the Arbuckle suite. Roscoe, emerging from his morning bath, was introduced to the gown salesman by Fischbach. Together with Lowell Sherman, they sat and chatted for a while.

During the course of the conversation Fortlouis mentioned seeing Virginia Rappe in the foyer of his hotel, and asked if any of them knew the young lady. All three men did. Fischbach felt that his friend must have made a mistake, that Virginia was down in Los Angeles. The question was resolved when Fischbach phoned the Palace and had Virginia Rappe paged; a few moments later she was on the phone. Fischbach invited her to join him and the others, and she accepted. A brief confusion almost kept Virginia away. She thought Roscoe and his friends were staying at the Palace, but when she asked for their room number at the Palace reception desk, she learned they weren't. The desk suggested she try the St Francis; Arbuckle was unlikely to be staying anywhere else. She reached Fischbach and got the room number. Then, at 11.50 a.m., she, Maude Delmont and Al Semnacher drove out of the Palace parking area.

They arrived at the St Francis just before noon. Virginia and Maude got out of Semnacher's car. As they turned to enter the St Francis, Virginia spoke to Al. 'I'll take Mrs Delmont with me, and you can come for us in about twenty or thirty minutes, and if we don't like the party, we'll return to Los Angeles immediately.' Al nodded and drove off into the busy Labor Day traffic.

In the foyer of the St Francis, Virginia hesitated for a moment. Arbuckle and his friends didn't know Maude Delmont, and Virginia was reluctant to appear with an unknown and uninvited guest. She told Maude to wait in the foyer until she was paged. After taking the elevator to the twelfth floor, Virginia walked along the corridor to Room 1220 and knocked. Fred Fischbach let her in.

Roscoe, Fischbach and Sherman knew that Virginia Rappe had played small parts in a few movies; that she lived with Henry Pathé Lehrman, the man who had tangled with Charles Chaplin at Keystone; and that the young actress was a woman of easy virtue.

There was a great deal more they didn't know – that very few people knew.

Virginia Rappe was born in New York in 1894. Her mother, Mabel Rapp, was a part-time chorus girl and possibly a prostitute as well. Her father may have been a well-known Chicago banker or a member of the House of Lords, among others – her paternity was uncertain. Whoever he was, he did not feel inclined to marry Mabel. And Virginia's mother died in New York in January 1905, leaving her 11-year-old illegitimate daughter an orphan.

A grandmother in Chicago took the young girl under her wing, but her supervision was clearly far from perfect. Between 1908, when she was fourteen, and 1910, when she was sixteen, Virginia appears to have had a total of five abortions. Then in 1910 she gave birth to a baby girl, which her grandmother placed in a foster home. In November, 1911, Virginia's grandmother died and Virginia went to live with a family friend, Mrs J.

Hardebach. By 1913 she was a successful commercial model working in various Chicago stores. That year the Chicago *Examiner* interviewed Virginia Rappe (she had added the 'e') for a story they called 'New Ideas for Girls to Earn Their Living'. Among her suggestions: to become a shopper for a rich family, or to work in a wealthy home 'counting the silver, sending it to the repairer and reporting to the mistress'.

After the article came out, she went to Europe with a friend, Helen Patterson. On the return voyage the girls created a sensation on the steamer *Baltic* by dancing the tango in their nighties. It turned out they were fully dressed beneath the nighties, but the male passengers were unaccustomed to seeing anything but a rare glimpse of feminine ankle. When the boat docked, the girls were surrounded by reporters, one of whom asked Virginia to display a harem trouser undergarment. She replied, 'Oh dear! I must refuse to show them except at the shoe tops.'

By the time of the San Francisco Exposition in 1915 she had acquired a reputation as a fashion expert and was being introduced to San Francisco high society by her friend Sidi Spreckles. Press accounts of her engagement to a visiting member of the Argentine Commission refer to her fiancé as 'dashing Alberto M. D'Alkaine'. Presumably he carried on dashing until he was back in South America. He never married Virginia.

In 1916 she moved to Los Angeles, where she met Henry Pathé Lehrman. He told her, 'I can get you into the movies.' They became lovers and shortly afterwards Virginia was working as a three-dollar-a-day extra at Keystone.

It was common knowledge at Keystone that Virginia and Lehrman were having an affair – he was her 'fiancé', though he clearly had no intention of marrying her – and it was soon common knowledge that they both had a venereal disease. Mabel Normand at first thought, naively, that it was something like typhoid. Mack Sennett's reaction when he heard about it was to ban

Virginia from the lot and have the area where she worked fumigated.

By 1918 Virginia was considered 'one of the best dressed girls in the movies', although 'best-undressed' might also have applied. (It was said that Virginia tended to strip at a party after she had had something to drink. There seemed to be a connection between this and a chronic bladder infection.)

Virginia graduated from crowd scenes when Lehrman gave her roles in some of his productions. Two of the films she was featured in were *Twilight Baby* and *The Punch of the Irish*. She photographed well, but was hardly a serious rival to Sarah Bernhardt. At the time of Roscoe's party in 1921 she hadn't worked for nearly two years, and was being kept by Henry Lehrman.

Very little of this was known to Roscoe and his friends that Labor Day weekend. All that concerned them was that Virginia was 'good fun'.

By 12.30 p.m., Maude Delmont had also joined the party. Breakfast was ordered, the bootleg liquor opened, and everyone was having a good time. Roscoe was in superb form. He repeated the story his friend Bebe Daniels had told him about her recent arrest and imprisonment for speeding. More people showed up, including two show-girls who would find it a particularly memorable party: Alice Blake came at 1.30, and Zey Prevon at 1.45. Alice had been invited by Lowell Sherman, and had taken it upon herself to invite Zey, who also answered to the names Zey Preven, Zeb Provost, Zeh Pryvon, Zey Pryvon and Sadie Reiss.

Roscoe and Lowell had both been in pyjamas when people started dropping in. Lowell got dressed, but Roscoe remained in pyjamas and a bathrobe. On the last day of shooting in Hollywood he had backed into a hot stove and burned his backside, so pyjamas were preferable to a tight-fitting suit. Before any women arrived, Roscoe had asked if it would be proper to receive them so casually, and Fred Fischbach had assured him it would be OK.

Virginia, in the party spirit after three glasses of 'orange blossom' (gin and orange juice), felt like dancing. Roscoe phoned the management for a Victrola, and soon they were playing the popular songs of the day: 'Second-hand Rose', 'Three O'Clock in the Morning', 'On the Gin Gin Ginny Shore' and others.

Just before 2.00 p.m. Al Semnacher came to collect Maude and Virginia. Neither was in a mood to leave, and Al resigned himself to the fact that he would not be seeing Los Angeles that day. He drove Alice Blake over to Tait's Café for an afternoon rehearsal, then returned.

It was later said that no-one else came to this party. In fact, at least another seven people came whose names have never been made public before this: Mabel Pearson, May Fellows, Effie McMorrine, Maud Parsons, Dollie and Gaston Glass, and Minnie Edwards. They and some prominent San Francisco citizens who also attended were successful in covering their tracks. Showgirls Betty Campbell and Dollie Clark joined the party later. Jack Lawrence brought more bootleg liquor from Gobey's Café; Victor, the hotel's famed chef, put in an appearance; and at least five waiters and numerous bellboys were in and out all day, the bellboys rewarded with dollar bills from Roscoe. There were endless orders for crushed ice and orange juice, essential for the bootleg gin. The phone was in constant use.

Fred Fischbach took off in Roscoe's car just before 2.00 p.m. He drove to the beach to look at some seals he was thinking of using in his next movie.

Roscoe's suite consisted basically of three rooms. Room 1220 was the reception room of the suite and therefore where the partygoers tended to gather. On one side of it was Room 1219, a bedroom shared by Fred Fischbach and Roscoe. On the other was Room 1221, Lowell Sherman's bedroom. Both bedrooms had bath-rooms attached. With so much alcohol being consumed, both bathrooms had constant visitors, a fact that was to prove important later.

At 2.30 p.m. Alice Blake returned; her rehearsal had been cancelled. Then Mae Taube arrived. She had arranged to go for a drive with Roscoe at 3.00 p.m., but Fred Fischbach had not yet returned with the Pierce Arrow. Assuring Mae that his friend would not be long, Roscoe returned to his role as life of the party, assisted by Maude Delmont, who in two hours had drunk ten double Scotches. Mae Taube left, after promising to return at about 3.15.

The liquor was having an effect on Virginia, too. She began to tell her troubles to Roscoe. She complained that Henry Lehrman, the impetuous lover, was proving a rather reluctant husband. Despite her constant pleas for marriage, he refused to legalize their relationship. She told Roscoe that she was broke, that she hadn't worked for nearly two years, that the only things she owned were the clothes she was standing in. Roscoe knew this was leading up to the inevitable touch for a loan, and he assured her that he would give her some money before she left the party. Then she dropped a bombshell: it wasn't just a few dollars she needed; it was a great deal of money. *She was pregnant, and she was sick. She needed money to have an abortion, and she wanted to have the abortion as soon as possible.*

Roscoe was shocked. He tried to persuade her to have the baby and, if she did not want to keep it, to have the child adopted. Virginia was adamant. She wanted an abortion. Roscoe suggested that she talk it over with Henry Lehrman – surely he would be delighted at the prospect of becoming a father? Wasn't this, perhaps, the way to get that wedding ring on her finger? But whoever the father of the child was, and Virginia was not divulging that, she paled at the thought of telling her fiancé: if he learned the truth, her hopes of marriage would be finished. 'Don't tell Henry,' she pleaded. 'He must never find out. I just want to quietly have an abortion while he's in New York. By the time he comes back, it will be all over, then perhaps I can get him to marry me.'

It was obvious that Virginia had made up her mind to have the abortion performed in San Francisco as soon as possible. Illegal abortions, even in an open city like San Francisco, were expensive in 1921, over $2,000 at least. Roscoe told her that he did not carry that kind of cash around with him, but that if she contacted him at the studios in Los Angeles during the coming week, he would see what he could do. Whether Roscoe intended to give her the money or was just playing for time, nobody will ever know. Events were about to take the problem out of his hands.

The party was in full swing by now, with dancing, giggling, and shouting. Roscoe acted out some of the comedy routines from his three latest movies. The man who was paid millions to make the masses laugh entertained a privileged few for nothing.

At about 2.45 p.m. Zey and Alice saw Virginia weave her way through the dancing bodies toward Room 1221, and Lowell Sherman's bathroom. Maude Delmont and Lowell Sherman were in the bathroom together and refused to open the door. Virginia knocked on it, and said, 'Open the door, Maudie. Let me in.' Maude replied, 'Go to the other bathroom. I am changing my dress.' It was getting hot at the party – too hot for Maude Delmont, who took off her dress and put on a pair of Lowell Sherman's pyjamas. Virginia gave up, and came back through the reception room on her way towards Roscoe's bedroom.

Ten minutes later, Roscoe glanced at the clock on the mantlepiece in Room 1220, saw that it was three o'clock, and realized with a start that Fred would be back soon with the car. Roscoe was still in his pyjamas. Being so casually dressed in his own rooms was one thing; he could hardly ride with Mae Taube through the streets of San Francisco dressed like that. He put 'Three O'Clock in the Morning' on the Victrola, walked into his bedroom, and shut and locked the door. Then he stepped over to the bathroom to wash before dressing. The bathroom door was not locked, but something was blocking it and he could not open it fully. Virginia Rappe was kneeling on the floor, vomiting into the toilet, groaning and reeling.

Roscoe slid into the bathroom and held her steady while she vomited, then picked her up, shut the toilet, and sat her down on the toilet seat. He asked her if there was anything she needed. Clutching her stomach and wincing in pain, she told him that she had these sick spells from time to time. Roscoe gave her a glass of water, which she drank; she asked for another and drank half of that. Then he helped her up and into the bedroom, and sat her on the single bed. Telling him that she just wanted to lie down for a while, she flopped down on the bed, her head towards the bottom. Roscoe lifted her legs on to the bed, then went back to the bathroom to wash up. A fastidious man, Roscoe regularly took three baths a day.

When Roscoe came back into the bedroom, it was 3.09 p.m. He heard Virginia moaning, but she was nowhere in sight. She had rolled off the small bed on to the floor between the single and double beds. There was not enough room for Roscoe to get around by the bedside and pick her up, so he pulled her up into a sitting position, then, lifting her up, stretched her out on the double bed. She promptly turned over on her left side, vomited on the pillow and down the side of the bed, and started to groan again.

Roscoe hurried to the door, unlocked it, and went into the central reception room, 1220, in search of Maude Delmont. It was 3.10 p.m. *He had been absent from the party for ten minutes.*

Maude was nowhere to be seen; she was still closeted with Lowell Sherman in the bathroom of Room 1221. Roscoe told Zey Prevon that Virginia was sick, and Zey hurried into the bedroom. At that moment, Maude Delmont emerged from Sherman's bedroom. Roscoe told her what had happened, and she and Roscoe followed Zey into Roscoe's bedroom.

Virginia was sitting up on the edge of the double bed, fully dressed. She then began tearing at her clothes and frothing at the mouth. Roscoe felt the general effect was of someone in a terrible temper. She began to rip her clothes from her body, and screamed, 'I'm hurt! I'm dying. I know I'm dying!' Pieces of her clothing flew in all directions as she tore at her dress, her stockings, her garters and her shirtwaist. Maude and Zey tried to restrain her. She moaned and screamed.

Roscoe turned from the window and spoke to Zey: 'Get her out of here, she makes too much noise.' The girls' attempts to restrain the hysterical Virginia were in vain. One of her sleeves was hanging by a few threads, and she kept pulling at it, trying to remove it. Laughing, Roscoe moved towards her and ripped off the sleeve, saying, 'All right, if you want that off, I'll take it off for you.'

Zey pushed him away, saying, 'Stop that Roscoe, she's sick.'

Roscoe was not impressed. 'She's not sick,' he said. 'Just putting it on.'

Ira Foutlouis, meanwhile, was still in the reception room getting drunk on the bootleg liquor. Roscoe walked out and saw him and decided he'd had enough of the garrulous gown salesman for one day. He spoke to Lowell Sherman, who quietly told Fortlouis that he had to leave the party because reporters were coming up to interview Roscoe. Slightly aggrieved, Fortlouis exited.

At that point, Mae Taube arrived, ready for her car drive. A few words with Roscoe and a look in Room 1219 convinced her that Roscoe was going to be slightly delayed.

A few moments later, Fred Fischbach came back from viewing the seals. He had left a fairly quiet party and returned to a madhouse. Told that his friend Ira Fortlouis had 'left', he walked down the hotel corridor, caught up with Fortlouis, exchanged a few words with him, and returned to the Arbuckle suite. He entered the bedroom he shared with Roscoe, and saw Maude and Zey trying to restrain Virginia in her hysterical strip. The two women began to remove her clothes, which by now were in shreds.

Zey suggested that they stand Virginia on her head. She'd apparently read somewhere that that was the thing to do when someone became hysterical. Fred, who was a giant of a man, obligingly jumped on the bed, caught hold of Virginia's ankles, and suspended her now-nude body in space. If nothing else, it stopped her screaming for a while. Then Alice Blake reappeared on the scene. Where she had been and whom she had been with, are still unknown. Maude suggested they dip Virginia in a cold bath. Fischbach, the gentle giant, picked Virginia up, carried her to the bathroom, and immersed her in very cold water. Nobody seemed sure how long she should be left there. After a while, Zey got anxious and suggested Virginia be removed. Again Fred picked her up and carried her back, placing her on the single bed.

Alice Blake proposed they try bicarbonate of soda; she happened to have some in her bag. They mixed it with water and gave it to Virginia, who had lapsed into a kind of stupor. She drank it, not knowing what they had given her, and immediately vomited the mixture.

Next someone suggested lumps of ice. The St Francis Hotel in 1921 could boast that it had dispensed with the old-fashioned method of serving ice chipped from large blocks. It could offer ice cubes. Maude wrapped the ice cubes in a towel and put it first on Virginia's head, then on her abdomen. The other girls placed ice over Virginia's body.

If these wide-ranging treatments seem bizarre, remember that most of the party guests were intoxicated in varying degrees. Maude, flapping about in Lowell Sherman's yellow silk pyjamas, was totally drunk. The alcohol, together with Virginia's hysteria, was hardly conducive to cool behaviour in any of the guests.

While the ice was being applied, Roscoe re-entered the room. Virginia had started to scream again. He picked up a piece of ice and asked Maude what the hell she was doing. Weaving, Maude shouted, 'Leave her alone, I know what I'm doing.' Roscoe put the piece of ice back, on Virginia's vulva, remarking as he did, 'This will make her come to.' It had no effect, however.

Roscoe moved to the window and glanced out to see if people could hear the commotion. Maude Delmont let out a piercing scream. Roscoe turned and shouted back, 'Shut up or I'll throw you out of the window.'

It was obvious that the do-it-yourself cures were having only a detrimental effect. Roscoe went back into the reception room, where Mae was still patiently waiting, and said, 'Mae, do me a favour, please. Would you phone down below and get the manager up here? We can't leave her screaming like that all day.'

Mae phoned the main desk. A few moments later one of the assistant managers of the St Francis Hotel, Harry Boyle, hurried to the luxury suite.

Meanwhile, Roscoe had gone back to his bedroom and told Maude to get out of Sherman's pyjamas and into her dress before the manager appeared. This Maude did.

A few minutes later, Assistant Manager Harry Boyle knocked on the door of Room 1221, and was let in by Roscoe, who was talking to Mae Taube. The time was 3.30 p.m. Roscoe explained to the manager that Virginia had had three drinks and had become hysterical. Boyle was taken to Roscoe's bedroom, where the others were doing what they could for the still-nude Virginia. Roscoe asked the manager if he could have another room for the sick girl. Boyle immediately said yes.

Taking Fred Fischbach's robe from a closet, Roscoe draped it around the girl and picked her up. He and Boyle, accompanied by Maude, went out into the corridor and made their way towards the new room, 1227. Virginia's body was soaking wet, and Roscoe had difficulty supporting her. Boyle took the girl from him and placed her in a bed in the new room. When Roscoe asked the manager to get a doctor, Boyle assured him that he would do so immediately and would let the movie star know the outcome of the doctor's visit. Satisfied that he had done all he could, Roscoe returned to his own suite. Meanwhile, Maude had collapsed on the bed next to Virginia and had gone to sleep.

Back in Roscoe's suite, the party picked up again. Reinforcements arrived – showgirls Betty Campbell and Dollie Clark. Roscoe and Mae had by now abandoned their plan to go for a car ride, although Roscoe promised to take Mae to dinner in the hotel restaurant that evening.

Harry Boyle had trouble locating a doctor. The hotel doctor, Dr Arthur Beardslee, could not be found. Eventually Boyle located an alternative, Dr Olav Kaarboe. Boyle called him at 4.30 p.m., and he was at the hotel by 4.45. On the way up to Virginia's room Harry Boyle told him that there had been 'a gay party in Mr Arbuckle's suite and the lady has had too much to drink'.

Dr Kaarboe entered Room 1227 with Boyle. Maude was on one bed, Virginia on the other. Virginia was as Boyle had left her, covered by the bedclothes. Maude was lying on top of her bed, naked from the waist down. Boyle pulled her dress down and shook her gently to wake her. Dr Kaarboe asked Maude what had happened. Maude, sleepy, did not like being bothered. 'Oh, I guess it was just a little too much party,' she yawned. 'Virginia just had a little too much to drink and got drowsy. There's nothing the matter with her.'

Dr Kaarboe asked Virginia how she was feeling. She didn't answer, so he lifted her head from the pillow and repeated his question. He asked her if she was hurt, and she merely turned her head away from him. He examined her and found normal pulse and normal heart reaction, and the strong odour of alcohol on her breath. It appeared to the doctor that no special medication was called for; she had simply had too much to drink. He examined her body and found no marks or bruises on it. He asked her if she had been injured in any way, but apart from turning her head away, she didn't respond. She was obviously not in any pain: she lay still, not writhing or clutching her stomach. Indeed, her hands were under her head and she gave the impression of being pleasantly drowsy. Dr Kaarboe asked if anything special had happened, and repeated his question about whether Virginia had sustained any injury. Maude's answer to both questions was negative. Maude gave the doctor the impression that she 'was indifferent and just wanted to be left alone'. Kaarboe told Maude that if she needed any further help, she should call.

Harry Boyle and the doctor walked over to Roscoe's suite. Roscoe asked the doctor how Virginia was. Dr Kaarboe said that there was nothing seriously wrong with the girl, that it was just a case of drinking too much. Declining an invitation to stay for a drink, the doctor and the assistant hotel manager left.

The party was still going strong. Irvan Weinberg, another friend of Fred Fischbach's, phoned. Weinberg had with him a young actress, Doris Deane, whom he wanted to introduce to Fred and Roscoe. While speaking to her, Fred casually mentioned Virginia's 'ripping her clothes off and carrying on'. Doris, a nondrinker at the time, shyly declined the invitation to come up to the suite. She and Fischbach discovered that they were both going back to Los Angeles by boat the next day, and Fred promised to introduce her to Roscoe.

On the Victrola, Marion Harris was singing 'I've Got the Wonder-Where-He-Went-and-When-He's-Coming-Back Blues'. Lowell Sherman chased Betty Campbell into his bedroom. Betty quickly locked herself into the bathroom and stayed there until Sherman had retreated and she was able to join the main party. Then Sherman chased Dollie Clark into his bedroom, threw her on the bed and dived after her, but Dollie rolled out of the way and rushed out to Roscoe. Both showgirls told

Arbuckle what had happened. He told them that some of the guests were obviously feeling the effects of the bootleg liquor, and roundly criticized Sherman, declaring, 'If you want to have an orgy, then get your own apartment. Don't do it in mine.' Roscoe assured the two girls the incident would not recur. Both girls were later to comment on his kindness, and also on his concern about Virginia.

Roscoe crossed to one of the windows in the reception room as dusk approached. Looking out across the city, he asked, 'What's life all about?' He turned to the partygoers. 'I'll jump out of this window if somebody will jump with me. Come on, who's going to jump with me?' Not surprisingly, there was no reply. The highballs he had been drinking had made him melancholy. 'If I jumped out of this window,' he said quietly, 'everybody would talk about me tomorrow. The day after, they'd go to the ball game.' The room was suddenly quiet. The situation could go many ways. Then Roscoe hunched his shoulders and grinned his famous foolish grin. Everyone laughed and the party swung into action again.

At ten minutes to seven, an uninvited guest arrived – George Glennon, the hotel detective. Having been advised of Virginia's illness, he had decided to check out the situation; he knew that a hotel guest who becomes ill on the premises has an unfortunate tendency to blame the illness on the hotel. First, Glennon had gone to see Virginia, but he found her asleep. He talked with Maude, who assured him that everything was fine. There were no problems, nobody was to blame for Virginia's illness – it was due to 'too much party'. Reassured, Glennon dropped in at the party and talked to a number of the guests. Without exception they confirmed Maude's statement. Convinced that nothing untoward had happened, Glennon departed.

At ten minutes past seven, Virginia had another visitor, the house physician of the St Francis, Dr Arthur Beardslee. He had returned to the hotel and had been told of

Virginia's illness and of the colleague who had been summoned in his absence. Like George Glennon's, Dr Beardslee's call was merely routine. And, like Glennon, Dr Beardslee was a realist about what went on in the city; he was sophisticated, a club man, a man about town.

As a result of Glennon's visit to the room, Virginia had awakened. She was in great pain. When Dr Beardslee examined her, she held her stomach and complained of severe pain in the lower abdomen. Having examined her reflexes, the doctor tried to palpate and percuss her abdomen – that is, to feel and to tap it with his fingers. Virginia cried out at the slightest touch of the doctor's hand. So that he could finish the examination, Dr Beardslee gave her an injection of morphine and atropine. While he waited for the injection to take effect, he asked Maude Delmont to tell him what had happened. Maude told the doctor about the party and said that Virginia had been attacked by Arbuckle. She was interrupted by Virginia, who vigorously denied that this was true. In answer to the doctor's questions, Virginia said that Roscoe had neither attacked her nor attempted to have sexual intercourse with her. Beardslee then examined Virginia, concentrating on her abdomen.

Dr Beardslee was later to swear an oath that at this point in Virginia's illness he was not able to form an opinion, but that '*I knew I was dealing with a surgical abdomen. It was self-evident. It was an abdomen which would require surgical interference. An operative case.*'

If Dr Beardslee knew that the evening of 5 September, his subsequent behaviour was extraordinary. He left Virginia Rappe's room. He did not tell either woman that Virginia should be hospitalized immediately. He did not say that an operation was needed. He prescribed no medicine or treatment. He did nothing.

In Roscoe's suite the party continued. Roscoe, Lowell Sherman, and Fred Fischbach left and joined Mae Taube for dinner in the hotel restaurant at 8.00 p.m.; after dinner they went to the ballroom. Uninhibited by their host's temporary absence, the partygoers in Room 1220 carried on, joined now and then by new guests. Having tired of her role as nurse and recovered from the effects of her earlier attack on the whisky supply, Maude returned to Room 1220 with renewed vigour.

At 8.45 p.m. Dr Beardslee returned. While he had made his rounds at the St Francis Hospital, the sick girl had been on his mind. Maude was called away from the party and joined the doctor in Room 1227.

Virginia was quieter now; the injection had had an effect. She was resting, so Beardslee did not examine her. Maude told him that the young woman was all right now, and he left.

Roscoe returned to his suite with his dinner guests to find Maude Delmont reeling around the room. She poured out a half-pint of gin, drank it all at once, and shouted at Roscoe that he had had no right to go to dinner without taking her with him. 'I'm not playing bloody nurse to that sick creature. I want to have some fun.' So saying, she took off her clothes.

Roscoe had never met this woman before the party; now he had seen more of her than he cared to. He phoned for the hotel detective, George Glennon, and asked him to send Maude back to the Palace Hotel, and to arrange for a nurse to look after Virginia. At 11.45 p.m., George Glennon appeared and, taking Maude Delmont with him, went to question Virginia Rappe directly.

'Do you believe that the St Francis Hotel is in any way responsible for your present condition?'

'No. They are not responsible,' she replied.

'Did Mr Arbuckle hurt you?'

'No. He never hurt me.'

'Then who hurt you?' Glennon asked.

'I do not know,' a puzzled Virginia answered. 'I may have been hurt by falling off of the bed.'

At the time Virginia made these statements she seemed to be suffering no pain and to have a clear head. When he had recorded this conversation in his notebook and felt that he had done all he could, the hotel detective joined Maude Delmont in a drink.

Obviously enjoying each other's company, Maude and the detective left Virginia in Room 1227 and went to Roscoe's suite. The party was finally over. Roscoe and Fred Fischbach were packing their cases, preparing to return to Los Angeles the next day. When Maude and Glennon came in looking for more drinks, Fischbach told them to help themselves. Taking the remains of the Scotch, they returned to Room 1227, had a meal sent up to the room, and, as instructed by Fischbach, had it put on Roscoe's bill.

At one o'clock in the morning, Virginia woke again and began to writhe in pain. Glennon quickly summoned Dr Beardslee. Virginia complained bitterly of the pain which was still emanating from her lower abdomen. Dr Beardslee gave her another injection of morphine and atropine, then re-examined her.

He examined her pulse, heart, and reflexes, and generally went over her body. Apart from a bruise in the upper region of her left arm, which was of no consequence, her body was unmarked. He concentrated on her stomach. The abdomen was sensitive and rigid. She could hardly bear to be touched. Again Dr Beardslee left without discussing the possibility of hospitalization.

The hotel detective kept Maude company until nearly four o'clock in the morning. In the Arbuckle suite, all was quiet.

At five o'clock in the morning, Maude summoned Dr Beardslee from his bed. Virginia was once again in severe pain. Beardslee gave her a third injection of morphine and atropine, he gave her an enema, and then because she had not urinated at all since she had become ill the previous afternoon, he catheterized her with a glass catheter which Maude Delmont later described as 'the biggest one I have ever seen.' Beardslee said later that the catheterization 'produced a scant amount of urine, about five ounces, and it was tinged with blood. It was old blood, very dark, almost of a coffee-ground consistency.'

He was also to say of this visit: 'The facts were self-evident at this time. I knew I was dealing with a lesion of the bladder, and from the signs and symptoms, and the scanty urine tinged with blood, I knew that her internal condition was at least complicated by bladder trouble. A ruptured bladder, I suppose.'

Dr Beardslee was also to say that at no time during any of his four visits to Virginia Rappe did he see any evidence that she was suffering from intoxication. Yet after this examination, Dr Beardslee left, again without telling either woman of his conclusions, without mentioning hospitalization, without administering any drugs or medicine except atropine and the pain-killing morphine, which merely masks the patient's true condition.

Maude Delmont had by now become dissatisfied with Dr Beardslee. She telephoned Dr Melville Rumwell and asked him to take over the case. He said he couldn't until Maude told Dr Beardslee that his services were no longer required. With medical etiquette satisfied, Dr Rumwell called on the two woman at 8.45 a.m. on Tuesday, 6 September.

First he got a history of the case from Virginia and Maude. Virginia repeated what she had told her two previous doctors – Rumwell was her third in less than twenty-four hours – and added that she had been vomiting through the night. She told him that when she was sick, the pain extended from her lower abdomen right up to her chest. Rumwell questioned her closely, but she was unable to throw any light on her illness. After her initial collapse, she simply did not remember what had happened. Rumwell felt her pulse and found it strong and regular. He examined her abdomen; there were no marks on it, no signs of violence. His diagnosis was that she was suffering from alcoholism.

His case notes for 6 September read: 'Patient gives

history of having been intoxicated last night. She does not remember just what happened, complains of pain in abdomen, vomiting, some trouble with the urine. Dr Beardslee was in attendance and was asked to withdraw from case. His bill was paid at the office of the St Francis. Used hot applications and stopped the use of morphine.'

Maude was beginning to convince herself that Roscoe was to blame for Virginia's condition. She had no evidence to justify such a belief, and all of her conversations with Virginia indicated the contrary. But Maude felt aggrieved. When she had staggered into Arbuckle's suite the night before, asserting that Roscoe should have taken her to dinner, she had been told in no uncertain terms what to do with herself. That she had then been ejected from Roscoe's suite by the hotel detective had not warmed her to the comedian, and by Tuesday she was beginning to harbour a deep resentment. She continually told Virginia that Arbuckle was to blame for everything and must be made to pay for everything; that although Virginia could remember nothing, she, Maude, knew what had happened. It didn't matter that she and Sherman had been in a locked bathroom at the time. Maude *knew* that Roscoe had attacked Virginia.

The repeated accusations were not without effect. At three o'clock on Tuesday afternoon, Nurse Jean Jameson came to care for Virginia. She found the young woman in a hysterical condition. Virginia told the nurse all about the party. She also said that 'She thought Arbuckle had thrown himself upon her.' She asked the nurse to examine her abdomen to see 'if anything is broken'. The nurse carried out an external examination and found nothing. A short while later Virginia asked, 'What do you think could have happened? What could be broken in my insides?'

Nurse Jameson quickly realized that she could give little credence to any of Virginia's statements or questions, since they fluctuated so wildly. At one point Virginia declared that she could not remember whether she had been dragged into the bedroom by Arbuckle; at another time, she said that she had definitely been dragged into the bedroom (Maude suggested this idea). She asked the nurse if Arbuckle had sexually interfered with her, asked Nurse Jameson to examine her vagina and the surrounding area. The nurse did, and found nothing. Nurse Jameson felt she was dealing with a patient hysterical because of an excess of alcohol.

Roscoe, having paid the hotel for all of the weekend expenses, drove Lowell Sherman and Fred Fischbach to Pier 7 to catch the ferry to Los Angeles. It was a leisurely way to make the return journey: the steamer *Harvard* sailed at 4.00 p.m. and didn't reach Los Angeles until late the following morning. At the pier, Roscoe drove his massive car on to the boat and parked, then strolled to the rail with Sherman and Fischbach to watch the other passengers come aboard.

Among one group of passengers, Fred spotted Irvan Weinberg, the friend who had called the day before, saying he wanted Fred and Roscoe to meet Doris Deane. Now Fred and Roscoe were introduced to Doris and her mother, who had been seen off by Lee Dolson, a business associate of Doris's father.

Fifteen minutes after the steamer had sailed, a steward came to the cabin that Doris shared with her mother, with an invitation for the two women to join Roscoe and his friends for dinner in the stateroom, which Roscoe had reserved. Doris recalled for me that first evening:

> He was the most charming man I ever met. During dinner I discovered that I was out of cigarettes. I smoked Melochrino at the time. Now you would think a big star like that would snap his fingers to get somebody running to him. Not Roscoe. He just got up quietly, excused himself for a moment. When he returned, he gave me a carton of cigarettes. He was so different to how one imagines a big movie star. I don't just mean that he was kind and considerate; he was certainly that. But his range

of conversation was very extensive. Quite a number of other big stars that I've met in my life have just one topic, themselves. He talked of many things that night. About music. The theatre. Literature.

This meeting took place a mere twenty-four hours after the party. Roscoe was calm and at ease. The man Doris Deane saw that night could not have done what he was soon to be accused of. At one point, the men discussed the way Virginia had torn off her clothes at the party and how she had acted afterwards. Lowell suggested after dinner that he and Roscoe retire to their cabin for a drink, but Roscoe declined and added quietly, 'And this lady doesn't want a drink either. It's a pity she wasn't at the party yesterday instead of some of those who were.'

Roscoe made a date to take Doris to the Majestic Theater in Los Angeles that coming Saturday evening, but it was a date he wouldn't be able to keep, because by then Virginia Rappe would be dead. They had planned to see a play called *The Ruined Lady*. It was only one irony among many.

The fact that Roscoe and Doris met that day has been secret until now. Roscoe could not know then that he would eventually marry Doris Deane – and that one day her friend Lee Dolson would hold the comedian's fate in his hands.

While Roscoe talked of many things that evening on the steamer *Harvard*, Virginia Rappe proved equally voluble. She had become exhausted with nervous excitement, and was experiencing hysterical pain, which moved all over her body: first she felt pain in her heart, then in her bladder, in her back, and in her stomach. The nurse thought they were all caused by 'gas, from alcohol'.

Virginia talked about getting money from Roscoe. Nurse Jameson later assumed this was because the sick girl in some way blamed Arbuckle for her condition, but from the remarks she made, it seems clear that she was recalling her conversation with Roscoe at the party, when she had asked him for money to pay for an abortion. At one point the nurse heard her say, 'It won't do any good for me to go to Henry Lehrman and ask for money. He'll turn me down.'

Pregnancy was just one of Virginia's problems. She was also suffering from an unpleasant vaginal discharge that she did not want Dr Rumwell to know about. She had told Rumwell that it was leucorrhoea. Nurse Jameson knew better. She asked the girl for an explanation, and Virginia said, 'I have had a running abscess for six weeks.' Nurse Jameson pressed her for more details, saying, 'You couldn't have got that from Arbuckle in a day because that takes at least ten days.'

Virginia replied, 'I got this abscess from excessive intercourse with my sweetheart.'

Dr Rumwell asked her several times if she was suffering from a vaginal infection or if she had ever been infected. The girl would only admit that she had had leucorrhoea.

On Wednesday a second nurse was brought on the case, Vera Victoria Cumberland. Catheterizations, enemas and hot compresses on the abdomen were con- tinued, and a new treatment added: a Murphy drip.

Maude told Nurse Cumberland that Arbuckle had 'jumped on Virginia and crushed her bladder', but in answer to the nurse's questions, she admitted that she had no evidence to support this accusation, that she had not seen anything, and that Virginia had not told her anything. Dr Rumwell had told her that the girl had a ruptured bladder, and as far as Maude was concerned, Arbuckle was to blame.

It was later said that Maude had this attitude because she smelled money – big money, because she had stumbled on a gold mine in the rich comic. When the party was over, she and Al Semnacher had gathered up the girl's torn clothing; after it disappeared, parts of it were traced to both of them. Maude's repeated insistence that Roscoe was to blame may have been calculated to ensure that, when the girl recovered, she would agree with Maude's version of what had actually happened. This is mere speculation.

What is not is that on Wednesday, 7 September, Maude sent two telegrams, one to an attorney in San Diego, the other to an attorney in Los Angeles. The message in both was the same: 'WE HAVE ROSCOE ARBUCKLE IN A HOLE HERE. CHANCE TO MAKE SOME MONEY OUT OF HIM.' Roscoe's lawyer was later to uncover evidence that put Maude's suspicious behaviour in perspective.

Whether Virginia was party to a plot will never be known. She needed a fair sum of money for an abortion, but Roscoe had said he might give it to her anyway. Certainly the abortion was on her mind, though. She turned to Nurse Cumberland as she lay in bed and asked, 'Do you know of a good abortionist in San Francisco?'

At 9.30 p.m. on Wednesday evening, Nurse Cumberland wanted to call Dr Rumwell to report on Virginia's condition. Maude Delmont refused to let her, saying, 'Rummy doesn't want to be disturbed tonight. He has a crowd of company in the house.' After an argument, Maude reluctantly agreed to phone the doctor.

Nurse Cumberland was later to state that during the time she was nursing Virginia, the girl said that she had had intercourse with Roscoe, but at another time also insisted that Arbuckle had not assaulted her, and that she had not had sex with him. Virginia was as inconsistent with her second nurse as with her first. And treatment remained bizarre.

Nurse Cumberland resigned from the case on Thursday, because she thought that it was being handled in a negligent manner. She was disturbed because despite the fact that the first catheterization had drawn blood as well as urine, no cystoscopic examination had been carried out, no X-rays had been taken, and no vaginal smears made. The list of what should have been done and was not, was endless.

Nurse Martha Hamilton took over from Nurse Cumberland, who discussed Virginia's case with her replacement. During the last week of her life Virginia didn't seem to understand how she had become ill. She would say, 'I wonder if he fell on me,' or 'I wonder if he dragged me in.' By now, she had developed a bruise on her left hip and another on her right arm. She asked the new nurse, 'How do you think I got them?' Nurse Hamilton suggested that they might have been the result of the drastic amateur first-aid treatment, particularly the cold-bath ducking. At another point, Virginia said, 'I got those marks dancing.'

On Thursday, Dr Rumwell examined Virginia again. The nurses had particularly drawn his attention to the vaginal discharge. *He concluded that she had gonorrhoea.*

Having completed his examination, he decided that Virginia should be immediately hospitalized. Three days had elapsed since she had become ill at the party. Even now, when it was finally decided that the sick woman should be taken to a hospital, her medical story remained curious. She was not taken to a general hospital, but to the Wakefield Sanatorium on Sutter Street. *The Wakefield Sanatorium was a maternity hospital.*

Dr Rumwell was later to state under oath that he considered Virginia's condition to be the result of alcoholism, and that with the history of the bloody urine, there was a possibility of some lesion of the kidney.

Virginia was admitted to the Wakefield at 2.30 p.m. on Thursday. The treatment previously prescribed was continued, with the addition of morphine injections at four-hour intervals. A blood count was taken, and showed '17,200 whites, with 91% polys.' – a concentration of white blood cells that suggested generalized infection. Albumen and some red blood cells were present in the urine, which suggested further that the infection involved the urinary tract.

At 6.00 p.m. Dr Rumwell returned to the hospital and examined her. He then went to the theatre with his family. At 9.30 p.m. he returned to the Wakefield and found her condition was much worse. Virginia was complaining of pain in the lower abdomen, and when Dr Rumwell examined her, he noticed that it was more distended than before. Her pulse rate had increased considerably, and the doctor sensed that he was losing the battle.

Worried, Dr Rumwell called in a professor of surgery at Stanford University, Dr Emmett Rixford. Dr Rixford arrived at the Wakefield at 10.00 p.m. Dr Rumwell told him the history of the case and said he thought it was a case of peritonitis, which he personally believed might be due to a rupture of a pus tube. Dr Rixford examined Virginia. Her hands were cold, and her circulation was flagging. He confirmed Dr Rumwell's diagnosis: her condition was extremely dangerous. He debated with his colleague about operating on the sick woman, and they concluded that it would be best to give her opium, as an operation would probably result in her death on the operating table. They seemed to be allowing her to die, and the realization of this shook Maude Delmont. She insisted on calling yet another surgeon, Dr W. P. Read.

Meanwhile, Rixford and Rumwell tried to explain to Maude Delmont what they meant by a ruptured pus tube. The Fallopian tubes lead from the ovaries into the uterus. When there has been any genital infection, such as gonorrhoea, the infection passes up through the uterus, and there is often a closure of both the inlets and outlets of the Fallopian tubes. Very often a considerable amount of pus accumulates within the tubes themselves. They become torous and can rupture spontaneously. Though Virginia insisted that she did not have such an infection, the doctors had evidence that she did.

Dr Rumwell had considered since Thursday morning that Virginia's condition was the result of a ruptured pus tube, but at no time did he consider the possibility of immediate surgery. His view was that the best thing to do was to 'keep her quiet until the inflammatory process had subsided'.

Dr Read arrived at the sanatorium at 11.30 p.m. Having examined Virginia, he agreed with his colleagues that it was now too late for surgery.

The following day, Friday, 9 September, 1921, at 1.30 in the afternoon, Virginia Rappe died in the arms of her friend, Sidi Spreckles, who had introduced her to San Francisco high society in 1915.

Dr Rumwell, dissatisfied with his own diagnosis, then embarked on a course of action that rivals for inexplicability anything that had preceded it.

He arranged for an illegal post-mortem to be carried out on the body of Virginia Rappe, and he started arranging for the post-mortem examination an hour and a half before Virginia died. At noon, he contacted Dr William Ophuls, professor of pathology at Stanford University, told him that he had a 'very insecure surgical case', and asked him whether he could be ready to perform a post-mortem examination that afternoon. Ophuls agreed to undertake the examination. However, Dr Rumwell did not phone the coroner's office.

It was incumbent upon Dr Rumwell to obtain permission from the coroner's office for the post-mortem. To perform a post-mortem without such permission was no trivial breach of medical etiquette. By doing so, Dr Rumwell risked imprisonment, which raised serious questions.

By her own admission, Virginia Rappe was pregnant at the time of her collapse at the party. After days of botched medical attention she was removed to a maternity hospital. Why a maternity hospital? She died. An illegal post-mortem was performed immediately. Why? Had an illegal abortion been performed on the body of Virginia Rappe while she was still alive? Was the illegal post-mortem an attempt to cover up an illegal abortion?

We will never know. The forces of justice that would

be so intent on proving Roscoe Arbuckle guilty of murder did not at any time investigate the medical malpractice on Virginia Rappe – the malpractice which I am convinced caused her death.

In Los Angeles, Roscoe, oblivious of what had happened to Virginia since he had left San Francisco on Tuesday afternoon, was getting down to detailed discussions about his next film.

That Friday, life looked good to Roscoe. At the beginning of the week one of his latest films, *Gasoline Gus*, had opened at Grauman's Egyptian Theater. The reviewers had praised it, and the public loved it. By Friday afternoon, Roscoe had learned from Sid Grauman that the film had broken all previous box-office records.

When the doctors in the Wakefield began their illegal post-mortem, Roscoe was deep in discussion with a director, James Cruze, about the film they were about to make, *The Melancholy Spirit*, co-starring the lovely Lila Lee. Roscoe showed the director photos of Doris Deane, and Cruze was impressed; they agreed to see the young woman together early the next week. Roscoe phoned her and gave her the good news.

Roscoe Arbuckle did not know it then, but his movie career was finished. A career that had begun in 1908 was ending now in the Wakefield Sanatorium.

At 2.30 that Friday afternoon, Dr Ophuls began his illegal post-mortem examination of the body of Virginia Rappe in the operating theatre of the Wakefield Sanatorium.

There were two superficial bruises on her right arm, a superficial bruise on her left leg, and a slightly discoloured spot on one of her thighs. Dr Ophuls examined the rest of her body very carefully, including the vaginal area. Nowhere was there any evidence of violence. The abdomen was slightly distended; when it was opened, the cause of death was immediately apparent to Dr Ophuls, as well as to Dr Wakefield and Dr Rumwell, who were assisting him. Virginia Rappe's bladder was ruptured, and death was due to peritonitis.

The death certificate was signed, and the bladder was removed and placed in a specimen jar. Since death was officially linked to the ruptured bladder, this was understandable. What is not so easily explained is why the uterus, part of the rectum, the ovary and the Fallopian tubes were also removed – except that if an illegal abortion had been performed on Virginia Rappe, removal of these organs would ensure that all surgical evidence of that abortion had also been removed.

The body was sewn up and sent to Halstead's, a firm of undertakers in the city, and there the matter would undoubtedly have ended but for the morbid curiosity of a young woman who worked in Dr Wakefield's office.

That Friday afternoon, Deputy Coroner Michael Brown received a phone call from the Wakefield Sanatorium. The caller wanted to know, 'What time is the autopsy being carried out?'

'What autopsy are you talking about?' Dr Brown asked.

Before the woman could answer, he heard another voice whispering to her in the background. She gasped and hung up. Another employee of the Wakefield, Grace Halston, had just told the curious secretary that the post-mortem had already been carried out, unofficially.

Dr Brown, his curiosity aroused, telephoned the sanatorium. The woman who had called him answered the phone. He asked her what autopsy she had been talking about. He had received no news of a sudden or unusual death occurring at the sanatorium. She denied calling him, said, 'I'm sorry, I have no information to give you,' and hung up.

Dr Brown went immediately to the Wakefield Sanatorium and asked for the name of the dead person. The staff refused to give him any information and told him he would have to wait to see Dr Rumwell.

He waited.

Some time later, Dr Rumwell and Dr Ophuls came down the stairs carrying specimen jars containing parts of Virginia Rappe.

Dr Brown advised them that they had exceeded the law. Dr Rumwell muttered that he had been trying to contact the coroner's office but had had no success. Then turning to Dr Brown, Dr Rumwell, the man who had been responsible for Virginia Rappe's medical treatment during the last few days of her life, made a curious statement: 'I did not attend the woman, but was only called in for the autopsy.'

No news of Virginia Rappe's illness had leaked out in San Francisco. In fact, news of her illness and of the party in Roscoe's suite had been deliberately suppressed – not to protect Roscoe but to hide the fact that Roscoe had been able to obtain liquor in San Francisco's principal hotel. At first, no-one even connected Arbuckle with what had happened to Virginia Rappe.

When news of Virginia Rappe's death leaked out, reporters began to dig. They traced her illness back to the party at the St Francis; then they met a wall of silence. The police knew what had gone on, knew about the bootleg liquor, but the reporters drew a blank there, too. One does not kill the goose that lays the golden egg, and even in 1921, Prohibition was big business.

Baulked, the press dug up Maude Delmont. They found her very cooperative. Soon the fact that bootleg liquor was freely available in the heart of the city paled into insignificance. Within the hour, wire services had flashed the story around the world. In cities all over people read the headlines:

ACTRESS DIES AFTER HOTEL PARTY

GRILL FOR ARBUCKLE: ACTRESS DEATH QUIZ

FATTY ARBUCKLE SOUGHT IN ORGY DEATH

It had begun.

If those who controlled Prohibition in San Francisco were successful in suppressing information about the party for a while, then once the dam was breached by the press, there was a flood of information, most of it inaccurate, and sometimes patently exploitative.

For example, Maude, who had returned to her hotel room after Virginia's death, was strangely affected when she heard that the press wished to interview her. She collapsed, insisted on having a doctor, and took to her bed with 'nervous exhaustion'. The press was admitted to her bedside. Never in her life had Maude been the centre of such attention. It was an opportunity not to be missed:

> . . . Arbuckle took hold of her and said, 'I have been trying to get you for five years . . .' During the afternoon the party began to get rough and Arbuckle showed the effects of drinking. Virginia and I were in our room. Arbuckle came in and pulled Virginia into his room and locked the door. From the scuffle I could hear and from the screams of Virginia, I knew that he must be abusing her. I made every effort I could to get in the room, but I could not get through the door. Arbuckle had her in the room for over an hour, at the end of which time Virginia was badly beaten up. Virginia was a good girl. I know that she has led a clean life, and it is my duty to see this thing through.

About Roscoe she said, 'The brute! I don't see why such men are permitted to live.'

The press, especially the Hearst press, began to run special editions. A number of Hearst's newspapers ran as many as eight special editions per day. They would have been obliged to if only to keep up with Mrs Delmont.

Recalling the moment when Roscoe unlocked his

bedroom door (a moment, it will be remembered, when Maude Delmont was in another room with Lowell Sherman), she said, 'He had Miss Rappe's Panama hat on his head. She was semiconscious, screaming, "He did it! I know he did it! I have been hurt, I am dying!" '

This gem was preceded by Maude's assertion that she had telephoned for the manager and that Roscoe had only opened the door at Assistant Manager Boyle's insistence.

Recalling the period when Virginia was in the Wakefield Sanatorium, she declared that Virginia had said to her, 'Maude, Roscoe should be at my side every minute and see how I am suffering from what he did to me. And he should pay all the expenses for both you and myself.'

Having recalled Virginia's 'dying words', Maude put her hand to her head, leaned back on her pillow, and fainted.

In her official statement to the police, Maude gave a similar story, adding embellishments.

Mrs Delmont had serious contenders for the headlines, among them showgirl Alice Blake. Advised by the press and the police of what Maude had said, Alice topped it: 'She was entirely unclothed when we entered the room. We tried to dress her, but found her clothes torn to shreds. Her shirtwaist, underclothes and even her stockings were ripped and torn so that one could hardly recognize what garments they were. We could not dress her because her clothes were torn so.'

As in Maude's case, Alice Blake's remarks to the press were also in her first official statement to the police.

At 10.30 p.m. that Friday evening, Roscoe Arbuckle sat quietly studying the script for his next picture. The doorbell rang and his butler opened the door. Two dozen reporters charged past the butler, knocking him over. They poured all over the house, taking photographs and looking for Roscoe. Surrounding him, they began to fire questions based on the statements that had already been made in San Francisco by Maude and Alice.

'Who else was at this orgy you gave?'

'Did you rape her or was she agreeable?'

'How much did you pay the San Francisco police to keep it hushed up?'

'Is it true that you screwed five women during the afternoon?'

Roscoe held his hands up for silence. 'What in hell's name is going on, boys?'

They told him that Virginia Rappe was dead. They told him what was being shouted all over San Francisco. He was stunned. He had left Virginia, as far as he knew, recovering from the party, and now she was dead. The press insisted on a statement. He told them how he had driven to San Francisco with Lowell Sherman and Fred Fischbach, he outlined what the three of them had done on Saturday and Sunday, and then he continued:

> Shortly before noon Monday, a friend of Mr Fischbach's, with us in the apartment, remarked that he had seen Miss Rappe at the Palace, and desired to meet her, as he wished her to model some gowns for him.
>
> I told him that I knew her, and would make the introduction. She readily consented to come to the St Francis.
>
> After meeting the man, we had a few drinks. Miss Rappe had one or two drinks. She went into the other room of the apartment, and began tearing her clothes from her body and screaming.
>
> The other woman, Miss Delmont, and a companion rushed into the room. They put Miss Rappe into a tub of cold water. She cried out that gas had formed around her heart, that she couldn't breathe.
>
> I engaged another room in the hotel and moved her there. Then a physician was called; after he reported that she had quieted down, Mr Sherman and I went down into the dining room and danced the rest of the evening.
>
> We had already engaged passages on the *Harvard* to return to Los Angeles on Tuesday, and did so.
>
> I had not received any intimation that Miss Rappe's

illness was as serious as it turned out to be, and I am very surprised and shocked to learn tonight of her death.

Considering the circumstances and the time elapsed, the statement was amazingly calm and lucid, although incomplete.

When the reporters asked him to comment on Maude Delmont's allegations, Roscoe sagely observed: 'Mrs Delmont came back into my room after Miss Rappe was put to bed and began to get hilarious. I chased her out and suppose she is sore at me for that.'

When the reporters asked him what he intended to do now, Roscoe told them that he intended to return immediately to San Francisco to answer any questions the police cared to ask him. The reporters rushed away to reproduce his statements under three-inch headlines that proclaimed, 'GIRL STRICKEN IN ARBUCKLE'S APARTMENTS'.

Roscoe Arbuckle changed into a natty pair of green plus-fours and matching jacket. The phone rang. It was a very worried Joseph Schenck. He too had heard all manner of wild stories. Roscoe reassured him and told him that he intended to drive north immediately. Joe Schenck's mind moved fast and he talked even faster. He reminded Roscoe of the anti-Los Angeles feeling that existed in San Francisco, and pointed out that as a big star, Roscoe was particularly vulnerable. Anything he did was news. If he went on his own, he wouldn't get a minute's peace. Joe Schenck insisted that he take a lawyer with him. Roscoe couldn't see why he needed a lawyer, but to quiet Schenck down, he agreed. Schenck told his star to go to Sid Grauman's theatre and sit tight in the office while Schenck got busy on the telephone.

Roscoe had phoned the San Francisco police and they had asked him to return for routine questioning. At three o'clock Saturday morning, the Pierce Arrow glided out of Los Angeles and headed north, with Joe Bordeau at the wheel. Seven days had elapsed since Roscoe and his party had headed towards the Bay City for a weekend of fun. Now the mood in the luxury limousine was one of anxious uncertainty. With Roscoe were his lawyer, Frank Dominguez; his manager, Lou Anger; and Virginia's manager, Al Semnacher. Semnacher's presence in the car seemed to confirm Roscoe's innocence. Semnacher was not only Virginia's manager but also a close friend and confidant of the girl. He was also destined in the months ahead to become a prosecution witness.

Arbuckle and his entourage didn't realize what they were heading towards. The gentle city by the sea was on a rampage, for which Roscoe was to serve as scapegoat. Ignorant of the true facts about Virginia Rappe's death, the club women of San Francisco, custodians of the city's morals, began telephoning officials of the grand jury, the district attorney's office, the police chief, the mayor, the newspapers and everyone else they could think of. They demanded an inquiry. They demanded a trial. They demanded justice. They demanded vengeance.

And they commanded attention.

Maude Delmont added fuel to the fire. Recovered from her swooning spell, she summoned the press to her bedside again. They responded.

IT'S MY FAULT, DEAD ACTRESS'S GIRL CHUM CRIED

A year ago Virginia Rappe and Maude Delmont were fellow members in the glad play, Maeterlinck's *Blue Bird*.

Today the former lies dead under tragic circumstances and her chum is in a state of collapse, under the care of two doctors, in her room at the Hotel St Francis.

Maude Delmont is haggard and frantic, finding herself only in the administrations of a trained nurse as a result of the hectic merriment in the suite of Roscoe Arbuckle which led to the death of Virginia Rappe.

'How can I get over this? It's my fault! It's more than I can bear.'

Such were the words she uttered today, with a frantic clasp of the hand when a personal friend was admitted to her room.

STRICKEN BY GRIEF

She lay distraught, the grief and remorse pictured on her face contrasting with the gaiety of a kimono twisted about her shoulders. In bits and snatches, this is what she said.

'It's my fault. I took her there. We were pals. She was like a sister to me. We'd been close friends so long. What will my aunt say? How can I explain this? It's more than I can live through. I should have been more careful. I know this, there was no better girl than Virginia and I'm ready to say it no matter what comes. I'd rather it was I who died than Virginia.'

IN GRIP OF REMORSE

Her desire to express her remorse to a friend was keen, but fulfilment of it was cut short by Dr W. P. Read, who is attending her with Dr F. W. Callisan.

Dr Read, entering while she was talking, reiterated his order that no interviews be granted by her and said that discussion by her would only aggravate her condition.

She persisted for a moment, but the physician declared that he must be obeyed if he was responsible for her condition, and the friend to whom she had uttered her grief for the first time, departed.

This was the kind of nonsense with which newspaper readers, first of San Francisco, then of the nation, fed their feelings of righteous indignation.

Maude Delmont had met her 'lifelong friend' for the first time two days before the party at the St Francis.

Though Maude told the press that she was an actress, she was to give her occupation as 'beauty specialist' at the coroner's inquest, adding, 'I am not in business now.' Later she was to admit under oath that she was currently employed 'collecting subscriptions for a labour journal in Fresno' and that she, Al Semnacher and Virginia Rappe had motored from Los Angeles to Selma, a town 'fifteen miles south of Fresno', for the sole purpose of collecting subscriptions for the journal. She was also to admit that before this car trip she had 'never met [Virginia] before and knew nothing about her'.

A member of the management of the St Francis told the press that Arbuckle had been asked to leave the hotel after the party. The statement was untrue and beside the point, since Roscoe was already leaving the next day, but it was seized upon as further confirmation that the comedian was guilty.

On 10 September 1921, something happened that received only minimal publicity at the outset. Two cinemas withdrew Roscoe's films and replaced them with Mary Miles Minter movies. The two theatre managers explained that they 'did not want to be understood as passing judgement on Arbuckle before he has been given a hearing, but in view of the nature of the affair, we owe the withdrawal of his pictures to our patrons'.

The stage was set for Roscoe, who reached San Francisco shortly before eight o'clock on Saturday evening. The man who a week before could have had rooms at any hotel that took his fancy suddenly discovered he was *persona non grata*. Learning that he had been banned from the St Francis Hotel, he and his friends drove to the Palace Hotel, where Virginia had so recently stayed. The Palace refused him accommodation as well.

Dominguez contacted Charles Brennan, a San Francisco attorney, and while the two of them discussed the situation in the foyer of the Palace, Roscoe waited patiently outside. There he was besieged by reporters asking a dozen questions at once. He tried to answer them and was eventually rescued by Dominguez. When a reporter asked if the lawyers intended to take Roscoe to police headquarters for questioning, Frank Dominguez stated, 'There has been no warrant sworn for his arrest.

Therefore, there is no reason why we should take him there to be questioned.'

The problem of accommodations was about to be solved for Roscoe. While the reporters milled around looking for information, four police detectives appeared and ordered Dominguez to take his client to the Hall of Justice for questioning. Dominguez was caught off guard, before he could consider the implications of such an action; soon he, his client and the rest of the party plus the four detectives were on their way to police headquarters.

At the Hall of Justice, Dominguez and Arbuckle were shown into Room 17 on the ground floor at 8.30 p.m. Confronting the two men were the four police detectives and two assistant district attorneys named Milton U'Ren and Isador Golden. Civic hysteria had clearly affected the six men, who began firing questions at Roscoe; especially affected were the two assistant district attorneys, who began screaming at Arbuckle as soon as he walked into the room. Armed with statements from Maude Delmont, Alice Blake and others, they gave the impression that at least a dozen eyewitnesses had sworn that Roscoe had torn Virginia Rappe limb from limb. Dominguez immediately advised Arbuckle to make no statement whatsoever and to answer no questions. At that point, Dominguez was physically removed from the room. For over three hours, without a break – and without an attorney – Roscoe was given the third degree.

The crowd of reporters in the corridor grew thicker. The longer Roscoe refused to answer screaming accusations, the more enraged became the two assistant district attorneys. If the Arbuckle party at the St Francis had at times resembled a madhouse, so now did Room 17 of the Hall of Justice. Detectives rushed in and out; the two attorneys argued with each other and with the detectives. Orders were given, then countermanded, then given again. Throughout, Roscoe quietly declined to answer any questions.

Furious, Assistant DA U'Ren had Maude Delmont pulled out of her bed. If the movie comedian was proving uncooperative, Miss Delmont more than made amends.

Roscoe was advised that unless he answered all their questions they would charge him with murder – Maude Delmont was ready and very willing to swear out a murder complaint against the star. By now Roscoe could not have answered any questions if he wanted to. Stunned by the turn of events, he didn't even complain that for over three hours he had been kept in this room. Finally, at 11.45 p.m., he was allowed to go out into the corridor. As he moved towards Frank Dominguez, his lawyer put a finger to his lips, again counselling silence.

As Roscoe wearily slumped on to a bench, U'Ren burst from the room and shouted, '*You are under arrest on a charge of murder*.'

The excitement before this announcement had been intense; now it was explosive. Reporters shouted questions at everyone, some in the excitement of the moment even interviewing each other. Magnesium flares flashed continually, recording for the nation the moment when its most famous comedian was charged with the most serious crime a man could commit.

U'Ren discovered he was the centre of attention. The press clamoured for a statement, and the assistant district attorney gave them one: 'Roscoe Arbuckle has been charged under that section of the penal code that provides that *a life taken in rape or attempted rape is considered murder*.'

Standing beside U'Ren was Captain of Detectives Duncan Matheson. Directing his words at Arbuckle, who was standing a few feet away, Matheson said, 'Neither I nor Mr U'Ren nor Chief of Police O'Brien feel that any man, whether he be Fatty Arbuckle or anyone else, can come into this city and commit that kind of offence. The evidence shows that an attack was made on the girl.'

Arbuckle was taken to the fifth floor and formally charged with murder. He was officially photographed and described for the police record. Height: five feet ten inches. Weight: 266 pounds. Age: thirty-four years. Profession: actor. Hair: medium chestnut. Complexion: ruddy. Eyes: blue.

His valuables were stripped from him and handed to his attorneys. Then he was locked up in Cell 12.

Front pages all over the country were scrapped and reset. The Los Angeles *Examiner* of Sunday, 11 September, was typical, with three-inch headlines announcing the most sensational news of the day: 'ARBUCKLE HELD FOR MURDER!' Beneath, in print a third the size, it told its readers that 250 people were feared dead in San Antonio floods.

Other American newspapers, including the *Examiner*'s sister paper in San Francisco, reported that Virginia Rappe had, with her dying words, accused Roscoe of being responsible. This report, inspired by a statement from Nurse Jameson, would subsequently prove to be totally without foundation; but the man who owned both newspapers and many more besides did not deal in truth.

His name was William Randolph Hearst; he was later to be immortalized in Orson Welles's brilliant movie, *Citizen Kane*.

The Hearst press adopted an attitude towards the Arbuckle case that was criminally irresponsible. Feature articles, news stories and editorials in Hearst's newspapers had but one aim: to boost circulation. In the event, the policy was successful beyond Hearst's wildest dreams. He was later able to boast that he sold more newspapers reporting the Arbuckle case than he had since America entered the First World War (or as Buster Keaton overheard him say, since the *Lusitania* went down). His ruthlessness in boosting circulation was to have a significant effect on Arbuckle's fate, so it is worth pausing here to describe the man behind the press.

Born to massive wealth, Hearst decided, after being expelled from Harvard, that the world of newspapers needed his talents. Among his father's many possessions was the San Francisco *Examiner*, described by John Winkler in his official biography of Hearst as 'a sleazy little sheet'. Having persuaded his father to give him the newspaper, Hearst took it over in March 1887, the month that Roscoe was born. In a few years he had transformed the sleazy little sheet into a sleazy big sheet. His style of journalism was influenced heavily by Joseph Pulitzer, who had revived the 1830 penny-dreadful style of journalism. With an astute mixture of sex, scandal and sensationalism, Hearst achieved both success and – what was more frightening – power.

A well-known incident in 1897 illustrates the kind of power he was beginning to wield. That year he dispatched artist Frederic Remington to Cuba to draw sketches of alleged Spanish cruelty. Hearst had decided that he did not like the idea of a Spanish-dominated community so close to the shores of his beloved country. Remington appraised the situation in Cuba and cabled Hearst: 'EVERYTHING IS QUIET. THERE IS NO TROUBLE HERE. THERE WILL BE NO WAR. I WISH TO RETURN. REMINGTON.'

The reply came swiftly: 'PLEASE REMAIN. YOU FURNISH THE PICTURES AND I'LL FURNISH THE WAR. W. R. HEARST.'

Fifteen months later, after Hearst had waged a tremendous anti-Spanish propaganda campaign in his newspapers, the United States and Spain were at war over the issue of Cuba.

Hearst's xenophobia was almost paranoid; anti-British, anti-Japanese, anti-Spanish, he was against everything that did not fit in with his conception of what was best for America. Even the Hearst-sponsored biography by John Winkler admitted, after his death, that 'He never permitted himself to doubt his own infallibility. Politically he was so far to the right that by comparison men like Barry Goldwater and Spiro Agnew appear highly enlightened, reasonable men.'

Hearst once said, 'I determined to restore democracy in the United States.' Hearst had his own peculiar idea of what democracy was, though. What he tried to create through the tabloid press was a higher authority than the Supreme Court: trial by press. (And Roscoe Arbuckle would come to know what that meant.)

His brand of yellow journalism didn't meet with total approval. When he died in 1951, the *Manchester Guardian* wrote this epitaph: 'No man has ever done so much to debase the standards of journalism.' In September 1906, Wallace Irwin observed in *Collier's Weekly*:

> When he saw that puddles were the topics of the hour
> Willie got a muck rake of a hundred-donkey power,
> Started up a geyser, shrilly shrieking all the time:
> 'Don't you touch my mud! I've got a scoop on this here slime!'
> Frantic Willie, antic Willie, always on the jump,
> Willie found the muck rake slow and so he bought a pump.

What Willie bought was newspaper after newspaper; he built up the largest publishing empire in the world. At his peak he owned nearly fifty newspapers, periodicals and magazines, and countless radio stations. His net annual profit was over thirty million dollars. And he gave real meaning to the phrase 'battle for circulation'.

In 1918, for example, he bought the Chicago *Record-Herald* and merged it with a paper he already owned to create the *Herald & Examiner*. He appointed Dion O'Banion as circulation manager. O'Banion, a devout Catholic and a gangster, gathered a team of 'persuaders' whose sole function was to 'persuade' newsagents to take the Hearst paper and not its rival *Tribune*. Persuasion took the form of bombings, beatings and murder. O'Banion was murdered by the Capone gang in 1924. (Hearst wasn't alone in using force to boost sales; on 6 September 1921, the Los Angeles *Examiner* carried a story about a man beaten unconscious by a newsboy after he bought a paper from a rival newsstand and refused to buy one from him.)

In California, Hearst built a 'castle', San Simeon, a monument to bad taste, blending many different styles of architecture and filled with art 'treasures' from all over Europe. There he invited people like George Bernard Shaw and Winston Churchill, as well as royalty – such was the power of Hearst that although he could hire thugs like O'Banion, he was also the confidant of the rich and the powerful. He could make or break people, and he did.

But above all, he was interested in good copy – anything that would sell papers. Many of the people I interviewed who knew Hearst personally said he published without fear or favour. For example, Ben Lyon recalls, 'If you were his guest at San Simeon, even if you were a close, intimate friend, if you did anything newsworthy you would find yourself on the front page whether you liked it or not. News was news to W. R.'

Unless it was about Hearst himself. The Hearst papers were never to print stories about his liaison with Marion Davies. Although Hearst had a wife and five sons in New York, he installed Marion Davies at San Simeon. A former Ziegfeld Follies girl, she became his mistress in 1916 and maintained the relationship until his death in 1951. Through his film company, Cosmopolitan, Hearst tried to make her a big film star, but despite massive publicity for each of her films in the Hearst press, most of her films were disasters, both artistically and financially.

In August 1924, lawyer William J. Fallon would find himself on trial accused of jury bribing, a trial resulting from a sustained campaign in the Hearst press. Fighting fire with fire, Fallon would try to show the court that he had been brought to trial because he had information that Hearst was determined to suppress, documentary proof that a liaison Hearst had with 'a certain actress' had produced a number of illegitimate children. While every

Roscoe relaxing during shooting in 1921. His visitor is Bebe Daniels. The photograph was taken shortly after Bebe Daniels' sensational arrest and imprisonment.

The $25,000 Pierce Arrow complete with cocktail cabinet and toilet.

Above left, Alice Lake, Roscoe and Buster Keaton in *Fatty at Coney Island*. Above right, Roscoe in *Brewster's Millions*. These were just two of the movies that helped pay for the quarter-of-a-million-dollar house below.

The St Francis Hotel, San Francisco. The Labor Day party created reverberations that rivalled the 1906 earthquake.

Sid Grauman receiving the award of 'Regular Fellow' at a Hollywood party. Grauman, a life-long friend of Arbuckle's, behaved in a singularly irregular way when news of the scandal broke. Standing next to Grauman is Joseph Schenck. In the background are two more of the men who panicked when the hysteria swept through the country, Louis B. Mayer and Cecil B. De Mille.

Taken seconds after Arbuckle had been charged with the murder of Virginia Rappe. On the comedian's right is Detective Sgt Skelly about to book the star and place him in cell 12. On Arbuckle's left is Attorney Frank Dominguez.

William Randolph Hearst did not merely fabricate news. His newspapers also fabricated photographs. This one showing Roscoe behind bars was created by taking an ordinary still of the comedian and painting prison bars in.

Monday, 12th September 1921. Roscoe's first court appearance. Seated is Police Court Judge Daniel O'Brien. Behind him L to R are Defense Attorney Milton Cohen, Asst D.A. Golden, Detective Kennedy, Arbuckle and Defense Attorney Charles Brennan.

Two more examples of Hearst's conception of good journalism.
(Top) The comedian is shown as laughing and jolly upon his arrival in San Francisco for the Labor Day weekend. Arbuckle is then shown as the morose individual facing a murder charge.
(Below) A photo of Roscoe and a separate one of Virginia Rappe were re-photographed. Artwork added a cigar, a glass and a bottle of bootleg gin.

(Below left) The last photograph taken of Virginia Rappe.

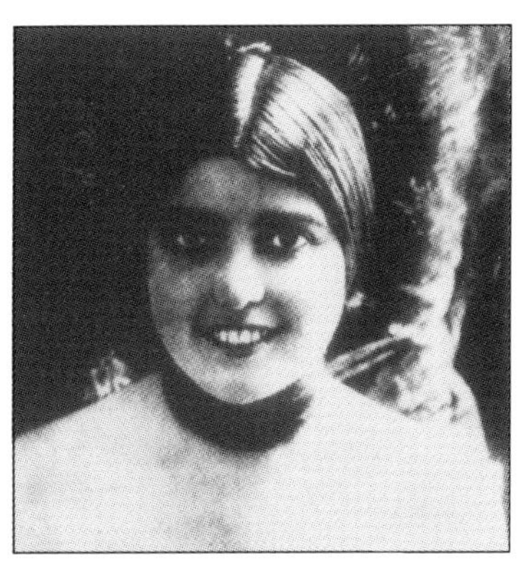

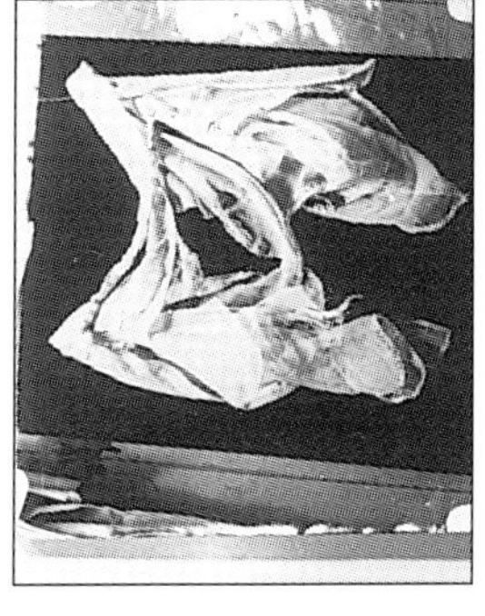

(Above) The torn underclothes of Virginia: photos such as this helped push circulation figures to record-breaking levels.

Minta, arriving in San Francisco at the behest of Paramount.

Her first meeting in prison with Roscoe. Upon the advice of defense counsel Minta sat next to her husband during the trials. She obeyed their instructions 'Dress simply and do not wear any jewelry'.

Frank Dominguez in action during the Police Court hearing. 'Put another big fat man next to Roscoe' Earl Rogers had advised. 'He won't look so conspicuous.'

The Women Vigilantes pause for a moment from fighting their way into the courtroom. Gavin McNab called them 'Stony faced women who haunt the courts, clamouring for blood, more blood.'

Asst D.A.s U'ren and Golden interrogating the comedian.

After eighteen days in the San Francisco jail, Roscoe was granted bail. With lawyers Brennan and Cohen he says farewell to Police Lieutenant Boland.

non-Hearst newspaper in the country carried front-page stories on the case, Hearst readers had to content themselves with headlines like 'HOTTEST DAY KILLS FIVE'; the Fallon trial was buried on an inside page, and all mention of Hearst deleted. Fortunately, the jury would not have to rely on Hearst's papers for information, and Fallon would be acquitted.

In later years, Hearst's affair with Marion Davies would become public knowledge. Asked about having both a wife and mistress, he would publicly admit, 'If the object is to decide who is the son of a bitch in this case, then I plead guilty.' I asked one reporter who knew Hearst well what he knew about the man's private life, and he quickly responded, 'My God, did he have a private life as well?'

But in 1921, at least, Hearst's private life was sacrosanct, although everybody else's was good copy. At the time of Virginia Rappe's death, Hearst's love affair was still a closely-guarded secret from the American public, though by then a number of rival papers had heard rumours of the liaison and had started digging. So for Hearst, the 'Arbuckle orgy', as his papers were quick to dub it, was a gift from heaven. By deflecting the unwelcome attentions of curious reporters from his private life, Hearst obtained breathing space for himself. While the champagne flowed freely at Hearst Castle, his papers raged against men like Arbuckle, who broke Prohibition law.

If the Arbuckle story gave him a personal out at the same time that it sold millions of papers, Hearst had yet another reason for the zest with which he attacked Arbuckle. Chauvinistic about his country, he was even more so about the city by the sea. If he loved anything in his life, Hearst loved San Francisco – and he wasn't about to have a film star come to his beloved city and mess it up.

Hearst was not alone in his civic pride. It was one of the things the prosecuting attorneys would appeal to when they made their pleas to the jury in the Arbuckle trials. Out of a long and curiously heartfelt rivalry between Los Angeles and San Francisco arose the question: how dare a movie star from Los Angeles use our fine city as a playground for immoral activities? Hearst and San Francisco were putting Hollywood on trial – and defending their own virtue.

While Roscoe Arbuckle sat in jail, newspaper readers were not only lapping up details about the fabulous Arbuckle party, they were also reading about Virginia Rappe, whom the Hearst papers represented as an amalgam of 'the girl next door', St Bernadette and Little Nell. (Hearst fed the prosecution strategy, which would be to present Virginia as a virtuous, healthy, even athletic girl. Defence strategy would be to present her as a diseased woman.)

Readers of the Hearst newspapers learned not only of Virginia's moral virtue, but of another American virtue: private wealth. According to one report, the late starlet had 'independent wealth as the result of oil investments'. According to another, she owned a great deal of property in and around Los Angeles. In fact, she lived in a rented bungalow, and her total assets at the time of her death were $134.

The Hearst press had no monopoly on nonsense. Newspapers from Los Angeles to New York printed one inaccurate story after another, and before anyone had set a foot in court, the nation rushed to judgement.

By Sunday, 11 September, the story was front-page news in Alaska, London, Paris, Amsterdam, Berlin, Tokyo, South America – all over the world.

Nowhere was Roscoe more the subject of discussion than in Hollywood. The news of his arrest on the charge of murder was greeted by those who knew him with stunned disbelief. To his fellow actors, Roscoe as a raping Bacchus was a case of serious miscasting. They felt the whole affair was a ghastly mistake that would soon be rectified.

Though Zukor, Lasky and the other Hollywood moguls shared the actors' stunned disbelief, they also experienced blind panic. Film historian Terry Ramsaye describes their reaction in *A Million and One Nights*: 'The smouldering gossip of corruption in the films broke into flame. New York film offices were stricken with terror. There were endless conferences. Lawyers scurried about. Press agents tore at their hair and typewriters. Statements flew and the wires to San Francisco were overloaded.'

Zukor and his colleagues at Paramount were not panicked by the thought that Roscoe was being propelled towards San Quentin's gas chamber. They were concerned about the three unreleased films Roscoe had just completed, which were expected to bring in a net profit of at least three million dollars and possibly as much as ten million dollars. At this time, in the US alone, thirty-five million people a week went to the cinema. Paramount's chiefs quickly realized that not only Roscoe but Paramount and the entire film industry were in grave danger. Every time an actor was involved in a scandal, the movement for censorship of the movies was strengthened; then as now, there was a strong tendency to judge a film star's acting by his private life, and it mattered little that an Arbuckle film was the epitome of innocent fun.

Sid Grauman, a friend of Roscoe's since his boyhood days in San Jose, was the first cinema owner to show the industry what the Arbuckle case was all about. Roscoe's feature film *Gasoline Gus* had been showing all week to record business. Grauman advertised it as 'positively the funniest comedy ever filmed'. After reading the Sunday papers, twelve hours after his friend had been charged with murder, Grauman withdrew the film without comment or announcement, proving, as Adela Rogers St Johns was to tell me much later, that 'Sid Grauman was not capable of being anybody's friend at any time'.

Coming as it did from a man everyone assumed to be close to Roscoe, the withdrawal of the film appeared significant: if anybody knew the truth, Sid did; Roscoe must have told him what really happened. In fact, since his return from San Francisco, Roscoe had not spoken to him. Sid Grauman had been home in bed at the time that Arbuckle had waited in his office for his attorney Dominguez, and at that time, in any case, Arbuckle had had no more idea of the circumstances surrounding Virginia's death than the press had. Now, however, the news of Grauman's action flashed to San Francisco, and at an emergency midnight meeting the owners of San Francisco's theatres decided to ban *all* Arbuckle pictures.

Although time and again the industry and the press leaped on statements damaging to Roscoe Arbuckle's case, they seemed indifferent to statements of support, no matter how important the source. At the time of Roscoe's arrest, Charles Chaplin was in London, making his first trip home since he had become world-famous. The press recorded his views on everything, so when news of Roscoe reached London, reporters rushed to Chaplin for a statement. He told them that the murder charge was 'preposterous'.

'I know Roscoe to be a genial, easygoing type who would not hurt a fly,' Chaplin said, and added more in a similar vein. Not a word of his opinion was printed. His views on a friend facing a murder charge, the views of the world's top comedian on his only serious rival for the crown, did not merit a line. One wonders what the press reaction would have been had his opinion been critical of Arbuckle.

In the meantime, back in the United States, there was fierce competition for newspaper coverage among several people: Maude Delmont, who added to her story daily; Henry 'Pathé' Lehrman, the late starlet's director-sweetheart; District Attorney Matthew Brady of San Francisco, who seemed to realize early on that as Roscoe's fortunes declined, his would rise; and Captain of Detectives Duncan Matheson. They were joined in their quest for publicity by America's club women and ministers, who were indulging in a national orgy of moral outrage.

Virginia Rappe's fiancé got massive coverage in the papers. Lehrman had been in New York at the time of the St Francis party. He was still there when news of Virginia's death reached him. Although he had no first-hand knowledge, he rapidly formed an opinion based on the press reports and a long-distance telephone call to Sidi Spreckles, who hadn't been at the party, but had been with Virginia when she died. He called a press conference at his hotel. To his surprise, Lehrman, who had faded into relative obscurity after his Keystone days, found himself playing host to over thirty reporters.

'I could not face Arbuckle. I would kill him. If he wants to live, he had better be punished,' Lehrman exclaimed as he strode up and down the room. He showed the reporters the cuff links he was wearing. They were inscribed, 'To Henry. My first and last sacred love. Virginia.'

He took a silk handkerchief from a breast pocket and, dabbing his eyes, continued. 'My prayer is that justice be done. I don't want to go to the Coast now; I could not face Arbuckle.'

Holding a large framed photograph of Virginia in one hand and a press clipping in the other, he quoted from the alleged affidavit of Nurse Jean Jameson. ' "She said she blamed Arbuckle for her injuries and wanted him punished." '

Lehrman paused, then said, 'That is just like Virginia. She had the most remarkable determination. She would rise from the dead to defend her person from indignity. Before she died, she kept saying, "Don't tell Henry. Don't tell Henry." That means one thing. She had lost the battle she made to defend herself.'

There is no record that any of the New York reporters suggested to Lehrman that Virginia's words may have carried quite a different meaning.

Lehrman was by now hitting his stride. 'Arbuckle is a

beast. I directed him for a year and a half. I finally had to tell him if he didn't keep out of the women's dressing room, I would see that he was through. He boasted to me that he had torn the clothing from an unwilling girl and outraged her.'

Lehrman did not tell the press that it was he who had been fired by Keystone. Nor did he explain why he continued, right up to the time of Virginia Rappe's death, to be a close friend of a rapist. He did, however, elaborate on Roscoe Arbuckle.

> That's what comes of taking vulgarians from the gutter and giving them enormous salaries and making idols of them. Arbuckle came into the pictures nine years ago. He was a bar boy in a San Francisco saloon. Not a bartender, a bar boy; one of those who wash glasses and clean cuspidors.
>
> Such people don't know how to get a kick out of life, except in a beastly way. They are a disgrace to the film business. They are the ones that resort to cocaine and the opium needle and who participate in orgies that surpass the orgies of degenerate Rome. They should be swept out of the motion picture business.

Lehrman continued with a vivid description of the virtuous Virginia. He said she would never attend a vile party, that her friends were stars like Charlie Chaplin (Chaplin had never met her). Lehrman told the press of the time he and Virginia had worked at Keystone and of her aversion to the star. He conjured up the scene in San Francisco.

> I can see now in my mind's eye how she must have fought him like a tiger, even if she had had a couple of drinks.
>
> I remember once when there was a terrible assault case in the newspapers. She said to me quietly: 'Henry, if anyone tried to do a thing like that to me, he'd have to kill me.'

He paused, shrugged his shoulders, and said, 'Well, she's dead.'

By tabloid standards it was great stuff. The press could not get enough of it. Lehrman, ever the frustrated actor, was giving the performance of his lifetime.

> I feel as though I had died and that my being here in these rooms isn't quite real. I haven't been out of these rooms since I got the wire that she was dead. But I want to live now and to see that justice is not cheated.
>
> Nobody can pull me off. Arbuckle has powerful friends, and much influence and money will be used to save him. But he will have me to reckon with, even if he succeeds in buying his freedom.

The interview finished with a plea to the Almighty. 'God,' prayed Lehrman, sinking to his knees and gazing at the ceiling, 'give me justice!'

Mack Sennett, after reading what Lehrman had said, retorted, 'In all the years that Roscoe worked for me, he didn't do a thing anyone could point a finger at. Fatty wouldn't hurt a fly. I never knew him to be mixed up in any brawls or to do an ungentlemanly thing towards any girl. He was a kind, good-natured fat man and a good comic.'

Sennett's remarks were not carried by any Hearst newspaper.

A few days after Virginia Rappe's death, Henry Pathé Lehrman left his hotel, secretly met his new girl friend, a model named Jocelyn Leigh, took her to a Manhattan shop and bought her a fur coat. This incident was not reported until Arbuckle's fate had been resolved, and only came to light then because Lehrman baulked at paying the bill for the expensive coat.

About Roscoe, Lehrman told his interviewers, 'I look to see him crumble. When he is alone in his cell and realizes the situation he is in, I expect to see him collapse.'

Lehrman was not alone in this expectation. Among

others who desperately wanted Arbuckle to break was DA Matthew Brady.

Brady had in fact been away from San Francisco at the time of Virginia Rappe's death and Roscoe's subsequent arrest. He returned to find that his subordinates had already arrested Arbuckle and charged him with murder – an action that was to change the course of events in the Bay City in the months to follow.

Matthew Brady was born in San Francisco on April Fool's Day, 1876, the son of a pioneer stationery merchant. He earned his law degree at Hastings College of the Law in 1899 and set up private practice the same year. Nine years later he was appointed to the Civil Service Commission, and served there until 1914, when San Francisco's Mayor James 'Sunny Jim' Rolph appointed him to the Police Court bench. In 1919, Brady ran against and defeated the incumbent district attorney, Charles M. Fickert, who was embroiled in the controversy surrounding the trial of Thomas J. Mooney and Warren K. Billings for the new 1916 Preparedness Day bombings.

At the time of Virginia Rappe's death, Brady, although no longer a member of the bench, was often referred to as 'Judge Brady', a nickname he did nothing to discourage. Brady had excellent relations with the press, as he was to demonstrate when he was back in the city on Sunday, 11 September.

On Monday, 12 September, the tabloids shouted:

BRADY SAYS EVIDENCE SHOWS MURDER

ACTOR SEIZED GIRL DURING CAROUSAL AND DRAGGED HER TO BEDROOM, DECLARES DISTRICT ATTORNEY

PROSECUTOR SAYS FILM COMEDIAN CRIED, 'I HAVE WAITED FOR FIVE YEARS AND NOW I'VE GOT YOU.'

The district attorney of San Francisco had decided to

fight this case not in the courts but in the tabloids. They featured a long statement from Brady.

'The evidence in my possession shows conclusively that either a rape or an attempt to rape was perpetrated on Miss Rappe by Roscoe Arbuckle,' the DA asserted. Having advised the world that Arbuckle was guilty of first-degree murder, the custodian of the city's law continued. 'Following this assault, Miss Rappe died as a direct result of the rupture of her bladder. The evidence discloses beyond question that her bladder was ruptured by the weight of the body of Arbuckle either in a rape assault or an attempt to commit rape.' Brady declared that Arbuckle had dragged the girl into his room exclaiming, 'I have waited five years and now I've got you.' He asserted that Arbuckle had remained in the locked room for over one hour, refusing to open the bedroom door despite repeated attempts from the other partygoers to get him to do so. The DA described Virginia's 'dishevelled condition' when the other guests gained admittance to the room. He told how the bed she was lying on was soaking wet, as were Arbuckle's pyjamas. He explained the reason for this: 'Undoubtedly this water in the bed and upon Arbuckle's pyjamas came from the ruptured bladder of Miss Rappe.'

Brady's statement to the press continued with the assertion, 'We also know that when the other members of the party went into the room, Miss Rappe was moaning in great pain and crying, "I am dying! I am dying! He killed me!" '

The district attorney concluded by saying:

> This is all the testimony that I desire to give out at the present time, but we have other testimony in our possession which, to my mind, conclusively proves the commission of this awful crime by Arbuckle.
>
> I desire to state to the people of San Francisco at this time that I will spare no effort to punish the perpetrator of this atrocious crime, although I will be opposed by the

cleverest lawyers and the greatest influence that money and fame can purchase.

Henry Lehrman whipped off to DA Brady a cable which Brady released for publication. It said in part:

> Party unknown to me wired me before, Mrs B. M. Delmont, had told me that she had accompanied Miss Rappe to Arbuckle's apartment and was alone with them at the time when Arbuckle, despite Miss Rappe's vehement and continuous protests, forced her into bedroom and locked door behind him.
>
> After Mrs Delmont repeatedly knocked at door, Arbuckle finally opened and stepped out. Mrs Delmont stated she found Miss Rappe in bed unconscious with her clothes off.
>
> For the sake of truth and justice please secure statement from Mrs Delmont immediately, as I am looking at the proper value of Miss Rappe.
>
> Please advise me when transfer of body to Los Angeles can be made. I am closest and most concerned relation of Miss Rappe.

Then Captain of Detectives Duncan Matheson issued a headline-catching statement of his own. Assuring the press that the prosecution had enough evidence to convict Roscoe Arbuckle and promising that they would 'go right ahead and convict', he said:

> This fellow Arbuckle is nothing but a dog. He got Virginia Rappe into his room. When he took her in he said, 'I've been waiting five years for this.' Then he assaulted her.
>
> They were in there an hour. She struggled for her honour. He overpowered her. When she was dying, he was appealed to to go and see her. He ignored the request. A man wouldn't treat a dog that way.
>
> This is a clean-cut case and it will be prosecuted as vigorously as any case ever has been in San Francisco.

The people of San Francisco are going to show that while they like clean fun they have no tolerance for parties like that at which Arbuckle attacked the girl. That party was wrong from the start.

Virginia Rappe was not operated on by the doctors handling her case because her mental condition was such, as a result of the attack, that she could not have stood an operation.

Everything Lehrman, Brady and Matheson said was based on what they were told by Maude Delmont. To compete for front-page attention, Mrs Delmont raised the ante with new details and with a large photograph of herself dressed in black, her hand on her heart. The caption read 'AGAIN DEMANDS JUSTICE'. Underneath, an interview with her was headlined 'ARBUCKLE DANCES WHILE GIRL IS DYING. JOYOUS FROLIC AMID TRAGEDY'.

'I wanted them to arrest Arbuckle here. I said, "Get that brute and throw him down in the cellar with the rats where he belongs."' What followed was a sustained vitriolic attack on Roscoe Arbuckle. Readers of the article learned from Mrs Delmont, 'I have been in the pictures for three years. I was with Sennett much of the time.'

She had never worked for Sennett. She had never worked in the movies.

For good measure, newspaper readers that Monday morning, 12 September, were treated to photographs of Virginia Rappe's torn clothing. The clothes had vanished at first; then, to the surprise of the police who had been hunting them, some had turned up in Maude Delmont's room, and the rest at the home of Virginia's manager, Al Semnacher. The police said the condition of the clothes indicated how savage Arbuckle's attack on the unfortunate girl had been.

No details were spared in accounts of Roscoe's life in prison. They described his shave, his breakfast, the comments he made while incarcerated.

But Roscoe maintained strict silence about the St Francis party. Dominguez had instructed him not to talk about it to anyone, and Roscoe was obeying instructions.

He adjusted quietly to prison life, reverting to the simplicity of his youth. He took a piece of wire and fashioned a coat hanger for his jacket. But he was still capable of the millionaire touch. The cell bunk was absurdly small for a man of his size, so he ordered new mattresses, not just for his cell but for every cell in the prison. He bought grapes for a cell mate who craved them.

Reporters dug into his past. They located his stepmother, who was still living in San Jose: 'STEPMOTHER ABANDONED BY ARBUCKLE SLAVES AT WASHTUB'. They located the Santa Ana grave of his mother: 'GRAVE OF ARBUCKLE'S MOTHER IS NEGLECTED, FINAL RESTING PLACE HAS NO HEADSTONE'.

Yet elsewhere the stepmother was quoted as saying, 'I don't see why my name should be connected with this horrible scrape. I am no relation of Roscoe's, and I have had enough trouble with the Arbuckles.' She told another reporter that Roscoe had offered her money and she wouldn't take it.

And a small news item revealed later that Roscoe had been paying for the upkeep of the grave from the time his mother died; the gravekeeper simply hadn't got around to doing his job.

Everything was fair game, or fair dirt, in this pre-trial 'fact-finding'. Newspapers wrote about his wealth, his cars, his parties, his separation from Minta, and about the 1917 Boston party, the one he didn't attend.

Taking their cue (and their evidence) from the newspapers, religious leaders around the country conducted trial by sermon, and in turn were given ample coverage in the newspapers. A Rev. John Snape of Oakland was quoted as saying from the pulpit:

Honours we seek are the honours of the world. We too

often make the mistake of bowing to some man in the world who may be a great star. Like Arbuckle. As far as his condition is concerned, if he is guilty as alleged, he should receive a court trial and justice be meted out to him.

If a moral leader goes down, it is a moral crash, but if a man foremost in lines of entertainment that can be capitalized and commercialized goes down, man loses nothing.

The shame of it all is that good people like you make possible the continuance of such a man before the public.

The morally outraged wanted satisfaction, and they didn't look for it from informed sources. Dr Ophuls, the man who had performed the post-mortem examination on Virginia Rappe in the Wakefield Sanatorium, issued a public statement. It was virtually ignored, despite its significance: '*The post-mortem examination showed a ruptured bladder, the rupture being due to natural causes. There were no marks of violence on the body. There was absolutely no evidence of a criminal assault, no signs that the girl had been attacked in any way.*'

Matthew Brady was to find out on Monday, 12 September 1921, how many lies had been told about the St Francis party.

That morning, Maude Delmont, flanked by the district attorney and his aides, appeared before Police Chief Daniel O'Brien and officially swore out the murder complaint. With cameras flashing and people fighting to get a look at him, Roscoe was escorted into the packed courtroom by his lawyers and officially charged with the murder of Virginia Rappe. Frank Dominguez and two other lawyers – Charles Brennan, of San Francisco, and Milton Cohen, of Los Angeles – had been retained to defend him in the preliminary proceeding. Roscoe was remanded in custody and returned to his cell.

Under increasing pressure from the club women of the city, the secretary of the grand jury, Harry Kelly, announced that the grand jury would investigate the case on Monday evening. DA Brady announced that he would ask the grand jury to indict Arbuckle for murder. Brady was taking out insurance. All he had to proceed with that Monday was the sworn murder complaint of Maude Delmont. A grand jury indictment would carry far greater weight during the preliminary hearings to determine if Roscoe should stand trial.

Zey Prevon (or Sadie Reiss or Zey Prevost) had been taken out of circulation by the police. In answer to enquiries about the lady, Captain Matheson said, 'Arbuckle has a load of money, and we are taking no chances on his reaching any of our witnesses. That is why we are keeping this person under cover.'

Brady supported Matheson. By now they were a popular duo. Brady told the press that a number of witnesses were being guarded because 'intimidation was feared'. At that moment, Zey Prevon was indeed being intimidated – by the DA's office.

The DA's office had wanted to postpone the coroner's inquest for at least three days. This did not satisfy Dr Leland, the coroner of San Francisco, who felt it should take place immediately. He could see no reason for delay. The inquest was set for Monday afternoon, despite the DA's objections.

Brady wanted to delay the official inquest because something had gone wrong with his case: it had collapsed. His star witness was a liar, and the foundation of his case was worthless.

Here is a summary of Maude Delmont's statement to the police: Arbuckle had grabbed Virginia outside his bedroom door and said, 'I've waited five years to get you.' Virginia had struggled to free herself. Arbuckle had dragged her into his bedroom and locked the door. From behind the locked door Maude could hear the struggle, and Virginia's crying out again and again for help. Maude had beaten and banged on the door. After an hour, Arbuckle had opened the door and rushed out into the main guest room, 'a terrified object', perspiring from the long struggle. She had rushed past him into the bedroom and seen the naked, dying Virginia Rappe in a state of unconsciousness. Virginia had fought off Arbuckle's advances as long as she could and then had been criminally assaulted. Arbuckle had ripped off the girl's clothes, and they lay scattered around the room, her panties and silk shirtwaist ripped to pieces. Virginia had screamed, 'I'm dying! I'm dying! Roscoe killed me!' Bruises covered her body, and there were 'two monkey bites' on her neck.

By Monday afternoon the DA, his staff, and the captain of detectives had issued dozens of public statements based on Miss Delmont's statement. By Monday afternoon the DA knew he had made a big mistake.

Maude Delmont had lied. The DA had statements from other people at the St Francis party that clearly showed that when Roscoe had entered his bedroom, Maude Delmont was locked in the bathroom of Room 1221 with Lowell Sherman. Her description of the struggle was worthless.

The DA had statements showing that Roscoe was not in the bedroom more than ten minutes, that Virginia was fully dressed when the others went into the room, and that she did not blame Roscoe. Indeed, Dr Beardslee, the second doctor to attend Virginia, swore that when he tried to discover what had happened, Maude Delmont declared that Roscoe had hurt the girl, and Virginia interrupted her to insist that she had not been hurt by Roscoe in any way. George Glennon, the hotel detective, indicated in his statement that a few hours after the party, he questioned Virginia Rappe, and she absolved Roscoe completely.

And the DA had a statement from Dr Olav Kaarboe, the first doctor to attend Virginia. Despite pressure from police officers to say that he had found the girl covered with bruises (testimony about police pressure would come out at a later trial), Dr Kaarboe insisted that there were no bruises on the girl, and that at the time he attended Virginia Rappe, Maude Delmont had said, 'Oh, I guess it was just a little too much party. Virginia just had a little too much to drink and got drowsy. There's nothing the matter with her.'

Brady had a clear choice that afternoon. He could publicly admit that an innocent man had been wrongly charged with murder, or he could go forward and try to build a case to justify the murder charge and the many statements he had made to the press. To have admitted error might have cost him his political career. He decided to go after a murder conviction.

The DA knew that his star witness, Maude Delmont, the woman who had sworn the murder complaint against Roscoe, must not take the stand when the case came to trial. If the defence cross-examined her, the case would be thrown out of court. Brady had to replace her. This was why Alice Blake and Zey Prevon were in police custody. The DA felt that, under pressure, both girls could be made to testify in a way that suited his case.

The statements of Dr Beardslee and George Glennon were simply suppressed. It didn't matter that a man's life was at stake, that justice would be perverted, that many people would suffer and careers be destroyed. This was advocate justice.

Before a trial, however, the DA first faced the hurdle of the coroner's inquest at which Maude Delmont *would* be asked to testify. He had fought for a postponement and lost. There was not enough time to 'process', to rehearse Maude Delmont. He had to gain more time.

The coroner's hearing began at 2.00 p.m. on Monday, 12 September. The first witness called was Maude Delmont. As soon as she had been sworn in, assistant DA U'Ren jumped to his feet. What follows is verbatim testimony.

U'REN: On behalf of the district attorney's office and on behalf of Judge Brady, the official adviser of the coroner, I desire to state that the district attorney's office thinks it inadvisable at this time to take the testimony of Mrs Delmont, and we request the coroner to postpone the taking of this testimony till tomorrow.

THE CORONER: What are the grounds, Mr District Attorney?

U'REN: The grounds are that this matter is now under investigation of the grand jury, and we desire to take this lady's testimony before the grand jury first. But in the interests of justice we think that the taking of this testimony at this time will seriously interfere with the district attorney's office and the work of discovering the truth in this matter.

The words flatly recorded above give little indication of U'Ren's aggressiveness and the violence of his delivery, which were to characterize his statements in the months ahead. Having heard this extraordinary request, Dominguez, Roscoe's chief attorney, rose to his feet and addressed the coroner.

On behalf of Mr Arbuckle I wish to say that we want this 'truth' developed now and during any stage of the proceedings wherein Mr Arbuckle may be involved on any charge presented against him. I cannot understand how the district attorney of this county, representing the people of this state, can suggest that a hearing which is absolutely legal and, as I understand the law to be, incumbent upon the coroner to hold, can in any way hamper any investigation of the charges made, and that is what we demand and that is what we ask for. Mr Arbuckle, represented by us, asks that this coroner proceed now and hear the testimony of the lady on the stand. We want all the facts. We want the people of this city, who are fair and honourable and just, to get the truth of this case. We want it published to the world. That is our position. And we believe that it is the legal right and not only that, but that it is the duty of this coroner now to go ahead and hear every person who may have any testimony to offer here and throw light upon the circumstances surrounding the entire matter.

Dominguez had no way of knowing how crucial the issue was. He did not have access to the many statements made to the DA's office. He knew only what Roscoe had told him. He was unaware that if Maude Delmont was obliged to testify, then by the end of the day Roscoe would be returning to Los Angeles totally exonerated. Dominguez only sensed that the DA had a reason for getting Miss Delmont out of that witness box and that it would not benefit Roscoe Arbuckle.

U'REN: Now, of course, Dr Leland, the charge against Mr Arbuckle is not being tried in this court nor will it be tried by the grand jury. It will be tried by a jury of twelve people when he will have his day in court. At this time the district attorney's office is investigating his case, is gathering the necessary evidence, and we state here that the taking of the testimony of this lady at this time will interfere with the gathering of all the evidence, which is not yet complete. And in that attitude the police department and Captain Matheson join with us in that request.

DOMINGUEZ: Mr Coroner, just a word. Captain Matheson is an executive officer of this state. Mr U'Ren is a distinguished prosecutor, making an effort to reveal the truth.

This is a process of revealing the truth, and that is all the defendant wants. And I cannot understand how a representative of the State of California – and this state, mind you, is the complaining witness here – can for a moment make any effort whatsoever to hamper an investigation of the facts in this case. It is the coroner's sworn duty to do it, and now on behalf of the defendant I demand that the coroner of this county proceed with this investigation.

THE CORONER: Well, I will state that so far as this matter is concerned, I have been in the coroner's office now for eighteen years. I have tried many cases, held many inquests. There have been very very many important cases in which murder charges were involved; cases far more important from the public standpoint than is this one. And it is the first time in the history of this office that I had the district attorney come forward and request that evidence be suppressed until they have completed their investigation. The law requires that the very nature of the coroner's office requires that an inquest be held right away, then and there, even beside the body, and that all the evidence be taken under those circumstances. It is a public inquiry in which the public are concerned. The coroner is not a prosecutor, that is true. He is supposed to take evidence from the standpoint of the accused as well as the other side. He is supposed to gather the impartial evidence then and there. And, of course, I am not entirely informed in regard to what this witness may know or whether we might secure from her some things she may possess that I am not acquainted with.

Dr Leland looked at the assistant DA and, speaking quietly, continued, 'I cannot see what harm it will be to go ahead and hear this woman's testimony now . . .'

In a rage, U'Ren jumped to his feet and interrupted the coroner. 'There is no objection on our part to proceed with this inquest.'

The coroner ignored the interruption and continued. He was clearly concerned that something improper and illegal was afoot. '. . . On the other hand, if witnesses – if a person charged or suspected is not to be given a full, free and public inquiry or investigation, why . . .'

Again the assistant DA jumped to his feet and shouted at the coroner. 'There is no intimidation like that on our part.'

Again the coroner ignored the outburst. '. . . It would be better to abolish the coroner's office entirely if it's function were not to be recognized by law. But there may be reasons why the witness should be withdrawn. An interested district attorney might well come forward and advise the coroner, "Don't hold this inquest. Suppress the evidence," and so forth. There might be many angles to it.'

U'Ren was physically restrained by his colleagues. What was important to the DA was keeping Maude Delmont's mouth shut until she had been told what to say – not indulging U'Ren's spleen. As his colleagues pointed this out to U'Ren, Dr Leland continued:

> I only know that in my experience, that during the bomb investigation here in San Francisco, the famous Mooney trial, that at the time the district attorney's office came forward and requested us to hold a sort of perfunctory investigation; simply find that a crime had been committed. Against my good judgement and against the judgement of most of the jury, we consented to follow the district attorney's dictate at that time. The captain of detectives was asked for his opinion, and it transpired that he agreed with the district attorney. During all the subsequent trouble over the bomb outrages the charge was continually hurled that the accused men were railroaded and that an injustice was done; that the district attorney's office did all sorts of irregular things; and even that the police department, the captain of detectives, performed irregular things.

It was ironic that Coroner Leland should refer to the irregularities surrounding 'the famous Mooney trial'. In April, 1922, only days after a decision was finally reached in Roscoe Arbuckle's case, Brady was to reveal that he had petitioned the governor of California, William D. Stephens, to free Mooney and Billings, men who had been found guilty of the death by bombing of a number of people during the Preparedness Day parade in 1916. Billings had been sentenced to life imprisonment and Mooney to hanging, a sentence that was later commuted to life imprisonment. After both men had served several years in prison, DA Brady admitted publicly that his predecessor, Charles M. Fickert, had obtained their convictions on 'flagrantly perjured testimony'.

The coroner continued:

> It has been my experience in this office that honesty is the best policy; through regularity of proceeding, the one side has no more right than the other. The defence may come forward and say, 'Well, we have reasons to believe so and so of the district attorney's office.' Now, I realize that the district attorney is the adviser of the coroner in these matters, I believe that serving the interests of the public and the interests of everybody at large there are more ways than one of looking at it.

U'Ren rose to his feet, barely controlling his temper.

> Yes, that is true. Now I think the situation is this: we have no desire to hamper any inquest by the coroner or to ask that this inquest go over. Our request is simply as to the order in which witnesses be introduced. As far as the holding of the inquest is concerned, this was originally set for Thursday, next Thursday. Then it was advanced until tomorrow, then it was suddenly advanced until this afternoon. *Now all I can say is in answer to your statement that you don't know all the facts, and we know that if the coroner proceeds at this time with the investigation of this witness and takes the testimony of this witness at this particular time, it is going to seriously interfere with the work of the district attorney's office*, and as your official adviser, as the district attorney of the City of San Francisco, we ask you to suspend the taking of the testimony of this witness until tomorrow. Now, that is all we ask.
>
> If you wish to proceed against our advice, do so; and accept the responsibilities.

The coroner flushed with anger at U'Ren's threat. 'I always accept the responsibility for my acts.'

Assistant DA U'Ren jumped to his feet and, pointing

a finger at Dr Leland, shouted, 'All right! I'll see that you do!'

The coroner repeated, this time loudly, that he was always willing to accept responsibility.

Frank Dominguez rose to his feet. He had seen many strange events during his years in the courts of California, but none stranger than this unabashed attempt by the district attorney of San Francisco to control an independent inquiry into a death.

> In the development of truth we all accept responsibility. I want to say now at this time that I have the utmost confidence and we all have in the honesty and integrity of the office of the district attorney of this county. And I want to say now, as a humble citizen of this republic, that the words of the coroner of this case have carried conviction to my heart that this republic will live. We are all anxious for the truth. This witness appearing now cannot injure the state's case, that is utterly impossible. She has never made any statement to any representative of the defendant. She has talked to the prosecution and to the police especially. And we want her now to make her statement here. These statements may be used as they see fit. She can be taken before the grand jury tonight or tomorrow. I want to say now that we brook the fullest investigation of the case and we want it. We are entitled to have the people of San Francisco know where we stand and what the facts are . . . And now is the chance of making a beginning, Mr District Attorney. Thank you.

But there was to be no beginning. The coroner announced that he was going to retire with the jury to consider the situation. Sometime later they returned. The coroner announced, 'Gentlemen, the coroner and the coroner's jury have agreed that the usual mode of procedure shall be followed in this case, that is, we should go ahead and hear the witnesses in the order in which we feel they should come sequentially.'

It appeared that Frank Dominguez had won this curious battle although he was ignorant of what was at stake. He rose and thanked the coroner.

But the coroner had something to add: 'And the case should be given a good, free and impartial investigation. But from the facts that the district attorney requests that simply the order of the witnesses, the sequence in which they shall be called, should be changed, we have consented to allow this witness to be called tomorrow morning at ten o'clock.'

There was an audible sigh of relief from the prosecution bench. District Attorney Brady himself stood up and thanked the coroner. He had come close to disaster. Without knowing it, Roscoe had lost an important round.

The first witness to give evidence at the inquest was Dr Olav Kaarboe, the first doctor called to the St Francis. Next came Harry Boyle, the assistant hotel manager. Both gave evidence supportive of Arbuckle.

Then Dr Melville Rumwell, who had replaced Dr Beardslee, gave his testimony. After outlining his involvement in the case, he made a statement that seriously weakened the DA's case: '*At no time up to the time that the laceration of the bladder was found did anything in connection with this case lead me to believe that any violence had been done whatever. I might add to this that at the time of the post-mortem, after the rent in the bladder had been found, the abdominal wall was examined and no evidence of violence was found within the walls itself either. No extravasation of blood. No bruises of the skin. Examination of the vagina equally failed to reveal any abnormality.*'

Dr Rumwell also testified that Virginia Rappe was not a virgin. Like the statement that Dr Ophuls had released to the press earlier, this important inquest testimony was virtually ignored by the press.

Dr Ophuls, the man who had performed the post-mortem at Wakefield, followed his colleague into the witness box. He confirmed Rumwell's evidence: apart from the ruptured bladder itself, there was absolutely no evidence of violence.

During my research into Roscoe Arbuckle's life I have discovered a recurring fable: that Virginia Rappe's bladder was ruptured by Roscoe when he pushed a bottle up her vagina. The details vary – whether it was a Coke bottle or a champagne bottle – but the impression remains. Those who know nothing else about the man will recall something like this: isn't he the fat man who raped a girl with a Coke bottle? Because of the positions of the bladder and the vagina, to rupture a bladder in such a manner would require virtually ripping the stomach apart, and no damage had been done to Virginia Rappe's stomach. Yet within a week, the Coke-bottle story was making the round of the clubs.

The fact is that several objects were inserted into Virginia Rappe in the last week of her life – but *they were put there by doctors and nurses.* Glass catheters – which are now banned by the medical profession – were used several times, as were rubber catheters.

The question that quite rightly occupied the mind of the coroner, Dr Leland, was, '*What caused the bladder to rupture?*' The following exchange between the coroner and Dr Ophuls has *never before been made public. Although the implications of Dr Leland's questions were staggering, they were never pursued at any subsequent hearing.*

THE CORONER: Could this tear that you found there have been made with a hard rubber catheter or a soft rubber catheter?

OPHULS: I don't think so.

THE CORONER: You don't believe it could have been made?

OPHULS: No, I don't think so.

THE CORONER: Could it have been made by a glass catheter or a metal catheter?

OPHULS: I doubt very much that it could, from the looks of it. It was not at all lacerated and it was clean.

THE CORONER: You understand the importance of this case, Doctor, do you? A great deal depends upon you, and the question of medical, ethical pride and all that sort of thing will come up against the liberty of a man, don't you see? On the one hand the question involved is: Could this have been made by faulty manipulation of a medical man, that is through instrumentation of a catheter? As opposed to this would hinge the life of a man, depending upon a possible act of violence, through the commission of an unlawful act. Looking at it impartially and under oath, taking all these things into consideration, would you say that, from the appearance as you found it, from all of the evidence as you found it there, that you would rather believe that it was due to some distributive force, not that of a catheter, you understand the use of a catheter by a medical man?

OPHULS: Yes, I would say so.

THE CORONER: Now, upon what do you base your conclusion?

OPHULS: Well, in the first place on the fact as I stated before that the opening in the bladder wall was not in any way lacerated, but was one single straight tear running more or less parallel to the bundles of the muscle fibres in the wall of the bladder. Then also it seems to me difficult to understand how any metal or glass instrument in going through the wall of the bladder would make just that kind of a tear in the wall, and then a comparatively small perforation in the peritoneum. I think one would imagine that if any such sharp foreign body had travelled through the wall of the bladder, it would have gone through the wall of the bladder and the peritoneum and made about the same kind of a hole in both of them.

We must remember that Dr Ophuls was here giving an opinion. I have consulted members of the medical profession who feel that such a course of events might have occurred. In fact, there are many points on which it would have been interesting to have contemporary medical opinion. For example, Dr Ophuls went on in his testimony to discount the possibility of the spontaneous rupture of the bladder due to overdistention. In his view, there never had been and never would be a spontaneous rupture of the bladder. But in fact, such cases have been recorded.

It was subsequently revealed that Dr Ophuls's opinions were based not on microscopic examination of the ruptured bladder, but on examination by the naked eye.

And he could not answer the main question: How did Virginia Rappe die?

Dr Rixford and Dr Read, who had been called in to consult at Wakefield Sanatorium just before Virginia Rappe died, each took the witness box and recounted his brief involvement with the case. Then the coroner adjourned the proceedings until Tuesday morning, when he could finally hear from Maude Delmont.

Still to come that Monday evening was the grand jury hearing.

At four o'clock Monday afternoon, DA Brady was able to devote his attention to rebuilding the case against Roscoe. Brady had one advantage: no-one outside his office knew the case had been shattered.

The DA studied the statements of the three partygoers who had ministered to Virginia when she needed help: Maude Delmont, Alice Blake and Zey Prevon. Delmont's testimony would be worthless. The defence could show easily that the woman was lying. But if the DA could get both Alice Blake and Zey Prevon to swear to some of Maude's allegations, he would have a solid case. They were the very people the defence would have used to discredit Maude. If they took a position that was damaging to Roscoe in their statements and subsequent testimony, the only person who could discredit their version would be Roscoe. It would be his word against theirs. Brady wanted one vital piece of evidence from the two girls. If he could get it, and the jury accepted it, Roscoe was a dead man.

Maude had stated that when she had rushed into the bedroom, Virginia had shouted, 'I'm dying! I'm dying! He killed me.' *The rule of evidence requires that if such a dying statement contains an accusation, it is only admissible in evidence if the accused was present at the time it was made.* It must have been made within his hearing. When this was pointed out to Maude, she promptly placed Arbuckle in the room and had him replying, 'You're crazy; shut up or I'll throw you out of the window.' *Testimony about the dying Virginia's accusation in Roscoe's presence was what Brady needed – not from Maude, but from Alice and Zey.* Studying their statements, he realized how big his problem was.

Alice Blake had been interviewed at Tait's Café shortly after Virginia's death was reported to the police. Her statement, though full of lurid details about Virginia's torn clothing (clothing that the police now knew had been torn off by the girl herself), contained nothing about a struggle or a criminal assault. She had declared specifically in her statement that she did not hear Virginia say that Arbuckle had killed her or hurt her. Alice said that all she heard the girl say was, 'I'm dying, I'm dying! I know I am going to die!'

Alice's initial statement also contradicted Maude Delmont's testimony that Roscoe and Virginia had been locked in the room for over one hour. Alice had left the party at 2.00 to attend a rehearsal at Tait's Café and had returned at 2.30 because the rehearsal was cancelled. The staff at Tait's confirmed this. Fred Fischbach had returned to confusion just after 3.00, and the assistant hotel manager had probably come to the room at 3.30.

Zey Prevon's statement was similar to Alice Blake's. Brady was faced with a problem.

He got detailed histories of both girls. Alice Blake came from a wealthy, upper-class family. Well-educated, she would probably be hard to break down. Zey Prevon, though worldly, came from a poor, working-class background. The DA reasoned that she would be a far easier proposition. He gave orders for Zey to be brought in for questioning.

Much of what follows here was not made public until Roscoe Arbuckle's second trial, but because it was to have so important an effect on the course of events, I relate it here.

Zey had been 'kept under guard' in the home of a DA's staff member since the previous day, ostensibly to protect her from witness-tampering. If the DA expected this to soften her up, he was sadly disappointed. Zey Prevon was asked to sign a statement containing the crucial allegation that she heard Virginia shout, in the presence of Roscoe Arbuckle, 'I'm dying! I'm dying! He killed me.'

She refused to sign. The whole weight of the DA's office was brought to bear upon the frightened girl. She was threatened, and subjected to third-degree questioning. She still refused to sign what she knew to be a false statement.

Time was running out for the district attorney. The grand jury hearing was due to begin soon.

The screw was turned tighter. Six men questioned Zey and told her that she had already made a statement containing the allegation. Astonished, she asked to see it. They showed her the statement she had given to Captain Matheson at police headquarters at 10.30 p.m. on Saturday night. It contained the vital remark, but it was not signed. She told them that it was incorrect.

Finally, time ran out. The grand jury hearing commenced with the testimony of Maude Delmont. Then, hoping that a public confrontation might succeed where the private interrogations had failed, assistant DA U'Ren hustled Zey to the stand.

Grand jury testimony is secret. Here for the first time is a verbatim record of the exchange between Zey Prevon and assistant DA U'Ren during the grand jury hearing that took place on the night of 12 September 1921.

U'REN: Then what did you do?

PREVON: We went into the room where Virginia was lying on the bed.

U'REN: What was her condition? What was she doing?

PREVON: She was just lying on the bed and started in to moan. Her hair was all down, I said, 'What is the matter with you?' She started to moan, she said, 'Oh, I am dying. I got pains, I know I am dying.' I said, 'You are not going to die, what is the matter with you?' So then Alice came running in.

U'REN: What did she do then?

PREVON: She didn't say anything more. She just kept moaning. She got up in bed then and started to tear her clothes off of her, she acted like she was crazy, she started to pull on her waist and started to pull on her cuffs. She pulled her waist nearly all off of her, she pulled her stockings clear off and garters.

U'REN: Did she have her shoes on?

PREVON: Yes, we took her shoes off. She said, 'I got a pain.'

U'REN: What part of her body was it she referred to?

PREVON: (*indicating heart*) Right here. She says, 'I got a pain around my heart.' Alice says, 'I think she's got gas pains.' Mrs Delmont went to put her dress on in the other room, and I got some carbonate of soda. No, we got her all undressed first, and the bed was all wet, so we took her from one bed to another bed, these two little beds, and laid her on the other bed. She started to rub her stomach and started to scream again; then she went completely out and we tried to put the carbonate of soda down her, and she threw it all up.

U'REN: Did she scream any more?

PREVON: Yes, sir.

U'REN: Were these the words she said – I am reading from a statement you gave to Mr Vernon [a notary public and stenographer] – 'Oh, I am dying, I am dying; he has killed me'?

PREVON: No, she did not say, 'He has killed me.' I did not hear her say that.

U'REN: And did you say, 'You are not dying, what is the matter with you?'

PREVON: She did say, 'I am dying. I am dying.' I said, 'You are not going to die, what is the matter with you?', but I did not hear her say, 'He has killed me.'

U'REN: You know this is a very serious matter, and you know that you are under oath?

PREVON: Yes, sir.

U'REN: Didn't you upstairs, within the last half hour, in the presence of Judge Brady, state that she said, 'He has killed me, he has killed me.'

PREVON: No, not 'He has killed me.' 'I am dying, I am dying. I know I am dying.' But I did not hear her say, 'He has killed me.'

U'REN: Didn't you, upstairs, in less than half an hour, say in the presence of Judge Brady and myself, state that she said that?

PREVON: No, because you wrote another paper today.

U'REN: I am not asking about any other paper. In the last half an hour upstairs – you made a statement last Saturday in the police headquarters?

PREVON: Yes, but they were all firing questions. I don't know what I said.

U'REN: Did you make a statement to me in the presence of Mr Howard Vernon, alone, at a little table, just the three of us, where you made a statement as to what occurred?

PREVON: I don't remember hearing 'He killed me'.

U'REN: I am asking you about last Saturday night.

PREVON: I don't remember of that.

U'REN: Don't you remember a statement last Saturday night?

PREVON: When I made a statement there, I don't remember.

U'REN: You did make a statement, yes or no?

PREVON: I don't remember.

U'REN: You don't remember whether you made a statement last Saturday night or not?

PREVON: Yes, sir.

U'REN: You were downstairs in police headquarters, were you not?

PREVON: Yes, sir.

U'REN: Don't you remember talking to me in the presence of Mr Vernon?

PREVON: I don't know who Mr Vernon is.

U'REN: The gentleman you saw upstairs just a few minutes ago.

PREVON: Yes, sir.

U'REN: To whom have you talked about this case since last Saturday night?

PREVON: No-one.

U'REN: Who has told you you did not have to sign any statement in this case?

PREVON: Nobody.

U'REN: Nobody?

PREVON: No.

U'REN: Who has told you you did not have to testify in this case unless you wanted to?

PREVON: I knew I have to testify. I was here as a witness.

U'REN: Who has told you you did not have to testify in this case?

PREVON: There was nobody told me I didn't have to testify, they told me I didn't have to sign anything.

U'REN: Who told you that?

PREVON: My folks told me.

U'REN: What folks?

PREVON: My mother. I have a mother.

U'REN: That is the only person you have talked to?

PREVON: My mother or my brother.

U'REN: You have talked to nobody since last Saturday night respecting this case, except your brother and your mother?

PREVON: That's all.

And so it continued, with the assistant DA pounding away at the frightened young woman. Since Saturday Zey Prevon had either been closely followed, had been at home with her house surrounded by police, or had been in police custody. So the assistant DA knew precisely to whom she had talked in that period of time. He knew, for example, that she had had a brief conversation with Charles Brennan, one of Roscoe's lawyers.

As U'Ren's examination of Zey Prevon continued, she told the grand jury of the events that followed Virginia Rappe's collapse at the party. Again and again her testimony was interrupted by the assistant DA. If he could not get the testimony he desired from the girl, he was determined that the grand jury should hear it some way, often through the technique of starting a question with, 'Didn't you tell me downstairs that . . .' Again and again he returned to the crucial piece of evidence, Virginia Rappe's so-called dying allegation. Again and again he told the grand jury that Zey Prevon had stated she heard the accusation. But he could not break Zey Prevon down. Doggedly she clung to the truth. She had not heard the remark. She had not stated to anyone that the remark had been made.

A man's life hung in the balance in that grand jury room. Questions came at Zey Prevon from two assistant DAs, U'Ren and Golden, and from several grand jury members. Her resistance began to break.

> U'REN: Now, I am going to ask you again, if you did not upstairs this evening, in the presence of Mr Howard Vernon, a notary public, state that in Mr Arbuckle's presence, in Room 1219, Miss Rappe was yelling, 'I am dying, I am dying; you killed me'?
>
> PREVON: No, she did not say, 'You killed me.' 'I am dying, I am dying. I know I am dying. I am going to die.'
>
> U'REN: I asked you if you did not tonight, upstairs in this building, in the presence of myself and Mr Howard Vernon, state that in Mr Arbuckle's presence in room 1219 Miss Rappe was yelling, 'I am dying, I am dying; you killed me'? Did you make that statement, or not?
>
> PREVON: I did not say, 'You killed me . . .'

At this point Zey Prevon broke down and sobbed. No-one went to her assistance. She had no attorney in the room, no friend, no relation. The grand jury and the district attorney's staff waited. Still sobbing, Zey went on.

PREVON: I don't remember.

A JUROR: Did you notice any marks on her neck?

PREVON: No, sir, I did not.

ANOTHER JUROR: How long have you known Mr Arbuckle?

PREVON: I met Mr Arbuckle three or four times, but he did not remember me, because he has met so many people, but I told him who I met him through when I went up to the St Francis, but I knew Fred Fischbach.

ANOTHER JUROR: Are you in the movie business?

PREVON: I used to be, not now.

ANOTHER JUROR: Has anybody approached you and told you how you should testify before this jury?

PREVON: No, sir.

JUROR: Has anybody told you, after you gave certain testimony in the district attorney's office that they claim you did, has anybody said you should not give that testimony?

PREVON: No, sir.

JUROR: Do you mean to say that the district attorney's office is telling an untruth when they make that statement?

PREVON: No, they are not telling an untruth.

JUROR: The gentleman says you made such a statement tonight?

PREVON: Maybe I made a mistake myself, but the district attorney's office didn't.

JUROR: You made a certain statement Saturday night. Now you deny it? Did you make a false statement Saturday night?

PREVON: I never made any statement. I never wrote anything down. Maybe I did make a mistake when I said a few things.

JUROR: You never signed any statement whatever?

PREVON: No, sir.

JUROR: Did anybody approach you and tell you how you should testify?

PREVON: No, sir. Not a soul.

JUROR: Any friend of Mr Arbuckle's, or anybody?

PREVON: No, sir, nobody; that is true.

ANOTHER JUROR: What clothes were on Miss Rappe when you went into the room?

PREVON: She had all her clothes on.

JUROR: A skirt?

PREVON: A skirt and a little green blouse and a little white blouse underneath it.

JUROR: All her clothes were on?

PREVON: Yes.

ANOTHER JUROR: Was she intoxicated?

PREVON: No, she was not intoxicated.

U'REN: Last Saturday night, about the hour of 10.30 or 11.00, did you in the office of the captain of detectives, on the first floor of the Hall of Justice, in the City and County of San Francisco, didn't you tell me in the presence of Mr Howard Vernon, a stenographer, that after you had kicked on the door, that Miss Rappe said, in the presence of Roscoe Arbuckle, 'I am dying, I am dying; he has killed me. I am dying.' Did she say that?

PREVON: She said, 'I am dying, I am dying, I know I am going to die,' but I don't remember her saying . . .

U'REN: (*interrupting*) I am putting the direct question whether or not you did not tell me that under the circumstances that I have related?

PREVON: No. Well, if I did, it is a mistake.

U'REN: Just answer yes or no, if you made that statement to me?

PREVON: If I did, I don't remember, because I don't remember her saying, 'He killed me.'

U'REN: I ask you the direct question, yes or no, whether she made that statement in the presence of Roscoe Arbuckle?

PREVON: I don't remember whether Roscoe Arbuckle was in back of me, or whether he was in the other room at the time, because I was so busy attending to her I don't know whether he was there in the room back of me, or whether he was in the other room, I don't know.

U'REN: I am going to ask you whether tonight in the Hall of Justice in Room 12 on the fourth floor you did not state to me in the presence of Judge Brady and Howard Vernon that Miss Rappe screamed and yelled in the presence of Roscoe Arbuckle in Room 1219 of the St Francis Hotel on Monday, 5 September, as follows: 'I am dying, I am dying; you killed me.' Didn't you make that statement tonight in this hall?

PREVON: Tonight?

U'REN: Tonight. Answer yes or no.

PREVON: No.

U'REN: What?

PREVON: No, I did not say, 'You killed me.' There is a statement there I gave to Mr U'Ren, he just wrote it up in his own hand on yellow paper upstairs.

U'REN: I am not talking about any statement written out, I am talking about an oral statement you made tonight so that your recollection may be entirely fresh, an oral statement you made?

PREVON: She said, 'I am dying, I am dying, I know I am going to die,' but I didn't hear her say, 'You killed me.'

GOLDEN: Did Miss Rappe ever say, did Miss Rappe ever use the words 'You killed me'?

PREVON: Not that I remember, no. 'I am dying. I am dying.' This is what she yelled.

GOLDEN: Did Miss Rappe ever use the words 'He killed me?'

PREVON: No.

GOLDEN: Did you ever tell anybody that Miss Rappe said, 'You killed me,' yes or no, please?

PREVON: I don't know. You have it written down there.

GOLDEN: Did you ever tell anybody?

PREVON: I don't know.

GOLDEN: Listen to it.

PREVON: I don't know.

GOLDEN: Listen to the question.

PREVON: I don't know.

GOLDEN: You cannot say you did not tell until you have heard the question. Did you ever tell anybody that Miss Rappe said, 'You killed me'?

PREVON: I don't know.

GOLDEN: If you did, have you forgotten?

PREVON: I must have forgotten.

GOLDEN: Did you ever tell anybody tonight, before you came here to testify as a witness, that Miss Rappe used the words 'You killed me'?

PREVON: I don't know.

GOLDEN: Did you ever tell anybody tonight in this Hall of Justice that you came here to testify as a witness that Miss Rappe used the words 'He killed me'?

PREVON: No.

At this point Zey Prevon broke down again. Golden asked, 'What is it?' Zey merely shook her head and cried.

Golden said, 'Please answer the question so the reporter can get the answer.'

Zey answered, 'I don't know.'

At this point, on Golden's instructions, the previous question was read out again. Zey sobbed.

PREVON: Not that I can remember.

GOLDEN: You remember, don't you, that only a short time ago, perhaps not more than an hour or two ago tonight, that you were talking about this case to Mr U'Ren and Judge Brady, don't you? You remember that?

PREVON: Yes.

GOLDEN: And where was it that you and Judge Brady and Mr U'Ren were talking about this case a little earlier tonight in this Hall of Justice?

PREVON: I don't know, upstairs.

GOLDEN: It was on the next floor above?

PREVON: Yes.

GOLDEN: The next flight of stairs up?

PREVON: Yes, sir.

GOLDEN: Do you remember the fact that at that interview between yourself and Mr U'Ren and Judge Brady, and during the course of the time you were being questioned by either of those gentleman, you were asked whether or not you said to anybody that Miss Rappe declared that someone killed her?

PREVON: I never said 'He killed me,' tonight upstairs.

And so it went. At 2.00 a.m. the DA had Zey Prevon's mother and brother roused from their beds and brought before the grand jury. He threatened to charge Zey with perjury. He threatened to charge her mother and brother with subornation of perjury, because they had warned Zey against signing statements she did not agree with. Still Zey clung to her statement.

In a fury, the DA adjourned the grand jury hearing after the jury advised him that they were not prepared to return a murder indictment against Roscoe Arbuckle. The proceedings were suspended. The grand jury would be reconvened the following evening.

At four o'clock in the morning, the DA and his colleagues were still hammering away at the girl in the Hall of Justice. Finally, enraged, Brady ordered her thrown into prison – a threat he hoped would break her. He knew that to arrest her he would have to charge her, and to charge her with perjury would be tantamount to destroying his case. Faced with prison, Zey did not yield. She would not put the rope around Arbuckle's neck. Brady, making a play of relenting, said that she could go home for the night, but that she must return at ten in the morning for further questioning. Accompanied by *fifty* members of the police force, Zey, her mother, and her brother went home for a few hours' rest while the police surrounded the house.

The fact that Zey Prevon was refusing to testify as the DA demanded had leaked out. Brady issued another statement to the press:

Whether or not Zey Prevon will be arrested and charged with perjury will depend on further developments. I am convinced, however, that perjury has been committed by her.

I am convinced that undue influence and pressure of a sinister character have been brought to bear on her and other witnesses.

In spite of these efforts to thwart the ends of justice, the investigation will proceed and no effort will be spared to bring the guilty ones to their just deserts.

Whenever wealth and influence are brought to the bar of justice, every sinister and corrupt practice is used in an effort to free the accused. It is always easy to convict a poor man. The wealthy malefactors are the ones who find means of using their wealth to advantage. Wealth and influence should not count in favour of a defendant, neither should they count against him. This case should be handled just as the cases of the other gangsters are handled.

In the morning a member of the DA's staff took Zey back to the Hall of Justice. Again she was subjected to the third degree, this time by U'Ren. He gave her a freshly-typed statement to sign; since it contained the damning accusation, she refused. Under more questioning she repeated that all Virginia had said was that she was dying. She added that neither she nor Alice Blake had attached any importance to Virginia's remark 'because we thought she was suffering from gas pains. That is why Alice Blake gave her bicarbonate of soda.'

At the end of the morning U'Ren came out of the room exasperated. He spoke to the reporters gathered in the corridor. Among them was Ed 'Scoop' Gleeson, who recently told me, 'U'Ren said that he intended to give Miss Prevon one more chance and that if she did not testify to what he wanted, he would have her placed in custody.'

At this stage, Alice Blake was brought into the DA's

office for further questioning. She refused to incorporate the crucial 'dying statement' into her testimony.

Now the DA played one girl against the other. Alice, Zey was advised, had testified that Miss Rappe had said Arbuckle killed her (for which complaint, it will be remembered, Alice had prescribed bicarbonate of soda).

'I never heard her say it,' Zey Prevon retorted. 'If Alice says that, then her ears hear differently than mine.'

Meanwhile Alice was told that Zey had finally agreed to cooperate and that they had proof that Arbuckle was guilty. She was threatened. Finally, Assistant DA Golden appealed to the woman in Alice Blake. He told her that girls like Virginia were nothing but dirt under the feet of men like Arbuckle. He asked her how she could possibly question the sincerity of the district attorney's office.

'Don't you know,' pleaded Golden, 'that we would be down here making the same kind of fight if you were the victim?'

Then Golden played his ace. The DA's office had discovered that Alice Blake had an illegitimate child. They told Alice that unless she cooperated the authorities would take her child from her. Alice Blake crumbled. But even then she insisted on a compromise. She agreed only to state that Miss Rappe had said, 'I'm dying. He *hurt* me.'

The news was carried to Zey Prevon that Alice had 'come through' to that extent. Zey, frightened and overcome with weariness, said, 'I never heard Virginia say it, but if you want me to say I did, I will.'

Her statement was handed to her with the words 'He killed me' crossed out. Zey wrote in 'He hurt me' and signed the statement.

While this charade was being played out in the Hall of Justice, Maude Delmont was finally testifying at the coroner's inquest. The previous evening, without any cross-examination by Roscoe's lawyers (defence lawyers are not permitted to attend the secret grand jury hearings), she had given the grand jury the works. Now however, she had to be more careful. Her testimony at the inquest was not only in public, it was being given in front of Roscoe and his lawyers. Maude still managed to tell a distorted tale to the coroner and his jury. But some of her omissions from her earlier statements are particularly interesting.

To the press, the police and the grand jury, she had portrayed Roscoe's struggling and pulling Virginia into his bedroom, exclaiming as he did, 'I've waited five years for you and now I've got you.' Not a word of this was uttered at the coroner's inquest.

To the press, the police and the grand jury, she had told how Virginia could be heard, behind the locked door, screaming to protect her virtue. To the coroner's jury, Maude Delmont said there had not been a sound from the bedroom. (Later she changed her mind and said there were a few screams.)

She told the coroner's inquest, as she had told the press earlier, that Arbuckle had only opened the door after she, Maude, had phoned down to the management and got Boyle, the assistant manager, up; that the door was opened only at Boyle's insistence. She had made an entirely different statement to the police.

To the press, the police and the grand jury, she had said she found Virginia naked, her clothes torn to pieces by Roscoe and scattered all over the room. To the coroner's jury, Maude recounted that when she entered the room, Virginia was fully dressed.

To the press, the police and the grand jury, she had described the love bites on Virginia's neck, and the bruises all over her body. During her testimony at the coroner's inquest, the love bites and bruises disappeared. So it went on.

It is little wonder that DA Brady and assistant DA Golden were later to remark, '*Mrs Delmont was not called to give evidence during the trial because we cannot believe a word she says.*' *Yet this is the woman who had, with the full cooperation of the DA's office, sworn out the murder complaint*.

Maude Delmont did not confine her act to the coroner's court. In a nearby detectives' office, after she had given her testimony, she approached Al Semnacher and demanded that he pay her bill at the St Francis. Al refused. She asked him what she was going to do about all of her baggage. Virginia Rappe's former manager remarked with a smile, 'Now, Maudie, you know the only baggage you have is that little handbag you're holding.' Enraged, Maude hit him round the face with her handbag and had to be physically restrained by detectives.

Semnacher's testimony at the coroner's inquest included the surprising admission that he had taken Virginia Rappe's torn panties back to Los Angeles because he thought they would 'make a nice car rag'.

One of the nurses who appeared on Tuesday was Vera Victoria Cumberland, who testified, among other things, that Virginia had admitted on one occasion that she had had intercourse with Roscoe in the locked bedroom. The nurse then testified that on another occasion Virginia had said that she had not had intercourse with Arbuckle. Miss Cumberland never gave evidence at Roscoe's trial. This may have been because she claimed not only to have received this information from the dying girl, but also to be the grand-daughter of Queen Victoria and 'a countess in her own right'.

The coroner, Dr Leland, tried all day to get Zey Prevon and Alice Blake into the witness box. Both girls had been subpoenaed, but each time he asked the DA to present them, he was told that they 'were not available' and that Zey Prevon in particular, having been questioned until 4.30 a.m., was 'not in a condition to attend the court that day'. In fact, *both girls were still being grilled in the Hall of Justice*.

The coroner retired with his jury to decide if they could arrive at a verdict without hearing the evidence of Zey Prevon and Alice Blake. They concluded that they could not. Severely criticizing the DA, the coroner demanded that the two women testify. The DA's office assured the coroner that the women would testify the next morning.

Meanwhile, at 8.00 Tuesday evening, 13 September, the grand jury hearing was reconvened. There were just two witnesses, Zey Prevon and Alice Blake.

Like the previous grand jury testimony recorded in this book, what follows has never before been made public. It shows what a good job the DA's office had done on Zey Prevon.

U'REN: You testified here last night?

PREVON: Yes, sir.

U'REN: Now, do you desire to add to your testimony? Do you desire to change your testimony?

PREVON: Yes.

U'REN: I will ask you whether or not since your testimony last night you read over for the first time the statement which you made to me in the office of Captain Matheson on last Saturday night at 10.30 p.m. in the presence of Detective McGrath, Captain Matheson, Howard Vernon, stenographer, and George Duffy [one of the DA's assistants]. You have read that over today for the first time in the form of questions and answers?

PREVON: Yes, sir.

U'REN: Last night in reply to certain questions, and particularly in reply to a question regarding what was said by Miss Rappe, do you desire now to state what was actually said by her?

PREVON: Yes, sir.

U'REN: In Room 1219 of the St Francis Hotel in the presence of yourself and Alice Blake and Roscoe Arbuckle?

PREVON: Yes, sir.

U'REN: What did she say?

PREVON: She said – do you mind reading my statement?

U'REN: Well, now, what did she say?

PREVON: She said, 'I am dying, I am dying,' but I don't

know – I am so nervous I cannot talk. Can you not read the statement that is on there?

U'REN: I will hand you the statement, Miss Prevon, and ask you if you have read over that statement as given to me in the form of questions and answers that has been reduced to writing. Will you look at it, and look at the signature, and look at the corrections you have made.

PREVON: 'He hurt me.'

U'REN: What is a complete statement of the cry Miss Rappe made in your presence?

PREVON: I am dying, I am dying, I know I am dying; he hurt me.'

Following her testimony, Zey was led in hysterical condition from the room; she fainted in the anteroom.

So finally, and only then by the skin of his teeth, assistant DA U'Ren had got it on the record. Even at the last moment Zey Prevon had faltered. U'Ren had been obliged to hand her her own statement, point out the crucial line, and allow her to read it into the record.

The doctored statement of Zey Prevon was then read in its entirety into the record. After hearing corroborating evidence from Alice Blake, the grand jury retired to consider the verdict.

After several hours the jurors returned and told the district attorney that without more evidence they were not prepared to indict Roscoe Arbuckle for murder. The DA asked them to reconsider their verdict without further evidence. They came back after another hour to announce that they had voted twelve to two for a manslaughter indictment.

It must have been apparent to the DA at this point that the most serious charge he could pursue through the courts with any hope of success was one of manslaughter, for which Arbuckle, if found guilty, would get a maximum sentence of ten years. But Brady wanted to pursue a murder charge, which, if successful, would carry with it the death sentence.

*

It might help to understand Brady's strategy to consider the legal possibilities open to him under California law.

The grand jury had met as an accusing body, an adjunct of the prosecutor's office, to determine if there was sufficient evidence to support the charge of murder. The district attorney could take Roscoe to trial on the basis of the grand jury indictment, but he could only take him to trial for manslaughter, as the grand jury had failed to return an indictment for murder.

Or if he wanted to, he could under California law 'file an information' charging the defendant with murder, if a preliminary examination held by a magistrate of a lower court determined that there was reasonable cause to believe that the defendant had committed the murder and should be made to answer for it in a superior court.

In other words, DA Brady could take Roscoe to trial on the basis of the *grand jury indictment* or he could *file an information* against him. California is one of the states in which the DA has these two options. The question was, could he get Roscoe Arbuckle to trial on the charge of murder by filing an information?

Brady announced that he would consider the situation and reveal his decision by the end of the week.

Meanwhile, the coroner's inquest continued its investigation into the cause of Virginia Rappe's death. If they found reason to suspect there had been foul play, they would recommend a course of action to the district attorney.

On Wednesday, 14 September, the coroner's inquest reconvened. The first witness to be sworn in was Zey Prevon. Waiting to follow her into the witness box was Alice Blake. Brady had no intention of letting either girl give testimony. As Zey Prevon's grand jury testimony indicates, the DA was walking a tightrope with both girls. They had come through with the testimony he needed for the grand jury, but it had been close. He needed time to 'run things through' with the girls before they were obliged to give their testimony publicly. As Coroner Leland turned to begin his questioning of Zey Prevon, Brady stood up.

THE DA: Dr Leland.

THE CORONER: What is it, Judge?

THE DA: Dr Leland, as your legal adviser and as the district attorney of the City and County of San Francisco, I desire to enter a formal protest against placing these two girls upon the stand at this particular moment. We think that the function of the coroner's jury is first, to determine the cause of death in a case of this kind; and secondly, to bring home to the proper public officials that a crime has been committed. The grand jury of the City and County of San Francisco has considered this phase of this matter and is evidently satisfied that a crime has been committed. They returned an indictment, charging him with the commission of the crime of manslaughter. Any further hearing in this matter will have no effect except to act detrimentally to the case of the people of the State of California; and I therefore protest against placing these two girls upon the stand at this particular point.

THE CORONER: When do you want them placed on the stand, Judge?

THE DA: As far as we are concerned, we think there is ample evidence before you at the present moment to justify this coroner's jury in retiring and bringing forth its findings.

For Coroner Leland, this was the last straw. For three days his official function had been subverted by the district attorney's office. The DA had failed to produce witnesses, had insisted on changing the order in which witnesses appeared, and now was resisting the coroner's attempts to hear evidence from two crucial witnesses who had been subpoenaed to attend and give evidence. Angrily, the coroner asked Brady why he had not made this statement yesterday, why he had allowed a third day's hearing that he knew he was going to object to. The DA said he had 'been busy'. The coroner exploded:

> Last evening, I put up to the jury that very question, as to whether they believed that with the evidence at hand, they could bring in a verdict. They felt they would like to hear the evidence of some other people who were present at that party. There are many things, Judge, which enter into the possibility of the cause of death. We have for example the condition of Miss Rappe when this witness on the stand entered the room. There are many other features, which might be straightened out by hearing from other witnesses.

At this point the coroner could not resist some irony.

> THE CORONER: It is not our wish to discommode or interfere with the cause of justice. I think, myself and the jury realize, Judge, that the district attorney's office deserves a great deal of credit for the energy that they are displaying in this particular case.
>
> But the people themselves have rights, Judge. We feel that you are engaged in a prosecution, the defendants, possibly have certain rights . . .
>
> THE DA: (*interrupting*) Doctor . . .
>
> THE CORONER: Just a moment. If prosecutions were allowed to go along entirely in the hands of prosecutors, why, there would be very little justice. So I myself can't see possibly how the testimony of these two women, who are only participants in this affair, how it could affect the case any more than the testimony of others that have been here.
>
> THE DA: Dr Leland . . .

But the coroner was not to be stopped. It was obvious to him that this case had become a crusade for the DA, a crusade in which the rules of justice had been abandoned.

THE CORONER: We are only too willing to assist, and if you can demonstrate that we will not be doing an injustice to the other side, to the defence, why, I am only too willing to work with the district attorney. I think we all appreciate, District Attorney Brady, that you are acting very very energetically in this case, more so than any case that I have seen for a long long time. We have had many murder cases here, important cases, and I must say that this one is being approached very energetically, perhaps too energetically.

The argument grew in acrimony. Brady lost his temper and shouted at the coroner that Arbuckle should take the stand and give evidence. He had to be reminded by the coroner: 'You, as my legal adviser, should instruct me to tell you not to enter into the argument of the case at the present time.' Frank Dominguez joined in with a long plea to develop the full truth, appealing again to the 'people of this city, noted because of their generosity and magnanimity and love of fair play'.

But eventually the DA won. Even though the coroner's jury had said they could not and would not reach a verdict without hearing the testimony of the two girls, even though both girls had been subpoenaed to give evidence, Zey Prevon and Alice Blake did not testify.

At four minutes past twelve, the coroner's jury retired to consider its verdict. This is what they decided:

That said Virginia Rappe came to her death from peritonitis, caused by a rupture of the urinary bladder. Said rupture was caused by the application of some force which, from the evidence submitted, we believe was applied by Roscoe Arbuckle. We, the undersigned jurors, therefore charge the said Roscoe Arbuckle with the crime of manslaughter.

We, the jury, recommend that the District Attorney of the City and County of San Francisco, in conjunction with the Grand Jury, the Chief of Police and the Federal

Prohibition officials, take steps to prevent a recurrence of affairs similar to the one in which this young woman lost her life, *so that San Francisco shall not be made the rendezvous of the debauchee and the gangster.*

A stunned Arbuckle was escorted back to his cell, where his brother Arthur and his sister Nora were waiting to talk to him. Roscoe stared at them like a sleepwalker. Nora pulled him out of his trance with a question: 'Did you do it, Roscoe?'

Her famous brother looked at her squarely as he replied, 'No, Nora, I didn't. I didn't touch the girl.'

It was apparent to Arthur and Nora that he was in a state of deep shock. His world had collapsed around him. When they left, Roscoe began to go through a sheaf of telegrams from well-wishers all over the country. The hate mail had not yet begun.

He was not yet aware of the fury he was creating outside the jail and the inquest room; of the panicked attempts of Paramount executives to save him, so they wouldn't go down with him; of the hasty efforts of many in the film world to dissociate themselves from Arbuckle, as if they would suffer guilt by association; of the greedy rush of creditors to get what they could while he still had something left; and the almost maniacal fervour with which club women, moralizers, and organized religion hastened to condemn him and cried for vengeance – cheered on by the nation's newspapers.

When Roscoe was arrested and when the grand jury hearings and the coroner's inquest had begun, the Paramount executives were faced with a problem: whether to back Roscoe up or to quietly dissociate themselves from him. In the end they played it both ways. They did not confront the issue face on and take a public stand on Roscoe's behalf, but they did quietly help Roscoe behind the scenes, using their power and money to get him the best defence they could.

Jesse Lasky, the vice president of Paramount, had immediately contacted Minta Durfee Arbuckle, from whom Roscoe had been separated for over four years. Roscoe with a wife by his side in San Francisco would present a better image than Roscoe with a wife in New York. Minta was staying at Martha's Vineyard, a quiet resort island in Massachusetts. Lasky told Minta that Paramount would pay her $5,000 plus expenses to rush across the country as the loyal wife coming to her beloved's aid. Minta accepted. She had planned to come anyway.

On Wall Street, despite constant buying by Paramount brokers, the price of shares for Famous Players stock was falling. It would continue to fall from a high of ninety before Roscoe's arrest to forty. This was hitting Paramount where it really hurt – in the cash register. The movie executives could not understand why Roscoe was still in prison two days after his arrest. They wanted him out, as fast as possible. Every hour that he remained in jail was doing terrible damage not only to his image but to that of the entire film industry.

What they needed was heavy artillery. Adolph Zukor got on the phone: 'Get Clarence Darrow for Arbuckle's defence.'

No amount of money was to be spared in obtaining Darrow or anyone else who could prepare an effective defence – not only to save Roscoe's neck, but to protect the industry's huge profits. But there was not enough money in Fort Knox to persuade Clarence Darrow to take the case: he valued his freedom.

Clarence Darrow – who was to become one of the world's most famous lawyers for his defence of Leopold and Loeb, the Scottsboro boys, and Scopes in the monkey trial – knew that if he appeared in a San Francisco courtroom in 1921, he risked jail. As a result of the notorious *Times* bombing case in Los Angeles in 1916, Darrow had stood trial himself, charged with two counts of jury bribing. What saved him from imprisonment for the first trial was not his own eloquence but the courtroom brilliance of one of the country's finest criminal lawyers, Earl Rogers, who won an acquittal for Darrow. For the second trial, Darrow virtually dispensed with the services of Rogers, to whom he had admitted in private his guilt on both counts. The result was a hung jury that voted 8 to 4 for a verdict of guilty. At this point, the district attorney of Los Angeles, John Fredericks, gave Darrow an ultimatum: Either agree that you will never again practise law in the state of California or I'll put you on trial again. Darrow got out of California, fast.

Paramount, having been turned down by Darrow, decided to hire the man responsible for his acquittal at the first trial, Earl Rogers. Or rather they tried to.

Joseph Schenck and Harry Brand (Paramount's executive in charge of publicity) called on Earl Rogers with a check for fifty thousand dollars, intended merely as a retainer. Rogers was told to name his own fee for defending Roscoe Arbuckle. Confident that he would take the case, the two men left.

Earl Rogers had been fighting alcoholism for years and was a sick man. He had lost the battle and was dying. For a short while he was very tempted by the case – a chance for one last hurrah. He knew Roscoe personally and liked him. Their paths had first crossed shortly after the San Francisco earthquake. Rogers, then at the peak of his powers, had taken on the attorney general of the United States in the courts and had won his case. In the years that followed, Earl Rogers had watched Roscoe become the epitome of the American Dream, the boy who made good. And now he saw Arbuckle at the centre of an American nightmare. As he considered the situation, he became coldly angry. All over the United States an appalling rush to judgement was taking place. Before Roscoe had had an opportunity to defend himself in court, he had been tried and found guilty by the American public. Earl Rogers decided to take the case. His doctors decided otherwise.

Sadly, Rogers prepared his daughter Adela for what was to come: 'Arbuckle's weight will damn him. He is charged with an attack on a girl, which resulted in her death. He will no longer be the roly-poly, good-natured, funny 350-pound fat man everybody loves. He will become a monster. If he were an ordinary man, his own spotless reputation, his clean pictures would save him. They'll never convict him, but this will ruin him and maybe motion pictures for some time. Tell Joe Schenck I can't take the case – the doctors won't let me – but to prepare Hollywood for tornadoes.'

It was an uncannily accurate prophecy. For the past seven years Roscoe's career had made nonsense of the saying that 'Nobody loves a fat man'. Now the scales were tilting in the other direction: 'Fatty', the figure of innocent fun, was now Fatty the rapist, the sexual degenerate. And once that image was evoked, it tended to linger.

This was the story of beauty and the beast, of violation of the innocent, and it was a story the American psyche of 1921 seemed to need. Americans, watching the loosening of morals, were afraid of what would happen to them – and to their daughters. Roscoe Arbuckle walked right into a myth in the making and gave it form.

As the coroner's inquest and the grand jury heard testimony, people all over the country were quick to make their views felt.

Mrs Hardebach, with whom Virginia had lived in Chicago and who later had been Virginia's housekeeper in Los Angeles, said, 'This monstrous thing against a good and beautiful girl should be prosecuted to the limit of the law.' Claiming to be Virginia's aunt, though she wasn't, she went on: 'Roscoe Arbuckle is guilty; any other thought would be inconceivable to one who had known Virginia Rappe.' Her views were featured prominently in the Hearst press, although she admitted, 'I know no more than the newspapers tell.'

More than a couple of Arbuckle's Hollywood friends ran for cover. Tom Mix put down his six-guns long enough to attack Arbuckle, and say, 'We don't want such men amongst us.' Another film cowboy, William S. Hart, objected later in the week to being tarred with the same brush as Arbuckle.

Denouncing the affair as 'disgraceful', the virile Hart said, 'Why did those men remain outside the room and let Arbuckle get away with it? Why did they run away with her clothing? What kind of men are they? Was there not a drop of red blood in their veins, that they could sit by and allow such a thing to happen? Why brand the entire industry when one man gets in bad? The crime was not committed because the man was a motion picture star. The same man would have done the same thing whether he was a manufacturer, hod carrier, bank president or minister of the gospel.'

As a member of the Los Angeles Athletic Club, Roscoe had, over the years, given large amounts of money to keep the club functioning. Early that week Hearst newspapers reported a statement by the president of the club, William Garland: 'When I read the newspapers this morning, it occurred to me that Mr Arbuckle might be a member of the club. The club secretary confirmed my suspicions.' Garland thought the party 'a filthy, revolting affair', although, he added, 'None of us are without sin and it is not becoming in anyone to throw stones at a man in great trouble; and that is not my intention.' He called a meeting, which voted to expel Roscoe.

It was to become the formula: 'I am not saying that the man is guilty; that remains to be seen. But I don't want anything more to do with him.'

On Monday, the Board of Censors in Memphis, Tennessee, banned all Arbuckle movies 'until the actor clears himself'. Roscoe was guilty until proven innocent. The mayor of Medford, Massachusetts, imposed a ban. A number of theatres in New York withdrew his films. The Exhibitors Association in Michigan banned the films. Chicago, Philadelphia, Portland, Pittsburgh and Buffalo all announced bans – some imposed by the authorities, some initiated by the exhibitors themselves. The exhibitors were breaking their contracts with Paramount, and the authorities were exceeding the law under the Constitution. No-one could justify the ban on the basis of anything *in the films*. Moreover, there had not at this time been one public demonstration against Arbuckle at any showing of his movies. By their actions, the local authorities and exhibitors fed the mounting public impression of guilt.

On Tuesday there were bans in six hundred theatres in New York, and in the entire states of Missouri, Pennsylvania and Kansas, although immediately prior to the ban in Kansas, Roscoe's appearance on the screen in Topeka had been greeted with loud cheers. There was only one film holdout, and it was in Honolulu. Local citizens there had appealed to the mayor to ban all Arbuckle movies, and he had refused to do so, saying, 'Roscoe Arbuckle's guilt has not yet been proven and he is entitled to a presumption of innocence.'

The New York Times, which was to become a relentless critic not only of Arbuckle but of any person or group who tried to help him, recorded each further cancellation and ban. With front-page headlines like 'ARBUCKLE DRAGGED RAPPE GIRL TO ROOM, WOMAN TESTIFIES', the staid New York daily competed with the tabloids, lending authority to the attack.

On Tuesday, the Anti-Saloon League in Washington announced that it intended to carry out a full investigation into the affair, and recommended that Arbuckle be prosecuted for violation of Prohibition law. The league needn't have bothered. On Monday, Prohibition agents had announced that a full investigation would be made about the alcohol consumed at the St Francis party. A special assistant to the US attorney general was already on the job.

On Monday, a furniture company served papers of

attachment for twenty-five pieces of Roscoe's furniture, worth $7,000. The company, claiming that Roscoe had not paid the bill, wanted the money while it was still obtainable.

On Tuesday, a Los Angeles interior decorator served a writ claiming that the star owed him $12,000.

The Moral Efficiency League announced that it was collecting evidence that would tie Arbuckle to a series of drug orgies.

As Frank Dominguez, his lawyer, would point out later in court, Roscoe was being persecuted: people were blaming him for everything. A Presbyterian minister in Pittsburgh, Dr Allen, said, 'The moving picture is poisoning the youth of America and they are slipping away from the Sunday school, the Christian endeavour and the Church.' He felt that Roscoe and his like were to blame for the fact that 'there have been over one million divorce cases in the past twenty years'.

Professor William McKeever, a Kansas Presbyterian, said, 'There should be martial law in the cities until the mad mob spirit is taken out of the movies.'

But the mob spirit seemed strongest among club women, who rallied to the issue with a unanimity as startling as it was vehement. The view of Miss Jennie Partridge, president of the County Federation of Women's Clubs, was typical: 'I think I can voice the opinion of the whole of San Francisco when I say that it is a disgraceful occurrence and most terrible thing that any girl should have to suffer as she suffered from man's ruthlessness, and the matter should be investigated to the utmost *and Arbuckle made to suffer*.'

Mrs W. S. Berry (a 'prominent Red Cross worker and club-woman') declared, 'I think it is one of the most atrocious things that has ever occurred here, and if Arbuckle is guilty he should receive the full penalty of the law. It is on a par with the gangster outrage. They received their punishment and he should receive his. Money should not be allowed to make any difference.'

To the club women, the whole affair was an outrage against womanhood and San Francisco, and they were intent on seeing that justice be done, no matter how famous and rich the defendant. They intended to watch the proceedings to make sure they hadn't been fixed.

Perhaps the most active watchers were the Women's Vigilant Committee of San Francisco, whose presence and pressure were felt through all of Roscoe's ordeal. On Monday, they demanded a meeting with Chief of Police Daniel O'Brien to discuss the 'Arbuckle case'. On Wednesday, while the coroner's jury was deliberating, O'Brien addressed them: 'It makes no difference whether Arbuckle is just a labourer, a film star or king of the South Sea Islands, he will be prosecuted the same as any other man.' He got a standing ovation, and the women began to chant, 'Punish Arbuckle. Punish Arbuckle.'

Speaker after speaker went to the rostrum at the Women's Vigilant Committee meeting. It appeared that Roscoe had personally outraged every woman in San Francisco. From among several hundred applicants, eighteen women were selected to attend Arbuckle's trial in a body and 'give moral support to the women witnesses who are called upon to give testimony'; this was done 'in the interests of justice'. One of the members proposed a resolution condemning Arbuckle, but the president of the Women's Vigilant Committee, Dr Mariana Bertola, dissuaded the meeting from passing it, because to do so 'might affect the qualifications of any of us who may be called to serve on a jury to try Arbuckle'. The implications were clear, the resolution withdrawn.

With similar pressure, the women's groups succeeded in getting the next hearing on the murder charge moved to a women's court, thus assuring that they would get maximum priority seating. (The idea behind the women's court was to allow women to give detailed testimony about sexual incidents under conditions which would minimize their embarrassment; thus all men were excluded from women's court hearings except those present on official business.)

The women's groups also organized the public laying out of Virginia Rappe at Halstead's Undertakers, a move to ensure that public indignation would be kept at a high pitch.

If the women's groups were implying that Roscoe, with all of his money, could buy his way out of a tight spot, others would suggest the same – and Matthew Brady presented himself as the brave district attorney who would fight moneyed criminals to the wall.

When the coroner's jury recommended that Roscoe be tried for manslaughter, Henry 'Pathé' Lehrman sent the following telegram to Brady, who issued it for publication by the press:

> For the sake of our God and justice to men, don't let justice be cheated. It brought tears of rage into my eyes when I read your speech that influence and wealth are brought into play to bar justice. I cried because you told the truth in spite of the pressure of gold to stifle it. You are convinced from the facts, and I from knowing him that Arbuckle killed Virginia Rappe as a result of his attack, and I think, just to be able to boast, 'Oh, I had her, too.' Now, don't let them cheat justice! For God's sake, don't! He is guilty. I held court with the facts known and my conscience convicted him.

The mayor of St Paul sent a similar wire, which Brady also issued for publication: 'In the name of all decent people, I thank you for your earnest action in Arbuckle case. Latest reports indicate Arbuckle money is overcoming State testimony. Do not falter. Fight this to a finish. If Arbuckle is not punished the movie business is done, for decent people are tired of the eccentricities of genius. Go the limit and win praise of all good people.'

And Brady's reply was published as well (the wires

could have gone via Hearst papers): 'Assure you and good people of St Paul that in spite of Arbuckle's money and influence, the case will be prosecuted most vigorously. Depend upon me to do full duty as district attorney to thwart any attempt to defeat justice.'

While the 'funniest man in the world' sat in his cell, souvenir hunters stormed his Los Angeles home, which the press was calling 'Arbuckle's Historic Jazz Palace of Pleasure'.

It was clear, not only from the banning of his movies around the country, but from what people were saying officially, that Hollywood, in its fear and panic that this scandal would strengthen the movement towards censorship, was already inclined to throw Roscoe to the wolves. Frank Woods, of Famous Players-Lasky, and head of the Screenwriters Guild, was asked by a member of the Los Angeles City Council: 'In your opinion, will producers use Roscoe Arbuckle in the pictures again, if he should be acquitted?'

Famous Players-Lasky was part of Paramount, Roscoe's company, so Woods's reply had special significance:

> No, not unless there should be a complete vindication. I think his day is over. I do not think he will ever appear in pictures again, and it's right that it should be so . . .
>
> Poor, unfortunate Fatty Arbuckle has been his own worst enemy. He has been guilty of the worst of follies, the folly of trying to be a good fellow. But no-one of us that know him believe him to be guilty of intentional injury or assault of the girl. But public opinion has convicted him of being a loose-living man and a bad influence, and his motion picture plays have been removed from exhibition. *Censors could not order their removal for they are clean, but the exhibitors have withdrawn them voluntarily.*
>
> Arbuckle made the mistake of thinking that in eating and drinking lay all the joy of life. As to his parties out

at his house in Los Angeles, believe me, many prominent citizens would have been glad of an invitation and to have gone with their wives to those parties. Now that he is down, some of those same prominent citizens are jumping on him with hobnailed boots. I do not believe in prejudging.

The president of the Motion Pictures Directors Association, William Desmond Taylor, also joined the public debate on censorship: 'I have listened with amazement to the charges of these ministers that we are debauching the morals of the youth of this city. We have not been cleaning house for very long, just a few months. In those few months we have cleaned house with a vengeance.'

A few months after Taylor made these remarks, he was murdered, and the investigation into his death and the surrounding circumstances revealed a lifestyle that would give moralists and club women a great deal to be indignant about.

Meanwhile, another central figure in the Labor Day party was to learn the meaning of this new kind of censorship – censorship not of the film, but of the actor's life. At the time of Roscoe's arrest, Lowell Sherman had expressed amazement; he couldn't understand what the fuss was all about. On Thursday, 15 September, the day after the coroner's jury decision, he learned what it was to mean to him personally. He had been contracted to star opposite Gloria Swanson in a big movie, but now Famous Players-Lasky announced that he had been released from the contract 'at his own request' – which was the first that Sherman knew about it. Within six months Sherman, a competent actor, found himself frozen out of the motion picture business, and was forced to declare bankruptcy.

The Rev. Neal Dodd, pastor of Hollywood's Little Church Around the Corner, having said, 'It is not for us to judge,' advised his congregation: 'I want to warn movie girls against the dangers of visiting men in their hotel rooms, the men clad in pyjamas and serving liquor . . . The real essence of this Arbuckle matter, however, is a general lowering of the moral standards in this country. The teaching of morality to children has gradually fallen off so that the situation is fraught with horrible results.'

From New York, Henry Lehrman cabled instructions to the San Francisco undertaker to ship the body of Virginia Rappe to Los Angeles for burial. With it were to go one thousand pink tiger lilies from Henry, and 'Before you cover her sacred remains for ever, just lean over and whisper into her ear a little message. Tell her, "Henry said he still loves you." She will hear.'

His floral tribute, which bore the words 'To my brave sweetheart from Henry', was impressive. So was the bill for it. Henry refused to pay and was eventually sued by the undertakers. Lehrman told New York reporters that he would not travel to LA for the funeral because he was 'too busy'. In April 1922, two weeks after Roscoe Arbuckle's 'legal' trials were over, Henry Lehrman drove to Santa Ana with his latest girl friend, Jocelyn Leigh. There they were married by Judge Cox, the man who had put Bebe Daniels in jail. Immediately after the wedding, Lehrman moved his bride into his Los Angeles bungalow, the one that he had so recently shared with Virginia Rappe.

While all around him was ceaseless activity, for Roscoe himself there were only a small cell and his own thoughts. On Thursday his lawyer, Charles Brennan, brought good news: he had been advised that the following day the DA would drop the murder charge and proceed with the grand jury indictment of manslaughter. This would mean bail for Roscoe. It was the best news he had heard since his return to San Francisco. But if he could have been an observer in the district attorney's office that afternoon, his spirits would have soon sunk again.

Brady called a long conference involving his staff, the

captain of detectives, and many other officials, to discuss which charge to proceed with. The majority of those present favoured proceeding with the grand jury indictment for manslaughter. There was not a scrap of evidence to justify proceeding with a murder charge. To file an information for murder and have it thrown out by the police court judge might seriously jeopardize their chances of success with the lesser charge. Brady saw the wisdom of this, but he wanted a murder trial. The DA was a politically ambitious man. If he could convict Arbuckle of murder, he could run a successful campaign for the governorship of California as 'the man who cleaned up the movies'. But before Brady could reach those heady heights, Arbuckle had to be convicted of murder. And for that to happen, there had to be a murder trial. If at the lower court proceeding the police magistrate were to reject the prosecution's evidence . . .

At 4.00 p.m. on Thursday, 15 September, an important discussion took place. The district attorney of San Francisco, Matthew Brady, called on Police Judge Sylvain Lazarus, the man who had been appointed to hear the committal proceedings on the murder charge.

DA Brady asked Judge Lazarus to guarantee that if the DA proceeded with the murder charge, the judge would hold Arbuckle to answer to that charge in the Superior Court. Before the judge had heard anything from the defence, before any witnesses testified or any evidence was presented, Brady wanted a commitment from the judge. 'I want to file the charge of murder. I want you to guarantee to me now that you will hold Arbuckle to answer to that charge in Superior Court.'

Judge Lazarus asked the DA what evidence he had against Arbuckle to justify such a guarantee, and Brady enumerated the 'facts' against Roscoe Arbuckle. Before their meeting ended, Judge Lazarus had given the guarantee. Based on what he had heard, he assured the DA that he would hold Arbuckle to answer on the murder charge.

★

The evening papers announced that Arbuckle had received an anonymous death-threat letter. The same papers predicted that the following day the murder charge would be dismissed and Roscoe granted bail. So certain were Roscoe's lawyers that he would be released that they booked two compartments on the 'Lark' express to assure Roscoe of a comfortable ride to Los Angeles. The $25,000 Pierce Arrow was still being held by Prohibition officials on the grounds that it might have been used to convey liquor illegally from Los Angeles to San Francisco.

Another member of the St Francis party was in the news that Thursday afternoon. Before Virginia Rappe's death, her manager, Al Semnacher, had been in the process of getting a quiet divorce. Now anything any guest at that party did was news. The divorce proceedings had been halted so that Semnacher could be in San Francisco to give evidence. Newspapers reported that Al was suing for divorce because his wife had permitted another man to help her wash the dishes and wind the clock, and these 'undue attentions' to the other man had caused him mental anguish.

On Friday morning, 16 September, the Women's Vigilant Committee packed the court of Judge Lazarus. Row after row was filled with middle-aged women dressed in black and carrying sandwiches to fortify themselves during what they thought would be a long day.

'Case No. 5, continued calendar, Roscoe Arbuckle, charged with murder.'

Those words were the cue for Roscoe, flanked by his attorneys, to enter the court. Matthew Brady rose and said, 'In the case of the people of the State against Roscoe Arbuckle, charged with murder, I may say that the people are ready.'

The words hit Roscoe like a thunderbolt. Frank Dominguez immediately rose to his feet and asked for a ten-day adjournment. After a brief argument, a six-day adjournment was granted. Stunned, Roscoe was hurried from the courtroom and returned to his cell.

Too much was happening too fast for Roscoe to comprehend. In San Francisco Bay lay the island of Alcatraz, soon to become the base for the most notorious maximum security prison in the world. As Roscoe sat in his cell, a cheerful guard stuck his head through the bars and called out, 'Hey fat boy! Don't you wish you were taking a ride to the island for the rest of your life instead of a trip to San Quentin?'

If Roscoe were found guilty, he would be executed at San Quentin.

Friday evening, 16 September, the district attorney authorized an examination of the suite at the St Francis. No act so clearly demonstrates the incompetence with which the Rappe case was investigated by Brady's staff. Brady called in a man named E. O. Heinrich to examine Roscoe's party suite for fingerprints. Heinrich ordered the rooms sealed – a full eleven days after the St Francis party, seven days after Virginia Rappe's death, and six days after Roscoe's arrest – a clear case of locking the stable door after the horse has bolted. Obviously, many people had had access to the rooms in the interim.

In one of the numerous articles it ran the day after Brady's pronouncement, Hearst's Los Angeles *Examiner* detailed what it called 'Four Possible Verdicts Open in Actor's Case'.

> 1. Murder in the first degree without recommendation by the jury calls for the death penalty.
> 2. Conviction on the charge of murder in the first degree with a recommendation by the jury, carries life imprisonment.
> 3. A verdict of murder in the second degree means an indeterminate sentence of one year to life imprisonment.

4. A verdict of manslaughter is punishable by imprisonment from one to ten years.

Nowhere did it mention a fifth possibility – acquittal.

In Thermopolis, Wyoming, the owner of the Maverick Theatre, despite protests from the local purity league, showed one of Roscoe's movies. One hundred and fifty cowboys, some of them still on their horses, burst into the packed cinema and shot up the screen, then dragged the film out to the street and burned it. It turned out that the cinema manager had arranged the whole affair for publicity.

In Hollywood, Paramount writer Zelda Crosby was found dead in her apartment. Her suicide had nothing to do with Roscoe Arbuckle, but her mysterious death did nothing to stem the tide of anti-Hollywood feeling.

Organized religion wasn't content that Roscoe's films be burned; clergymen seemed to foresee his soul done to an eternal crisp as well. Preachers in Los Angeles competed for advertising space with other branches of Sunday show business. And on Sunday, 18 September, some of the pulpits offered stiff competition to the cinema:

'The Arbuckle Booze Party. Shall We Censure All Movie People?' (Temple Baptist)

'Jungleman or Gentleman?' (First M.E. of Hollywood)

'The Unpardonable Sin' (South Park Christian)

'Rainbow Chasers' (Westlake Presbyterian)

'Moral Degeneration' (First Congregational)

'Movie Stars and the Ten Commandments' (Immanuel Presbyterian)

'Is Arbuckle a Sample or a Warning?' (Westlake Methodist)

'Is the Prohibition Amendment to the Constitution a Mistake?' (Central Baptist)

'Some Prohibition Problems – Wild parties and Debaucheries' (Wilshire Blvd. Christian)

'A Modern Daniel Among Lions' (Wilshire Presbyterian)

The Rev. John Roach Straton attacked 'moral infamy' in New York, and his sermons were said to 'surpass vaudeville'. Theatre managers loved to be attacked by him, as a pulpit attack increased box-office takings dramatically.

Roscoe was by now deluged with mail and cables from people all over the United States. Some of this was hate mail, but most of the letters were from people declaring their belief in his innocence. These people did not speak from church pulpits or fill the columns of Hearst papers with their views; they were just ordinary people. They were not moulders of public opinion, but part of the public whose opinion was being moulded by stories like this written for Hearst by someone named Lannie Haynes Martin:

> FLOWERS BEDECK BIER OF 'BEST-DRESSED GIRL'
>
> Little Virginia Rappe, 'the best-dressed girl in the movies', whose up-to-the-minute clothes have been the admiration and the envy of thousands, wears today the oldest known garment in the world. It is a shroud.
>
> Today her body lies in state, from 10 to 4 in the Strother and Dayton undertaking establishment on Hollywood Blvd. Tomorrow morning at 10.30 a simple burial service will be read by the Rev. Frank Rodenbush of St Stephen's Church. Miss Everett Matoon and Miss Jessie Pease will render a few sweet and tender old-fashioned melodies, and then the remains of the girl whose death has shocked the nation will be placed in the Hollywood cemetery. Wrapped in her winding sheet of sheer white silk, a sheaf of dead white roses on her breast, her lips parted, showing her pearly teeth, there is still some of the old-time beauty and sweetness in her face, but the sparkle of her eyes, her chief charm, lies forever dimmed beneath her heavy lashes . . .

The piece ends:

. . . Today hundreds will pass through this flower-decked chapel and view the body. In that throng will be the kindly sympathetic, the friendly acquaintance, the screen worshipper, the merely morbidly curious. Will any of these remember another dead Virginia who lay in state in the Forum of Rome? The Virginia slain by the hand of her own father to save her from the rapacious embrace of the licentious Claudius? Will any pause and recall that the death of Virginia was the means of ending the corrupt saturnalia of ancient Rome, which is said to have had no parallel until the present day. Would not this dead girl now, whose every impulse is said to have been wholesome and kindly, whose life is said to have been given to defend her honour, would she not feel that her life and death had not been in vain if those who read her story would be influenced to saner, simpler living, would see as she saw at the end how furile it is to seek gaiety and pleasure which are not 'within the law'.

With exquisite, albeit probably unconscious irony, the article began with two lines from *Lays of Ancient Rome*. Virginia Rappe, the 'lay' of modern Los Angeles, had now been sanctified by Emperor Hearst.

The club women of Chicago condemned Roscoe Arbuckle, saying that Virginia Rappe had been 'made a martyr to the gay life of the film colony'. They demanded a federal investigation of Hollywood.

While eight thousand people filed past the body of Virginia Rappe at the Los Angeles funeral parlour, DA Brady went to the St Francis Hotel with a number of the female party guests, telling reporters that he was going to 'get the lay of the land'. All week he claimed that the defence was tampering with witnesses. He invoked a grand jury hearing into the matter, but nothing of consequence came out about witness influencing.

Meanwhile, Brady's colleagues to the south were equally busy exposing vice in the city of the angels. Suddenly the Los Angeles jails were filled with ladies of the evening, and at least one woman whose only crime was 'window shopping'.

As the day of the police court proceedings neared, the Arbuckle case became the stone upon which a thousand axes were ground. In Geneva at a League of Nations debate on white slave traffic, a Danish delegate blamed the Arbuckle party for an increase in the traffic of women. The Swiss authorities, alarmed at the prospect that their young maidens might be abducted, promptly banned Roscoe's films throughout the country. There was also by now a nationwide ban of his films in Great Britain.

Curiously, the French took a different line. Roscoe had always been tremendously popular in France, and now exhibitors were obliged to order more prints to cope with the demand for his films.

While the coroner's inquest and grand jury hearings had been going on, Roscoe's wife, Minta Durfee, had prepared herself for the journey to be by his side. In New York she had issued statements declaring that Roscoe was innocent, that he was just a big overgrown boy spoiled by success. Mabel Normand, who was in New York at the time, called on her to express outrage at the treatment being handed out to her co-star of former days.

Minta's passage across country took on the aspect of a royal tour, with interviews en route and with newspapers reporting on her daily progress. When reporters questioned her about her five-year separation from Roscoe, she said ruefully, 'Our marriage wasn't wrecked. It was warped. Eight years of never being out of each other's sight would put a blight on most marriages.'

Minta and her elderly mother stopped over in Chicago and dug up evidence on the early life of Virginia Rappe. Then they resumed their journey by train.

As the train went through Utah, it was pursued by a low-flying aeroplane. Minta and her mother looked up from their compartment to see a keen reporter with a megaphone trying to get an interview.

By the time the two women arrived in San Francisco,

there was huge public interest in Minta's reunion with Roscoe. Try as they might, the forty reporters who met her at the train could not get a statement. Two of Roscoe's lawyers had boarded the train in Sacramento and instructed her to maintain total silence. When she met Roscoe in the city prison, the reporters, shouting and swearing, were kept outside.

Roscoe held his arms out to her. Smiling at him, she remarked, 'Why, honey, you've been holding out on me.'

Roscoe's laughter filled the room. Then, holding Minta in his arms, he said simply, 'I love you.'

It was the first time since his arrest that Roscoe had laughed. While his name had been dragged through the gutters, he had remained silent. His lawyers had protected him somewhat from the hysterical bigotry that was sweeping the country. They had kept out-of-town newspapers from him and had tried to appear cheerful and confident, but the man was no fool. Accustomed to laughter, now he heard sniggers. Soberly he told Minta of his incredulity, of how he awoke each morning imagining for a moment that he was back in his West Adams home and had had a horrible dream – until the bars on his cell brought him back to reality. 'Why me?' he asked. 'Last week I was the man they all loved. Now I'm the man they love to hate.'

During their long trip across country, Ma Durfee had said repeatedly, 'Ye shall know the truth.' Now they did. They sat quietly with Roscoe as he told them what had really happened at the party.

Forty-eight hours before the police court hearing was to begin, the September issue of *Photoplay* magazine hit the stands. It contained an article that predated the Labor Day party – an interview by Adela Rogers with Roscoe Arbuckle, called 'Love Confessions of a Fat Man'. Ordinarily it would have been an amusing piece; under the circumstances, it was bitterly ironic. Only two weeks had elapsed since Virginia Rappe's death, yet the interview was published, and from it the newspapers picked up several quotes that were peculiar in the context of what had happened: 'It is very hard to murder or be murdered by a fat man . . . I prophesy that the fat man is about to have his day. He will be sought, chased, even mobbed, because there will not be enough of him to go round, not individually, but as an institution.'

One thing the Los Angeles *Examiner* did not pick up was Roscoe's answer to Adela's question 'Are you afraid of women?' He had replied, 'You bet I am. You just bet I am. So is everybody else that wears pants on the outside in this land of the free and the home of the brave. Women are free and we are brave. The 19th Amendment [votes for women] is only the hors d'oeuvre to the amendments they will pass now that they have found out they can.'

The same day the Hearst papers quoted the *Photoplay* interview, they also quoted a similar July interview published as 'Those Modern Misses' in *Pearson's Weekly,* an English publication. The two stories were in adjoining columns, next to a story headed 'REPORT SHOWS WAVE OF CRIME AGAINST WOMEN', which reported that an unprecedented crime wave, marked by attacks on young women, was sweeping California.

As the date of the police court hearing drew nearer, Frank Dominguez had many consultations with Earl Rogers. Rogers urged him to concentrate on the medical evidence, insisting that the key to Virginia's death lay in that area, and stressing the importance of clearly understanding the medical testimony.

Dominguez didn't know it yet, but there was a movement to replace him. Adolph Zukor and Joseph Schenck, disturbed that Dominguez hadn't got Arbuckle released on bail, had contacted Rogers, asking him to suggest a replacement. Rogers had advised Schenck to give Dominguez a chance, pointing out that, apart from anything else, 'With Frank Dominguez, you have another big fat man. Next to him Roscoe doesn't look so conspicuous in court.' (In Los Angeles, Frank Dominguez was a big man not only physically but politically. A member of one of the original Spanish land-grant families in California, he was well known and respected. If there was any aristocracy in the state, the Dominguez family was assuredly part of it.)

On the eve of the police court hearing, the president of the Women's Vigilant Committee, Dr Mariana Bertola, received a standing ovation at a mass meeting when she said, 'We have here a criminal worth millions, which was built by the cheapest kind of buffoonery. We have been responsible for that buffoonery for we have countenanced it and laughed at it.'

On Thursday, 22 September, five hours before the case opened on the second floor of the Hall of Justice, the building was packed with women. Nearly one hundred police were on duty, trying to keep a semblance of order as the women elbowed each other to get close to the court doors. The first eleven to be admitted were a delegation from the Mothers Club, who came with sandwiches and cake. In a few moments, the court was packed. Women scrambled over seats, sat on benches, on the window sills, on the floor and on desks.

As Frank Dominguez entered with his colleagues, he found himself standing next to Mrs W. M. Hamilton, the vice-president of the Women's Vigilant Committee. He remarked to her, 'I hope you ladies will suspend judgement until all of the testimony in this case has been brought out.'

Giving him a look that would have killed lesser men, Mrs Hamilton replied, 'That is our intention. But we expect all of it to be brought out.'

At that point Roscoe was brought in from his cell. This was the first glimpse most of the women present had of him. Minta Durfee recalled that moment for me: 'When the Vigilantes saw him, they started to applaud. This was Roscoe Arbuckle, the beloved comedian. The applause was automatic. The leader of the Women's Vigilant Committee, Mrs Hamilton, called out, "Women of

America, do your duty!" At that they all stopped applauding and began spitting.'

After the judge, the lawyers and Roscoe had posed for press photographs, what passed for a court hearing in San Francisco in 1921 got under way.

A few hours before the police court hearing was to begin, Al Semnacher, Virginia's manager, had caused a sensation by announcing in Los Angeles that Roscoe had told him the day after the party that he had pushed a piece of ice inside Miss Rappe's vagina. Hearst headlines announced: 'TORTURE OF VIRGINIA RAPPE CHARGED!'

Roscoe had placed the cube of ice on the sick girl's vulva *in front of at least three witnesses*, and one of them, Zey Prevon, had already given details of the incident in her original statement to the DA, but the DA made a big play of Semnacher's story, saying this was the key to the case, the 'atrocity' that had caused Virginia Rappe's death. This piece of evidence would hurry Roscoe Arbuckle to his execution. He wired money to Semnacher to ensure his appearance in court.

Semnacher said that the ice incident had taken place in the locked bedroom and that Roscoe had described it to him, Fred Fischbach and Lowell Sherman.

Sherman, who had been playing hide and seek with the authorities for nearly a week, popped up in New York and denied Semnacher's allegation. He also said that he had considered at the party that the only thing ailing the sick girl was 'that she had a little bun on [was drunk] and was suffering from indigestion'.

As soon as Semnacher's story was made public, Buster Keaton contacted Arbuckle's lawyer, Frank Dominguez, and explained to him that sometime before the St Francis party, he had advised Roscoe that the quickest way to tell if somebody was feigning illness was to place a piece of ice against the person's thigh and hold it there. Keaton was anxious to go on the witness stand and give this testimony. Frank Dominguez told him and other Hollywood stars who wanted to testify for their friend that the San Francisco populace would resent their presence in the Bay City, that there was even bitter feeling in the city against him, Dominguez. 'The local people think the case should have gone to one of their own lawyers. They would discount your evidence and consider you merely Arbuckle's front men.'

During the second day of the hearing, the DA produced Al Semnacher, who had in the past forty-eight hours been elevated to 'star witness' for the prosecution. Unfortunately, Al's memory failed him in the witness box. There were so many facts he couldn't remember, that within a short time, he was deemed 'a hostile witness' to the prosecution. And to assistant DA U'Ren's chagrin, Semnacher now testified that Roscoe's conduct towards the women at the party was 'gentlemanly'.

However, Semnacher did persist with his account of the 'ice incident'. When asked why it had not featured in his statements to the police shortly after the death of Virginia, he said simply, 'I had forgotten all about it.' Assistant DA Golden wanted to know where Roscoe had put the ice. Embarrassed, Semnacher at first refused to reply, then wrote his answer down. Golden glanced at the piece of paper, then read aloud, 'In her snitch' – slang for vagina. He repeated the words several times, each time louder.

The next morning, the headline in the Los Angeles *Examiner* was 'ICE ON ACTRESS BIG JOKE TO ARBUCKLE'.

On Monday, 26 September, California sweltered in a heat wave that pushed the thermometer up to 110 degrees in some places. It was nothing compared to the heat Frank Dominguez turned on in Judge Lazarus's court that day. He had Al Semnacher recalled to the stand. After covering some of the ground they had already gone over, Dominguez changed direction. He began to ask how well Semnacher had known Virginia Rappe, implying that it was intimately. He asked how well Semnacher knew Maude Delmont – and this time there was no innuendo. It was apparent that Dominguez had evidence of an affair between the two. He began a series of questions that the district attorney objected to as irrelevant.

Frank Dominguez turned to Judge Lazarus and, pointing at Semnacher, said, 'We intend to prove that this man, acting upon the suggestion and instigation of Mrs Delmont and a third person, conceived the idea and carried out the plot of taking Miss Rappe's torn clothing to Los Angeles, and later with these articles in their possession, of extorting money from Roscoe Arbuckle.'

There was an immediate uproar. Despite objections from several assistant DAs, Dominguez continued. 'It is my duty to prove the existence of and to establish these facts and I am prepared to do it. I will then establish the intimate relationship between this witness and Mrs Delmont.'

The district attorney and his assistants were on their feet, shouting objections.

The judge commented: 'I am not going to try the character of every witness here.'

And that was that. Dominguez was not allowed to develop his thesis.

I am convinced that until Virginia Rappe's death became public knowledge, Maude intended to play the badger game on Roscoe. (There are variations on the badger game, but basically a man is lured into a bedroom by a young woman, and when both are either naked or making love, a photographer appears, takes a few revealing shots and leaves quickly. The man is shown copies of the photos and asked to pay up, unless he wants his wife, boss, *etc.*, to see the photos. Invariably, he pays up.) Maude's behaviour, from the time of the party until reporters surrounded her after news of Virginia's death had leaked to the press, was consistent with the premise that she intended to extort money from Roscoe. At no time did she call the police or tell them that her beloved friend Virginia had been raped or assaulted by Roscoe. Not only had she and Al Semnacher squirrelled away some of Virginia's torn clothing, but she had sent the two telegrams to Los Angeles, saying, 'WE HAVE ROSCOE ARBUCKLE IN A HOLE HERE. CHANCE TO MAKE SOME MONEY OUT OF HIM.' Moreover, those who followed the trial at close range tell me that Dominguez (who is dead now) had between twenty and forty affidavits from Maude Delmont's previous victims. Dominguez had only to wait for the prosecution to put her on the witness stand.

DA Brady announced at the end of the day's hearing that he had summoned the grand jury to investigate the charges made by Dominguez. The grand jury now had enough work investigating aspects of the Arbuckle case to occupy it for months.

By now every newspaper had teams of reporters and feature writers covering the case. They ran articles by sob sisters, crime reporters, gentlemen of the cloth, leading club women, and famous writers like Guvernor Morris and G. K. Chesterton. The Arbuckle case had become an industry for writers.

All of them awaited eagerly the appearance of the state's most important witness, Maude Delmont, who had sworn out the murder charge against Arbuckle.

On Tuesday, 27 September, the prosecution produced Alice Blake and Zey Prevon. During cries of witness-tampering the previous week, there had been no mention of either girl. The reason was simple; they had been both held – illegally – at the home of one of the DA's assistants. They would continue to be held there, against their will, for months.

After both women had testified, Brady produced a surprise witness, Josephine Keza.

Josephine Keza worked as a maid at the St Francis Hotel. On the afternoon of the party she had been on duty on the twelfth floor. At the police court she testified, among other things, that she had heard a woman's voice coming from Roscoe's bedroom. 'The first noise I heard was a woman's voice saying, "No, no. Oh my God!" Then I heard a man's voice say, "Shut up." '

The testimony visibly shook Roscoe and his wife at the defence counsel's table.

Then Golden said, 'That is our case.' Of Maude Delmont, not a sign.

Roscoe's chief attorney leaped to his feet, saying vehemently, 'We demand that the complaining witness be put on the stand. In the interests of truth and justice we demand it. We demand that Mrs Delmont be put on the stand that we may cross-examine her. She is the person who swore to the warrant. She is the chief witness. I never heard of a case in which the complainant was not produced – in this case the person who has charged the defendant with a most heinous crime.'

Assistant DA Golden had his answer ready: 'Mrs Delmont is a mere witness in this case. The issue is not between her and Roscoe Arbuckle. It is between Arbuckle and the people of the State of California. The district attorney is quite within his legal rights if he decides that her testimony is not needed at this time to perfect his case. The evidence that we would have her give would be merely cumulative to that already heard.'

'You don't dare put her on the stand,' shouted Dominguez. 'You fear to give me the opportunity to tear to shreds the fabric of vicious falsehoods which she has tried to weave about this defendant.'

Judge Lazarus was as astonished as Dominguez. Addressing Golden, the Judge said, 'I must express my astonishment. I had hoped that the Court would be given the benefit of hearing the testimony of the complainant, whose name has been so frequently interwoven in the evidence thus far adduced.'

Dominguez spoke again. 'What we want is the truth. We are entitled, by every right, to hear what Mrs Delmont has to tell.'

Assistant DA Golden replied that they all wanted the

truth – that the defence knew much of it but had not made it public, which was of course a perfectly legal course for the defence to adopt, until there was a trial. Golden continued, 'What testimony we have heard, literally has had to be dynamited out of reluctant witnesses, all of whom were guests of Arbuckle at his party, and all of whom, if they dared to go that far, would much have preferred to deny that they were even present.'

All the more reason, one would have thought, for calling Maude Delmont, who by the greatest stretch of the imagination could not have been called a 'reluctant witness'. Judge Lazarus was obviously deeply troubled:

> This has taken me as much by surprise as the defence. I certainly expected that Mrs Delmont would be placed on the stand. I feel that I should have been supplied with the evidence of Mrs Delmont before coming to a decision. However, the prosecution of the case rests entirely with the district attorney, and I see no way, now that persuasion has failed, to bring her in and place her on the stand. I regret exceedingly that the district attorney has not seen fit to place her on the stand. It is evident that she is an important witness. I can't force the prosecution to put her on the stand, still I feel in all fairness I should have more facts upon which to base a decision.

At the coroner's inquest assistant DA U'Ren had shown contempt for the coroner. Now Golden reminded Lazarus of the limit of his authority: 'You are sitting merely as a committing magistrate and not as a trial judge.'

Judge Lazarus eyed Golden coldly and said, 'I must advise you gentlemen of the prosecution that you are taking a chance on a motion to dismiss; you are travelling very close to the line that may cause me to dismiss the charge.'

Judge Lazarus had become increasingly appalled at the

flimsiness of the DA's case. He had told the DA before the proceedings began that Arbuckle would be held to answer on the charge of murder if the DA had overwhelming evidence of Arbuckle's guilt and delivered the goods in court. District Attorney Brady had failed to deliver the goods.

For a moment, Arbuckle's case hung in the balance. On Roscoe's behalf, Milton Cohen moved to dismiss the charge. His motion was followed by another display of acrimony from Golden. The motion was denied and the hearing adjourned until the following day.

All that remained were defence witnesses, if Dominguez planned to call them at this stage, and then the judge's finding.

The following morning Dominguez rose and said that he intended to submit the case without calling any witnesses. He attacked the prosecution again for its failure to put Maude Delmont on the stand. Golden rose to argue the merits of the prosecution's case, but was immediately silenced by the judge, who said that he did not want to hear argument from either side. He had reached his decision.

DA Brady smiled. He knew what the decision was. Hadn't he arranged it before the proceedings began?

Judge Lazarus began to analyse the evidence. His analysis quickly wiped the smile from the district attorney's face. Of Al Semnacher, he observed, 'His testimony was perfectly worthless. Semnacher occupied two days of the court's time and his testimony might just as well have not been taken as far as its value is concerned. There were other witnesses, called by the district attorney, whose evidence was equally worthless.'

With regard to the piece of ice and its significance, the judge remarked, 'As a remote connection, evidence has been introduced here referring to a certain vulgar and ribald conduct of the defendant. But this was a matter which happened later; that had no connection. I cannot feel that the defendant would have so acted if he had realized at the time that the lady was in the desperate condition that subsequently developed. *Anyhow, that thing, although abhorrent, had nothing to do with any injuries, any possible injuries, received by the deceased.*'

Judge Lazarus dealt with the torn clothing of Virginia Rappe. 'She was clutching at her clothes, and with the assistance of her lady companions, they were removed. The garments have been introduced in evidence here, badly torn, which, at the time of their introduction I thought might have some application to the charge against the defendant. But the testimony of the prosecution witnesses afterwards developed that these clothes were torn by the deceased herself.'

The judge dealt with the bruises upon the body of Virginia. 'Photographs were introduced here in evidence showing various bruises on the body of the deceased, but Dr Beardslee, who had numerous opportunities, testified that the only bruise he saw was one on the arm.'

Slowly, systematically, the judge demolished the district attorney's case. He was frequently interrupted by assistant DAs U'Ren and Golden, who challenged his conclusions and were rebuked by the judge. The prosecution's zeal for getting Arbuckle to trial did not stop at entering into argument with the judge while he gave a verdict.

Only one piece of testimony had impressed Judge Lazarus. 'There is only one witness whose testimony has any direct bearing. I refer to the chambermaid. Without that evidence I doubt very much whether the testimony would justify holding Mr Arbuckle on any charge.'

Even there the judge had reservations. 'However and despite the fact that she heard Miss Rappe say, "No. No. Oh my God!", we must remember a possibility which is suggested in a line from Byron: "And saying she would ne'er consent – consented." [*sic*]'

One of the judge's remarks turned the DA's face to stone. 'I do not find any evidence that Mr Arbuckle either committed or attempted to commit rape.'

Again and again the judge criticized the district attorney for not producing Maude Delmont and for failing to provide adequate evidence against Arbuckle.

'The court has been presented with the merest outline; a very skeletonized description of what, if anything, occurred in the apartment . . . The district attorney has frankly admitted that he has presented just enough facts, perhaps I might say barely enough facts, to justify my holding the defendant on the charge which is here filed against him.'

Judge Lazarus saw issues that far transcended the guilt or innocence of Roscoe Arbuckle:

> In this case we have a public lesson. This case is larger than the district attorney would have us to understand, and I had really hoped that this humble police court would be the avenue through which a full and complete revelation would be made concerning absolutely all the facts and circumstances, so that the public, at least, not alone in this city, but of the entire world, would have the opportunity to determine the guilt or innocence of this man whose celebrity has travelled, and I shall say justly travelled, to the four quarters of the globe.
>
> A man who gives joy and pleasure to his fellow men is more valuable I should say in the scheme of creation even than lawyers and judges and other people who add more to the gloom of existence . . . But I say that this is really an important case. We need not disguise that fact, or beguile ourselves into the idea that we are handling just the ordinary trivial case . . . *We are not trying Roscoe Arbuckle alone*; we are not trying the screen celebrity who has given joy and pleasure to the entire world; we are actually, gentlemen, *in a large sense trying ourselves.*
>
> *We are trying our present-day morals*, our present-day social conditions, our present-day looseness of thought and lack of social balance. The issue here is really and truly larger than the guilt or innocence of this poor, unfortunate man; the issue is universal and grows out of conditions which are a matter of comment and notoriety

and apprehension to every true lover and protector of our American institutions.

In such a manner during the late afternoon of Wednesday, 28 September 1921, it was determined that Roscoe Arbuckle was to become the scapegoat for the Jazz Age. The judge decided that there was not sufficient evidence to send Roscoe to the Superior Court to answer the charge of murder. However, he added, 'I have decided to make a holding on the ground of manslaughter, feeling that there is enough in the conduct of the defendant justifying some possible defence or explanation on his part.'

Shaking with anger, DA Matthew Brady strode from the court with his assistants scurrying in his wake. The courtroom erupted into cheers. The women who had come to see the rope put around Arbuckle's neck now shouted and clapped their approval. Sentiment in the court had shifted dramatically towards Arbuckle. While Judge Lazarus had spoken, every interruption from U'Ren and Golden had been greeted with hisses from the women. Appalled, the leaders of the Women's Vigilant Committee tried to control their members, but without success. Only twenty-four hours previously, their president, Dr Bertola, had told the press that in her opinion the evidence more than justified a murder trial. Now she declared that she was 'well pleased with the verdict of Judge Lazarus'.

Arrangements were made to release Roscoe on bail pending the manslaughter hearing. He had been in prison for eighteen days.

Roscoe collected his personal effects from the police cell and emerged to find a cheering crowd. He was surrounded by hundreds of people, mainly women, all of whom wanted to shake his hand and touch him. There were shouts of 'Hurrah for Fatty' and 'Good for you, Fatty' and 'We're with you, Fatty' and 'Hit 'em with a pie, Fatty' and 'Attaboy'.

Those who heard the meagre evidence presented in Judge Lazarus's courtroom – even though they had entered the courtroom eager for a more severe judgement – left feeling more well-disposed to Roscoe Arbuckle. Personal feelings aside, there were many who could not understand the insistence with which the prosecution case had been pursued. Judge George B. Harris, of San Francisco, recently told me, 'I've always wondered about the stability of the prosecution in this case. Why the prosecution in the first place? If it had been John Jones, he would never have been prosecuted. It was the spectre of Hollywood. It was a witch-hunt.'

This contemporary view was held by many in the early twenties, but not by all. Among those who thought justice had miscarried were the Hearst newspapers, which gave much space to Brady's peevish remarks. Brady launched a bitter attack on Judge Lazarus which the Hearst papers headlined: 'IF ARBUCKLE WERE UNKNOWN HE'D BE HELD FOR MURDER,' BRADY DECLARES.

Arthur Brisbane, Hearst's right-hand hack, editorialized:

> The learned Judge in the Arbuckle case says not Roscoe Arbuckle but ourselves, our morals, our present-day social standards are on trial. Mr Chesterton, fat and forceful, discovers in the Arbuckle case much wickedness on the part of America generally. The learned Judge and the clever Englishman perhaps attach too much importance to Mr Arbuckle. Brutality usually lacks intelligence and is therefore unable to gratify its tendencies. It hasn't the money. Occasionally, as in the case of Coal Oil Johnny, Arbuckle and others, money comes rapidly, without restraining intelligence, and what Zola describes as the 'hog asleep in each man' breaks out and disgraces itself. But it doesn't disgrace everybody.

The New York Times was equally distressed that the charge against the comedian had been reduced. The

Times questioned the decision 'respectfully but a little pressingly' and criticized the people who had responded to Roscoe at the end of the hearing. An editorial was headed 'HOW CAN ANY WOMAN BE PLEASED?'

The following day, Roscoe went home to Los Angeles – to Hollywood. At every stop on the way, large crowds waved and cheered at him. It was reminiscent of his 1917 train journey across the nation – except then he had suffered acute physical pain; now he was psychologically wounded. The past nineteen days had marked him deeply. Sitting in his San Francisco cell, he had sensed the hysteria he was causing. Now, returning home, he wondered how he would be received by the film colony.

Many have written of the moment when he stepped off the train in Los Angeles, and the story they usually tell is the same: that he was greeted by a howling mob who spat on him, and that the heart of the man died then. His closest friend, Buster Keaton, described the crowd as 'a hate-frenzied mob of fifteen hundred men and women who seemed to want only to get close enough to tear him to pieces. And they yelled at the fat man they had loved so much a few weeks before, "Murderer! Big fat slob! Beast!" and "Degenerate bastard!" Some in the crowd had come to cheer him, but they were drowned out in the din.'

To friends like Buster, it may have seemed an unfriendly crowd, but in fact the reception was so impressive and generally so favourable to Roscoe that some newspapers hinted the next day that the crowd had been made up of 'supers', or as we call them now, extras. Half of Hollywood was there, including not only Buster Keaton, but also Bull Montana, Viola Dana, Eileen Percy, Natalie Talmadge and Hank Mann. One woman stood on a crate and denounced Roscoe, but few took notice of her.

Accompanied by his wife, Roscoe returned to his millionaire's house. It was Minta's first look at her husband's home. She oohed and ahed at the magnificence of it, which to Roscoe now seemed meaningless.

He asked her to choose a suit for him to wear. Minta pulled open the large doors of his wardrobe and counted fifty-seven suits. Roscoe smiled as he watched her counting, then remarked, 'You know, Minty, when I first met you I had just one suit. Remember? A brown one. I was a lot happier then.'

In the years between those two moments the American public had made Roscoe Arbuckle a superstar and had turned on him when it appeared he didn't deserve their adulation. Perhaps they even took pleasure in thinking, 'How the mighty have fallen.'

Motion Picture News, on 24 September, had warned actors that they were not artists, and had continued, 'You are mere photographic types . . . you think you have been touched by divine fire, whereas you have only been touched by Celluloid . . . If you don't protect yourselves, the same forces that made you will rise up and put you out of business overnight, destroy you in the very same magic way that you were created.'

While Roscoe had endured the police court hearing in San Francisco, forces were rising to destroy not only him but the entire industry. The St Francis party and its aftermath had been eagerly seized upon by those who wanted to destroy the film industry. Some wanted films banned from existence; others proposed censorship. At the heart of the industry, the city council of Los Angeles was moving towards censorship of all films. By the time Roscoe came home, the battle had been well and truly joined.

Through his papers, William Randolph Hearst had proclaimed himself a bitter opponent of censorship. He also announced that Metropolitan Films, which he owned, would *not* be making five million dollars' worth of movies in the coming year in Los Angeles if the city council brought in censorship. Myron Selznick rallied to the fight by announcing that, if censorship became a reality, his company would withhold the making of four million dollars' worth of films in the city.

William B. De Mille wrote a long open letter to the leader of the censorship lobby in Los Angeles, a certain Dr Briegleb. The good doctor objected to the religious persuasion of many of the film moguls. As he put it, 'When the Jews get together to say what my boy and girl shall see on the screen, then I am going to fight.'

Apparently, what Dr Briegleb had in mind was a group of Christians getting together to tell people what they should or should not see on the screen.

On 1 October 1921, reformers got further confirmation of the film world's iniquity. The Boston courts delivered their judgement on the charges of corruption that had been made against DA Tufts: he was found guilty and removed from office. There was no mention of Roscoe Arbuckle in the judgement, but there was considerable comment about Adolph Zukor, Jesse Lasky and the other movie moguls who had attended 'an orgy of drink and lust'.

The Hearst papers ignored this report of scandal among the moguls. At the time, they were preoccupied with convincing reformers that the men who ran the film industry were models of propriety, set on cleaning their own house. As Murray Schumach was to observe in his book on film censorship, *The Face on the Cutting Room Floor*, in rather a different context, 'The unwilling alliance of greed and idealism is one of the most fascinating ironies of the movie censorship story . . . No political issue has ever made stranger bedfellows.'

The film industry did not fight the censorship lobby in a united fashion. In many ways, the industry's reaction was one of blind panic. As a direct result of the Arbuckle case, the film companies inserted a 'morality clause' in all contracts, which stipulated that actors would 'conduct themselves [*sic*] with due regard to public conventions and morals and will not do anything tending to degrade him (her) in society or bring him (her) into public hatred, contempt, scorn, or ridicule, or tending to shock, insult, or offend the community or outrage public morals or decency, or tending to prejudice the company or the motion picture industry.' Violation of the clause would ensure immediate dismissal. Many film companies even inserted a 'retrospective morality clause': if something from an actor's past came to light and upset the public, the actor was fired. *Morality clauses are still used in contracts today*.

As for Roscoe: Zukor and Lasky simply stopped paying him. Famous Players-Lasky advised him that he was in 'breach of contract for failing to appear on the set for the filming of *The Melancholy Spirit* on the first day of shooting'. (Roscoe had been locked in a San Francisco cell.) He was further told that he was 'suspended until you are cleared'.

Having resolved Roscoe's financial situation to their satisfaction, if not his, they then fired his lawyer, Frank Dominguez. Paramount had put limitless funds at Dominguez's disposal and felt that Roscoe should have got a full acquittal at the police court. Dominguez had had his chance, and he blew it. He was replaced by a San Francisco attorney named Gavin McNab.

McNab was one of the city's leading attorneys and a powerful political force. He virtually ran the Democratic party there. He had once put up for election to the city council a man named Billy Hines. Hines was an affable man with no knowledge of politics, whose main talent was the ability to bow from the waist to lady customers at the store where he worked. He also sang 'The Laughing Song' for amateur theatricals. When he began campaigning and people asked him policy questions, his response was to take a deep breath and sing, 'Ha, ha, ha, ha, ha, ho, ho, ho, ho.' While other candidates analysed rising taxes and the cost of living, Billy was a lot of fun. He got elected.

An Irish tailor named Kellerher came soon after to see McNab. He was a dab hand at the Irish jig. He told McNab that if Hines could laugh his way into office, he, Kellerher, should be able to dance his way in. McNab agreed. So did the citizens. Kellerher was elected.

These were two of many stories illustrating McNab's power. Furthermore, the film industry had had direct opportunities to see him in action.

When in April 1920, the Nevada attorney general had said that there was collusion in the March divorce of Mary Pickford, McNab had stepped in and saved the day.

A few months later he had been called on to defend the heavyweight champion of the world, Jack Dempsey, who had been accused of draft dodging. The state's principal witness against Dempsey was his former wife, Maxine Cates. San Francisco reporter Edward 'Scoop' Gleeson introduced Dempsey and his manager, Jack Kearns, to McNab, and outlined the case against the fighter. The canny Scottish lawyer said quietly, 'I can't go into the court with the case of a prizefighter versus a whore.' But when Gleeson told him that the Pathé film company had $200,000 tied up in a series of films starring Dempsey, McNab murmured, 'Well, that's different. A case of invested capital. Maybe there's a way of handling that.' He took the case.

The blank cheques Paramount waved under his nose were tempting, but McNab didn't take the Arbuckle case until he had made a full personal investigation and convinced himself that Roscoe was innocent.

He declined to discuss his fee with the press, except to say, 'My charges in this case are no more than I ordinarily receive in cases involving the same amount of work and a similar responsibility.' (He had asked $35,000 for the Dempsey case.)

McNab quickly found himself earning his fee. On 22 October, Roscoe was rearrested for having violated Prohibition law at the St Francis party. He went to San Francisco again and was released on bail; the hearing was suspended until after the manslaughter trial. (In 1922, Roscoe pleaded guilty to violating the Volstead Act and was fined $500.)

Driving back to Los Angeles after that hearing, Roscoe went through a red light. A motorcycle policeman pulled him over to give him a ticket, but when he recognized the comedian, he said, 'Roscoe Arbuckle! Hell, you've got enough trouble. On your way and good luck.'

On returning to their West Adams home, Roscoe and Minta discovered that in their absence a number of bugging devices had been installed, the house had been searched, and letters had been taken away. It turned out that a member of Roscoe's house staff was in the pay of the police. She was promptly fired.

As a result, Roscoe's lawyers hired private detectives to guard him around the clock. A number of Brady's detectives spent a lot of time watching Roscoe's detectives.

Roscoe was under siege in his own house. On his lawyers' instructions, only Minta was allowed to answer the phone. Bus and coach trips were organized by local companies to view Roscoe's home. Minta Durfee recalled, 'They would go by and, seeing the greenhouse, would point at it and shout, "Look! There's Arbuckle's own private film studio." '

Except for the police informer, Roscoe's staff remained loyal to the man they called 'the Chief'. His family and staff gathered protectively around him, trying to blot out the ordeal that lay ahead. Roscoe would putter in the kitchen and make huge beef stews with his sister-in-law Marie on the cook's night off.

During this period the butler, a Negro named Munroe, was due to become a Mason. It was a big moment in the man's life. On the night of his initiation, he spruced up and left the house with his wife, who was the cook. Marie cooked the meal that night, and the family sat eating quietly, each alone with his own sad thoughts. Then they heard someone playing the piano softly as a woman sang

'When Irish Eyes Are Smiling'. Munroe and his wife had come back to 'cheer up the Chief'.

The Vigilant Committee of San Francisco, which had been silent for nearly two weeks, acted again on 12 October. It passed a unanimous resolution opposing the exhibition of Roscoe's films in the United States *for ever*. The final part of the resolution read: 'Regardless of the fact that Arbuckle may be proved innocent of the police charge, his immoral conduct marks him as a person unfit to appear before the American public.'

Ministers continued their attack on Roscoe and what he represented. One referred to him as a 'towering monument of iniquity'. Another said, 'The anti-Christ is here among us.'

Roscoe was quoted as saying, the day after the Vigilant resolution, '. . . The loss of friends, the shame, the stories, the rumours about me, the attitude of the American public, the sermons of the ministers, to say nothing of the loss of money – you'd be glad to get it over with too . . . I know the American public is fair and square and when it finds out all about this case, it will give me a square deal.'

DA Brady had been busy since the police court hearing, collecting 'new and invaluable evidence'. He had sent teams of detectives and attorneys all over the country to get background evidence on Roscoe. Men were sent to Boston to check on the infamous 1917 party. Others were sent to Chicago, New York, Washington and Kansas. Brady and U'Ren were themselves investigating Roscoe's activities in Los Angeles, with the full cooperation of LA's district attorney, Thomas Woolwine, who was himself under investigation on charges of corruption. The purpose of this nationwide search was to find information that would damage Roscoe's defence by showing him as a degenerate, a man without morals.

Every available man was mustered in the task and outside agencies were used as well, including the famous

Pinkerton Detective Agency. Among the Pinkerton men searching for dirt was Dashiell Hammett, who didn't find any dirt, and who maintained a firm belief in Roscoe's innocence from then on. It is said that he drew on the Arbuckle case to create some of the characters in *The Maltese Falcon*. Certainly both Arbuckle and Brady lent themselves to fictional representation.

During these investigations, Brady told the press that he had 'overwhelming evidence that shows what kind of a man Roscoe Arbuckle really is'. Indeed he did. *One hundred men working diligently all over the country were unable to discover any unsavoury facts about Arbuckle.*

In fact, their investigations must have uncovered a great deal to support Arbuckle. It was clear from the medical evidence, for example, that Virginia Rappe was probably suffering from gonorrhoea at the time of the party in Roscoe's suite. If Arbuckle had had sexual intercourse with the girl in Room 1219, he would almost certainly have contracted the disease. Yet during the three and a half weeks he was in prison he was examined regularly by the prison staff and at no time during his incarceration did he display any symptoms of the disease. The incubation period for gonorrhoea is short; within two days to three weeks symptoms appear. And theoretically Roscoe had been exposed to the disease several days before his arrest.

The Hearst press leaped on a report that Brady's Chicago investigators had discovered details of an attack that Roscoe had made the previous year on a woman and a bellboy in a Chicago hotel. They ran the headline, 'NEW ARBUCKLE CHARGE. GIRL ATTACK IN CHICAGO LAID TO FATTY'. Subsequent reports indicated that Arbuckle had slapped a man's face because the man made improper remarks in front of female guests.

Milton Cohen, one of Roscoe's attorneys, observed, 'Fatty Arbuckle is the Dreyfus of America. He has been made the victim of a conspiracy based upon greed for political power, with no consideration of the injustice upon its victim. But like Dreyfus, my client will be vindicated.'

How long would that vindication take?

While Brady dug into Roscoe's past without much success, the defence – and the newspapers – found out what they could about other members of the St Francis party. They had already uncovered Al Semnacher's divorce proceedings. Now they concentrated on Virginia Rappe and Maude Delmont.

Some of the less innocent details of Virginia's past were beginning to appear in newspaper stories, and the defence was carefully tracking down details of her peculiar medical history both in Los Angeles and Chicago. Unfortunately, much of the information they turned up about doubtful aspects of her moral character could not be introduced at the first trials, either because it was not allowed as evidence or because the defense lawyers believed it would alienate the jury to defame the character of the dead starlet.

Maude Delmont was having problems of her own as a result of all the publicity surrounding the trial. A mislaid husband had turned up, a gentleman by the name of Cassius Clay Woods. They had been married only eight months when Mr Woods was arrested and charged with embezzlement. Maude had immediately started divorce proceedings, but had a problem in the form of yet another husband, James Hopper. A warrant for her arrest on the charge of bigamy was issued, but Matthew Brady intervened. It would hardly help his case if Maude were brought from prison to testify in the Arbuckle trial, so it was quietly arranged that Maude would not be arrested for bigamy until after the comedian's trial had ended.

Either way, it was a boost to the defence. If Maude testified, her own statement and pre-trial testimony were so full of holes that they could be used against her. Now the bigamy charge could be used to discredit her too.

As it turned out, she would not testify at all.

*

On 14 November 1921, the arduous process of jury selection began. Gavin McNab asked prospective jurors questions about virtually every aspect of the trial. Anyone admitting a connection with the Women's Vigilant Committee was challenged and disqualified.

After five days and forty-three people, the jury – seven men and five women – had been selected. Throughout the trial McNab would pay special attention to the expression on the face of one of the female jurors.

Roscoe's case was to be heard not only by the twelve jurors in that San Francisco courtroom, however. While they deliberated, he would be tried simultaneously by a jury of hundreds of millions of people all over the world. Every news syndicate in the country had representatives in that courtroom; details of the trial's progress would be flashed daily to newspapers in North and South America, Europe and Asia. In Chicago and Bombay, in Buenos Aires and Liverpool, men, women and children who had laughed at the innocent films of the world's most popular comedian would join the world jury of public opinion. Would the people who loved to laugh decide that Arbuckle should not make them laugh any more? From the moment of his arrest, two trials proceeded, one in a courtroom in San Francisco and the other at the world bar of public opinion. For Roscoe to survive, he had to win both trials.

The trial was presided over by Judge Louderback, who was recently described to me as 'a man who ran his courtroom with an iron hand. He was pompous and arrogant'. He was also destined to be the subject of a Senate investigation for corruption in the 1930s, when his career would be saved by the intervention of one of the members of the investigating committee, Louisiana's Huey Long. But that lay in the future as the trial of Roscoe Arbuckle began.

Apart from Gavin McNab, there were four other

attorneys involved in Roscoe's defence: Charles Brennan, Milton Cohen, Nat Schmulowitz and Joseph McInerney. For the state, Brady was assisted by U'Ren and a man new to the case, Assistant DA Leo Friedman.

On Friday, 18 November 1921, at precisely 2.00 p.m., Leo Friedman rose and made the opening speech on behalf of the State of California. He outlined to the jury the prosecution's version of events leading up to the moment of Virginia Rappe's death, saying among other things, 'We will prove to you that the defendant and Miss Rappe remained in Room 1219 for a period of time extending over possibly a half an hour to an hour.'

The crux of the allegations against Roscoe was contained in his closing remarks.

> We will prove to you that the defendant in this action made a wilful, unlawful and felonious assault upon and against the person of Miss Virginia Rappe; and we will prove to you that the assault was made by the defendant with the intent to rape and ravish Miss Virginia Rappe at that time.
>
> And we will prove to you beyond any question of doubt that as a result of this felonious assault made by the defendant upon this poor girl, we will prove to you that the bladder of Miss Rappe was ruptured.

Friedman went on to say that a result of Virginia Rappe's bladder rupture during that assault had been peritonitis, from which she had died. Having proved all of these 'facts' beyond all question of a doubt, he concluded, 'We shall request and expect at your hands a verdict finding Roscoe Arbuckle, the defendant in this action, is guilty of manslaughter as charged in the information.'

On the first Saturday, the trial was adjourned at midday so that members of the jury could attend an afternoon football game between the University of California and Stanford University.

The prosecution was first to call witnesses. Here I will touch only on highlights of the lengthy testimony.

Dr Arthur Beardslee, the hotel physician for the St Francis and the second doctor to attend Virginia Rappe, was called to the stand. He told the court that at his first examination he had given the girl morphine to ease her pain. The following exchange then took place:

> U'REN: What was your opinion at that time, after your examination, as to what ailed the patient?
>
> BEARDSLEE: Besides treating her in this manner, I tried to learn something about her history by interrogating this woman [Maude Delmont] that was attending her.
>
> U'REN: Well, do not give anything that was said, Doctor.
>
> MCNAB: We have no objection, Doctor; we want all the facts before this jury at any time.
>
> JUDGE LOUDERBACK: The Court does not desire to have the record filled up with anything that is not necessary.
>
> U'REN: And we are not going to try this case in that improper manner; we are going to try this case according to the rules of evidence, no matter what counsel says, and we do not want all this hearsay stuff in the record.
>
> JUDGE LOUDERBACK: Proceed.

And proceed U'Ren did. Aided by the judge, he had safely steered the witness away from the conversation that had occurred among Dr Beardslee, Maude Delmont and Virginia Rappe, 'hearsay stuff' that could destroy his case. He knew that the drunken Maude Delmont had told Dr Beardslee that Roscoe had attacked Virginia; he knew also that Virginia had contradicted Maude, declaring that Roscoe had not touched her. And he knew that when Beardslee had asked the sick girl if she had had intercourse with Arbuckle, Virginia had firmly said there had been no intercourse. Avoiding these points,

U'Ren turned again to the doctor's conclusions at that time.

U'REN: And what did you find out?

BEARDSLEE: I was not able to form an opinion at this time. I merely knew I was dealing with a surgical abdomen; it was self-evident.

U'REN: What do you mean by a surgical abdomen? Kindly explain that term to the jury.

BEARDSLEE: An abdomen which would require surgical interference, an operative case, in other words. And at this time I informed this lady that was caring for her . . .

U'REN: (*interrupting*) Well, I do not think you can give even that, Doctor, because conversation that occurred there would be hearsay testimony at this time.

MCNAB: We are not making any objection to any information he obtained from anybody.

JUDGE LOUDERBACK: The Court is not going to let hearsay and rumour go into the record anyhow. We are going to try this case upon the real issues.

BEARDSLEE: The facts were self-evident at this time. I knew I was dealing with a lesion of the bladder, and from the signs and symptoms, and the scanty urine tinged with blood, I knew that her internal condition was at least complicated by bladder trouble, a ruptured bladder, I suppose.

Nobody asked the questions that begged to be asked: *If Virginia Rappe had been operated on at the time Dr Beardslee arrived at his conclusions, might she have lived? Why wasn't she operated on right away?*

At the police court hearing, Frank Dominguez had tried to establish why Dr Beardslee did nothing. The prosecution had objected, and the objections had been sustained. Dominguez had also asked Dr Beardslee why, when he had been replaced by Dr Rumwell, he had not advised his colleague of his conclusions. In Dr Beardslee's view, it was a question of medical etiquette: if your patient is seriously ill, it is bad form to tell an incoming doctor your opinion of the patient's condition.

When McNab on cross-examination tried to bring out the conversations that the doctor had had with both women, U'Ren objected again and again. These conversations that occurred only a few hours after Virginia became ill were, in the opinion of the assistant DA, hearsay evidence and inadmissible. (The DA was later able to introduce in evidence conversations that Al Semnacher had had with both women over twenty-four hours after the conversations with Dr Beardslee.)

The curious matter of the illegal post-mortem at the Wakefield Sanatorium was touched on a number of times during the trial. It became evident that the defence considered a deal had been made between the DA's office and the physicians involved. Only Dr Rumwell had been arrested and charged with performing an illegal autopsy (and ultimately the DA did not proceed with the charge). Dr Wakefield, who had given permission, and Dr Ophuls, who had actually performed the autopsy, were never charged. *All three doctors were prosecution witnesses*, and so was the nurse who had assisted Dr Ophuls.

The situation raised many questions regarding medical ethics. There was the matter of Virginia Rappe's pregnancy. She had asked Roscoe for money for an abortion and had asked one of her nurses for the address of an abortionist. When she was finally admitted to a hospital, it was a maternity hospital. Immediately after her death an illegal post-mortem was performed. Why? Why was the illegal autopsy performed in the operating theatre of the hospital? Why wasn't official permission obtained? Why were attempts made to keep the autopsy secret from the coroner's office?

More basically: was it possible that Virginia Rappe died because of medical malpractice?

The questions would never be answered.

On Monday, 21 November, the state produced two of its star witnesses, Zey Prevon and Alice Blake. For seven weeks both girls had been kept in 'protective custody' in the home of George Duffy, one of the DAs assistants. No-one had had contact with them except members of the DA's office. From time to time during that period they had been brought into San Francisco and 'processed'.

Roscoe Arbuckle had been charged with manslaughter not only as a result of the police court hearing, but also as a result of the grand jury hearing. Under California law, the DA could proceed on the basis of one or the other of the charges, though not both.

He had proceeded on the police court charge, for one reason: he hoped to exclude the grand jury testimony of Zey Prevon from the trial. In the event, the gambit failed. McNab succeeded, after a long and bitter battle, in getting Zey's grand jury testimony read into the trial record, and it damaged the state's case. In the witness box she gave the testimony that U'Ren and Brady wanted her to give, including the allegation that Virginia had said, 'I am dying, I am dying. He hurt me.' But it was clear that her evidence had been changed under pressure from the prosecution.

Furthermore, Gavin McNab got Alice Blake's original statement to the police read into the court record. Nowhere was the remark 'He hurt me'.

And although both Zey and Alice testified that Virginia had said, 'He hurt me,' the usefulness of their testimony to the DA's case was weakened when they both went on to say that the statement had been made *after* Virginia had torn her clothes, had been stripped, had been suspended naked in midair by Fred Fischbach, and had been dumped in an ice-cold bath by Fred and the girls. The 'he' could have been Fred Fischbach instead of Roscoe.

The DA's next witness was Jesse Norgaard, who in 1919 had been a janitor at Henry Lehrman's film studios in Culver City and who had an interesting tale to tell. Before he told it, the defence objected strenuously about the relevance of testimony set so far in the past, but Roscoe, who had nothing to hide, intervened and told his counsel to allow Norgaard to testify, even though McNab had been tipped off that Norgaard would give testimony indicating that Arbuckle had attacked Virginia Rappe in 1919.

U'REN: Now, while you were employed as janitor you stated that you had a conversation with the defendant about Miss Rappe. What month and year was this?

NORGAARD: The month of August 1919. I went into his office to get my hat and he says, 'Have you got the key for Miss Rappe's room?' and I said 'Yes.' He says, 'Let me have it; I want to play a joke on her.' I said, 'No, sir, you cannot have it.' He said, 'I will trade you this for the key,' and he had a bunch of bills in his hand.

U'REN: Did you see the denomination of those bills?

NORGAARD: Yes, I seen two twenties and one ten.

U'REN: Were there any other bills?

NORGAARD: Yes, there were other bills, too.

U'REN: What did you say to that proposition that he submitted to you?

NORGAARD: I said, 'No, sir,' and walked out.

Laughing, Gavin McNab rose and asked U'Ren, 'Is that the rape that counsel has been talking about?'

U'Ren replied, 'You know that is not rape, Mr McNab. That is all.'

Under cross-examination Norgaard revealed that this event had lain dormant in his mind, and he had not thought it significant until he 'read in the papers about this affair'.

Hotel maid Josephine Keza, on the basis of whose police court testimony Roscoe was standing trial, repeated her story about a woman's voice shouting, 'Oh my God, no, no, no!' (the order of the words changed with each telling) and a man's voice answering, 'Shut up.' But it was shown that she had heard this exchange

(Above): Zey Prevon. Below: Alice Blake. After the D.A.'s office had applied third degree the two women finally agreed to commit perjury.

Bambina Maude Delmont. Thwarted in her attempts to blackmail Arbuckle, she told a tale of 'Rape and Murder'. She never repeated the story in a courtroom.

The San Francisco District Attorney called it 'A million-dollar defense team'. L to R: Nat Schmulowitz, Gavin McNab, Milton Cohen, Roscoe, Charles Brennan, Joseph McInerney.

R to L: Asst D.A. U'Ren, Asst D.A. Friedman and District Attorney Matthew Brady. Brady's pre-trial investigations were later described by McNab as 'An Apache running wild'.

The first trial jury. The camera shy lady is Helen Hubbard, who, when the jury retired to consider its verdict, declared that she would 'Vote guilty until Hell freezes over'. Seated immediately in front of Mrs Hubbard is the foreman August Fritze. His life was threatened because he voted 'Not guilty'.

Roscoe Arbuckle during his three-hour cross-examination. Behind him can be seen the hotel doors leaning against the court wall.

After a seven-month ordeal Roscoe stands with the jury whose verdict was: 'Acquittal is not enough for Roscoe Arbuckle. We feel that a great injustice has been done him...' Ma Durfee and Minta are immediately to the star's right.

Banned from the movies, the comedian sails for the Orient from San Francisco.

Forced by Will Hays to keep behind camera and
to change his name to William Goodrich.

A scene from *His First Car*, a two-reel movie directed by Roscoe in the mid-twenties. The adults are Doris Deane, soon to become his second wife, and his nephew Al St John. Ironically, the Women's Clubs in the USA voted the film 'the best short movie of the year'. They did not know that Arbuckle and William Goodrich were one and the same person.

One of the few who dared at this time to be publicly photographed with Arbuckle was child star Jackie Coogan.

between 2.00 and 2.30 p.m., and prosecution witnesses had established that Virginia had not entered Roscoe's bedroom before 2.50 p.m.

Miss Keza's testimony was to confuse matters further. The defence established that when she heard the remarks and heard the girl screaming, she also heard the sound of many people in Room 1219. If one assumes that her estimate of the time was incorrect, then it would seem that what she heard was the other partygoers attending to the sick girl. She was certainly an obliging witness; before she finished she had agreed with the prosecution's suggestion that although she had first heard the scream at 2.00 p.m., it had continued unabated until 4.00 p.m. However, the assistant hotel manager had supervised the removal of Virginia to Room 1227 at 3.30 p.m.

U'Ren introduced photographs of the dead girl covered with bruises, and insisted that they be shown to the jury – the sole purpose of introducing them.

Even the hotel doors of Room 1219 were brought into court, accompanied by E. O. Heinrich, who claimed to be a consulting criminologist and fingerprint expert. Heinrich had, on Brady's instructions, ordered the room sealed eleven days after the party had taken place. Apparently one month after Virginia's death Heinrich removed both doors and transported them to his laboratory in Oakland. Under questioning by U'Ren, Heinrich's credentials sounded impressive. Then Gavin McNab questioned him.

MCNAB: What cases have you testified in in this state?
HEINRICH: In this state?
MCNAB: Yes.
HEINRICH: None in this state.
MCNAB: So you have never testified in the State of California on fingerprints for any district attorney.
HEINRICH: No, sir.
MCNAB: Where else have you testified in the Superior Court, or a court of criminal jurisdiction?

HEINRICH: In the State of Arizona and the State of Washington.

MCNAB: How often have you testified on fingerprints in the State of Washington?

HEINRICH: Once.

MCNAB: How often in the state of Arizona?

HEINRICH: Once.

MCNAB: We challenge the expert as an expert.

U'Ren then offered to have Heinrich take the fingerprints of every member of the jury, have them secretly numbered by the court reporter, shuffled, then handed to Heinrich, who would be able to tell which fingerprints belonged to which juror. McNab had a better idea. 'I will accept it on this basis, if the Court please: that the fingerprints be put upon a door; that a chambermaid take a rough cloth and rub them every day for eleven days . . .'

The courtroom erupted in laughter, but the judge overruled McNab's objection and allowed Heinrich's testimony. U'Ren began calling his witness 'Professor'.

The professor had discovered some fingerprints on the doorknob of Room 1219. He believed that one of them was Virginia's. Superimposed on it, according to Heinrich, was Roscoe's fingerprint. The implication as elicited by U'Ren was clear: a desperate struggle at the door.

During a recess, McNab asked Roscoe if he accepted that they were his and Virginia's fingerprints. Roscoe's reply was short and to the point. 'I'm damned if I do. They're trying to say I screwed the poor girl against the door.'

In cross-examination, McNab drew from Heinrich the admission that he could not positively say that the fingerprints on the door belonged to Virginia and Roscoe, merely that they were 'similar'.

In an attempt to establish that Virginia Rappe had been healthy upon her arrival at the party, the state produced Mrs Hardebach and Joseph Rideaux.

Mrs Hardebach had been Virginia's housekeeper in Los Angeles. Her testimony described an athletic girl. Not a minute went by, according to Mrs Hardebach, without Virginia going for three-mile walks, dancing, or tossing medicine balls around the living room. Virginia also did gymnastics and never had a moment's sickness.

Under cross-examination by Milton Cohen for the defence, Mrs Hardebach remembered that there had been an abscess of the girl's vagina, which had cleared up after a few days of flaxseed poultices.

Joseph Rideaux was a masseur and physical-culture trainer who had taken five-mile walks and thrown medicine balls with Virginia. In the witness box, Rideaux went through a series of medicine-ball exercises that he had done with his late client. He said they had also performed 'muscle-resistant exercises' together – sometimes on tables, sometimes on the floor – and had done many breathing exercises together. His testimony indicated that Virginia was a 'powerful and resistant woman, with a fine pair of lungs'.

At this point in the trial, the prosecution asked that the jury be taken to see Roscoe's suite at the St Francis, and that Judge Louderback appoint a medical commission to examine Virginia Rappe's bladder.

And that was the case for the People of the State of California against Roscoe Arbuckle.

On the afternoon of Thursday, 23 November, Gavin McNab rose to make his opening statement on behalf of Roscoe Arbuckle. Within minutes he observed, 'It is the duty of the State, as you have heard, to present a case beyond any reasonable doubt. That burden, we feel, the State has miserably failed to perform.'

Assistant DA Friedman took exception to this, and the judge advised McNab to confine himself to what he intended to prove.

McNab went on. 'Well, I will give you in part what we propose to prove. We intend to show you by the best evidence that it is possible to produce, the words of the dead girl at or about the time of the sad events, exonerating this defendant. We will present a witness whose testimony will be direct in his communication with the young girl, and we shall ask the district attorney to produce a sworn statement of that witness given to him at the beginning of these proceedings . . .'

After another interruption by Friedman, he again picked up his thread. 'We will show you by physical facts; you will see the rooms of the St Francis tomorrow; you will see the small room in which nobody could have uttered an exclamation whatever that could not be heard on either side . . .'

This time U'Ren interrupted to complain that McNab was being argumentative. The judge agreed. Roscoe's attorney went on.

> We will show you the St Francis rooms. We will prove to you that the door entering into the hallway was open at all times of that day, that the window of that room faced another open window, and that it was open the whole day long; and that people from one side could look in and people from the other side could go in and out.
>
> We will show you by the clock itself, by the testimony of the facts, because there is no more inexorable fact in nature than time, that this man could not have been in the room more than ten minutes.

McNab said the defence intended to produce every person who had attended the party. He continued.

> MCNAB: We will present you a solemn line of facts, and after all it is facts that run the world; truth is the strongest and most just thing in the world.
>
> JUDGE LOUDERBACK: Mr McNab, you are getting into argument.

Gavin McNab called his first witness, the hotel detective George Glennon, who had interviewed the sick girl a short while after her collapse at the party. The detective's testimony could have given a powerful boost to the defense case. In his statement to the police, Glennon had told of an interview with Virginia Rappe that he had recorded in his notebook the night of the St Francis party:

GLENNON: Did Mr Arbuckle hurt you?
RAPPE: No. He never hurt me.
GLENNON: Then who hurt you?
RAPPE: I do not know. I may have been hurt by falling off of the bed.

Not only had the DA suppressed Glennon's statement, but Captain of Detectives Matheson had threatened to prosecute the hotel detective for 'dereliction of duty as a special policeman drinking on duty', and he had been fired by the St Francis Hotel. When Glennon realized that the prosecution was not going to use his statement, he took it to McNab.

Now he was sworn in, and Gavin McNab began his examination. Glennon recalled that on the day of the party he had made two visits to the bedside of Virginia Rappe and that he had had a conversation with her in the presence of Maude Delmont. *That was all he was allowed to recount*. The DA objected to the details of the conversation as well as to details of his statement to the DA being given in evidence because they were 'incompetent, irrelevant, immaterial, hearsay evidence'. Despite McNab's pleas, Judge Louderback ruled in favour of the DA.

George Glennon was not allowed to give crucial testimony about his notebook entries either at this point or later.

The next defence witness provided light relief. Kate Brennan, a hotel maid, gave the judge and jury a demonstration of door-polishing, the object being, Heinrich or no, to prove that fingerprints could not possibly have remained on the door of Room 1219 after Kate Brennan had finished with it. She had cleaned the room after the party, and, if she had not been physically restrained, would have cleaned the fingerprints off the exhibit door in the courtroom.

The resident of the room next to Roscoe on that fateful day had been located. This woman had been in her room with her daughter for the entire period of the party and had heard considerable noise from Roscoe's suite. She had heard phones ringing and being answered, but she had not heard the remarks that Miss Keza, the chambermaid, said she had heard, nor did she hear Virginia call out, 'He hurt me' or 'He killed me'.

When a Nurse Martha Hamilton testified for the defence, the prosecution was again successful in stifling testimony. Nat Schmulowitz, one of Roscoe's lawyers, tried to question the nurse about the vaginal discharges of the sick girl. The testimony was not allowed. Absurdities about medicine balls and five-mile walks were admissible evidence. Relevant information that the detective and nurse had obtained directly from Virginia Rappe during the last week of her life was not. Similarly, conversations that Dr Olav Kaarboe, the first physician to attend Virginia, had had with both her and Maude Delmont, were not allowed.

Then Fred Fischbach took the stand and told of his involvement at the St Francis party. Under cross-examination he was asked how he had grabbed Virginia to remove her from the bath. He turned and, advancing on Judge Louderback, said, 'I grabbed her by the arm. May I show you?' The judge swung round on his chair and ducked, saying loudly, 'No, you illustrate on someone else.' Obligingly, Fred left the witness box, picked up the court reporter and, dangling him in midair, went on testifying as the reporter (I am told) wrote shorthand in a suspended position. The excitement became too much for one juror, who asked to be excused for a moment.

When Dr Melville Runwell testified, U'Ren and Friedman fought again to keep out vital testimony concerning the doctor's conversations with Virginia Rappe. For once they failed. It was established that at no time had the sick girl told the doctor that Roscoe was to blame for her condition. It was also established that after several days' attendance on the girl, Dr Rumwell concluded that whatever else she was suffering from, she had a venereal disease, gonorrhoea.

This was the first evidence to indicate clearly that Virginia was not a virgin.

Rumwell was followed by a strong defence witness, Irene Morgan. Miss Morgan, a nurse and masseuse, had been employed by Virginia the previous year as a housekeeper-nurse. She had preceded Mrs Hardebach, the old family friend who had come to live with Virginia and who had presented the girl to the court as a healthy, indeed an athletic girl.

Miss Morgan's testimony presented a different picture of the starlet. She told the court that Virginia had frequently experienced agonizing abdominal pains, which were relieved with hot packs over the pelvic cavities. Virginia would cry out in pain when voiding urine and often had to be catheterized. When the girl was in pain, she would double up, screaming, 'My God!'

At this, U'Ren rose to his feet, wanting the testimony ruled out as hearsay. It was. Miss Morgan went on to describe Virginia's condition after she had taken a drink. 'She would tear her clothes off, virtually all of them. Sometimes she would run out into the street naked. I would have to go after her and bring her back in.'

During the trial, there was a sensation when Irene Morgan was found lying on the bedroom floor of the hotel where she was staying. She had been poisoned. The DA did not complain about 'witness-tampering' this time. Fortunately the nurse recovered, but it was rumoured that she had been threatened with both death and kidnapping if she testified on Roscoe's behalf.

Another witness the defence brought forth to testify about Virginia's attacks was Minnie Neighbors, who a month before Virginia's death had been taking the waters at Wheeler's Hot Sulphur Springs at the same time that Virginia was there. She testified that on several occasions Virginia had had attacks similar to those described by Nurse Morgan. Minnie Neighbors was arrested by DA Brady and charged with perjury, a charge that dangled over her head through Roscoe's trials and was then dropped as soon as there was a court decision. With the perjury charge as a weapon, Brady had one less defence witness to worry about.

The key issue that had to be resolved was how the bladder of Virginia Rappe had ruptured. To this end a great deal of medical evidence was heard during the trial. Of the sixty witnesses who gave testimony, eighteen were doctors (among those was Dr Sheils, the man who had coined the term 'Dementia Americana' in the Harry Thaw murder trial). In fact, the medical testimony was so confusing and contradictory that Judge Louderback had appointed a commission of three doctors to examine Virginia Rappe's bladder and report back to the court.

The opinions of the eighteen doctors varied enormously: the bladder could have ruptured spontaneously, or due to internal force, or due to external force. It could have ruptured because of the rough handling of Miss Rappe by the party guests as they tried to administer first aid, especially when she was swung upside down by Fred Fischbach, or when she was plunged into the cold bath and her muscles contracted. It could have ruptured when she fell off the bed, or when she vomited, or when she tried to urinate. It could even have ruptured after a violent sneeze.

Dr Ophuls – who at the post-mortem had judged by the naked eye and not after a microscopic examination of the bladder – testified that in his opinion there had never been and would never be a spontaneous rupture of the bladder due to overdistention. But I have consulted members of the medical profession who say there are well-documented cases of spontaneous rupture.

In addition, of course, there was the possibility, which was never pursued after the coroner's inquest, that Virginia Rappe died as a result of medical malpractice – incorrect diagnoses and inadequate treatment. There was even the possibility that the bladder had been ruptured by a glass catheter. And certainly looking back on the evidence now, one wonders what effect an illegal abortion would have had on the girl's diseased bladder. Just what *did* go on at the Wakefield Sanatorium?

The defence set out to establish that Virginia Rappe had suffered from inflammation of the bladder for many years and that this chronic cystitis could have caused the bladder finally to rupture.

The testimony of one defence witness after another indicated that the dead girl had a long history of illness. The defence had done its job well. They were able to cover the girl's medical history as far back as 1907.

They were forced to fight every inch of the way in introducing the medical history into the trial record. Every piece of evidence that looked favourable to Arbuckle was resisted strongly by the DA's assistants. Thus it took a legal argument lasting nearly two hours before the defence deposition of a Dr Maurice Rosenberg of Chicago was allowed in as evidence.

When Virginia Rappe was living in Chicago, she was hired in 1913 by Mandel Brothers to model in a fashion show. The store manager there testified that three times in a two-week period she suffered severe attacks from 'bladder trouble', which had bothered her as early as 1907. After she had ripped off the dress she was modelling and collapsed to the floor, the store doctor, Dr Toohey, sent her to the hospital. She was subsequently examined by Dr Rosenberg, whose trial deposition indicated the following:

Her bladder at the time of the 1913 examination was

severely inflamed. A urine examination revealed a large quantity of pus cells and some blood cells. Dr Rosenberg's conversations with the girl established that she had experienced great pain urinating for a number of years. He diagnosed her condition as 'chronic cystitis', and began to treat her for the bladder ailment, but she did not finish the treatment. He also warned her against drinking alcohol, but she continued to drink.

After further attacks of acute pain in 1914 she had called a Dr S. Graves to her Chicago apartment. A sworn deposition from Dr Graves was entered as evidence in the trial. He gave the same diagnosis Dr Rosenberg had: chronic cystitis. He advised her that her recovery would depend on careful treatment and 'even more careful conduct on your part. It will be necessary for you to remain in bed for several weeks on a very restricted diet and you must totally abstain from any alcoholic beverages. I must also advise you that any form of mental or physical excitement is forbidden'. Virginia had told the doctor that she considered the treatment 'too much trouble'.

Several witnesses were called to testify to incidents in which Virginia screamed and moaned, clutching at her body and tearing her clothes off. The defence suggested that her impromptu stripping at Hollywood parties was probably caused by cystitis attacks.

It appeared that after her treatment by Dr Graves in Chicago in 1914 she had never again received proper medical attention – she had a fear of doctors and surgery that transcended normal apprehension.

The defence had depositions from two women living in Chicago that revealed sensational details about Virginia's early life. In 1908, when 14-year-old Virginia was living in Chicago with her grandmother, she had had an abortion. Four months later she had another. Between 1908 and 1910, she had a total of five abortions. Then at the age of sixteen – according to a midwife whose deposition was entered at a later trial – she gave birth to a baby girl, which her grandmother arranged would be brought up by foster parents.

Details about the abortions and the illegitimate child were not submitted in evidence during the first two trials because the defence feared that to defame the girl's character would alienate the jury – and because Roscoe objected to the idea. Therefore it was impossible to suggest a connection between the abortions and the girl's health. Thus the reputation of the dead woman was preserved at the risk of a man's life.

However, the defence had established that the girl was not in prime health at the time of her death.

Roscoe's attorneys now sought to discredit the testimony of the prosecution's fingerprint expert. They recalled E. O. Heinrich to the stand.

McNab's staff had been digging into Heinrich's activities at the time he had removed the doors of Roscoe's suite and taken them to Oakland. Under questioning, Heinrich admitted that he and his secretary, Salome Boyle, had spent many hours alone together in the Arbuckle suite. The courtroom's laughter at this admission increased when Heinrich admitted that he and Salome had introduced themselves to the St Francis Hotel management as 'Sherlock Holmes and Dr Watson'.

Besides making Heinrich appear ridiculous, the defence suggested the possibility that the fingerprints on the doorknob could belong to 'Holmes and Watson'.

Then the defence put its own fingerprint expert on the stand. He stated categorically that the fingerprints were forgeries and offered to demonstrate in court how they had been forged. The DA objected to the demonstration. His objection was sustained, and Judge Louderback ruled that the defence's fingerprint expert was not an expert, thereby invalidating his evidence.

While a legal battle was being waged in the courtroom, a more private battle was being fought behind the scenes.

From the outset Roscoe had insisted that he be allowed to testify in his own behalf. Since his arrest, his attorneys from Dominguez on had insisted at all times that he remain silent. Now Roscoe was equally insistent that he be allowed to take the stand and tell the truth. Schenck and Zukor insisted that Roscoe be kept off the stand. Gavin McNab and his colleagues were split on the problem. While they realized that Roscoe had nothing to hide, they feared that he would fall apart, or be made to appear absurd, by the pounding cross-examination of the DA's staff.

For weeks Brady had insisted publicly that Arbuckle would not take the stand and give evidence. 'He wouldn't dare,' said Brady. 'We would tear him to shreds. If he gets on that stand, he will be shown for the liar, rapist, and murderer that he is.'

Roscoe pointed out to Schenck and Zukor and to his lawyers that it was his liberty that was at stake, his reputation that was being destroyed. He had grown sick at heart as one by one his friends turned away from him, and as women's clubs and ministers all over the country attacked him. At no time had he been given an opportunity to answer back, to state his case. Now he insisted on that opportunity. And two of his attorneys, Milton Cohen and Charles Brennan, threatened to walk off the case unless Roscoe was allowed to take the stand.

At 10.30 a.m. on Monday, 28 November, Gavin McNab said quietly, 'Mr Arbuckle, will you take the stand, please?'

The soft-spoken request caused a sensation. Even the press had been confident that Arbuckle would not testify. Before Roscoe was sworn in, the courtroom was packed.

In the early morning Minta and her mother had walked to court. It was part of defence strategy: no ostentation, no signs of wealth. Limousines were not used; the rings on Minta's hands were covered by her gloves throughout the trial. Roscoe was dressed conservatively.

As the two women had walked towards the Hall of

Justice, a gunshot rang out from across the street. Minta fell. A bullet had grazed her leg, causing slight bleeding. Ma Durfee helped her hysterical daughter to her feet and said, 'If we are going to be killed like Lincoln, then let's live like him. Now come along, Minta, or we'll be late.'

The leg wound was bandaged up by a court nurse. When Roscoe was told what had happened, he became enraged, but McNab pacified him, telling him the place to retaliate was in the witness stand, calmly, and with no display of histrionics. No word of the murder attempt was leaked. McNab feared that if it was, the lynch mood that had inspired the attack might spread to the jury.

Thus advised, Roscoe Arbuckle took the stand.

The verbatim testimony that follows is taken not from newspapers of the period, but *directly from the court transcript, a transcript thought to have been officially destroyed nearly fifty years ago.*

Everyone I have talked to about the case has said that Roscoe Arbuckle was an impressive witness. The atmosphere in the courtroom throughout the four hours he was in the witness box was electric – but he gave his evidence simply and directly.

Of those four hours, less than twenty minutes was spent in direct examination by defence counsel. Except for refuting Jesse Norgaard's testimony about the keys to Virginia Rappe's dressing room, Roscoe spoke mainly about the events leading up to and following Virginia's collapse at the party. The famous pyjamas and bathrobe, along with his slippers and socks, were entered as evidence and handed to the jury for their consideration. Led by his attorney, Roscoe described the moment when he had first discovered Virginia in the bathroom of Room 1219.

ARBUCKLE: When I walked into 1219, I closed and locked the door, and I went straight to the bathroom and found Miss Rappe on the floor in front of the toilet, holding her stomach and moving around on the floor. She had been vomiting.

McNAB: How do you know she had been vomiting?

ARBUCKLE: I saw it in the bowl and there was the odour of it.

McNAB: What did you do? Explain to the jury all the circumstances which occurred in the bathroom of 1219.

ARBUCKLE: When I opened the door, the door struck her, and I had to slide in this way (*illustrating*), to get in, to get by her and get hold of her. Then I closed the door and picked her up. When I picked her up, I held her and she vomited again; I held her under the waist, like that (*indicating*), and by the forehead, to keep her hair back off her face so she could vomit. When she finished, I put the seat down, then I sat her down on it.

Roscoe went on to describe how he had wiped her face and given her several glasses of water. After recapitulating all that had gone on until he had summoned help from some of the other partygoers, he described to the absorbed courtroom what he and the guests had found on re-entering his room: 'Miss Rappe was sitting on the edge of the large bed, tearing at her clothes in this fashion [*illustrating*], tearing and frothing at the mouth, like in a terrible temper . . .'

Arbuckle was interrupted by Friedman, who objected to 'terrible temper' as a conclusion on the part of the witness. Judge Louderback agreed. Roscoe picked up his narrative again:

I say, she was sitting on the bed, tearing her clothes; she pulled her dress up, tore her stockings; she had a black lace garter, and she tore the lace off the garter. And Mr Fischbach came in about that time and asked the girls to stop her tearing her clothes. And I went over to her and she was tearing the sleeve of her dress, and she had just one sleeve hanging by a few shreds, I don't know which one it was, and I said, 'All right, if you want that off, I'll take it off for you.' And I pulled it off for her, then I went out of the room.

Roscoe then dealt with the ice incident:

> I went in there, and Mrs Delmont was rubbing her with some ice. She had a lot of ice in a towel or a napkin, or something, and had it on the back of her neck, and she had another piece of ice and was rubbing Miss Rappe with it. Massaging her. There was a piece of ice lying on Miss Rappe's body. I picked it up and said, 'What's this doing here?' She [Maude Delmont] says, 'Leave it here; I know how to take care of Virginia.' I put it back on Miss Rappe where I picked it up and I started to cover Miss Rappe up, to pull the spread down from underneath her so I could cover her with it, and Mrs Delmont told me to get out of the room and leave her alone, and I told Mrs Delmont to shut up or I would throw her out of the window, and I went out of the room.

Quietly, so quietly that frequently the only sound to be heard was the court reporter's pen on paper, the events of the St Francis party were narrated from Roscoe's point of view.

But this testimony had been elicited through the gentle questioning of his own lawyer. How would Arbuckle fare under cross-examination?

The man Brady had chosen to cross-examine the comedian was Assistant DA Leo Friedman. Friedman was a young man, talented, ambitious, and very determined. The questions he asked Arbuckle had been prepared by Brady, U'Ren and Dr Boyer, one of the state's medical advisers on the case. From the moment the well-briefed, good-looking Friedman rose to his feet, it was clear that he intended to break the defendant. Everyone I have interviewed who observed the trial said that Friedman's unbridled hostility and viciousness 'made the jury wince'. He made the most innocuous question sound like an accusation.

He would ask Roscoe one question over and over again, varying it only slightly, repeating, repeating – and then he would switch abruptly to an apparently unrelated series of questions and start over again. If the technique was meant to confuse Arbuckle, it failed. Friedman began by asking about Jesse Norgaard in 1919, then switched suddenly to questions about the precise time that Virginia Rappe had entered the Arbuckle suite. Roscoe merely answered the questions as they came.

When Friedman referred to the pyjamas, bathrobe, slippers and socks that Roscoe had been wearing, he walked over to the exhibit table and touched them gingerly, as if he expected the devil himself to leap out of the clothes. He dwelt on them, as he also dwelt on the illicit liquor consumed at the party, taking pains to show Roscoe as a pyjama-wearing, whisky-drinking movie star.

Another item that held particular fascination for him was the Victrola.

> FRIEDMAN: Now, from the time that Miss Pryvon [sic] entered Room 1220 and you saw Miss Rappe go into Room 1221, as you have testified to, what was being done in these rooms?
>
> ARBUCKLE: Well, people were eating, drinking, the Victrola was brought up, and that is about all, just general conversation.
>
> FRIEDMAN: Well, who suggested that the Victrola – who, if anyone, suggested that the Victrola be brought up?
>
> ARBUCKLE: Miss Rappe.
>
> FRIEDMAN: Miss Rappe suggested that?
>
> ARBUCKLE: Yes, sir.
>
> FRIEDMAN: And whom did she suggest that to?
>
> ARBUCKLE: To me.
>
> FRIEDMAN: And what did you say?
>
> ARBUCKLE: She suggested that we get a piano, and I said, 'Who can play it?' Nobody. Then I said, 'Get a Victrola.'

FRIEDMAN: And who, if anyone, sent for a Victrola?
ARBUCKLE: I telephoned for it.
FRIEDMAN: You phoned for it?
ARBUCKLE: Yes, sir.
FRIEDMAN: And you say the parties had been drinking up to this time. Had you indulged in anything?
ARBUCKLE: I was eating my breakfast.
FRIEDMAN: You didn't drink anything?
ARBUCKLE: Yes, sir, after breakfast.
FRIEDMAN: And what were you drinking, gin or whisky?
ARBUCKLE: I was drinking highballs.
FRIEDMAN: And after the phonograph was brought into the room, or the Victrola, what was done by the people in Room 1220?
ARBUCKLE: Well, they danced.
FRIEDMAN: Did you dance?
ARBUCKLE: Yes.
FRIEDMAN: And how long did this dancing and drinking keep up?
ARBUCKLE: All afternoon, until I left, and some after that, I guess.
FRIEDMAN: All afternoon long?
ARBUCKLE: Yes, sir.
FRIEDMAN: What time did you leave the room?
ARBUCKLE: I went downstairs about eight o'clock in the evening.

Having established that Roscoe had been in the hotel dining room and then the ballroom until about midnight before returning to his suite, Friedman suddenly changed tack and went back to breakfast time. Ten minutes later he was back to Victrola again and asked a further *thirty* questions about it. In asking how Maude Delmont came to be at the party, Friedman asked the same question, with variations, twenty-eight times.

As Friedman hurled questions at Roscoe, he shouted, waved his arms, and lifted his eyes to heaven. In contrast, Roscoe remained composed; the repetition, histrionics and courtroom rhetoric didn't fluster him. The seven men and five women of the jury never removed their eyes from Arbuckle during his testimony, and if they were looking for nervousness or signs of guilt, they watched in vain. Moreover, of Arbuckle the buffoon there was no trace – although his frequent gestures and his facial expressions reflected his experience in silent films.

As one observer at the time put it, 'He showed himself, both under direct examination by McNab and cross-examination by Leo Friedman, to have one of the most swiftly-working brains in the courtroom.'

The cross-examination lasted over three hours. His lawyers purposely refrained from interrupting with objections, so that he seemed alone and unprotected from the barrage of questions, as if he were being hounded by the state. It made his testimony all the more impressive.

The pre-trial evidence of prosecution witnesses had indicated to the DA's office that Roscoe had not been alone with Virginia for more than ten minutes – and to have done all he was alleged to have done in ten minutes was virtually impossible. Somehow Friedman had to extend those ten minutes. Roscoe had testified under direct examination that he looked at the clock on the mantelpiece of Room 1220, saw that it was three, realized that he had better change for his car ride with Mae Taube, and went to his room. When Friedman came to this episode in his cross-examination, he asked *over two hundred* questions about it. Still he couldn't shake Roscoe. Finally Friedman shouted, 'Isn't it a fact the clock was not going?'

ARBUCKLE: No, sir.
FRIEDMAN: Was it your clock?
ARBUCKLE: No, sir, the hotel clock.
FRIEDMAN: It was going?
ARBUCKLE: Yes, sir.
FRIEDMAN: Had you taken any occasion at any time to see whether or not the clock was correct?

ARBUCKLE: I know two positive times I looked at the clock. It was going all right.

FRIEDMAN: It was going?

ARBUCKLE: Yes, sir. That is when Miss Blake left for Tait's, and at three o'clock when I went into 1219.

FRIEDMAN: Do you know whether or not the clock was correct?

ARBUCKLE: Well, everything else in the hotel is pretty good; I suppose their clocks ought to be all right.

This observation produced laughter and applause in the courtroom, and the bailiff ejected ten people. A few moments later, when Friedman had established that the clock was electrically controlled, he abandoned that line of enquiry.

The assistant DA sought contradictions in Roscoe's story, but failed to confuse him. Friedman raged; Roscoe remained calm.

When the day's hearing was finished, spectators in the courtroom cheered the comedian.

The battle continued – and battle indeed it was. The DA had pitched himself against the film industry in general, and Roscoe Arbuckle in particular. He was determined to win his case.

When it was time for the prosecution to call rebuttal witnesses, E. O. Heinrich made his third appearance in the witness box. Under questioning by the prosecution lawyers, he told what he had found on the floor of Roscoe's suite. The defence objected, deeming irrelevant the fact that Heinrich and his secretary, Salome, had crawled around on the carpet for hours. When U'Ren answered that the reason for the testimony was to show that the maid had not cleaned the floor, McNab convulsed the court by saying, 'Offer the floor in evidence if it is an issue in this case.'

The floor was not entered as evidence, but what Heinrich had found on it was, even though he had not examined it until two weeks after the party. What had Heinrich found on the floor? Dust, a number of hairs, a couple of hair clips, and a white feather two inches long.

To rebut Nurse Morgan's testimony, Mrs Hardebach, Virginia's housekeeper, was brought back, and other prosecution witnesses were produced; they swore that Virginia had always been a healthy girl. Someone was lying somewhere. The jury would have to determine who it was.

Perhaps realizing that he was being bested in the courtroom, the DA once again took his case to the press with a statement: 'I'll put a stop to this perjury and witness-bribing, whether or not Arbuckle ever goes to jail. If Roscoe Arbuckle is acquitted, then I'll open the doors of San Quentin to the Howard Street gangsters.' The DA was referring to a notorious gang that had recently been convicted of charges ranging from protection racketeering and white slavery to murder.

Brady's comments were quoted to McNab, and he was asked for a reply. He said, 'If it is true that the district attorney says that he will free the so-called Howard Street gangsters in the event that Arbuckle is acquitted, he'd better lose no time. If he used the same tactics in securing a conviction in the gangster cases as he is using in the Arbuckle trial, he'd better get busy at once. When is he going to start "putting a stop to perjury and witness-bribing"? My advice to the district attorney is that he had better start house-cleaning for himself. He impounded Alice Blake and Zey Prevon, and their testimony could not bear the closest scrunity.'

The Hearst newspapers printed the DA's remarks, but not the defence attorney's reply.

Virginia Rappe's bladder was brought into court. Roscoe, appalled, turned to Milton Cohen and objected, 'It's a disgusting thing to do. What they're doing is obscene.'

Obscene or not, the bladder was entered as an exhibit. Then the commission of three doctors appointed by the court to examine the bladder gave its findings. The three doctors confirmed what the defence had contended from the outset: the bladder was diseased, and there was evidence of chronic inflammation of the mucous membrane which extended into the muscle.

Virginia Rappe's bladder was cystitic, and cystitis is one of the predisposing conditions to a rupture of the bladder.

After the testimony of the medical commission, there ramained the closing arguments and the judge's instructions to the jury.

At this point the bailiff in charge of the jury's welfare complained to the judge about what he considered intimidation of the jury by members of the district attorney's staff and members of the San Francisco police force. Policemen and assistant DAs had on a number of occasions just happened to bump into jury members on their way to and from the court, and had engaged them in friendly conversation. When the jurors had lunched together, members of the DA's staff always chanced to be at the next table.

With the testimony over, Gavin McNab rose and made public an offer he had been making to the DA for days. He offered to let the case go to the jury without closing arguments, to let the facts speak for themselves. The DA refused. Each side was allotted four hours to make its closing arguments. By the rules of American jurisprudence, the prosecution was allowed two bites at the cherry and the defence one. Leo Friedman would speak first for the state, then Gavin McNab for Roscoe, then Milton U'Ren for the state.

Leo Friedman began by reminding the jury why they were there.

> We are here to try Roscoe Arbuckle upon the charge of manslaughter, and that is, that he is charged that during the month of September of this year, he feloniously and

> without malice killed one Virginia Rappe, a human being. We are here to try Roscoe Arbuckle; not Roscoe Arbuckle the comedian, not Roscoe Arbuckle the hero of a thousand laughs, not Roscoe Arbuckle the nationally-known figure, but Roscoe Arbuckle the man. And we are here to try Roscoe Arbuckle, I say the man, the calloused man, the man who can stand in the face of suffering and laugh; the man who can be in the presence of one who is almost in the agonies of death, and play jokes and pranks upon that person. We are here to try Roscoe Arbuckle, the man who had no thought when he saw a woman writhing and moaning in pain in his room, no thought only to get her out of his room, and no thought of calling medical help and medical attendance to relieve that suffering. That is what we are here for.

It was fine courtroom rhetoric, addressed not only to the jury, but also to the packed courtroom and the news-hungry world outside. Friedman asserted that the prosecution had proved beyond all doubt that Roscoe had caused Virginia's bladder to rupture. He made great play of the incident with the ice, and of the fact that Roscoe had had a Victrola brought to the suite to play records on. Every defence witness was attacked, either as 'mistaken' or as 'guilty of perjury'. Of the many doctors who offered testimony at the trial, those whose testimony was favorable to the state were 'good, reliable and fair witnesses', and those favourable to the defence were 'incompetent, arrogant, or just plain fools'. Curiously, the assistant district attorney referred a number of times to Maude Delmont, citing her actions and her remarks in support of the state's case against Arbuckle, even though she hadn't testified.

Friedman was savage in his attack on Roscoe, whose testimony, he said, was 'perjury'. He criticized the comedian for not telling everybody at the party what was wrong with the sick girl, as if Roscoe could have known, and concluded:

Why his silence day after day, and day after day until we were called here in court, and a jury impanelled, and then for the first time anyone not in his confidential employ heard the story of so simple an explanation? Why should this man allow a charge of this kind to be placed against him? Why should this man allow his reputation to be dragged up and down this great nation, if all that happened was that Miss Rappe was sick, and fell off the bed? And if you believe that that is not true, if you believe that Arbuckle falsified to you upon the stand, if you believe the medical testimony in this case, if you believe the witnesses for the People, and if you believe the writing on the wall, you must return a verdict finding Roscoe Arbuckle guilty of manslaughter as charged in this information.

After a ten-minute recess, Gavin McNab rose to begin the only speech allowed to the defence. The time was 5.30 p.m. Since the court would adjourn at six, the unity of the speech would be broken. McNab was one of the most eloquent public speakers in the state. But Friedman had shouted; McNab spoke quietly, not to the public at large, but to the twelve people sitting in the jury box: 'May it please the Court, and the ladies and gentlemen of the jury box: King David the Psalmist said, "In my house all men were liars." Had he listened to Mr Friedman, he might have said that in anybody else's house, everybody was a liar, but it seems to me needlessly cruel to make the attacks upon the witnesses that have been made upon the women in this case.'

There was applause from the spectators, and the bailiff asked a number of people to leave. McNab moved into a spirited defence of the female witnesses, particularly of Nurse Morgan, who had been subjected to a scathing attack by the prosecution in an attempt to break her down.

He reminded the jury of a California rule of evidence:

evidence that could be produced but was not produced was presumed in law to be against the party who did not bring it before the jury. He continued, 'You have heard throughout this record the name of Maude Bambina Delmont, interwoven with the web and woof of this case as being the complaining witness. Why has not the district attorney produced this woman, so long associated in gathering evidence?'

McNab paused to let the implications of what he had said sink it, then went on: 'Why has he not placed this witness on the stand, so you, the jury, might see her and hear her? Why substitute for Maude Bambina Delmont? Why are you insulted by an incantation in front of a door, while someone summons spooks from out of the ancient woodworks, to tell you the finger stories of long ago, instead of having you see the living flesh?'

Leaving the subject of the missing Maude for the time being, McNab observed that the defence had not needed to produce witnesses from Chicago and LA to testify to Virginia's predilection for tearing her clothes off. One of the prosecution witnesses had done the job for the defence.

When McNab got to the question of how long Roscoe had been in the room with Virginia, he presented a powerful argument. Using the *prosecution evidence* and a number of model clocks, McNab demonstrated to the jury that Roscoe and Virginia had been in the room a maximum of ten minutes.

There had been ample testimony throughout the trial, much of it from prosecution witnesses, to justify the contention that Roscoe could not have been alone with Virginia for more than ten minutes and was probably with her for less than ten minutes.

Alice Blake had said, 'I left the hotel and went down to Tait's around two o'clock. I think I arrived back [at the party] around 2.30 . . . I think it was fifteen or twenty minutes afterwards' [that Miss Rappe left Room 1220].

Al Semnacher had said, 'Just before three o'clock I left

the party to go for a short drive with Mr Fortlouis. At that time everybody was present in the main reception room.'

Zey Prevon had said, 'I do not know the exact time that Virginia Rappe left the room. It was between 2.30 and 3.00 . . . She went into Room 1221. She went to the bathroom. She was knocking on the bathroom door for Mrs Delmont to open the door. She said, "Open the door, Maudie. Let me in." [Maude] said, "Go to the other bathroom. I am changing my dress." [Then Virginia] came through Room 1220 and went into Room 1219.'

Fred Fischbach had said, 'I had to leave . . . at fifteen minutes to two . . . When I returned . . . Miss Rappe was in kind of an hysterics – an hysterical condition, and tearing her clothes, and gritting her teeth, and more of an hysterical laugh . . . I was not in the rooms over twenty or twenty-five minutes from the time I returned from the beach to the time I left . . . until Mr Boyle was called, about twenty or twenty-five minutes.'

Harry Boyle had said, 'I was called by Mrs Taube to Room 1221 at three or three thirty in the afternoon.'

And finally, a Mr R. C. Harper of the Golden Gate Film Studios in San Francisco had come to the hotel and waited in the corridor outside Arbuckle's room 'at about 2.30 or 2.45', and had left the St Francis at 'about 3.15'. 'I walked up this corridor here a ways and then I confined my walk right across the face of the corridor so that I could see if Mr Arbuckle came out. I walked up and down here, and then I stood with my back against the wall over here a while, and then I walked again, but I was there approximately about 35 or 40 minutes – 35 minutes.' Mr Harper had come with a business proposition for Roscoe Arbuckle, whom he didn't know. As he waited in the hall, he heard music and laughter from the suite inside, and about 15 or 20 minutes after his arrival he saw Fred Fischbach (whom he identified in the courtroom) get out of the elevator and go into the suite.

He saw no maid listening at the door. He heard no screams.

McNab then took up the subject of the dead girl's athletic abilities – abilities the DA had been diligent in establishing – and turned the DA's point around. Surely a young amazon would have been able to manage at least a shout if Roscoe had been trying to rape her in the small bedroom – but none of the partygoers had heard shouts, nor had the woman in the next room, an independent witness. He reminded the jury of the evidence that had been presented to show that Virginia was not a healthy, athletic woman, and summarized what he felt to be the main point for the jury to consider:

> This man went in the room, and either he found the giantess that has been described by the prosecution, or he found a sickly, broken woman, as has been testified to, in these convulsions, by Mrs Bates, by Mrs Davis, by the nurse Miss Morgan, and by Mr Semnacher, their own witness. If he found what other people found occurred to that young lady after she had taken wine, there isn't any circumstance that would have caused even a brute to have attacked her, because human nature is human nature. And that woman, lying there, writhing and vomiting, would not have excited the passions of the lowest beast that ever was called man. You have to take one theory or the other; there isn't any escape from it. If she was in that condition, no man would have touched her. And if she was in the condition of a giantess and an athlete, no man could have touched her without the knowledge of everybody in that part of the building, and in the period of ten minutes nothing could have been done.

McNab moved on to the prosecution's criticism of Roscoe for declining to make any statement until the trial. He countered by criticizing the DA for the methods he had resorted to. By nature McNab was a quiet man. He gestured frequently, but his voice was soft, except on one subject: the treatment of Zey Prevon and Alice Blake by the DA and his men. The first time he touched on this he remarked, '. . . and I want to say from the evidence in this case, that I believe the district attorney representing the People in this case has paid less attention to the processes of law than the processing of witnesses.'

Apparently McNab was not raising his voice simply for effect. I have since interviewed people who were close to McNab at the time, and they have told me he was outraged that members of his profession had acted the way the DA and his staff had acted.

Now he developed his attack on the DA's treatment of the two girls: '. . . in San Francisco . . . district attorneys have taken witnesses and put them in private prisons. I thought that when Dickens wrote *Little Dorrit*, that private imprisonment had ceased, but I have learned since that in some places, witnesses are taken into custody on the grounds that these witnesses are such as can be tampered with. Now what class of witness can be tampered with? Not a reliable witness; certainly not.'

He went on: 'If the practices that have been developed in this trial, in this state, are to characterize San Francisco justice in the future, then some of us will emigrate to America from San Francisco. Perhaps we will go to Oakland, or some place else.'

This brought another round of applause from the spectators. The bailiff ejected another twelve people, whose seats were quickly filled.

Slowly, quoting testimony to back up his assertions, he demonstrated how the evidence of Zey Prevon and Alice Blake had been fabricated by the district attorney and his staff. He observed that if Roscoe had made a statement when he had returned to San Francisco with his attorney, Frank Dominguez,

> God knows what these witnesses would have been processed to testify against him as to other facts.
>
> Why, had he given that statement, Mr Heinrich would have discovered that he was under the carpet and

listening. And Miss Keza, the official listener for the prosecution, the chambermaid who testified that she was listening at four doors and two rooms at one and the same time, and who seems to have had, with an ear at one keyhole, and an eye at a crack, her nose into everybody else's business there at the St Francis hotel – well, with that form of creation of testimony, it is not pleasant to consider what would have happened to Mr Arbuckle had he told them anything at all.

Roscoe's attorney attacked the prosecution for preventing the testimony of three doctors and three nurses, all of whom were prepared to swear on oath that at no time did the sick girl accuse Roscoe of attacking her. He attacked the DA for stifling the evidence of George Glennon.

True to form, the DA's staff continually interrupted McNab's closing speech. Then, at six o'clock the trial was adjourned until the following morning.

When the defence attorney rose to speak the following day, it was as if there had been no interruption. He told how Dr Kaarboe, Dr Rumwell, and Dr Beardslee had been kept from giving crucial evidence concerning their respective conversations with Virginia.

He quoted Professor Huxley as saying, 'Since the history of human events began, the mind of man has been the same.' There was, he said, little difference between what was being done in the name of justice towards Roscoe and what had been done in centuries past when Justice Coke had found people guilty of witchcraft and condemned them to the flames.

McNab went through the DA's case point by point, witness by witness, and continued to emphasize the absence from the trial of the complaining witness Maude Delmont, and the treatment of Zey Prevon and Alice Blake by the DA's office.

He insisted that the jury be given copies of the grand jury testimony of Zey Prevon and, describing the DA's behaviour at the time of the grand jury hearings, said, 'The emancipation of Lincoln had been suspended. And . . . the Constitution of the United States, which could not deprive people of life, liberty, or the pursuit of happiness without process of law, was suspended, I say, in San Francisco.'

Towards the end of his speech he returned again to the question of the length of time that Roscoe had been alone with Virginia Rappe. 'You have heard the old saying that "Time waits for no man". You have heard sometimes of people killing time, but no man ever lived that did, because time kills every man. *And on time alone, measured by the prosecution's testimony, there are but ten minutes for it to happen.*'

He contrasted the character of Roscoe, who had entered the box and told his story, with that of Maude Delmont, who 'instituted these matters with the district attorney and now has vanished from the scene'. A few moments later he concluded his speech.

The final prosecution speech by U'Ren was in the style of his colleague Friedman. U'Ren began by insulting Gavin McNab, then said he did not intend to answer the attacks that McNab had made upon the DA and his staff concerning Zey Prevon and Alice Blake. He was, he said, 'going to leave my reputation in the hands of this jury without defending either myself or my office.'

Essentially U'Ren then covered the same points Friedman had covered, although he cloaked them in more elaborate imagery and portrayed Roscoe as a booze-drinking womanizer to be kept away from women, children, and San Francisco.

> We find that on the afternoon of September fifth of this year a Babylonian feast was in progress in the St Francis Hotel . . . And this man, who, Mr McNab says, had made the children of the nation laugh, this man appeared in pyjamas before that mixed crowd and stayed in pyjamas all afternoon. My God! Make the children

laugh! As Mr McNab uttered those words, the thought flashed into my mind: What would the children of America think, and what would the mothers of America say, if they could have seen that man that afternoon in pyjamas, surrounded by his lords and ladies, pouring wine and drinking booze? Oh, my friends, this is a false issue, trying to appeal to you by making the children laugh. What hypocrisy! What hypocrisy for this man of such a nature as that to even assume to deceive the children of America with his antics, while underneath his skin lay the rotten nature that has been shown in this case.

Roscoe's attorneys were 'a million-dollar array of counsel'. Roscoe himself was 'a moral leper'.

'Oh, if the children of America could have seen Roscoe Arbuckle put ice in the private parts of Virginia Rappe, how they and their mothers would have laughed with glee! Oh, my friends, this man who makes the world laugh – who makes the world laugh. Thank God, he will never make the world laugh again.'

U'Ren quoted Pudd'nhead Wilson, the 'fingerprint expert' in Mark Twain's novel, in support of the state's expert, Heinrich. Clearly the state believed that the fingerprints on the doorknob in the St Francis hotel room represented the writing on the wall for Roscoe.

'And as I studied those fingerprints, I thought again of the feast of Belshazzar. You remember that in the Fifth Book of Daniel is recorded the story of the feast of Belshazzar, the Babylonian king, how he sat in his palace surrounded by his lords, and as I thought of that story I thought of the words that "God moves in a mysterious manner [*sic*], His wonders to perform." And I believe, as I stand here, that God was instrumental in some way in placing those finger marks upon that door, so that the guilt of Roscoe Arbuckle would be established beyond any and all reasonable doubt.' Milton U'Ren then read from the Fifth Book of Daniel, concluding, 'And that night Belshazzar the king was slain, and the Medes and

Persians took possession of his kingdom and divided it; and that night Roscoe Arbuckle's kingdom, as the king of humour, fun, was ended. He has been weighed in the balance and found wanting. God has remembered his kingdom and finished it. And his kingdom and he no longer reigns [*sic*], he no longer reigns, thank God.'

A few moments later he closed with these words:

> We ask you to do your duty as men and women of San Francisco. We ask you to do your duty so that when you meet your fellow men, you can look them in the eye.
>
> We ask you to do your duty so that when you return to your families, you can take them to your breasts; and we ask you to do your duty so that when you take your little children upon your knees that you will know that you have done what you could to protect them from this defendant and from all the other Arbuckles in the world, now existing, and yet to come.
>
> And we ask you to do your duty so that this man, and all the Arbuckles of the world, will know that the womanhood of America is not their play thing.

After Judge Louderback explained the legal position on points raised in evidence the jury retired to consider its verdict on Friday afternoon, 2 December, at 4.15 p.m. The courtroom and the corridors of the Hall of Justice remained packed.

What happens in the confines of the jury room is theoretically sacrosanct, but during my three years' research into Roscoe Arbuckle's life I discovered what happened that weekend in December, when the jury deliberated about Roscoe's guilt or innocence.

A number of ballots were taken, showing a nine to three majority for acquittal. It became apparent that the majority favoured acquittal, two were undecided, and one woman, Mrs Helen Hubbard, was convinced of Arbuckle's guilt.

Not only was Mrs Hubbard convinced of his guilt, but

she refused to discuss the evidence and told the others that she intended to vote guilty 'until hell freezes over'. When August Fritze, the foreman of the jury, and the others began to discuss the case, she put her hands to her ears, to avoid hearing the discussion.

Eventually the vote became eleven to one for acquittal. At 11.05 p.m., having reached no verdict, the jury members were locked up in their respective bedrooms for the night.

On Saturday, 3 December, the jury reconvened. A year earlier to the day Roscoe Arbuckle had arrived in Paris to a hero's welcome. Now one woman was determined that no-one should consider him a hero again.

In another part of the Hall of Justice, Maude Delmont had been arrested and charged with bigamy. About the Arbuckle trial she said, 'I have lost all interest in the verdict.'

In the jury room, pressure mounted. One juror, Mrs Winterbur, told the others, 'I don't know what to do. Sometimes I think he is guilty and sometimes I think he is innocent. If only I knew more about the dead girl's character, then I might be able to decide more clearly.'

So much for unwritten rules about attacking a dead woman's character.

Mrs Hubbard told her colleagues, 'I believe Arbuckle is guilty. I believe those fingerprints on the door were accurate, and it is my opinion that when Arbuckle held Virginia Rappe against the door her bladder ruptured. Right there is where I think it all happened, I don't believe his story; I think it is entire fabrication.'

Foreman Fritze called her 'a stubborn woman'. Turning her back on the jurors, she replied, 'I've made up my mind and intend to stick to it if we are here for a thousand years.'

She refused to look at the exhibits. She refused to read the trial transcript.

The jury room had been bugged. The news reached DA Brady that Mrs Hubbard was the lone holdout.

Fearing that she might be persuaded to change her mind, he asked the judge to dismiss the jury. The judge declined; he wanted to give them more time.

Somehow, while this exchange took place, Roscoe found himself locked out of the courtroom. He banged on the door.

A voice from within asked, 'Are you attached to this court?'

Roscoe replied, 'Not very deeply.'

In the jury room, nothing changed. Ballot after ballot, the vote was eleven to one for acquittal. Mrs Hubbard was as immoveable as the Rock of Gibraltar. On Sunday, 4 December, another round of balloting showed no change in her vote.

At noon, having been out forty-four hours, the jurors returned to the courtroom. They told Judge Louderback that they were hopelessly deadlocked. Their final vote had been ten to two for acquittal, one of the men having decided to keep Mrs Hubbard company. The jury was discharged.

DA Brady announced that there would be a second trial as soon as possible. The whole process would have to be gone through again.

One woman had prevented a verdict of acquittal. Why?

In this book, the photograph of the first jury clearly shows all of the facts but one. The woman hiding her face from the camera is Mrs Hubbard. From the moment she was sworn in, everything that followed – testimony from sixty witnesses – was as naught.

Mrs Hubbard's mother-in-law, Sarah Hubbard, was the first California Regent of the Daughters of the American Revolution. Mrs Hubbard's husband was an attorney who had business connections with the DA's office. Gavin McNab had realized early in the trial that he had let a vigilante (in spirit if not in fact) slip through in jury selection, and he warned his client about it. After the non-verdict, McNab said:

From the time she was sworn in as a juror, it was the unanimous opinion of the defence that the expression on her face was that of intense hostility and prejudice toward every defence witness and defence action.

We concluded that, regardless of any juror, or all the other jurors, she would hang the jury and produce a mistrial, and we so advised the defendant.

Although it is a mystery how the diligent defence team allowed Mrs Hubbard on the jury, there was nothing mysterious about the effect. In Hollywood the news of the hung jury was greeted with stunned disbelief. The film colony had followed the trial closely and had been confident that Roscoe would be acquitted. Reaction to the surprising turn of events foreshadowed what would happen in Hollywood years later, with the 'Hollywood Ten'. King Vidor was one of many members of the film colony who recalled for me the effect of the jury's decision:

> There was panic like you have never seen in your life. The only comparable thing to it that I can recall was the hysteria that followed Pearl Harbor. The snowball effect of Roscoe's case in terms of nationwide reaction was incredible. The movie bosses just didn't know which way to turn. There were meetings in New York. Meetings in Los Angeles. Meetings in Boston. Louis B. Mayer said to me, 'If this pressure keeps up, there won't be any more film business.' It wasn't a case of moving to Florida or New York. The moguls firmly believed they faced a total, complete, and permanent closure. The order of the day was to stem the tide of comment, criticism and general indictment of the industry.

Jackie Coogan, then a child star, also recalled that time: 'The whole motion picture industry was in that dock with Roscoe. Hollywood front offices decided to go moral. Guys were told to cut themselves down to two or three mistresses. Zukor, Lasky and Schenck would go which way the dollar pointed.'

And the dollar pointed directly at respectability.

Bootlegging had operated successfully behind a front of drycleaning establishments – why couldn't the movies? What the moguls needed was a respectable manager to run the shop at the front while they got on with their business. They took their cue from organized baseball. A year before, to change its public image after a scandal involving the Black Sox and a World Series 'fix', the association of baseball owners had hired Judge Kenesaw Mountain Landis as 'tsar' of baseball to publicly erase the image of corruption in the sport.

Roscoe's trial ended on 4 December, when the jury returned to the courtroom. Four days later the Hollywood moguls made a decision, the effects of which are still with us. To ward off the external censorship which they had fought against for years, the moguls decided to appoint their own tsar: Postmaster General William Hays.

Hays, a forty-one-year-old pillar of Presbyterian respectability and chairman of the Republican National Committee, was largely credited with President Harding's victory at the polls in 1920. Harding had achieved a stunning success and had rewarded Hays with a seat on his Cabinet. The film magnates were impressed. Joe Schenck suggested that a man who could persuade the majority of the people in the country to elect Harding to the Presidency would make an ideal front man for the film industry.

While Roscoe's trial drew to a close, Hollywood took out insurance in the form of a letter to Hays signed by twelve of the most powerful men in the business, including Zukor, Fox, Goldwyn and Lewis J. Selznick. The letter was to be delivered only if Roscoe were found guilty, but when the news reached them of the hung jury, they waited no longer. A hung jury, even one that had voted ten to two for acquittal, was bad news.

On 8 December, Selznick and Saul Rogers, attorney for the Fox Film Corporation, delivered the letter to Hays personally. The signatories, 'striving to have the industry accorded the consideration and dignity to which it is justly entitled', realized that in order to achieve their aims it would 'be necessary to obtain the services of one who had already, by his outstanding achievements, won the confidence of the people of this country'.

In Hollywood, everything has a price. The price the letter-writers put on the realization of their ideals was 'One hundred thousand dollars a year under a commitment satisfactory to you for a period of three years'.

The 'three years' would become three decades. Hays accepted their offer in mid-January and remained as 'tsar of films' until 1950. *Variety* hailed his appointment as 'the biggest thing that has happened in the screen world since the close-up was first evolved'.

Although Hays didn't officially take up his position as front man to the industry until March 1922 – in 1922 the Motion Picture Producers and Distributors Association of America, MPPDA, was created and came to be known as 'the Hays Office' – his effect was felt in Hollywood in early January of that year. Attendance at filmland's churches swelled; the projection rooms at various studios were packed, too, by order of the studio executives. King Vidor described one of those projection-room meetings:

> I remember that all the directors were called into the projection room. Louis Mayer was there. Suddenly he said, 'Right, roll.' Up on the screen came a number of clips; they were all from the latest movies that we had made that were just about to be released. When they'd all been run through, Mayer turned to us and said, 'I've had all those scenes cut from your movies. Those are some of the reasons that we've brought Hays into the industry.'
>
> Now, believe me, they were so panicky that they had cut anything and everything that anyone could conceivably take offence to and a good deal more besides.

It wasn't until 1930, with the creation of the Motion Picture Production Code, that the industry began formally to regulate itself. For the time being, Hays' most important role was to create good public relations for the industry and in this capacity he may have been effective. Creation of the Hays office did seem to head off the censorship movement.

Ironically, while Hays was selected to rescue Hollywood from its most serious scandal so far because of his ultra respectability, his former employer, President Harding, would be remembered in history for scandals of his own, especially for the oil fields at Teapot Dome, Wyoming. While Roscoe was being tried for manslaughter – but really for a wrongful life in general – the man in the White House was having an extramarital affair with Nan Britton that would eventually result in the birth of a baby girl.

Meanwhile, the President was fascinated with the Arbuckle case and would follow it every day on the radio, sometimes interrupting Cabinet meetings to hear the latest developments. (Perhaps it was from those radio accounts that he learned of San Francisco's Palace Hotel, where Virginia Rappe had been staying when she was invited to Roscoe's party – and where the President was to die in 1923.)

While President Harding maintained a mistress in the White House (and while Hearst maintained one in San Simeon), the DA of San Francisco prepared for the second trial of America's 'looseness of morals'.

After the first trial had resulted in a hung jury, Brady and his staff made a song and dance about jury-tampering – alleged attempts to persuade Mrs Hubbard to change her vote. Brady called for a grand jury hearing into the matter. He did not do as much for August Fritze, the jury foreman, whose life had been threatened. In fact he called the foreman 'a blackguard'. This may have been in response to Fritze's saying that the prosecution's case was 'an insult to the intelligence of the jury. They asked us to substitute conjecture for facts. Human liberty and American rights should depend, not upon guesses of anybody, but upon evidence.'

Not every official in San Francisco thought justice was being served by a second trial. *Even Leo Friedman, who was one of Roscoe's principal prosecutors, was later to say, 'The case should never have been brought in the first place.'*

Not only was much of the DA's case based on conjecture, but a number of people had come to the conclusion that Arbuckle was innocent, among them Chief of Police Daniel O'Brien, who said privately to Minta Durfee and to Jackie Coogan's family (it would have been impolitic to say so publicly), 'Roscoe Arbuckle is innocent of everything. He should never have been put in prison. He should never have been charged with anything.'

The Women's Vigilant Committee was less reticent and took a different view, which the press picked up: 'This committee recommends that the vigilants express their appreciation and thanks to Mrs Hubbard for her courage and conviction and fearless stand in this case.' The club women said that Roscoe 'should have shown more humility at the end of the trial'; they attacked the defence attorneys and criticized the other eleven jurors for not 'joining in praise of Mrs Hubbard'. They praised the judge for 'keeping the trial clean', and congratulated the prosecution. When their remarks drew criticism, they insisted that 'we are not biased in any way'.

Roscoe Arbuckle's second trial began on 11 January 1922, the day Hays's appointment as industry watchdog was officially announced. Arbuckle was protected by his family, friends and lawyers from the curious public, but those close to him saw that this was not the same old Roscoe Arbuckle. Reporter Ed Gleeson and writer Guvernor Morris were both outraged at Roscoe's treatment since his arrest.

Ed Gleeson told me, 'By the second trial Roscoe was

almost in a comatose state. I have never seen a man so changed in such a short space of time. I had met him a number of times before the whole affair at the St Francis. He was such a funny man. His comedy was so inventive. Off screen, he was a prince, a wonderful person, the best-natured man I ever met. But by the time the second trial began, he was totally shattered.'

Selecting the jury for the second trial took even longer than the first time, because it was so hard to find twelve men and women who had not read or discussed the case, and had not formed definite opinions. After seventy-nine people had been questioned, and sixty-seven rejected, a jury was sworn in and the trial could begin.

Judge Louderback, who had presided over the first trial, also presided over the second. Much of the evidence was simply a repeat of the first trial, but there were some notable differences. Alice Blake's memory failed her on the crucial evidence that she had given against Roscoe in the first trial.

Zey Prevon went further than 'I don't remember'. Under cross-examination, she broke down and told the story of how the evidence had been forced out of her and Alice Blake. Despite protests from Brady, U'Ren and Friedman, she told the whole story. The DA tried to have his 'star witness' labelled hostile. The judge ruled against him.

At the first trial, when the defence had tried to establish that the fingerprints 'Sherlock' Heinrich and Salome 'Watson' had discovered were forgeries, the defence witness's testimony had been discounted on the ground that he was not an 'expert'. This time the defence produced two men whose expertise was beyond question. The first of them, Milton Carlson, declared categorically that the fingerprints were fakes, and swore that they had been placed there after the doors had been moved to Heinrich's laboratory in Oakland. Carlson demonstrated not only that there were no similarities between the prints on the door and Virginia's and Roscoe's, but that there were a number of similarities between the prints on the door and those of E. O. Heinrich.

The second defence expert was the policeman in charge of San Francisco's fingerprint bureau. He confirmed the evidence already given by Milton Carlson.

Jesse Norgaard took the stand and retold his tale of Roscoe's attempt to bribe him for the key to Virginia's dressing room in 1919. His story was somewhat discredited by the testimony of the secretary of the film company involved. The secretary declared that Norgaard had never had a special key to Virginia's dressing room, but that in any case a duplicate set of keys to every room in the studio had hung in a place that was accessible to everyone, including Roscoe.

Furthermore, since the first trial the defence had dug into Norgaard's past, and when the former janitor was recalled to the stand during the second trial, McNab established that Norgaard had been arrested for bootlegging in 1918, that he had assaulted an eight-year-old girl, and, most sensational of all, that he was in fact a fugitive from a chain gang.

As McNab developed these facts, U'Ren and Friedman cried, 'Shyster lawyer. Shyster lawyer!' Unruffled, McNab continued his cross-examination. When he had finished, Judge Louderback severely censured the assistant DA's, warning that any more conduct like that would be considered contempt of court.

During the second trial, the defence produced even more witnesses who testified to Virginia's predilection to strip after a drink.

Mrs Nigel Barry told of attending a party given by director Allan Dwan in Hollywood on 21 April 1921. The party was held 'to see the eclipse of the moon', but the partygoers had also been treated to Virginia's stripping and 'throwing herself on an ottoman'.

Eugene E. Presbray, long-haired, dressed in a buckskin suit, and described as a 'dramatic author of Hollywood', recounted an incident at the Hollywood Hotel in 1917, when Virginia had torn off her clothes after a couple of drinks.

Of the many witnesses who told similar stories, perhaps the most significant was Mrs Portnell, who described an incident that had occurred on her ranch on 3 September 1921, just before Virginia had left for San Francisco and death. There was no way for the DA to shrug that off as occurring in the 'dim and distant past'.

The trial had moments of bizarre comedy. The bailiffs were kept busy ejecting people from the court for laughing, but when E. O. Heinrich went through his act with the hotel doors again, one of the bailiffs joined the laughter. Judge Louderback ordered him to throw out the people causing a disturbance. The bailiff refused, asking, 'What do you expect me to do when he keeps pulling all that comedy stuff?' The bailiff himself was ejected.

The DA tried to have the testimony of Kate Brennan, the hotel maid, thrown out on the grounds 'that she has once been an inmate of an insane asylum'. The judge rejected the motion, on the basis that even lunatics can polish doors.

And at one point the trial was delayed while Judge Louderback performed a marriage ceremony in his chambers.

The irony was lost on Roscoe, for whom each day was an ordeal.

After the prosecution had read into the record Roscoe's entire testimony from the first trial, the defence lawyers decided there was no point in Roscoe testifying again. What was the point of duplication, they argued. They overlooked the effect upon the jury of seeing and hearing the defendant – especially Roscoe, who was effective on the witness stand – and of evaluating his testimony firsthand.

Confident that there would be a prompt acquittal, McNab rose to make his closing speech and said, 'The jury has had all the facts. It is unnecessary to weary the jurors with further argument. We therefore submit the case for the defence without argument.'

McNab had committed a serious error. Most of the jurors thought he was conceding defeat. On 1 February, at 3.45 p.m., the jury retired to consider its verdict. The initial balloting was nine to three, *but this time the majority favoured conviction.*

It was soon apparent that among those who found Roscoe guilty, a determining factor was McNab's failure to make a closing speech. The jury spent all of the following day in discussion. There was less acrimony among the jurors at the second trial than there had been among those at the first. The voting on the second day was ten to two for conviction. Just two men held out. One of them, Clem Brownsberger, indicated that he would change his vote if the other man would, but the other man would not.

On 3 February, the jurors returned to court and declared that they were deadlocked. They were dismissed.

Brady announced that Roscoe Arbuckle would be tried for a third time.

Even if one takes into consideration McNab's important decisions not to make a final speech and not to have Roscoe testify, the jury's deadlock was astonishing – especially since the first jury had leaned heavily towards acquittal. At the second trial the state's case had disintegrated when the 'processing' of Zey Prevon and Alice Blake was revealed. The state's case was weakened, and the defence's case was considerably strengthened, yet on the whole the second jury had taken the reverse point of view from the first. Why?

For one thing, it had taken seventy-nine prospective jurors to get twelve who were acceptable. When all of the potential jurors from Judge Louderback's court had been exhausted, the state had then turned to the jurors from another court, that of Judge Louie Ward. (Under the rules of jurisprudence then operating, jurors served more than once.) The men and women from Judge Ward's court were 'case hardened' – they had already served in a number of trials. Moreover, they had established a reputation of being, in the words of Ed Gleeson, 'a convicting jury'.

Just as Mrs Hubbard had stood in the way of Roscoe's acquittal in the first trial, so now one man stood in the way of Roscoe's conviction, and assured a hung jury at the second trial. The man who played Mrs-Hubbard-in-reverse was Lee Dolson, the very man who, the day after the Labor Day party, had come to the ferry to see Doris Deane and her mother off to Los Angeles – the day Doris Deane met Roscoe.

Dolson had never met Roscoe, but when it began to seem likely that he might serve on the second jury, he phoned Doris Deane. She told me of that telephone conversation.

> He said, 'Dodo, it looks like I might be called for jury service on Roscoe Arbuckle's case. I want to ask you what kind of a man is he?' I said, 'Lee, he's a marvellous man. This is a horrible thing that's going on. It's just horrible. He doesn't deserve what they are doing to him.' I told Lee about the evening on the boat. Of how Roscoe had been. I remember clearly saying, 'Lee, that man is innocent. I'll stake my life on it.'

U'Ren had talked at the end of the first trial of God moving in a mysterious way, His wonders to perform. Little did U'Ren know . . .

Once more Roscoe, his wife, his friends and relatives returned to Los Angeles, to await the third trial. They found the city in an uproar. On 1 February, while the second jury had been considering its verdict in Roscoe Arbuckle's trial, William Desmond Taylor had been murdered in his Hollywood home.

The Taylor murder had everything. Nobody would

have dared to write a scenario like it. Taylor, a suave Englishman, had been a leading director, president of the Motion Pictures Directors Association, and one of his industry's spokesmen on the censorship issue (I quoted him earlier when he spoke about Hollywood cleaning its own house). Whenever famous people came to Hollywood, Taylor had invariably been the man chosen to meet them. Nor had his charm been reserved for visiting VIPs; at the time of his death he had been having affairs with at least four women. In his boudoir on Wilshire Boulevard police found not only his body but also hundreds of pairs of panties, each of them labelled with the owner's name and the date they had been 'removed'.

There was also evidence indicating that Taylor had indulged in witchcraft, and had had more than a passing interest in drugs. Police found huge piles of love letters and many photographs showing Taylor making love to a variety of women. (The photographs may have been taken by his valet, Edward F. Sands, who vanished, never to be seen or heard from again.)

Other evidence poured into LA when the news of the murder hit America. William Desmond Taylor was not Desmond Taylor at all, but William Cunningham Deane-Tanner, from County Cork, Ireland. He had run an antique shop in New York with his brother Denis, had married one of the Floradora Girls, and had later deserted his wife and daughter.

There were many suspects. There was Taylor's homosexual butler, Henry Peavey. There was the valet, Sands, whom Taylor had said he fired for forging cheques and stealing clothes and jewellery. There was Taylor's brother Denis, who had abandoned his wife and two daughters in New York, in the family tradition. Like Sands, he had now vanished – so it was impossible to check the theory that Denis and Sands were one and the same. There was Mabel Normand – Mack Sennett's lover for many years and Roscoe's co-star from Keystone days – who was 'friendly' with Taylor. There was Mary Miles

Minter, one of Hollywood's most popular stars, whose name had been linked with his. And there was her mother, Charlotte Shelby, who had been practising firing a .38 calibre gun, the kind that killed Taylor. There were two gentlemen known as 'Harry the Chink' and 'Wong Wong Lee'. There was the possibility that Taylor had been killed for giving information about drug traffic to narcotics agents. And, as if there weren't enough legitimate suspects, within six weeks three hundred men and women, some of them in Europe, had confessed to committing the crime.

Into this madhouse came Roscoe, seeking peace and quiet. The fact that Mabel Normand, an old friend, had often called at his house since his arrest, was seized on after Taylor's murder as 'highly significant', particularly since Mabel had been the last person, except for Charlotte Shelby, to see Taylor alive. It was lucky for Roscoe that he was in a San Francisco courtroom at the time of Taylor's death.

Just as the identity of Taylor's murderer is an open secret in Hollywood, so is the fact that the moguls of the industry prevented any arrests for the murder. King Vidor explained to me: 'Ethics went out of the window. Bribes were handed out all over the place in the Taylor case. The cover-up was entirely organized by Hollywood. To fight it was like taking on the United States government. Remember, these men were all-powerful, you could not fight them. For example, I once heard De Mille tell an actor, "You will never work in another studio. You will never again act before a camera." The man never did.'

Nobody has ever been charged with the murder of William Desmond Taylor. In many ways it is not surprising that so many people were quick to believe that Hollywood could and would try to 'fix' Roscoe's case.

Excitement was not confined to Los Angeles. Maude Delmont was out of prison and out of one of her marriages, and had taken the Arbuckle show on the road.

Baulked by DA Brady from playing a leading role in San Francisco, she had opened in a one-woman show at the Empress Theater in Kansas City.

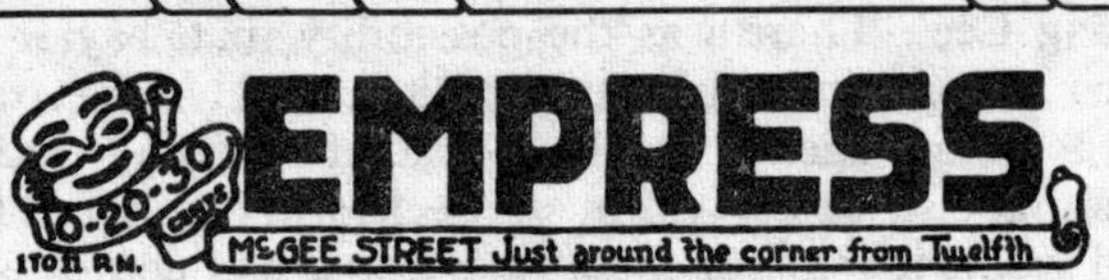

E-X-T-R-A!

Mrs. Maude "Bambina" Delmont

Herself–

THE WOMAN WHO SIGNED THE MURDER CHARGE AGAINST ARBUCKLE

The Most Sensational Act on the American Stage

Mrs. Delmont will tell of the famous Arbuckle-Rappe murder case.

She will rip wide the screen which hides Hollywood and the movie colony.

Her's is a story for Every Father and Mother, every Young Man and Young Woman in Kansas City

HEAR HER SEE HER

THE COMPLAINING WITNESS IN THE ARBUCKLE TRIAL

No Increase in Prices. 10-20-30 CENTS.

A $5,000 Act at-Pre-War Prices

E-X-T-R-A!

Unlike Maude, Zey Prevon had had more than enough of the whole affair. Knowing that to remain in San Francisco would mean another ordeal in the witness box, she fled to New Orleans. When she was traced to her hotel by Brady's bloodhounds, she escaped with her suitcases through a third floor window. Members of the hotel staff admitted that they had heard her say something about going to Cuba.

The third trial of Roscoe Arbuckle began on 13 March 1922. Gavin McNab had learned a bitter lesson from the second trial. This time there was no soft pedalling, no taking for granted that the result was a foregone conclusion. His cross-examination of Alice Blake was so intense that she collapsed on the stand. At another point in the trial, when Judge Louderback – who for the third time was sitting in judgement on the case – made a number of rulings that McNab felt grossly unfair to Arbuckle, the defence lawyer roundly criticized the judge. Judge Louderback remarked sharply that perhaps McNab was 'not so familiar with criminal procedure as you are with civil matters'.

McNab was on his feet in a flash. 'Never again do I wish to appear in a criminal trial if these are the methods ordinarily employed.'

Roscoe went to the stand and gave his account of the party. The defence was leaving nothing to chance.

On one important point, Virginia Rappe's past life, the prosecution played into the defense's hands by insisting on making the details public. For the first time the full facts of her early life were revealed.

On 24 March, in the midst of the trial, Roscoe 'celebrated' his thirty-fifth birthday. McNab turned to him at the beginning of the day's proceedings and wished him 'happier returns than today'.

In this as in the other trials, there were moments of comedy, provided this time by the judge. One of the jurors had to receive dental treatment. The judge, observing gravely that the law demanded the jury be kept intact once a trial had begun, ordered the twelve jurors, two alternates and the bailiff, en masse, to the dentist's office.

On 12 April, Gavin McNab made his closing speech to the jury. As in the first trial, he went through the evidence point by point. He described Brady's behaviour in the initial stages of the police investigation as 'an Apache running wild'. He said the DA's office, in the early days of the case, 'was surrendered to Mrs Maude Bambina Delmont, the complaining witness who never witnessed', and that the DA and his staff had then 'manufactured evidence'.

McNab accused U'Ren of harbouring venom towards the comedian. 'Because Arbuckle did not fall on the shoulder of U'Ren when he returned from Los Angeles, he was dragged to the Hall of Justice. If he had told any kind of story to U'Ren that would have given the district attorney's office an opportunity to build up a case on perjured evidence, by this time Arbuckle would have been hanged.'

Referring to the vigilantes, Gavin McNab described them as 'stony-faced women who haunt the courts, clamouring for blood, more blood'.

At ten minutes past five on the afternoon of 12 April, the jurors filed out to consider their verdict. Five minutes later a stunned court was told they had arrived at their verdict. Quickly the court reassembled. The verdict, written on a piece of paper, was handed to the judge, who read, 'We the jury find Roscoe Arbuckle not guilty of manslaughter.'

The courtroom was in an uproar, with cheering and cries of 'hurrah!' Eventually silence was established, and the foreman of the jury asked the judge for permission to read out a statement from the jury. The jurors had taken an immediate standing vote when they retired. The five minutes had been spent writing out the statement that the foreman, Edward Brown, now read:

Acquittal is not enough for Roscoe Arbuckle. We feel that a great injustice has been done him. We feel also that it was only our plain duty to give him this exoneration, under the evidence, for there was not the slightest proof adduced to connect him in any way with the commission of a crime.

He was manly throughout the case, and told a straight-forward story on the witness stand, which we all believed.

The happening at the hotel was an unfortunate affair for

which Arbuckle, so the evidence shows, was in no way responsible.

We wish him success, and hope that the American people will take the judgement of fourteen men and women who have sat listening for thirty-one days to the evidence, that Roscoe Arbuckle is entirely innocent and free from all blame.

The statement was signed by the jury of twelve and the two alternate jurors. What followed in the courtroom and in the corridors of the Hall of Justice was like the fade-out happy ending to a Hollywood movie. It had been seven months since Roscoe Arbuckle had been charged with the murder of Virginia Rappe. Although swift justice is guaranteed in America by the Constitution, nowadays – when the judicial process is so extended that, by the time the verdict is in, the public has forgotten what was at issue in the case – it is hard to imagine how a man could undergo three trials in only seven months. Those months had been a nightmare for Roscoe, but now he had been given the kind of sweeping exoneration that comes to few men placed on trial for a serious charge. Once more he would be able to make the millions laugh. He was a free man.

So ended the case of *People of the State of California v. Roscoe Arbuckle*.

The trial had cost him over $700,000. Never a frugal man, Roscoe at the time of his arrest had had less than $20,000 in the bank. Joseph Schenck had loaned him the rest of the money. Because Zukor had stopped his salary on the day of his arrest, and because his new feature films had been held back and others had been withdrawn from distribution, he had lost perhaps $600,000 in income. That put the total immediate cost to Roscoe at over a million dollars. (The cost to the state was also extremely high.)

In psychological terms and in terms of his career in the movies, the cost was so numbing and enormous that he wouldn't begin to comprehend it for years.

But 12 April 1922, was not the time to assess damage, merely to feel a sweet relief. As the crowds milled around the comedian, he was questioned about his future plans. Laughing, he told reporters that he had put on nearly thirty pounds during the seven-month ordeal, and the weight would have to come off before he even thought about motion pictures.

He continued, 'I will be able to go on with my work if the public wants me. If the public doesn't want me, I'll take my medicine. But, after the quick vindication that I have received today, I am sure the Americans will be fair and just. I believe I am due for a comeback.'

So, it seemed, did everyone else.

In New York, Jesse Lasky expressed delight and said that a new Arbuckle picture would be released immediately. 'The manner in which the public receives this picture will determine whether Arbuckle is offered another contract,' Lasky added.

Joseph Schenck said, 'Arbuckle will return to the screen at once, and I think the public will welcome him.'

Matthew Brady, district attorney of San Francisco, made his shortest public statement in seven months: 'I am an American citizen and I take off my hat to the verdict of an American jury.'

News of Roscoe's vindication swept through the film colony. Charles Chaplin, Douglas Fairbanks, Mary Pickford and Mabel Normand were only four of the stars who expressed delight at the acquittal and confidence that Roscoe would quickly return to the screen. Some felt, 'He is going to be more popular than ever.'

Even as they expressed this confidence, a Los Angeles cinema scrapped the feature it was showing and replaced it with *Crazy to Marry*, an Arbuckle feature film. The cinema was packed at every showing.

The following day a New York theatre put on *Gasoline Gus*, the new feature that Sid Grauman had pulled off his screen seven months before. There was a full house at every screening.

News of this reception was relayed to Roscoe in San Francisco. He turned to Minta and said, 'Looks like I'm going to be a comedian again instead of a tragedian.' He had just had his first good night's sleep since his arrest.

Another of his feature films opened in San Francisco on the first weekend after his acquittal, and played to capacity business.

Roscoe returned to his West Adams house a happy man. He and Minta had reconciled their differences; the press photographed him at the piano with Minta as she played 'Spring Song' while he accompanied her on a kazoo.

On Sunday, 16 April, Will Hays and millions of other Americans celebrated Easter Sunday at church.

Two days later Hays made public his first major decision since becoming official watchdog of the film industry. It had been just six days since a jury had wholeheartedly voted for Arbuckle's acquittal.

On 18 April 1922, Hays banned Roscoe Arbuckle from the screen.

PART THREE

AFTER

So it was that on 18 April 1922, Will Hays topped the injustice of the previous seven months with an act so unfair that all of Hollywood was stunned. Why did Hays do it? Why, when a jury of twelve citizens had found Roscoe innocent, did Hays find him guilty?

He didn't. The time would come when the Hays Office would be known in Hollywood as 'the terror machine', but in mid-1922 Hays was still only a front man. The decision to end Arbuckle's career was made by the men for whom Roscoe had earned millions of dollars: Adolph Zukor and Jesse Lasky. Thirty years later Hays would say that the greatest lesson he had learned in life was 'that it is possible to change public opinion', but in April 1922 he bowed to the heads of Paramount in their decision to trade Roscoe for peace with vociferous ministers and with women's and civic groups. Roscoe as sacrificial lamb would save the industry he had done so much to create.

Even before the third trial was over, it was clear which path Zukor and Lasky would take; Roscoe's guilt or innocence was irrelevant. The fact was, his trials had crippled the box office. Roscoe had to go. But Zukor had a problem: if Paramount banned his films, it would face a revolt within the industry. The film colony had become convinced of Roscoe's innocence, and if his own company were now to betray him, Hollywood would take a long time to forget.

Zukor needed someone to do the job for him. He went

to Will Hays and told him why he thought the ban was necessary. Hays thought Zukor should announce the ban and said so, but Zukor had an answer for that: 'No, Will, let the Association give it out. That will show that the Association means business.'

Hays, naively impressed with this argument, recalled years later in his autobiography, 'Even that early in the game Adolph Zukor had passed the stage in which profit was the primary concern of his activity. If any man ever had the "alma mater" spirit for the industry which had made him, and which he had largely made, that man was he.'

So Hays, not Paramount, bore the criticism when the industry learned that Roscoe had been banned. Not only did Paramount retain the industry's confidence, but Hollywood felt sympathetic towards the men who had been responsible for the decision to ban Arbuckle – after all, hadn't they just lost their biggest box-office star? Zukor and Lasky played to their audience, feigning surprise when they heard Hays's announcement. In fact, hours before the Hays ban was made public, Zukor issued a press statement announcing the release of the three Arbuckle features, 'as we are confident that the American public is eminently fair and realizes by this time that Arbuckle has been the victim of unfortunate circumstances'.

Zukor said this, knowing that Hays's announcement would nullify it. Nevertheless, Zukor stood to lose a great deal of money on Arbuckle films, starting with three million dollars net rental profit on the three unreleased movies. As a result of the Hays announcement, contracts with over ten thousand exhibitors were rescinded. Based on average box-office takings on Arbuckle films before Virginia Rappe's death, this meant *a projected loss of over one hundred million dollars*.

It is hard to imagine astute businessmen like Lasky and Zukor willingly terminating the career of their biggest star, knowing that they stood to lose such vast sums of money. Certainly they didn't arrive at their decision through moral conviction; only fear of a worse fate made it possible. They were terrified that the American public, 'eminently fair' or not, would turn against them – and 'public' was only another word for box office.

Panic at this possibility – and also at the possibility of some form of government control of the industry – was to surface time and again over the years in forms of self-censorship unique to Hollywood. In 1941 Nicholas Schenck, Joseph's brother, approached George Schaefer, the head of RKO, on behalf of Louis B. Mayer, and offered $842,000 for the master print of *Citizen Kane*, with the intention of destroying it. Schaefer refused to consign the film to the incinerator, but despite critical acclaim the film fought against overwhelming odds: many cinemas refused to show it, the Hearst press refused to carry ads for it, and several people associated with it became marked men and women. Pauline Kael in *The Citizen Kane Book* explains that men like Mayer feared that 'the Hearst press would reveal some sordid stories about the movie moguls and join in one of those recurrent crusades against movie immorality, like the one that had destroyed Fatty Arbuckle's career. The movie industry was frightened of reprisals'.

Never strong on moral courage, the Hollywood moguls were frightened above all of economic reprisal. This fear was to paralyse filmland again when, between 1947 and 1953, Congress and other groups investigated Communism in Hollywood. Ten people (the Hollywood Ten) were imprisoned for contempt of Congress, for refusing to tell the House Committee on Un-American Activities if they were Communists or if they knew who in Hollywood was. After an initial feeble protest against the investigation as an invasion of privacy, industry leaders met in New York in 1947 and agreed not to hire anyone 'politically dangerous'. The political blacklist which developed as a result of this agreement ruined the careers of countless hundreds in the industry, the innocent along with the 'guilty'; many of them never knew what had happened, since the details of the blacklist were by then a secret carefully guarded by studio executives.

Roscoe at least knew why his acting career was being ended, even if the ending of it was unjust and unconstitutional (and a precedent Hollywood would all too easily follow again). Nevertheless, there was a straight line from Roscoe's banishment to the later blacklisting of the Hollywood Ten. Roscoe was the first Hollywood star denied the right to work because of behaviour the film industry felt the public wouldn't countenance. Soon he was to have plenty of company. In the summer of 1922 the Hays Office prepared a list of nearly two hundred people who were to be eased out of the business because they represented risks to filmdom's image – not because of their politics, but because of habits like drug use, which contributed to the image of Hollywood as sin city.

At the time of Roscoe's persecution, an actual physical blacklist existed – I have seen a copy of it. By the mid-thirties, the physical list no longer existed. By then writers and actors were eliminated over a quiet game of bridge or golf, and in any case there was less need for care, as Hollywood was not being watched with the same intensity of moral fervour. When McCarthy and the Red Menace panicked everyone in the late 1940s, the blacklist was resumed, but this time it was refined to perfection and focused on politics instead of personal morality.

The blacklists of the 1920s and of the 1940s and 1950s shared an important feature: the studios could get around them if it was economically beneficial to do so. In matters of protecting the industry from moral and political corruption, it was appearances that counted. After the congressional investigations, writers like Albert Maltz, Dalton Trumbo, and Ring Lardner, Jr, would work again; they would simply do so under different names and at a tenth of their regular salaries. For an actor, of course, this would be impossible. But even Roscoe would find work, directing under a pseudonym.

Ironically, the day the ban on Roscoe's films was made public, the Women's Vigilant Committee released a statement drafted the day before, expressing the group's intention not to take any official action against Roscoe's films – in effect, the group seemed to have accepted the jury's verdict. Nevertheless, after newspapers carried stories of the ban, the Hays Office was flooded with letters and cables of congratulations from club women and ministers.

The press, though, had questions. Newspapermen asked Hays to comment on the statement the jury had issued after acquitting Roscoe. Hays declined. They asked him if the ban was permanent. Hays responded: 'The purpose of this Association is to attain the highest possible standards of motion picture production and to develop to the highest degree the moral and educational value of the industry.'

Not everyone thought the way to attain those standards was by compounding an injustice.

Ole Hanson, former mayor of Seattle, called Hays's action 'un-American and worthy of medieval despotism'. He continued,

> It is a principle of our American government that all men stand equal before the law in the matter of freedom and liberty of action.
>
> It is a matter of the gravest importance that this principle be upheld. The entire censorship movement is in line with a prohibitive and restrictive tendency that will result in a reaction that is bound to be fraught with grave dangers to our country. A few self-appointed guardians of our actions are attempting to reduce us to the status of slavery.

A sense of outrage swept Hollywood, but as Jackie

Coogan observed, 'Hays was like President Coolidge – no sense of humour, but he did have the power.'

Coogan, like many stars I interviewed, still felt angry about Roscoe's treatment: 'This loss of something so newly acquired by the man was devastating. He had millions of fans. He was such a funny man. That such talent should be destroyed by backwoods bigotry is a terrible crime. Roscoe's story shows what happens when bigotry and censorship get into the arts. My father was stunned. I can remember him walking round the house saying, "He's such a great entertainer. God, what have they done to such a gentle man?" '

Ironically, Coogan also recalled, 'When Hays was brought in, I was the first person he was photographed with, for publicity purposes. Not for me. For him. Good for his image to be seen with a loveable child star.'

According to Babe London, 'Hollywood was up in arms about the deal that Roscoe got – to be acquitted, then crucified.'

Adela Rogers St Johns observed more ambivalence: 'Everybody rallied behind him – the people of Hollywood, that is. They did it because they were aghast. Then came the realization for them: they might be next. People began to run like little puppy dogs, running scared. They were only concerned with protecting their own fortunes. They might lose all their pretty toys. It was always "good old Roscoe" in private, but in public they were never seen with him.'

King Vidor, who was to witness other stages of Roscoe's fall from grace as well, concluded: 'If they had stood firm behind Arbuckle, they could have saved his career. Damn it all, the man was acquitted.'

But if Hollywood stood behind Arbuckle at all, it was to hide.

Mrs Toll, president of the Ebell Club, a large women's club in Los Angeles, said:

> I hesitate to bring such a sordid note to such an occasion

as this, but I have been feeling so strongly my own distress at the manner in which this man is lionized and the reception given his pictures here in this city – amounting, apparently, almost to hero-worship – that I felt I must do something.

My conscience troubled me that I was slow to act, and now the statement of Will H. Hays that he will bar these pictures takes a load from my conscience.

Hollywood did not argue. Hays had relieved many a conscience, including that of someone at *The New York Times*, which on 20 April maintained in an editorial that the ban would meet with 'wide and cordial approval', then continued, 'Picture plays in which Arbuckle is the most prominent figure are not to be displayed . . . Carefully-preserved obscurity best becomes the heir of the particularly squalid drama . . . Fortunately . . . fellows of the baser sort will not have an opportunity to disease themselves and the rest of us by applauding the man the jury pronounced "not guilty".' Even *The New York Times* was willing to abandon constitutional rights if they stood in the way of righteousness.

Three days later Roscoe made his first public statement about the ban. Acknowledging that his destiny was controlled by Famous Players-Lasky and Hays, he said, 'I shall do everything possible to cooperate with the leaders of the industry. In the meantime, I shall prove to the world by my conduct that I am entitled to an opportunity to earn my living in the only profession I am equipped to follow, and shall patiently and hopefully await the final opinion of the American public, in whose sense of fair play I have never lost confidence.'

His public confidence belied private reality. As Adela Rogers St Johns put it, 'He was absolutely shaken to his boots. He didn't seem to be functioning. Mabel Normand and I thought there was still a lot of hope, that eventually the business would stand behind him.'

But Roscoe saw no hope. The Hays ban had broken

him, and now his world was shattered. His reconciliation with Minta was short-lived; within two months after his acquittal she had left his palatial West Adams residence and returned to New York. He lost his cars, his servants, and most of the friends who had eagerly attended his parties a year before. He was forced to sell his West Adams home to Joseph Schenck to repay some of the money he owed him for trial costs. His manager, Lou Anger, rented the house from Schenck, and Roscoe lived in his former home as Anger's guest.

Ironically, the film he had been scheduled to make at the time of his arrest, *The Melancholy Spirit*, was renamed *One Glorious Day*, and Will Rogers, a friend of Roscoe's, was asked to replace him in the lead.

Roscoe wandered on to film lots and chatted with former friends and colleagues, but as the weeks went by, they showed less inclination to talk to him. One of the few who remained loyal was Buster Keaton, for whom Roscoe now wrote a film script which was to become a classic. Traditionally, Keaton and Eddie Cline are credited as the writers, but in *The Frozen North* it was actually Roscoe who adapted an idea he himself had used earlier – and, in the process, got mild revenge on one of the people who had turned on him at the time of his arrest. In *The Sheriff* Roscoe had burlesqued Douglas Fairbanks. Now the target of Roscoe's humour was Wiliam S. Hart, the wooden hero of a thousand wooden Westerns, and a subject perfectly suited to the deadpan style Keaton had mastered since his return from the war. Unlike Fairbanks, Hart did not laugh at this parody of himself. After seeing *The Frozen North*, he refused to talk to Keaton for many years.

On the Sennett lot, Roscoe trained a new generation to throw custard pies. Audiences who laughed at the new scenes didn't know that the humour was tainted by the behind-the-scenes presence of Roscoe.

These activities, although pleasant, served also to sadden the comedian, reminding him that he was now only on the periphery of the movies. Quietly Roscoe packed a couple of suitcases and, with only his dog Luke, went to live in a cabin in the Sierra Madre. There he read everything that had been said or written about him, and it didn't seem to be him they were talking about. For months he thought about all that had happened, trying to analyse why it had happened – and finally he decided that if people held the opinion of him that they seemed to hold, words would not change their minds. In his film-making he had displayed a keen awareness of the limitations of his audiences, realizing that there was no point in directing humour above the heads of moviegoers. Nevertheless, Roscoe had a simple faith in human nature. During his period of isolation in the Sierra Madre, he decided that he would show through his actions that he was a fit person to make the world laugh.

Having licked his wounds, he found himself yearning to be among people again – but not those who knew him and who would remind him of former glories. He sailed to the Orient, thinking that there he would be unknown and could lose himself, even as he re-established contact with humanity. But not for Roscoe the anonymity of foreign cities – wherever he went, he was recognized. In China, they pointed at him and gathered around him on the streets. In Tokyo, a minor story about him became transformed into headline news. Aboard ship he had badly injured his hand when he tumbled down a flight of stairs, and in no time the injury was reported as the result of a shipboard brawl. American newspapers quickly relayed the news: 'Honourable Fatty injured in battle with sake.' In Japan, Roscoe realized that perhaps the only place where he would be ignored was Hollywood. In Yokohama at the end of September, he boarded a ship bound for San Francisco.

On his return to the West Adams residence, he found sacks of mail waiting for him – thousands of letters from all over the world, expressing sympathy for what had been done to him and the desire that he would return to the screen.

Apparently the same people who wrote to Roscoe were also appealing to the managers of local movie houses all over the country, asking that Roscoe's films be shown again. Exhibitors began to canvass their patrons about whether they wanted Arbuckle pictures or not, and news soon reached Paramount that the results were overwhelmingly in favour of the comedian's return to the screen.

Zukor talked to Will Hays, and together they apparently decided that the 'high moral standards' Hays had spoken of would now best be preserved by Arbuckle's reinstatement.

Having banned Roscoe at Easter time, Hays announced just before Christmas that *the ban had been lifted*, that Arbuckle was free once more to work.

What reasons did Hays give for the decision?

'First, perhaps, was the fact that he seems completely chastened and that his conduct since he was barred from the scene last April apparently has been exemplary.' Hays would start 1923 with a clean slate. 'Live and let live is not enough; we will try to live and help live.' Speaking of 'the spirit of Christmas', Hays reminded the public that Arbuckle's movies 'were always clean and they brought laughs to millions'.

When Hays had reviewed the evidence to his own satisfaction, he explained to his fellow Americans, 'Still, again, it was felt that inasmuch as a jury acquitted him of the charges upon which he was tried, he is constitutionally entitled to the right of any citizen, especially to the right of working at the only thing he knows how to work at.' Having suspended both Roscoe and the Constitution in April, Hays was willing to reactivate them both on 20 December. The ban nearly bridged the gap between Easter and Christmas.

Roscoe was delighted. So were Joseph Schenck and Jesse Lasky.

Their delight was short-lived. About four hours after the announcement, the president of the Los Angeles Federation of Women's Clubs condemned the decision. (One marvels at the speed of the club's communication system – or at the ability of reformers to read the mass mind.)

Details of what happened in the next four weeks could fill a book. Reaction to Hays's decision made the reaction to Roscoe's arrest and trials appear almost benign.

The problem with reinstating Roscoe was that banning him in the first place had implied he had done something wrong. The ban suggested that Roscoe had been acquitted for lack of evidence, and not for lack of guilt – or at least that he was guilty of generally loose living, if not of the specific crime he had been tried for. In lifting the ban, Hays had not admitted the ban was a mistake; the implication was that Roscoe had tried to reform. And it was possible to interpret the reinstatement as a Hollywood whitewash.

The day after Hays announced his decision, the mayor of Boston said he would continue the ban in his city. He was joined in this decision by the acting mayor of Detroit, and by the mayor of Indianapolis, who said, 'It is a big mistake to make a hero out of a man who did the thing he did.'

Within two days, the following organizations – and another twenty not listed – had expressed opposition to the pardon, registering their collective 'disgust', 'outrage', and 'fury': women's clubs in Buffalo, Pittsburgh, and Philadelphia, and the Women's City Club of Chicago ('Let's have our fun and our fun-makers clean'); the Citizens Committee for the Massachusetts League of Women Voters; the National Education Association in Washington; the Church Federation of St Louis; the Illinois PTA; the Detroit Police Commission; and the Minnesota Film Exhibitors.

The State Church Federation in California sent Hays

the following telegram: 'The announcement that Roscoe Arbuckle is to reappear is incredible. We have only pity for one of his record, but to return him to the screen is to say, no matter how vile a man's record, yet we will approve of him as our entertainer. It is unthinkable. Our children have rights we must safeguard.'

Several Presbyterian elders warned the Presbyterian Hays: 'Your failure to maintain the ban on Arbuckle will mean a forfeiture of the respect and confidence of our people and, we believe, the forfeiture of the confidence and respect of all God-fearing, decent men and women.'

The Catholic Welfare Council resolved that there was no room 'for persons of the Arbuckle type' on the screen and asked all of its affiliates in the country 'to prevent the showing of Arbuckle films'.

In New York, the general secretary of the YMCA 'vigorously opposed Arbuckle's return'.

Protest knew no denominational boundaries. These groups were joined by the president of Temple University, the Rabbi Joseph Krauskopf of Temple Keneseth Israel in New York City, and the Women's Christian Temperance Union.

Even the warden of Sing Sing announced that Arbuckle's films would not be shown in the prison because 'they might be a bad influence'.

It was time for Roscoe's friends to stand up and be counted. The counting didn't take long.

Joseph Schenck was one of those who stood loyally by Roscoe, saying,

> It is not Christian-like of these ministers to condemn Arbuckle before he has been heard. He is willing to meet these ministers face to face at any time and at any place to defend himself.
>
> We have the profoundest respect for these men, but it is not fair in them to condemn him without giving him a trial; nor should they try to keep him down.

Schenck received powerful support from Gavin McNab, the Scottish lawyer who had defended Roscoe in court and who had been appalled at Roscoe's treatment during the seven-month ordeal in San Francisco. This new attack made a mockery of three trials, and McNab decided to fight back with positive action. He got together a group of San Francisco businessmen with a working capital of $100,000, and formed a film company for Roscoe. McNab would be executive producer and Roscoe would have a free hand making the company's films.

Showman Arthur Hammerstein told the press that the Sunday after the ban had been lifted he had shown an old Arbuckle movie at the Park Music Hall in New York. 'The public was so anxious to see him, they broke the doors down,' he said. He made public an offer he had made privately several months earlier, to buy the three unreleased Arbuckle feature films for one million dollars. Hammerstein said that if Famous Players-Lasky didn't want to sell the films, 'I will be willing to present these pictures in the United States, especially the eastern part of Pennsylvania, where they are so antagonistic, for the sum of ten per cent of the profits.'

By coincidence, a mere two days after Hays announced his decision, the news broke that Wallace Reid – the clean-cut film hero of his day, the handsome star every girl-next-door dreamed of marrying – was in a sanatorium to cure himself of drug addiction.

In the summer of 1922, when Hays had shown Zukor his list of nearly two hundred people who represented a threat to Hollywood's clean image, Zukor had spluttered when he saw the name at the top: Wally Reid, who was listed as risky because of 'morphine addiction'. Zukor had flatly refused to end Reid's career. One scapegoat was enough, and as Zukor had remarked, 'To lose Reid would cost us another two million dollars.' (Ironically, Reid had been scheduled at the time to make *Thirty Days*, a film which had originally been planned as a vehicle for

Roscoe.) Eventually Reid ended Zukor's dilemma: by the end of the year he was too ill to work, and by then the public knew why.

Illicit drugs were big business in America in 1921. There were an estimated five thousand addicts spending about 1.5 million dollars a year in Los Angeles alone. Reid's addiction was made public at the perfect moment for those who were protesting Arbuckle's reinstatement.

The New York Times saw each turn of events in more perspective than the civic and religious groups, but it hardly stood on the side of the angels in the matter of civil liberties for Roscoe. In an editorial on 22 December, the paper had described the lifting of the ban as 'a serious tactical blunder', and continued, with cynical realism, 'Arbuckle has become, through mischance, a symbol of all the vice that has been indulged in by movie people . . . Sometimes it is expedient that one should be sacrificed for his group . . . the only thing to do with a scapegoat . . . is to chase him off into the wilderness and never let him come back. It will do the picture business no good to have him tottering back into the parlour, bringing his aroma with him.'

The State Federation of Churches in New York endorsed these remarks and added: 'To give Roscoe "Fatty" Arbuckle another chance in motion pictures would be to defy the parents of America and to condone the capitalization of crime for financial gain, as well as to cripple the efforts to elevate the moral and artistic standards of the motion picture industry.'

Roscoe Arbuckle could take no more. He had remained silent under this onslaught, but on 24 December he issued a statement. Asking for 'fair play', he reminded his critics not only that he had been acquitted, but that his jury had sent a message from that courtroom declaring his absolute innocence to the rest of the country. Now part of the country was virtually refusing to abide by the law. He continued,

I am not only wholly innocent, but more than that. There is a higher law which deals with the spiritual side of mankind, and surely this Christmas time should not be the season when the voice of the pharisee is heard in the land.

It is not difficult to visualize at this time of the year, which commemorates the birth of Christ, what might have happened if some of those who now heartlessly denounce me had been present when the Saviour forgave the penitent sinner on the cross, in words that have more influenced the human race than any other words ever uttered. Would not some of these persons have denounced Christ and stoned him for what he said?

No-one ever saw a picture of mine that was not clean. No-one ever saw a picture of mine that was not wholesome. No-one will ever see such a picture of mine. I claim the right of work and service.

The sentiment of every church on Christmas Day will be 'peace on earth and good will to all mankind'. What will be the attitude the day after Christmas to me?

The day after Christmas, Roscoe found out. *The New York Times* attacked him in another editorial, saying in part: '. . . among the differences which separate members of the human race is that between those who get away with it and those who get caught . . . An odour clings to him: and it will cling no matter how he sprays himself with Biblical analogies.'

The General Federation of Women's Clubs, claiming to represent 2.5 million women and anxious to purify the country, cabled Hays: 'This organization stands ready to help any individual to rehabilitate himself, but not at the expense of the ideals of the nation. The youth of our country must be protected from a revival of interest in the degrading details of his trial and from continued discussion of immoral living associated therewith.'

Roscoe was banned in Omaha, Iowa, Ohio and Alberta. The bans were unconstitutional, but who was there to challenge them in the courts?

The president of Universal Pictures pleaded for Roscoe to be given a 'fair chance'. The Rev. John Roach Straton replied: 'You cannot purify a polecat, you cannot denature a smallpox epidemic, you cannot reform a rattlesnake . . . you cannot cure the organic disease of film corruption . . . with soothing syrup.'

Daily attacks from the pulpit and civic groups were reinforced by the press. On 8 January, *The New York Times* focused again on Fatty as a mere pawn in a game of illusion: 'The appearance [of the motion picture industry] was ruined by the Christmas pardon. The iniquity worked on the industry by this affair would be just as great if the acquitted Fatty were, and always had been, spotless as Sir Galahad. It is appearances that count.'

The New York Times at least admitted the possibility of Roscoe's innocence. The Adrian *Daily Telegraph* informed its readers, 'The "righteous gentlemen" behind the pardon talk as though the only question were that of being good to Arbuckle. What about the feelings and the morals of the millions before whom they propose to thrust Arbuckle's picture and personality?'

The Pittsburgh *Gazette Times* also ignored Roscoe's acquittal: '. . . to portray him on the screen is to place him in the light of having been guilty of a mere indiscretion which should be overlooked in the interests of art.'

The St Paul *Pioneer Press* wrote that Hollywood could only bring him back at 'the expense of jeopardizing the morals and mental integrity of millions of impressionable young persons. His prosperity is as nothing compared with the welfare of a generation'.

The Chicago *Post* recommended 'another kind of job; the fact that it might be less to his liking and considerably less lucrative would be good for his soul'.

Outlook was one of the national magazines to share the general horror: '[Arbuckle's] name and pictured face are odious to decent theatregoers . . . There is something revolting and abhorrent in holding this man up again as an amusing, even if vulgarly farcical, comedian.'

*

Hays records in his autobiography that there 'were others who commended my stand'. It would appear they were pitifully few.

The Denver *Times* applauded the Hays philosophy of 'live and help live' as being the 'very spirit of the golden rule'.

The Springfield *Union* saw the matter as 'a question of the attitude of the sinners towards the sinner' and reminded its readers that Jesus had told Peter to forgive his erring brother seventy times seven times.

Billy Sunday, the evangelist, whose daughter-in-law, Mae Taube, had been at the St Francis party, said publicly that what was being done to the man was 'un-Christian and evil. The forces of darkness have gained control in this country. This man is being destroyed by the greatest display of bigotry that I have ever seen in this country. There is a lynch mood in the land'.

During early January 1923, the storm raged unabated. For every call for fair play or justice there were ten demands for blood.

The Better Film Department, an offshoot of the San Francisco women's clubs, passed dozens of resolutions, cabling them all to Will Hays. The theme was constant:

> Whereas, many of the youth of our country are inclined to idealize the screen actors and actresses, and the moral development of our young people is of more importance than the welfare of any individual screen actor and
>
> Whereas, Roscoe Arbuckle has not proved himself to be a proper example for anyone to follow, despite his acquittal by a jury of the charge of manslaughter, and
>
> Whereas, we believe the standard of conduct of all motion picture actors and actresses will be elevated if an example be made of those who brazenly violate the moral code of a Christian nation, therefore . . .

To her credit, one San Francisco club woman who had

been an active watchdog at Roscoe's trials, Mrs. W. B. Hamilton, publicly opposed the mob rule she saw developing. She asked a meeting of Vigilantes, 'Where is your forgiveness?' Her question was greeted with boos and shouts of 'sob stuff!'

'I do not believe in taking the whole pound of flesh out of Arbuckle,' Mrs Hamilton went on, to continued jeers. 'Why should he be made to pay for the sins of the whole moving picture industry? As your representative, I attended the Arbuckle trials and I know that he could not have been convicted of manslaughter on the evidence presented. As long as he has been reinstated, what can be done about it, and why not give him his chance to make good as a man, anyway?'

Mrs Hamilton got her answer from Dr Mariana Bertola: 'Arbuckle can prove himself a man some other way. We have no objection to his running a teahouse in Japan or anywhere else. What we do object to is having him paraded before little boys and girls, to be idolized and emulated. I believe this move on the part of Will Hays is just a feeler to test women's sentiment, and believe that it would be fatal to the cause of decency to weaken in our demand for the punishment of these moral offenders now.'

For people like Dr Bertola, acquittal was not enough, after all.

Hays refused to change his stand, declaring that he would not be the 'single judge for 110 million people, or for a great industry and art' – although that, of course, is precisely what he had been when he had imposed the ban in April. The ban had implied that Roscoe was guilty of *something* – and if he was guilty, he must be punished, if not for his own good, then for the good of America, or at least to show the movie industry's good intentions.

After his Christmas Eve statement, Roscoe had returned to work – in *Handy Andy*, a two-reel comedy starring

Molly Malone and Roscoe (and financed by Gavin McNab). Before the cameras, he struggled to revive his comic ability, anxious to get down to what he knew best: making funny movies. Each night he returned to the West Adams house to find reporters waiting for a stinging retort to the latest vitriolic statements about him. Invariably he replied, 'No comment.'

Roscoe was prepared to fight it out indefinitely, but in mid-January Adolph Zukor and Will Hays appealed to him to bow out. There was no question of the ban being reinstated – the loss of face would have been disastrous. Hays and Zukor told Roscoe that the situation was crippling the industry and pointed out that, if the controversy continued indefinitely, it would hit the box office hard, causing a recession within the industry which would throw many of his friends out of work.

Towards the end of January, Roscoe had reached breaking point. He announced that he had signed a contract to direct motion pictures for a comedy film corporation and that he was 'done with acting'. His statement continued: 'My greatest ambition is to make people laugh and make them happy, and I can do it best as a director of comedies. This is my chance to make good in the right way and in the profession that I know and love, and in a way that will meet the approval of all. I start work at once, and from now on you will hear from me only through the medium of the comedies that I direct.'

Whether Arbuckle ever finished filming *Handy Andy* remains a mystery. Some sources say the film was scrapped, others that it was completed for foreign distribution. Roscoe's public statement came as 'a complete surprise' to Will Hays, who told the press:

> The natural and proper factors, operating in a natural way, have concluded this matter in a manner that should be satisfactory to all.
>
> I am sure that the industry will meet and rightly settle,

as they arise, all of the difficulties incident to its growth and development.

Roscoe was to be left no shred of dignity. The movie moguls decided that the name Roscoe 'Fatty' Arbuckle could not be used for the director's credit; Roscoe would have to use another name. He chose his father's, William Goodrich. Buster Keaton remarked that the moguls might prefer Will B. Good, a name that many film historians later said Roscoe did use; they missed the point that Keaton was simply making a sick joke. Many of the films Roscoe subsequently directed bear no director's credit; a number of film companies thought no name at all preferable to a nom de plume.

Between January and May 1923, Roscoe directed five two-reel films for a company called Reel Comedies. He was restless to perform himself. In January, with controversy about Roscoe at its height, he had received an offer from comedians Weber and Fields to star in a New York stage revue. He had turned it down, thinking at the time that he would still return to the screen, but after his decision to work in films only as a director, he reconsidered the possibility of performing in theatres and nightclubs. Finally he decided to accept an engagement in Chicago.

Roscoe's friends in Hollywood pleaded with him not to begin his comeback in Chicago, where he would be exposed to crippling hostility. Virginia Rappe's name was linked with the town. Although born in New York, she had spent most of her life in Chicago; during the trials, prejudice against Roscoe had been whipped to a fever pitch in the windy city by Hearst's Chicago *Herald & Examiner*.

After being reminded that feeling against him ran high in Chicago because of Virginia Rappe's death, Roscoe replied stubbornly: 'I want to be accepted, not just here in Hollywood, but everywhere. I'm not going to duck out of the tough spots. These people that keep knifing me, they don't know me. I'm not a rapist. I'm not a monster. I've got to get there and prove that to them.'

So in May 1923, Roscoe once again made the front page of the *Herald & Examiner*, this time with the news that he had been hired by the city's Marigold Garden for an eight-week engagement.

The nightclub had guaranteed Roscoe a minimum salary of $2,500 a week, and he needed every penny of it. Not only did he owe Schenck a great sum for trial costs, but he also had over $100,000 in tax debts, and he was still paying Minta handsomely. (He paid her between $2,000 and $3,000 a month virtually until the time of his death.)

It was to be his first stage appearance in ten years. Although he had begun his career on the stage in Santa Ana in the summer of 1895, he hadn't performed before a live audience since before his days at Keystone. He actually went into training for his comeback. He exercised and ran around the swimming pool of the West Adams residence in his track suit, toning up a body that had been inactive too long.

On the night of 4 June 1923, 2,500 people crowded into the Marigold Garden, buzzing with expectation. On stage was a big white screen. Suddenly the lights dimmed, and the audience grew hushed. A projector whirled; on the screen appeared a film of Roscoe, running hell-for-leather towards the camera – and the audience. The image grew bigger and bigger. Suddenly Roscoe himself plunged through the screen, executed a perfect pratfall, and landed on the stage.

For a moment, there was silence. Then the room filled with applause that went on and on. At one table, the mayor of the city cheered the comedian. At another, Al Capone cried as he clapped. (Roscoe was Capone's favourite film star; a photograph of the comic hung on a wall of his apartment until the gangster's death.)

Roscoe beamed and bowed to the audience throughout the ovation. When the noise had subsided enough for him to be heard, he said, 'I thank you from the bottom of my heart. It is the first real smile I have had in a long, long time.' Then he went into his act, a piece of trick comedy with two Indian clubs. The encores continued into the small hours of the morning.

The Chicago *Herald & Examiner* reported a 'bedlam of applause the like of which has never been equalled in the place'.

Not everyone was delighted with Roscoe's reception at the Marigold Garden. Two days later *The New York Times* carried an article headed 'THE FATTED CALF IN CHICAGO', which said in part: 'There was doubtless as much insincerity in the general outcry against Arbuckle as there is in the present rush to welcome him to the sheepfold . . . The public soon forgets . . .'

Two days later the paper could report that some of the public had remembered: plans for Roscoe to appear in Kansas City had met with protest. It seemed that for each step forwards, Roscoe was to take two steps backwards.

In the White House, President Harding had been replaced by President Coolidge, who summed up one of the nation's problems with this immortal line: 'When more and more people are thrown out of work, unemployment results.'

Roscoe knew how it felt to be 'thrown out of work'.

Film director James Cruze was one of the loyal friends who tried to help Roscoe, in a way that was courageous by the standards of the day. As the filmography at the back of this book indicates, in 1923 Cruze made *Hollywood*, a massive, star-studded feature film about the life of the film colony. Cruze had decided to make a public comment about what had been done to his friend, and he chose *Hollywood* to make it in. In one scene we see the back of an actor as he goes to a casting director's office. Seeing the actor approaching, the casting director hangs a sign: NO WORK TODAY. The actor turns and faces the camera. It is Roscoe Arbuckle.

Roscoe itched to appear in films again, but although the ban on his films – and on his further performance in front of the camera – had been lifted, the films were not shown in America, Great Britain, and Australia, among other countries. Frequently, rival film companies encouraged the agitation that kept his films off the world's screens – and out of competition with their own. Whatever the reason, he was unemployable as a screen actor and comedian. He continued to direct two-reel comedies and to appear on stage, but the strain on the man was showing. He began to drink.

Ben Lyon, who went to Hollywood in 1923, recalled for me the first party he attended: 'For me it was a fantastic experience. All of those people that I had paid my nickels and dimes to see were there: Viola Dana, Jack Pickford, Shirley Mason, Anna Q. Nilsson, Doug Fairbanks. This party had been going on for over twenty-four hours before I got there. One of the first things I saw was Fatty Arbuckle being carried out drunk. The party went on for another three days.'

Drink provided the man only temporary relief from the everyday struggle. In Newark, New Jersey, the police chief barred Roscoe from appearing at a local club. Roscoe took him to court, and the judge ruled in Roscoe's favour, saying, 'Roscoe Arbuckle, like any other man, has the right to make a living.'

Late in 1923, Roscoe once again met Doris Deane, the attractive young actress with whom he had shared dinner on the ferry from San Francisco to Los Angeles the day after the Labor Day party. Doris, whose real name was Doris Dibble, was the daughter of a man who manufactured and sold musical instruments. Born in Butte, Montana, in 1900, she had lived in New York and Chicago before her family moved to Pasadena, California. There she finished her schooling before she returned to New York, to dance with the Mary Morgan troupe. After playing small parts in several J. Stuart Blackton movies in New York, Doris went West again. She made films for MGM, Universal, and, from 1923 to 1925, on the Keaton lot. It was while working for Keaton that she re-encountered Roscoe – and that Roscoe and she fell in love.

At first her family was far from delighted. Doris's relatives didn't mind her friendship with Larry Semon, the film comedian, or with Jack Dempsey, but Roscoe's reputation made them afraid at first for Doris to be associated with him. They changed their minds when they met him. Roscoe, who was usually reluctant to talk about the affair at the St Francis, sat down with Doris and her family one day and related everything that had happened the day of the party. He told them about Virginia Rappe's pregnancy at the time of the party and gave details he hadn't even told Minta – details on which I drew for part of the background in Part Two of this book.

Doris soon realized how seriously Roscoe had been damaged:

> He was stunned. I remember him saying, 'A person can lose their money, their home, all of their possessions. These you can work for and reacquire. But when you've lost your good name, you've lost everything.'
>
> He was so easily hurt. He could not put it behind him. It was too much a part of his life. It had happened so suddenly, so instantly. He was at the height of his powers. He had so much more to offer and there he was being prevented from contributing to it.

Roscoe wrote to tell Minta that he loved Doris and wanted to marry her. Minta began divorce proceedings in November 1923, but it was nearly two years before Roscoe was free to remarry.

His friends in Hollywood were delighted at the romance, especially Buster Keaton and his wife, Natalie Talmadge. The four became inseparable.

In early 1924, Roscoe directed what many consider a film classic, Buster Keaton's *Sherlock Jr.* Most film historians who write of the filming of the movie follow the account given by Keaton in his autobiography: Keaton, determined to help his friend, got him a job directing *Sherlock*, but the assignment was a disaster. Roscoe was impatient and irritable. He snapped at everybody and reduced the leading lady to tears a dozen times. Keaton and Lou Anger arranged to ease Roscoe off the film so that Roscoe wouldn't know what they had done. According to Keaton, Roscoe was asked to direct *The Red Mill*, a spectacular feature starring Marion Davies, and Roscoe 'excitedly rang up Lou Anger in a dilemma'. He wanted to accept the offer, but didn't want to let Buster down. Anger told him to grab the chance; they would finish *Sherlock* without him. Roscoe accepted and everyone was happy.

Perhaps Keaton's memory was simply failing him when he told this story. Nearly three years elapsed between the filming of *Sherlock Jr* and the filming of *The Red Mill*, and according to Doris Deane, who was on the set while *Sherlock* was made, Roscoe directed the picture from start to finish, and provided the story idea as well.

Curiously, the film was inspired by the performances of E. O. Heinrich, the fingerprint expert who testified for the prosecution during Roscoe's trials. In the opening scene, Keaton recaptures to perfection Heinrich's courtroom performance with a magnifying glass. Roscoe had remembered the courtroom reaction to 'Sherlock' Heinrich and Salome 'Watson' and had used it to good effect in Keaton's film.

In May 1924, with the Keaton film finished, Roscoe signed to do a one-year tour of the Pantages circuit, a string of vaudeville houses that stretched across the United States. It was the second time Pantages had hired Roscoe; he spoke warmly of the stage act Roscoe had done for him years before in San Francisco and Seattle.

Now as Roscoe began his tour once again in San Francisco, he played to an audience that included District Attorney Matthew Brady. Little more than a year before, Brady had led the fight to imprison Arbuckle for the death of Virginia Rappe. Now he joined the San Francisco audience in a standing ovation.

Alexander Pantages was later to have some idea what Roscoe's experience had been like. On 9 August 1929, a 17-year-old girl named Eunice Pringle came to his office above the Pantages Theater in Los Angeles, looking for work. He declined to book her and she accused him of raping her. He was tried, found guilty, and sentenced to fifty years in prison. His lawyer, Jerry Geisler – a protégé of Earl Rogers – appealed to the California Supreme Court, and on the basis of his appeal they ordered a second trial. At the second trial it was established that Eunice Pringle, an aspiring actress, had attempted to compromise Pantages in an effort to get work on the Pantages circuit. Pantages was found not guilty.

Geisler's appeal to the Supreme Court was a brilliant piece of advocacy, resulting in an historical decision. He argued that it was prejudicial to the defendant to exclude testimony about the morals of the plaintiff, even though she was under age. (Until then, if the plaintiff were under age, the question of consent or moral character could not be made a trial issue.) Geisler argued that it was important for the jury to hear a discussion of her morals so that they could judge the reliability of her testimony. The Supreme Court agreed. Geisler was to make full use of this precedent in 1943, when he defended Errol Flynn against similar charges of rape.

During Roscoe's year on the road the general public accepted him, but he occasionally experienced hostility. One night in Long Beach, California – the city where he and Minta had been married on stage – he had already performed twice at Hoyt's Theatre and was due to go on again, when word reached him that the city council was at that very moment debating a petition to ban him from all Long Beach theatres. He jumped in a car and rushed to city hall, while an animal act opened the third show. Perspiring freely, and followed by a crowd that had gotten wind that something was going on, he rushed into the council chamber and asked for permission to speak. It was granted. He reminded the council members that he had been acquitted and said, 'Even District Attorney Brady told me after the trial that I deserved acquittal. Now I am here, earning a living in the only way I know how. I am still nearly $200,000 in debt to the people who stood behind me and believed in me enough to let me acquire that debt and much more.'

Cheers rang out through the council chamber.

Councilman Condit, the man who had filed the petition to ban Roscoe from the stage, stood up and said, 'If Mr Arbuckle is in debt to nearly $200,000, I am willing to contribute towards a fund that will get this poor boy out of debt, but I am not in favour of permitting him to appear before the men, women and children of Long Beach on a public stage.'

This was greeted with boos from the packed council chamber.

'I am not looking for charity,' Roscoe answered. 'I only ask the right to earn a living. I don't care for your money.' Pointing to the American flag that hung in the chamber, Roscoe continued, 'I am merely asking for what the flag guarantees me – truth, liberty and justice.'

With that, Roscoe dashed back to the theatre to take his top-of-the-bill spot as the penultimate act. After heated argument at city hall, the petition to ban Roscoe was thrown out.

Jackie Coogan recalled for me Roscoe's performance that year on the Pantages circuit: 'He used to play ukulele, sing songs, tell jokes and dance. For such a big man – God, he was light. When he danced, he floated. A first-class entertainer.'

In Atlantic City, New Jersey, Roscoe met Minta, who

was appearing in vaudeville at a rival theatre. He told her what he was feeling:

'My heart's in my mouth every time I walk out on the stage. I'm in a cold sweat waiting for the audience's reaction. I fear that they will call out, "Rapist! Monster! Murderer!" '

Roscoe paid all of Minta's hotel bills during that week in Atlantic City. Later in the year, when she went to Paris to obtain a divorce, he bought her a fur coat for the trip and paid a man to act as her protective escort. (In the 1920s, one went to Paris for a foreign divorce. When the French began to resist being thus used, Americans turned first to Mexico for divorces, then in the early 1970s to the Dominican Republic and Haiti.) On 27 January 1925, after almost seventeen years of marriage, Minta Durfee and Roscoe Arbuckle were divorced. They squabbled over alimony, but when I met Minta many years later, she still used Arbuckle's name, and after two weeks of interview, she remarked: 'I have only one last thing to say to you. If I had my whole life to live over again, I would marry the same man.'

On 16 May 1925, Roscoe married Doris Deane at the home of her parents in San Marino, California. Roscoe was ahead of his time; the word 'obey' was omitted from the wedding ceremony.

There was a distinguished guest list. Roscoe's best man was Buster Keaton, and the matron of honour was Buster's wife, Natalie Talmadge. Charlie Chaplin was there, as well as Natalie's sister Constance, and Constance's husband, Joseph Schenck, whom Roscoe now considered his best friend. Doris recalled: 'On Father's Day I sent flowers to Joe from Roscoe. When we were going to get married, Roscoe asked Joe Schenck for his approval.'

After a wedding reception in Buster's home, the couple went to live in a house owned by Schenck, on North Canyon Drive in Beverly Hills.

Doris encouraged Roscoe to believe in himself. He was

determined that he should once again be a top film comedian. But it would not be easy. Doris recalled that time for me:

> It was very trying. Yes, he was bitter. I tried to get him away from that feeling of bitterness. His name was Roscoe Conkling Arbuckle. He always signed his name Roscoe C. Arbuckle. When people asked him what the *C.* stood for, he would say, 'Crucified'.
>
> He had a lot to contend with. We were at a party one night at Billy Camp's over at Beverly. Roscoe was strumming on his ukulele, which he loved. Some people, out of the business, out of the profession, came over to him. He didn't like to be with anybody out of the profession. He had withdrawn. People in the business didn't point fingers at him; those outside did. This woman came up to him. First thing she does is ask in a loud voice, 'Hey, why are you called Fatty?' Then she said to him, 'This isn't a very lively party. I bet that one you gave in the St Francis was better.' Roscoe just froze. He told her to get away, to get out.

Another incident a few days after their marriage reinforced Roscoe's mistrust of people. A group led by a Mrs Murphy told Roscoe that unless he paid them $100,000, they would expose him as a man who neglected his family and refused to help his brother Arthur, who was supposedly having a rough time financially. Doris insisted on calling the district attorney's office, and plainclothes police officers exposed the conspiracy. Doris produced cancelled cheques to show the press that, far from neglecting his family, Roscoe had been generous with them. Roscoe refused to press charges against Mrs Murphy, fearing that 'to do so would only stir up a lot more publicity, and I don't want it'.

Roscoe refused to go out, except to work. On stage, after the initial moments of fear, he could lose himself in his act, and he had no trouble directing men like Lupino Lane on a film set. Among people in the industry, he could relax. When the public was around, he felt he had to be on guard.

Buster Keaton would bring the latest movies over to Roscoe's house, and they would watch them privately to see what other people in the business were doing. Eventually Doris persuaded him to go to the theatre and finally even to the cinema and to film premières. She recalled: 'You cannot possibly imagine the reception he used to receive when he began to attend film premières. When he was introduced on stage before the show, the audiences would rise in their seats. The applause was staggering, the reception accorded to him tumultuous.'

In August 1925, James Quirk, the editor of *Photoplay* magazine, ran a full-page editorial, which began: 'I would like to see Roscoe Arbuckle come back to the screen. More than that, I believe that the vast majority of the people in the United States, if they would stop to consider the matter, will share that desire with me.'

He wrote of the 'bitterness of the press', saying, 'No man since time began was ever tried in more adverse circumstances.' Reminding his readers that Roscoe was a great screen comedian and that 'there isn't a better comedy director in the world', he urged the public to right what was 'a great injustice'.

The public wasn't ready for fair play.

Roscoe was a member of the Masquers, a society for theatre and film people which planned in October 1925, to have a gala evening in the auditorium of Hollywood High School. One of the several comedy sketches on the programme involved Roscoe. When the board of education learned that Roscoe was taking part, it withdrew permission for use of the premises, saying it had had 'scores of protests'.

The incident affected Roscoe deeply. It had been over three years since his acquittal, and he was still being punished for a crime he didn't commit.

Roscoe's arrest in 1921 had interrupted his career at its

peak. He had had less than four years to establish himself with Comique – from March 1917, when he began *The Butcher Boy*, until September 1921, when he was arrested for the death of Virginia Rappe. Now his career lay in the shadow of four comic stars whom posterity would consider the comedy élite of the silent era – Keaton, Chaplin, Langdon and Lloyd. In the decades to come, Roscoe would seldom be mentioned except in connection with the scandal – and rarely seen. But all four comic greats were indebted to him, either for his direct help in their lives, or for the influence of his work on theirs. Who is to say how his career would have developed had his professional life as an actor not ended prematurely?

Buster Keaton never failed to acknowledge his debt to Roscoe. More important, Keaton tried to keep Roscoe's hope alive. Towards the end of 1925, Buster was making a feature called *Go West*. One day he showed up on the set at the Educational studios, where Roscoe was directing two-reelers, and spoke quietly to Roscoe. Babe London, who was making a film for Roscoe, recalled what happened next:

> Buster turned to me and said, 'Come over to the studios tonight and wear your rompers, Babe.' (I used to wear rompers a lot in those days, playing small children.) 'We're going to have a few laughs,' Buster said.
>
> That evening, Roscoe and I went over to Buster's studio. I didn't know what it was all about or what was going to happen. We sat around for a while in Buster's dressing room, more like an apartment than a dressing room – kitchen, dining room, dressing room. A man could live there; Buster frequently did. I remember Roscoe and I were sitting in the corner at a big table. After a while Roscoe got up and tried to get past me, tried to squeeze between me and the table. Now, as you can see, I'm a big woman. I was known at one time as the female Fatty Arbuckle. Roscoe tried to get past me and got stuck. He sat down on my lap facing me. He looked at me, looked

around at Buster and his crew, who were roaring with laughter, then he looked back at me and said, 'Hey, Babe, you know, I believe we could do it. It wouldn't be much of a thrill, but it would be a hell of a laugh.'

[Roscoe went out of the room and] after a while he returned, dressed as a woman. God, he made a better woman than I do. Then he and Buster told me what it was all about. Roscoe was going to play my mother, and we were going to shoot a scene for *Go West*. We went out on to the set, a big department store. Roscoe did the most incredible falls. He'd dive over the counter and come up smiling. To Buster and him the whole thing was a laugh. We're right there in the film. It was their way of thumbing their noses at the people who had decreed that Roscoe could not appear on the screen.

Roscoe was working for Educational Pictures, directing two-reelers, which by 1925 were the poor man's film. (Ironically one of the first of these, *His First Car*, which Roscoe did not direct under his own name, was voted the best short of the year in a women's club competition.)

He hadn't lost his sense of humour, on or off the set. In one short that he made with Doris, a scene called for her to land hard on her backside. Roscoe, unhappy with the comic timing of the fall, shot take after take, all day long. Doris recalled: 'By the end of the day I was as stiff as a plank, and very bruised, but we finally got it into the can. When I got back to our home, I saw that Roscoe had had the dinner table laid for one. I asked him where I was supposed to eat. He just pointed at the mantelpiece. There was my meal laid out – candles and flowers, everything. He looked at me and smiled, 'Thought you might prefer to stand this one out, dear.'

Doris tells another amusing story of a memorable evening in March 1926. They had been invited to Keaton's for dinner, and after the meal Roscoe, who had just bought a new Lincoln, said, 'Let's take a little ride.' Doris and Natalie, in full-length evening dresses and fur coats, trooped out and sat in the back while the men climbed in front. Doris recalled:

We began to chat on the drive, Natalie and I. The boys up front seemed to be immersed in something. Well, time went by, and suddenly I said to Pops [her name for Roscoe], 'We seem to have been driving a long time. Where are we?' Buster turned to me with that exquisite deadpan face of his and just said one word: 'Yosemite'. They had driven us over four hundred miles.

Now, Yosemite Park was not open to the public at this time. They were still building the highway through, using convict labour from San Quentin. The boys had decided to take a little surprise vacation. There we were, in the middle of nowhere, in fur coats and evening dresses. By now it's morning. We stopped at a drugstore near Yosemite and picked up a few things. The boys told us that they intended to spend a few days in the park. Well, now, no women were allowed in the area because of the convict labour, but of course the prison road camp sergeant in charge of the road works recognizes Buster and Roscoe. He just told us to duck down in the back seat so that the convicts didn't get too excited at seeing real live women, and we drove through. The lodge was open, just. We had a marvellous time. Real back-to-nature stuff.

Then the word comes through that we have been forbidden to leave. Word had got out that there were two women in Yosemite, in a prohibited area. The State Highway Commission said that all roads were closed to us until they had had a full investigation. The boys discussed the situation. Roscoe had to get back to Hollywood to begin direction on a new movie, and Buster was due to start work, too. They didn't really have time to wait for the open season. So they rang up the railroad. There was a track running through the reserve. They hired a whole train, a Pullman car for us, and a flat wagon to put the car on. The train pulls into Yosemite, then pulls out again with all of us and the Lincoln on board.

By mid-1926, Roscoe and Doris were frequent visitors to the San Simeon castle of William Randolph Hearst, the newspaper baron whose editorials had helped to build public feeling against Roscoe in 1921 and 1922. At one dinner party they attended, Hearst made the classic remark: 'I never knew any more about your case, Roscoe, than I read in my newspapers.'

Hearst's mistress, Marion Davies, had wanted Roscoe to direct one of her feature films, and he got his chance with *The Red Mill*, a movie based on the musical comedy by Victor Herbert and Henry Blossom. The film went into production for MGM in late 1926, with Miss Davies starring and 'William Goodrich' directing (and with Owen Moore, Mary Pickford's first husband, in the cast). It looked as if Roscoe had finally made the big step from two-reelers to feature films.

Throughout her career Marion Davies had struggled to maintain her own identity, to be considered more than merely an adornment of the multimillionaire. Because of Hearst's insecurity and mistrust, it was not easy for her to find privacy.

On the set, Roscoe noticed a very large woman who was not part of the production. When he asked his assistant who the woman was, he learned that she was a former policewoman hired by Hearst to 'protect' Marion. She went everywhere that Marion went and gave Hearst daily reports on what Marion was doing. Hearst often visited the set, and when the policewoman followed Marion to the ladies' room, Hearst followed the policewoman. He would wait outside the ladies' room until the two women emerged; then the three of them would walk back to the film set.

Hearst was also watching Roscoe, and apparently he didn't like what he saw. King Vidor told me what happened:

> During the shooting, they became worried about Roscoe's direction. They became very concerned with his

work. Hearst sent for me and persuaded me to go on to the set and supervise and generally watch what was going on, keeping the film on agreed lines. It was an awkward situation for both of us. It was terrible. They had apparently got Roscoe's consent, but it was still one hell of a situation. I had to be there, on set, all the time until the movie was finished. Roscoe was obliged to consult with me about setup, every shot. I don't know what Hearst and the moguls were making a fuss about. The job he was doing was all right. I never had any conflict with Roscoe about the situation. The man was too gentle for that; he never got in conflict. I didn't get any money for the assignment. Hearst gave me a diamond-studded watch. I've still got it.

The film was a success, but at a cost to Roscoe. King Vidor's presence on the set weighed heavily against the encouragement he had steadily received from Doris, and from friends like Buster Keaton and Natalie Talmadge, Joseph Schenck, James Cruze and his wife, actress Betty Compson.

Doris tried to persuade Roscoe that he had a talent for directing features, but it was a slow business convincing a man to believe in himself when he had been systematically stripped of his self-confidence: 'If I had been older, I might have been more able to cope with the situation. I'd had a number of poison-pen letters when I married him. They didn't bother me, but they upset him terribly. For me, some of the time it was like being a mother to a baby. I tried so hard to be gentle, but it was hard, very hard, day after day. He began drinking very heavily. So did I. For him it was an escape. For me it was a relief. I just was not equipped to repair the damage that had been done to that man.'

Roscoe finished *The Red Mill* early in 1927, and was under contract to Famous Players-Lasky to direct *Special Delivery*, a feature starring Eddie Cantor and William Powell. Again there were problems. The story, written by Cantor, centred on a mail robbery, and halfway through filming the Hays Office advised the producers that the government would not permit even a comic mail robbery to be shown on the screen. The story was rewritten by committee, never an ideal method for developing comedy, and comedian Larry Semon, an ex-boyfriend of Doris Deane's and a friend of Roscoe's, was brought on the set to 'assist' in much the same way King Vidor had assisted on the set for *The Red Mill*. Despite these problems, however, the film was fairly successful and lit a spark of hope in Roscoe.

In March 1927, hope flared when he signed a contract worth nearly three million dollars with Abe Carlos, an independent film producer – a contract, moreover, which called for Roscoe not to direct, but to perform – to be once again a film comedian. A film was to be made in Berlin and released internationally, in the United States as well as elsewhere. Shooting would start towards the end of the year.

Roscoe was determined to get out of debt. A number of people had suggested that he take the easy way out and declare bankruptcy, but Roscoe was horrified at the idea of reneging on debts to friends. Doris took care of his accounts now, since money had little real meaning for him. As Doris recalls, 'Roscoe just earned it and let me look after it. I remember showing him how to write out a cheque eventually.' It was beginning to look as if the debt would be paid off.

With his star in the ascendant, Roscoe began a fourteen-week tour of the Pantages circuit.

At the same time, the news reached the press that his second marriage was falling apart. Both Roscoe and Doris denied the divorce rumours that filled the newpapers, but their friends knew better. The marriage wasn't over yet, but it was damaged beyond repair.

Two incidents that occurred on the vaudeville tour illustrate two recurring themes in Roscoe's life: his generosity in helping people in whom he spotted talent, and the apparent eagerness of others to misinterpret his behaviour.

In Cleveland an eager young man asked Roscoe to help him get a start in show business. The young man did a song-and-dance act that impressed Roscoe, who urged him to go to Hollywood. Roscoe gave the fellow a list of people to contact, saying, 'Tell them I said you're good. They'll give you a break.' He called up friends to tell them to watch out for a talented youth named Bob Hope.

The other incident occurred in Milwaukee. Roscoe was later to tell the story: 'I was talking with some of the stagehands in the alley behind the theatre, and I told them a joke, and to kind of illustrate it I put my hat on the side of my head and walked funny. The evening papers came out with the big headline that Roscoe Arbuckle was seen staggering drunk at the stage entrance to the Pantages Theatre.'

As Doris insisted during my interviews with her, 'Sure he would drink, sometimes very heavily, but never, and I mean never, when he was working. He considered that to drink while you were working was unprofessional.'

On 9 June, Roscoe turned to the legitimate stage in a play called *Baby Mine*, which opened at Chanin's Theatre in New York. In the play with him was a young actor whom Roscoe had recommended to the management as a 'boy that's going to go a long way'. The boy's name was Humphrey Bogart.

Doris was on the West Coast, but Minta Durfee was in the audience for opening night. The first act went well in the packed theatre, but there was something about Roscoe's movement that puzzled Minta, so she went backstage during the intermission to see what was wrong.

> He had put on a Kid McCoy belt [a corset] to hold his stomach in. It was crippling him. I insisted that he take it off. I told him, 'You've always been a big man. You've picked a fine time to try to hide the fact.' I helped him undress. He had just got down to his underpants when

Humphrey Bogart came in. Confronting Bogart was Roscoe in his underpants and me in my furs and jewels.

Bogart didn't say a word, just stood there with his mouth going in that way of his.

Roscoe turned round and said, 'I'd like you to meet my wife, Minty.'

Bogart said, 'I thought your wife's name was Doris.'

Roscoe was a bit nonplussed, then he said, 'Well, it is, but this is my wife too.'

Bogart's mouth began to twitch again, then he said, 'Well, I suppose it's OK. You're big enough to have two wives.'

Everything Roscoe did now was a test of one kind or another. In *Baby Mine* the question was whether Roscoe would be accepted in the serious theatre. Intolerance was still in the air in America in 1927, as two men not far from New York, Sacco and Vanzetti, were soon to find out.

The day after the play opened, *The New York Times* reported that the applause at the end of the first night was 'of almost record length'. Roscoe, they said, gave a 'fairly satisfactory performance'. Coming from the *Times*, which had been hasty in reporting bad news about Roscoe, such faint praise was praise indeed to the comedian.

During the New York run, Abe Carlos told Roscoe that there was a snag in the film deal. Both Carlos and Joe Schenck wanted Roscoe to fire his agent, Sidney Cohen (Lou Anger was now Buster Keaton's studio manager). They didn't want Cohen involved in Roscoe's future; if Roscoe wanted the film job, he had to let Cohen go. Roscoe thought it over for a few days, then told Carlos, 'I can't tell the guy I don't want him around. It would hurt his feelings.'

That was that. The film deal was scrapped. Roscoe's dream of working before the cameras was once again just a dream.

★

With rumours of their divorce appearing almost daily in the newspapers, Roscoe and Doris sailed for Europe in early 1928. He had been booked to appear in a variety show at the Empire Theatre in Paris. I would like now to correct another part of the Arbuckle myth that sprang up at this time.

Buster Keaton in his life story says that Roscoe was booed from the Paris stage – not because the French objected to the scandal that was for ever linked with the name of Arbuckle, but because 'the French just did not find the once-great comic funny any more'. American newspaper clippings from the time tend to support Keaton's view.

The facts, according to Doris Deane, are far more interesting, and my research in Paris tends to confirm what she told me.

Roscoe had been told by the management that he would be playing to an English-speaking audience drawn from the many Americans and Englishmen in Paris. But the audience began to heckle Roscoe in French as soon as he started his act on opening night. He was playing in English to a group that seemed to understand only French. Roscoe told the theatre management that night, 'Right, I want my act translated into French. Get me somebody who is bilingual.'

By the following evening he had the routine word-perfect in French, thanks to his ear for languages. He finished his run at the Empire Theatre to capacity business.

Roscoe returned to New York in May 1928, and played vaudeville again. Doris Deane recalled:

> More than anything he wanted to return to the screen. He kept on and on trying to get people in the industry to employ him. Not to direct – he got as much of that kind of work as he wanted, more than he could handle. He

wanted to perform, to get in front of that camera and be funny. It was as if he was only half alive, that he knew the only way to be a whole man again was in front of the camera, making the millions laugh. He was such a shy man, such a gentle man. He had, for example, a very high sense of morality. I remember walking into the bathroom one night. He was naked, just getting out of the bath. He was very embarrassed. Now, we'd been married several years when that happened. Such a shy man. He would never make love to me with the lights on, never make love to me during the daytime. Said he never had and never would.

Doris continued: 'It got very bitter towards the end. We used to fight, not physically, but with words. I just could not cope with the situation. God, it wasn't his fault the marriage shattered. I hadn't taken on one man for better or for worse. I'd taken on the American nation, or at least quite a big part of it. I just didn't have the ability to cope with the problems that the constant rejections of the man created.'

In early August 1928, Roscoe and Doris were divorced.

As one door closed, another opened. Roscoe had become co-owner of the Plantation Club, a nightclub in Culver City, near many of the film studios. He had gone into partnership with two other men to reopen the defunct club. Word got around Hollywood that he was short of money and was struggling to get the club ready for opening night. The film colony, perhaps feeling guilty about having abandoned Roscoe once before, responded with unique enthusiasm.

Cedric Gibbons, the MGM art director who had designed the sets for *The Red Mill*, offered to plan the club's decor and to organize the workers, and refused to accept a fee. It was a gesture many would repeat.

If the roof had fallen in on the first-nighters at the

Plantation Club, the film industry would have been wiped out. Lew Cody grabbed the microphone to praise 'Roscoe "Fatty" Arbuckle, the funniest man in America!' Tom Mix, complete with six-guns and half a dozen 'pardners', took over the orchestra. Buster Keaton did an act. So did Mary Pickford, Douglas Fairbanks, Charlie Chaplin, Harry Langdon, Larry Semon, Ruth Roland, Marshal Neilan, Bebe Daniels, and the three Talmadge sisters. James Cruze, who hated dress suits and hadn't worn one for three years, put one on. Mabel Normand had a life-sized model of 'Fatty' made in flowers and presented it to him. Leatrice Joy gave Roscoe a plaque that read: 'We owe Mr Arbuckle a debt of gratitude. He has shown the miracle of patience without bitterness in a world of injustice.'

Roscoe went on the small nightclub stage and cried. Then he took a deep breath and did his routine. The ovation was reminiscent of that at the Marigold Garden in Chicago.

Amazingly, it was not just a one-night phenomenon. As the weeks and then the months went by, the film world competed to support its former golden boy. Million-dollar actors performed at the Plantation Club for nothing. Al Jolson sang thirty songs one evening. Fanny Brice sang. Jack Warner, the movie mogul who always referred to actors as 'those bums', sang – the only time he ever sang in public. John Barrymore, with many a drink under his belt, camped it up with thirteen-year-old Jackie Coogan. The Plantation Club became Hollywood's meeting place.

Roscoe would amble on to the stage and stamp his foot three times for silence. His comedy routines were shaded with poignancy:

> I met a girl on a train. She asked me, 'Excuse me, are you Mr Arbuckle?'
>
> I said to her, 'Why, yes, I am.'
>
> She said, 'Can you tell me how to get into the movies?'

'Pardon me, young lady, but can you tell *me* how to get into the movies?'

The stock market collapsed in 1929, and the following year Roscoe sold his nightclub business. He went back to directing movies, always hoping to make a comeback as a film comedian. One of the women he directed at Educational Pictures was actress Louise Brooks, who recalled for Kevin Brownlow's book *The Parade's Gone By* her memories of Roscoe in May 1931: 'He made no attempt to direct the picture. He sat in his chair like a man dead. He had been very nice and sweetly dead ever since the scandal that ruined his career. But it was such an amazing thing for me to come in to make this broken-down picture and to find my director was the great Roscoe Arbuckle. Oh, I thought he was magnificent in films. He was a wonderful dancer – a wonderful ballroom dancer, in his heyday. It was like floating in the arms of a huge doughnut – really delightful.'

Roscoe had been engaged to heiress Dorothy Wallace, but it was a short-lived affair. Now he was to meet a woman who would give him fresh heart – a beautiful young actress whose name was Addie Oakley Dukes McPhail, though she went by the shorter Addie McPhail.

Born in White Plains, Kentucky, in 1906, Addie was married to Lindsay McPhail, the songwriter and pianist. By 1930, she had starred in several movies, one of which Roscoe had just seen. He hadn't yet met her, but a few weeks later he was directing her in *Up a Tree* for Educational. He fell in love with her at once.

Unlike Louise Brooks, Addie did not find Roscoe a dead man. She recalled for me:

> When I met him he was a jolly, big-hearted individual. He was very forbearing with other people. He didn't like people to talk about what had happened. He didn't want sympathy. He didn't like people to call him 'Fatty'. He resented that, disliked it intensely – that was his screen

character – but even that he bore quietly. Once in a while, if he got overtired or had been drinking, he might get a little tetchy with certain people, but who doesn't? I think he was hurt, deeply hurt by what had happened – with the prejudice, with the intolerance, with the false friends.

Of course, Roscoe had genuine friends. Addie gave me a cable that comedian Joe Lewis sent to Roscoe when he was engaged at the Playhouse Theatre in Hollywood: 'I passed by the Playhouse Theatre and saw you billed so I passed by the Playhouse Theatre.'

Lewis also sent a wire telling Roscoe that he was an inspiration to every comedian in America, that whenever a comedian had a bad night, or died on stage and thought of throwing it in, he thought of Roscoe and what he had endured and the fact that he was still fighting.

The king of Italy was quoted in the press as asking, 'Whatever happened to Roscoe Arbuckle?'

It was a question that disturbed many people in the film business. They knew the answer and they didn't like it.

The Vitaphone Film Company released a film called *Stars of Yesterday*, a series of film clips of silent stars like Theda Bara and the late Rudolph Valentino. One clip featured Roscoe who, unlike Valentino, was very much alive and fighting to get back in front of the cameras.

In September 1931, *Motion Picture* magazine ran a three-page feature article headed 'Doesn't Fatty Arbuckle Deserve a Break?' It was the most serious effort there had been to alter the course of events. James Cruze was quoted as willing to direct Roscoe's come-back picture: 'I will not take a cent of salary for directing. It would be an honour and a privilege to be associated again professionally with the man I know Roscoe Arbuckle to be . . . My admiration is unstinted for the manner in which Roscoe has taken punishment that might have broken lesser men.'

Buster Keaton observed, 'I have seen Roscoe "take it

on the chin" for ten years. I have seen the grit, the gameness of the man. He hasn't gone about feeling sorry for himself. He hasn't asked others to feel sorry for him. He doesn't want or need sympathy. All he wants is a square deal – all he needs is common justice.'

The article recorded support for Roscoe from a long and impressive list of Hollywood people: Laurel and Hardy, Marion Davies, Marie Dressler, Lila Lee, Lew Cody, Betty Compson, and of course Joseph Schenck.

Two months later the magazine published a sample of the public response to the campaign. Some of the letters that came from all over took the form of petitions signed by hundreds of people. All of the letters said the same thing: the fans wanted Arbuckle back on the screen.

The comedian now had company on his vaudeville tour. Addie had given up the screen to be with the man she loved. She joined his act, and they toured the vaudeville houses of America and Canada. Here and there they met the opposition that Roscoe had been fighting since 1921. In Montreal, for example, the local women's club attempted and failed to get his stage act banned.

In February 1932, Roscoe received the phone call he had waited eleven years for. Jack Warner called to offer Roscoe the chance to make a talkie. He didn't ask him to write it, direct it, or give advice about it. Warner wanted him to perform. Still wary of public opinion, the Hays Office had limited the offer to one two-reel comedy. If the public received that favourably, the doors would be thrown wide open.

At 2.15 a.m. on 21 June 1932, Roscoe and Addie woke up the justice of the peace in Erie, Pennsylvania, and got married. Roscoe told the press, 'I'm walking on air. Addie is a wonderful girl.'

In August, Warner Brothers issued a press release about the film Roscoe was about to begin work on, describing him as 'once the most popular comedian in pictures'.

Mistress of San Simeon and William Randolph Hearst: Marion Davies. The still is from *The Red Mill*, directed by Arbuckle secretly, and sadly assisted by King Vidor.

The wedding of Doris and Roscoe. The group above includes best man Buster Keaton and his wife Natalie Talmadge.

Opening day at the Plantation Club, Culver City. Below: the larger-than-life model of Roscoe in flowers presented to him on the first night by Mabel Normand.

Addie McPhail, the third Mrs Arbuckle.

Opposite: 1925 party at Norma Talmadge's beach house in Santa Monica. *Top row, left to right:* Fatty Arbuckle, Mae Murray, Ward Crane, Virginia Valli, Ronald Colman, Bessie Love, Jack Pickford, Rudolph Valentino, and Pola Negri. *Second row, left to right:* Raymond Griffith, Chris Goulding, Louella Parsons, Lila Lee, Carmel Myers, Allan Forrest, Bert Lytell, Claire Windsor, Dick Barthelmess, Constance Talmadge, Beatrice Lillie, Al Hall, Mrs Jack Mulhall, Mrs John Robertson, Julanne Johnston, Agnes Ayers, John Robertson, Mrs Talmadge, Henri, the Marquis de Falais, Mickey Neilan, and Howard Hughes. *Seated, left to right:* 'Tony' Moreno, Prince David Mdivani, Charles Lang, Edmund Goulding, Marcel Desano, Manuel D'Arce, Harry D'Arrast, Doris Deane Arbuckle, Mrs Antonio Moreno, Eddie Kone, Natalie Talmadge, Mrs Sedgwick, Christine Francis, Allie MacIntosh, Kitty Scola, and Blanche Sweet.

The campaign to reinstate Roscoe drew widespread support from men who were in theory his rivals. Typical were the group above, pictured in a scene from *Hinky, Dinky Do*. Stan Laurel, Oliver Hardy, Jimmy Durante, Chuck Reisner and Buster Keaton.

After an eleven-year fight, Roscoe signs for Warners watched by Addie and film executive Sam Sax.

Back at work. A frozen frame from *Buzzin' Around*, one of the 'comeback' movies.

The last photograph, taken less than two months before he died, shows Roscoe and Addie arriving at Hollywood.

On 25 August 1932, Roscoe 'Fatty' Arbuckle climbed into a pair of his famous baggy trousers measuring seventy-five inches around his fifty-inch waist, slipped on an old pair of Number 12 elastic-sided canal-boat shoes, put the famous brown derby hat on his head, and walked in front of the camera. The film crew applauded as he walked on the set. Asked how it felt, Roscoe said quietly, 'It's a big thrill.'

In almost eleven years, he had paid off debts amounting to close to a million dollars. All he owed when he walked on that set was $5,000, and that too would be repaid within a few months. His marriage was happy. He had fought for his professional life against impossible odds, and he had triumphed. Forced to battle against bigotry and hysteria, he had seen the work of a lifetime swept away in days at the peak of his success. He had been attacked, scorned, and shunned, but he had survived, and although he had felt moments of private bitterness, through the eleven-year nightmare he had remained his own man. Only drink had provided temporary refuge as he struggled to live again as a film comedian.

Eleven years were ripped from his professional life, years that could have been rich in his comedy development. Now here he was in August 1932, beginning as he had begun for Mack Sennett at Keystone – with a comedy two-reeler.

The first person he saw as he walked on the set was Joe Henabery, who had directed Roscoe's successful 1921 feature, *Brewster's Millions*. It was a good omen.

Warners considered that first talkie two-reeler, *Hey Pop*, a success, and Roscoe was signed to make six more. If they went well, he would move on to features.

On 28 June 1933, Roscoe finished the last of the series of two-reelers. They had been successful. That day Warner Brothers had signed Roscoe to make a feature film, so that night there was double cause for celebration, since he had been married just over a year to Addie. They had dinner at a New York restaurant with the owner, Billy La Hiff, and with the boxers, Johnny Dundee and Johnny Walker. They all discussed the boxing match between Sharkey and Carnera that they planned to watch the following evening.

Addie remembered the evening well:

> We had a lot of fun that night. After dinner I played backgammon with Billy La Hiff while Roscoe chatted and joked with the others. He was very happy.
>
> I remember when we went back to the hotel, Roscoe was roaring with laughter over something that had been said at dinner. All the way up in the elevator he was laughing. He went to bed, still laughing. I went into the bathroom, and when I came back I talked to him, and he didn't answer. He was very peaceful. Looked as if he had fallen asleep. Then I realized he was dead.

In France one headline declared simply *FATTY EST MORT*.

Sid Grauman, the theatre-owner who had triggered the wave of banning of Roscoe's films, said, 'He was the Pagliacci of motion pictures, the original "Laugh, Clown, Laugh".'

Will Rogers, who had remained a loyal friend, said, 'Those who demanded their pound of flesh finally received their satisfaction. Roscoe "Fatty" Arbuckle accommodated them by dying, and from a broken heart. He brought much happiness to many, and never knowingly wronged a soul. The Lord will pass on his innocence or guilt now, and not the reformers.'

Joseph Schenck, deeply shocked at the news of Roscoe's death, said,

> All who have ever known the real Roscoe Arbuckle will always treasure the memory of the great, generous heart of the man, a heart big enough to embrace in its warmth

everyone who came to him for help, stranger and friend alike.

It was this quality which led to his downfall, after he had struggled from poverty to a fame in which the children throughout the world worshipped him. Those who knew him for the great artist he was, admired him. His was the tragedy of a man born to make the world laugh and to receive only suffering as his reward. And to the end he held no malice.

Roscoe Conkling Arbuckle died at 2.15 a.m. on 29 June 1933. Forty-six years old, he died of a heart attack in a hotel bedroom.

His career had ended in another bedroom, in the St Francis Hotel, San Francisco, on 5 September 1921.

That was the day the laughter stopped.

EPILOGUE

'One no longer speaks of him. One has already announced his death.' So commented one French newspaper at the time of Roscoe Arbuckle's death in 1933. And yet . . .

One evening in recently, I sat in the National Film Theatre in London and broke the law with two or three hundred other film buffs, watching *Leap Year*, one of the three Fatty Arbuckle films for which release was cancelled at the time of Virginia Rappe's death in 1921. In England, the ban placed on the screening of Roscoe's films in 1921 has never officially been lifted; indeed, when *Hey Pop*, the first of Roscoe's 'comeback' movies, reached England in January 1933, the twelve-year ban was reconfirmed and the film was not shown. The bigotry and injustice to which Roscoe had been subjected were not peculiarly American phenomena.

That such a ban still officially exists in England today is patently absurd. So is the fact that there have been so few Arbuckle revivals in America's film institutes and little theatres. Since his career was interrupted before he could fully develop his comic talents, we will never know how Roscoe Arbuckle might have measured up to the giants of silent film comedy, Keaton and Chaplin, Langdon and Lloyd. I do know that on that night in 1973 the National Film Theatre was filled with laughter. If there were a revival today of Arbuckle's films, I suspect the public would be delighted.

Hollywood has never had much of an historical sense. Perhaps eighty per cent of the films of the silent era have been destroyed, either in the studio fires that were frequent in those days of highly flammable film or in the ruthless housecleaning of studios that destroyed vast numbers of silent prints to make shelf-space for the 'talkies' they felt would render silent flickers obsolete. And some film historians have perpetuated the myth that those Arbuckle films which survived the general destruction were destroyed at the time of the Hays ban. But a good number of his films have survived and I feel it is incumbent on film institutes all over the world to allocate parts of their budgets to getting and showing prints of these films. We owe it to Arbuckle but more than that we owe it to ourselves.

Of the principal participants in the San Francisco drama, many have now joined Virginia Rappe and Roscoe Arbuckle in the grave.

Of the movie moguls whose fortunes Arbuckle helped to build, only Adolph Zukor remained as I wrote these words. I have since learned, however, that he died in 1976.

Roscoe's friend and mentor, Joseph Schenck, was also to see the inside of a jail cell. On behalf of a number of studio heads, Schenck made pay-offs of $50,000 a year to union racketeers Willie Biof and George Browne, the two men who controlled the stagehands' union. Over the years, these payments were covered up by the studio accounting departments. Finally, Biof and Browne were exposed and convicted, largely because of Schenck's cooperation with the government. Schenck himself was convicted of lying about his income tax returns and served over four months in prison before President Harry S. Truman granted him a full pardon. Throughout his ordeal, Hollywood stood loyally behind him; he in turn remained discreet about who had contributed to the union 'war chest'. Schenck remained a powerful and much-talked-about figure in Hollywood until his death in 1961, not least because of the role he played in the life of a starlet named Marilyn Monroe.

Matthew Brady, the man who had hoped to ride the Arbuckle case to glory, never did become the governor of California. A 'crusader' against gambling and drug traffic, he remained district attorney of San Francisco for over twenty years, making a name for himself not only for his prosecution of Arbuckle but also for his prosecutions in the Frank Egan and William Hightower murder cases. He was criticized during Prohibition for appearing too often in speakeasies, and was tried by the Bar Association for alleged payroll juggling, but he maintained an officially clear name and a solid popularity through six elections, until 1943. One issue of the election campaign that year was his rare appearance in court on cases he was prosecuting, a habit he had begun to develop as early as 1921, when Arbuckle was all too vividly aware of his presence behind the scenes. Brady was unseated in 1943 by Edmund G. 'Pat' Brown (who did later become governor of the state), but he was quickly appointed Deputy State Attorney General by Robert F. Kennedy, and was then elected a Municipal Judge in 1945. He served on the bench until his death in 1952 at the age of 76.

Of the three women Roscoe married, little was known when I began my research on this book early in 1972. One authority on silent films told me at the time, 'Arbuckle only married once.' Another said, 'Well, yes, he was married a couple of times, but both of the women died a long time ago.' Happily, I found all three of his former wives living in California. Sadly all of them have since died. Each was generous with her time and they were all remarkably frank in talking about their lives with Arbuckle, welcoming the opportunity finally 'to tell it as it really was'.

Minta Durfee Arbuckle was living in Malibu Beach and working as an extra on film sets when I met her in 1972. After Arbuckle's trials, she had set up a thriving business as a beauty expert but was to lose over a million dollars in the Wall Street crash. In the early thirties she returned to Hollywood, but for Charlie Chaplin's first leading lady there were no more major roles – she was still playing bit parts when she was over eighty. She died on 9 September 1975, at the age of 84. Curiously, Virginia Rappe had died on a 9 September – more than half a century earlier.

After her divorce from Roscoe, Doris Deane married a Beverly Hills banker and retired from work in motion pictures. 'I no longer had the will or the desire to be part of an industry that could treat a man of Roscoe's talent so shabbily,' she told me. 'He had it all and they took it all.' When I met her in 1972, she was living in extreme poverty. A charming and refined lady, she had never before given an interview about her life with Roscoe, but she talked to me with total candour. Perhaps she sensed that it was time to get things on the record. She died alone in her Los Angeles apartment in March, 1974. She was 75.

Like Doris Deane, Addie McPhail retired from the screen, when her marriage with Roscoe was ended prematurely by his death. 'Without Roscoe, there did not seem much point in continuing,' she told me. She too was living in Los Angeles at the time of my research, but unlike Roscoe's first two wives she was living in happier circumstances, active in charity work for the Motion Picture Country House and Lodge, a home for the elderly and sick who have spent their lives in the movie business. Minta had spent her last days there.

Much of Roscoe Arbuckle's world is gone for ever. Priests live now in his palatial West Adams residence. The 'jazz palace of pleasure' belongs to the Roman Catholic Church. Roscoe would have been amused to know this. Laughter came easy when Roscoe was around.

Will Hays is dead, too, but the work he began at the time of the Arbuckle trials continued for many years. In 1930, Hays set up the Motion Picture Production Code to 'govern the Making of Talking, Synchronized, and Silent Motion Pictures'. It is still a rare movie that is released without the Code seal of approval. When film censorship took hold, it took hold all over the world, though in different forms – as the British Board of Censors, as Italy's Ministry of Tourism and Spectacles, as Ireland's Department of Justice. Even Sweden has had government censorship of films for over fifty years. And if the Hollywood blacklist no longer exists in the form it once took, the shadow of fear has never left the offices of Hollywood's executives, who have run scared for more than half a century. The morality clause that is a standard part of every motion picture contract is still called 'the Arbuckle clause', a grim reminder of the Labor Day party that ended Roscoe Arbuckle's career and ruined his life.

Few remember the happy days of the fat man who was always good for a laugh. All we have left are a few old films, seldom screened, but shelved away here and there waiting to be seen by a new generation, waiting to make another generation laugh, waiting to remind that generation of the day the laughter stopped.

DAVID A. YALLOP
London, August 1991

FILMOGRAPHY

Compiled by Samuel A. Gill

An index to the films of Roscoe 'Fatty' Arbuckle, produced between 1909 and 1933, and including those made under his pseudonym William Goodrich.

This filmography is arranged chronologically by release date. It includes the following information in this order: final release title; working title (in parentheses); release date(s); copyright date(s); date the picture was finished or print shipped; number of reels; film length in feet; sound or colour (when applicable); series or brand name; identification number; copyright claimant; production company; distribution company; production credits; cast; character name or role (in parentheses); production information; variant spellings and alternate titles.

This filmography includes short and feature-length productions, films for which Arbuckle worked in a variety of capacities – actor, director, writer, adapter and possibly producer – and films for which Arbuckle used both his real name and the pseudonym William Goodrich. Disputed Arbuckle pictures and pictures intended for Arbuckle which he did not complete are included in the filmography but marked accordingly.

adapt	adapter	play	playwright
art dir	art director	pres	presented by
assoc pro	associate producer	pro	producer
		r	release date
asst dir	assistant director	scen	scenarist
c	copyright date	scen ed	scenario editor
cam	cameraman	sd	sound
cc	copyright claimant	sets	sets designer
		story	story writer
cont	continuity writer	sup	supervisor
dia	dialogue writer	sup dir	supervising director
dir	director		
dist	distributor	titl	title writer
fs	date finished or shipped	ward	wardrobe designer
film ed	film editor	writ	writer

SELIG (1909)

Arbuckle's Selig pictures were produced by the Selig Polyscope Company at the Selig western studio at 1845 Allesandro Street in Los Angeles (Edendale), California.

1
Ben's Kid. rl Jul 1909. 1 reel. 1,000 feet. Selig Polyscope Company (pro). *Francis Boggs (dir). James Crosby (cam).* Roscoe Arbuckle, Thomas Santschi, Harry Todd.

2
Mrs Jones' Birthday. r30 Aug 1909. ½ reel. 540 feet. Selig Polyscope Company (pro). Roscoe Arbuckle. Released on same reel with *Winning a Widow* (450 feet).

3
Making It Pleasant For Him. r29 Nov 1909. ½ reel. 380 feet.

Selig Polyscope Company (pro). Roscoe Arbuckle. Released on same reel with *Brought to Terms* (615 feet).

SELIG (1910)

4
The Sanitarium. r10 Oct 1910. 1 reel. 1,000 feet. Selig Polyscope Company (pro). Roscoe Arbuckle, Nick Cogley, George Hernandez.

SELIG (1913)

5
Alas! Poor Yorick. r21 Apr 1913. c17 Apr 1913. ½ reel. Selig Polyscope Company (pro/cc), *Colin Campbell (dir/writ).* Wheeler Oakman (Montgomery Irving), Thomas Santschi (Hamlet McGinnis), Lillian Hayward (Ophelia Jones), Hobart Bosworth (theatre manager), John Lancaster (player), Frank Clark (player), Roscoe Arbuckle (player in female costume). Released on same reel with *Canton, China* (educational subject).

NESTOR (1913)

Arbuckle worked four weeks in Nestor Comedies produced under the supervision of Al E. Christie by the Universal Film Manufacturing Company. Titles have not been found for these comedies, which were supposedly filmed in February-March 1913 at the Universal studio on Sunset Boulevard and Gower Street in Hollywood, California.

KEYSTONE (1913)

Keystone comedies were produced by the Keystone Film Company under the supervision of Mack Sennett and distributed by the Mutual Film Corporation on a state-rights basis. Arbuckle's comedies from 1913 to 1915 were produced at the Keystone studio at 1712 Allesandro Street in Los Angeles (Edendale), California, and filmed at the studio and in the general Los Angeles vicinity. A few comedies were filmed on location in other areas, such as *Fatty and Mabel at the San Diego Exposition* and *Mabel and Fatty Viewing the World's Fair* at San Francisco.

6
The Gangsters (The Feud). r29 May 1913. fs24 Apr 1913. 1 reel. Keystone Film Company (pro). Mutual Film Corporation (dist). *Henry Lehrman (dir)*. Roscoe Arbuckle, Fred Mace, Ford Sterling, Hank Mann, Al St. John. Variants: *Gangsters*; *The Gangster*.

7
Passions, He Had Three. (Country Boys). r5 Jun 1913. fs3 May 1913. ½ reel. Keystone Film Company (pro). Mutual Film Corporation (dist). *Henry Lehrman (dir)*. Roscoe Arbuckle, Mabel Normand. Variants: *Passions – He Had Three*; *Passions! He Had Three*; *Possums, He Had Three*.

8
Help! Help! Hydrophobia! (The Chemist). r5 Jun 1913. fs3 May 1913. ½ reel. Keystone Film Company (pro). Mutual Film Corporation (dist). *Henry Lehrman (dir)*. Roscoe Arbuckle, Peggy Pearce. Variants: *Help Help Hydrophobia*; *Help, Help, Hydrophobia!*

9
The Waiters' Picnic. (The Cheff)*. r16 Jun 1913. fs15 May 1913. 1 reel. Keystone Film Company (pro). Mutual Film Corporation (dist). *Mack Sennett (dir)*. Roscoe Arbuckle, Mabel Normand, Ford Sterling, Hank Mann, Al St John. Variant: *The Waiter's Picnic*. *(*sic*)

10
A Bandit. (A Bandit). r23 Jun 1913. fs21 May 1913. ½ reel. Keystone Film Company (pro). Mutual Film Corporation (dist). *Mack Sennett (dir)*. Roscoe Arbuckle, Nick Cogley.

11

Peeping Pete. (The Peep Hole). r23 Jun 1913. fs21 May 1913. ½ reel. Keystone Film Company (pro). Mutual Film Corporation (dist). *Mack Sennett (dir).* Roscoe Arbuckle, Mack Sennett, Ford Sterling, Nick Cogley.

12

For the Love of Mabel. (The Melo-Drame). r30 Jun 1913. fs6 Jun 1913. 1 reel. Keystone Film Company (pro). Mutual Film Corporation (dist). *Henry Lehrman (dir).* Roscoe Arbuckle, Mabel Normand. Variant: *For Love of Mabel.*

13

The Telltale Light. (The Mirror). r10 Jul 1913. fs16 Jun 1913. 1 reel. Keystone Film Company (pro). Mutual Film Corporation (dist). *Mack Sennett (dir).* Roscoe Arbuckle, Mabel Normand, Alice Davenport, Charles Avery. Variant: *The Tell-Tale Light.*

14

A Noise from the Deep. (A New Trick). r17 Jul 1913. fs23 Jun 1913. 1 reel. Keystone Film Company (pro). Mutual Film Corporation (dist). *Mack Sennett (dir).* Roscoe Arbuckle, Mabel Normand.

15

Love and Courage. (Rubes). r21 Jul 1913. fs25 Jun 1913. ½ reel. Keystone Film Company (pro). Mutual Film Corporation (dist). *Henry Lehrman (dir).* Roscoe Arbuckle, Mabel Normand.

16

Prof. Bean's Removal. (House Moving). r31 Jul 1913. fs11 Jul 1913. 1 reel. Keystone Film Company (pro). Mutual Film Corporation (dist). *Henry Lehrman (dir).* Roscoe Arbuckle, Mabel Normand, Ford Sterling. Variant: *Professor Bean's Removal.*

17

The Riot. (The Riot). r11 Aug 1913. fs25 Jul 1913. 1 reel.

Keystone Film Company (pro). Mutual Film Corporation (dist). *Mack Sennett (dir)*. Roscoe Arbuckle, Mabel Normand, Ford Sterling.

18
Mabel's New Hero. (The Baloon). r28 Aug 1913. fs2 Aug 1913. 1 reel. Keystone Film Company (pro). Mutual Film Corporation (dist). *Mack Sennett (dir)*. Roscoe Arbuckle, Mabel Normand. Also known as *Fatty and the Bathing Beauties*. *(*sic*)

19
Fatty's Day Off. (The Invalid). r1 Sep 1913. fs1 Aug 1913. ½ reel. Keystone Film Company (pro). Mutual Film Corporation (dist). *Wilfred Lucas (dir)*. Roscoe Arbuckle.

20
Mabel's Dramatic Career. (The Actress). r8 Sep 1913. fs12 Aug 1913. 1 reel. Keystone Film Company (pro). Mutual Film Corporation (dist). *Mack Sennett (dir)*. Roscoe Arbuckle, Mabel Normand, Mack Sennett, Alice Davenport, Ford Sterling, Virginia Kirtley, Charles Avery, Mack Swain. Also known as *Her Dramatic Debut*.

21
The Gypsy Queen. (The Gypsy). r11 Sep 1913. fs16 Aug 1913. 1 reel. Keystone Film Company (pro). Mutual Film Corporation (dist). *Mack Sennett (dir)*. Roscoe Arbuckle, Mabel Normand.

22
The Fatal Taxicab. (The Taxicab). r18 Sep 1913. fs21 Aug 1913. 1 reel. Keystone Film Company (pro). Mutual Film Corporation (dist). *Mack Sennett (dir)*. Roscoe Arbuckle, Mabel Normand, Ford Sterling. Variant: *The Faithful Taxicab*.

23
When Dreams Come True. (The Snake). r22 Sep 1913. fs26 Aug 1913. 1 reel. Keystone Film Company (pro). Mutual

Film Corporation (dist). *Mack Sennett (dir).* Roscoe Arbuckle, Mabel Normand, Ford Sterling.

24
Mother's Boy. (The Bears). r25 Sep 1913. fs1 Sep 1913. 1 reel. Keystone Film Company (pro). Mutual Film Corporation (dist). *Henry Lehrman (dir).* Roscoe Arbuckle, Nick Cogley. Variants: *Mother's Boys*; *Mothers Boy.*

25
Two Old Tars. (Yachting). r20 Oct 1913. fs22 Sep 1913. 1 reel. Keystone Film Company (pro). Mutual Film Corporation (dist). *Henry Lehrman (dir).* Roscoe Arbuckle, Nick Cogley. Original title, *The Sea Dogs,* changed to *Two Old Tars,* probably to avoid confusion with a Broncho two-reeler titled *The Sea Dog* (r21 May 1913). Also known as *The Sea Dogs.*

26
A Quiet Little Wedding. (Interrupted Wedding). r23 Oct 1913. fs25 Sep 1913. 1 reel. Keystone Film Company (pro). Mutual Film Corporation (dist). *Wilfred Lucas (dir).* Roscoe Arbuckle, Minta Durfee.

27
The Speed Kings. r30 Oct 1913. 1 reel. Keystone Film Company (pro). Mutual Film Corporation (dist). *Wilfred Lucas (dir).* Roscoe Arbuckle, Teddy Tetzlaff, Earl Cooper, Mabel Normand, Ford Sterling, Paul Jacobs. Filmed at automobile race track in Santa Monica. Variants: *Speed Kings; The Speed King;* Teddy Tetzlaff and Earl Cooper, *Speed King*; Teddy Tetzlaff and Earl Cooper, *Speed Kings.*

28
Fatty at San Diego. (A Jealous Husband). r3 Nov 1913. fs9 Oct 1913. 1 reel. Keystone Film Company (pro). Mutual Film Corporation (dist). *George Nichols (dir).* Roscoe Arbuckle, Minta Durfee, Phyllis Allen.

29
Wine. (Wine Making). r13 Nov 1913. fs18 Oct 1913. 1 reel. Keystone Film Company (pro). Mutual Film Corporation (dist). *George Nichols (dir)*. Roscoe Arbuckle, Minta Durfee, Ford Sterling.

30
Fatty Joins the Force. (Freak Coward). r24 Nov 1913. fs25 Oct 1913. 1 reel. Keystone Film Company (pro). Mutual Film Corporation (dist). *George Nichols (dir)*. Roscoe Arbuckle, Minta Durfee, Dot Farley.

31
The Woman Haters. (Yachting). r1 Dec 1913. fs4 Oct 1913. 1 reel. Keystone Film Company (pro). Mutual Film Corporation (dist). *Henry Lehrman (dir)*. Roscoe Arbuckle, Nick Cogley. Variant: *The Woman Hater*.

32
Ride for a Bride. (The Golf Ball). r8 Dec 1913. fs1 Nov 1913. 1 reel. Keystone Film Company (pro). Mutual Film Corporation (dist). *George Nichols (dir)*. Roscoe Arbuckle, Edgar Kennedy. Variant: *A Ride For a Bride*.

33
Fatty's Flirtation. (The Masher). r18 Dec 1913. fs13 Nov 1913. ½ reel. Keystone Film Company (pro). Mutual Film Corporation (dist). *George Nichols (dir)*. Roscoe Arbuckle, Mabel Normand, Minta Durfee, Hank Mann.

34
His Sister's Kids. (The Doctor's Cat). r20 Dec 1913. fs12 Nov 1913. 1 reel. Keystone Film Company (pro). Mutual Film Corporation (dist). *George Nichols (dir)*. Roscoe Arbuckle, Keystone Cops.

35
He Would a Hunting Go. (Hunting Story). r29 Dec 1913. fs30 Nov 1913. 1 reel. Keystone Film Company (pro).

Mutual Film Corporation (dist). *George Nichols (dir).* Roscoe Arbuckle, Grover Ligon.

KEYSTONE (1914)

36
A Misplaced Foot. (Comedy of Errors). r1 Jan 1914. fs3 Dec 1913. ½ reel. Keystone Film Company (pro). Mutual Film Corporation (dist). *Wilfred Lucas (dir).* Roscoe Arbuckle, Mabel Normand, Minta Durfee.

37
The Under Sheriff. (The Sheriff). r8 Jan 1914. fs17 Dec 1913. 1 reel. Keystone Film Company (pro). Mutual Film Corporation (dist). *George Nichols (dir).* Roscoe Arbuckle.

38
A Flirt's Mistake. (The Hindoo). r12 Jan 1914. fs18 Dec 1913. 1 reel. Keystone Film Company (pro). Mutual Film Corporation (dist). *George Nichols (dir).* Roscoe Arbuckle.

39
In the Clutches of the Gang. (The Disguised Mayor). r17 Jan 1914. fs11 Dec 1913. 2 reels. Keystone Film Company (pro). Mutual Film Corporation (dist). *George Nichols (dir).* Roscoe Arbuckle, Ford Sterling, George Nichols, Rube Miller, Edgar Kennedy, Hank Mann, George Jeske, Al St John. Variants: *In the Clutches of a Gang.*

40
Rebecca's Wedding Day. (The Sisters). r24 Jan 1914. fs31 Dec 1913. 1 reel. Keystone Film Company (pro). Mutual Film Corporation (dist). *George Nichols (dir).* Roscoe Arbuckle. Variant: *Rebeckas Wedding Day.*

41
A Robust Romeo. (The Wolf). r12 Feb 1914. fs22 Jan 1914. 1 reel. Keystone Film Company (pro). Mutual Film Corporation (dist). *George Nichols (dir).* Roscoe Arbuckle.

42
'Twixt Love and Fire. (The Finish). r23 Feb 1914. fs4 Feb 1914. 1 reel. Keystone Film Company (pro). Mutual Film Corporation (dist). *George Nichols (dir)*. Roscoe Arbuckle, Peggy Pearce. This picture should not be confused with the Keystone split-reel picture *'Twixt Love and Fire*, directed by Henry Lehrman and released 19 May 1913.

43
A Film Johnnie. (A Movie Bug). r2 Mar 1914. fs11 Feb 1914. 1 reel. Keystone Film Company (pro). Mutual Film Corporation (dist). *George Nichols (dir)*. Roscoe Arbuckle, Charles Chaplin, Minta Durfee, Virginia Kirtley. Also known as *Movie Nut; Million Dollar Job*.

44
Tango Tangles. (A Midnight Dance). r9 Mar 1914. fs17 Feb 1914. ½ reel. Keystone Film Company (pro). Mutual Film Corporation (dist). *Mack Sennett (dir)*. Roscoe Arbuckle, Charles Chaplin, Ford Sterling, Chester Conklin, Minta Durfee. Referred to variously as ½ reel, ¾ reel, 1 reel. Variant: *Tango Tangle*. Also known as *Charlie's Recreation*; *Music Hall*.

45
His Favorite Pastime. (The Drunk). r16 Mar 1914. fs19 Feb 1914. 1 reel. Keystone Film Company (pro). Mutual Film Corporation (dist). *George Nichols (dir)*. Roscoe Arbuckle, Charles Chaplin, Peggy Pearce, Harry McCoy, Hank Mann, Edgar Kennedy. Original release date changed from 12 Mar 1914 to 16 Mar 1914. Also known as *The Bonehead; Charlie Is Thirsty*.

46
A Rural Demon. (A Horse). r19 Mar 1914. fs25 Feb 1914. 1 reel. Keystone Film Company (pro). Mutual Film Corporation (dist). *Mack Sennett, Henry Lehrman (dirs)*. Roscoe Arbuckle. Original release date changed from 14 Mar 1914 to 19 Mar 1914.

Arbuckle received his first credit as director with *Barnyard Flirtations*; and with the exception of a few comedies directed by Charles Chaplin (*The Masquerader, The Rounders*), Mack Sennett (*The Little Teacher*) and co-directed by Ferris Hartman (*The Waiters' Ball*), Arbuckle received official credit as director of his own comedies from 1914 to 1920 for Keystone, Triangle-Keystone and Comique. Several individuals who assisted Arbuckle with direction on set and never received official credit include Charles Avery (ca. 1914-1915), Joe Bordeau (1915-1918), Andy Anderson (ca. 1916), Harry Williams (ca. 1916), Frank Griffin (1917), Herbert Warren (1917-1918), Buster Keaton (1917-1919), Al St John (1917-1919) and Glen Cavender (1918).

47
Barnyard Flirtations. (The Farmer's Toe). r28 Mar 1914. fs7 Mar 1914. 1 reel. Keystone Film Company (pro). Mutual Film Corporation (dist). *Roscoe Arbuckle (dir).* Roscoe Arbuckle. Variant: *Barnyard Flirtation.*

48
Chicken Chaser. (New Yard Lovers). r2 Apr 1914. fs13 Mar 1914. 1 reel. Keystone Film Company (pro). Mutual Film Corporation (dist). *Roscoe Arbuckle (dir).* Roscoe Arbuckle, Keystone Cops. Variants: *The Chicken Chaser.* Also known as *New Yard Lovers.*

49
A Bath House Beauty. (Bathing Picture). r13 Apr 1914. fs26 Mar 1914. 1 reel. Keystone Film Company (pro). Mutual Film Corporation (dist). *Roscoe Arbuckle (dir).* Variants: *A Bathhouse Beauty; A Bathing Beauty.*

50
Where Hazel Met the Villian. (Burglars Union). r23 Apr 1914. fs6 Apr 1914. 1 reel. Keystone Film Company (pro). Mutual Film Corporation (dist). *Roscoe Arbuckle (dir).* Mabel Normand. Variant: *When Hazel Met the Villain.*

51
A Suspended Ordeal. (Hung by a Hook). r9 May 1914. fs23 Apr 1914. 1 reel. Keystone Film Company (pro). Mutual Film Corporation (dist). *Roscoe Arbuckle (dir)*. Roscoe Arbuckle, Minta Durfee. Variant: *Suspended Ordeal*.

52
The Water Dog. (The Rescue). r18 May 1914. fs2 May 1914. 1 reel. Keystone Film Company (pro). Mutual Film Corporation (dist). *Roscoe Arbuckle (dir)*. Roscoe Arbuckle.

53
The Alarm. (Fireman's Picnic). r28 May 1914. fs16 May 1914. 2 reels. Keystone Film Company (pro). Mutual Film Corporation (dist). *Roscoe Arbuckle (dir)*. Roscoe Arbuckle, Mabel Normand, Al St John, Hank Mann.

54
The Knock-out. (Fighting Demon). r11 Jun 1914. fs29 May 1914. 2 reels. Keystone Film Company (pro). Mutual Film Corporation (dist). Roscoe Arbuckle, Charles Chaplin, Minta Durfee, Edgar Kennedy, Mack Swain, Al St John, Hank Mann, Alice Howell, George 'Slim' Summerville, Charles Parrott (later Charley Chase), Mack Sennett, Eddie Cline, Joe Bordeau. Variant: *The Knockout*. Also known as *Counted Out*; *The Pugilist*.

55
Fatty and the Heiress. (Love and Money). r25 Jun 1914. fs14 Jun 1914. 1 reel. Keystone Film Company (pro). Mutual Film Corporation (dist). *Roscoe Arbuckle (dir)*. Roscoe Arbuckle. Referred to variously as 1 reel, 2 reels.

56
Fatty's Finish. (Fatty's Flirtation). r2 Jul 1914. fs19 Jun 1914. 1 reel. Keystone Film Company (pro). Mutual Film Corporation (dist). *Roscoe Arbuckle (dir)*. Roscoe Arbuckle.

57
Love and Bullets. (The Assassin). r4 Jul 1914. fs22 Jun 1914.

1 reel. Keystone Film Company (pro). Mutual Film Corporation (dist). *Roscoe Arbuckle (dir).* Roscoe Arbuckle, Charles Murray. Also known as *The Trouble Mender.*

58
A Rowboat Romance. (Boating). r6 Jul 1914. fs23 Jun 1914. 1 reel. Keystone Film Company (pro). Mutual Film Corporation (dist). *Roscoe Arbuckle (dir).* Roscoe Arbuckle. Variants: *Row-boat Romance; Row Boat Romance.*

59
The Sky Pirate. (Up in the Air). r18 Jul 1914. fs4 Jul 1914. 1 reel. Keystone Film Company (pro). Mutual Film Corporation (dist). *Roscoe Arbuckle (dir).* Roscoe Arbuckle. Variant: *A Sky Pirate.*

60
Those Happy Days. (Cast Adrift). r23 Jul 1914. fs11 Jul 1914. 1 reel. Keystone Film Company (pro). Mutual Film Corporation (dist). *Roscoe Arbuckle (dir).* Roscoe Arbuckle.

61
That Minstrel Man. (Fanny's Jewels). r17 Aug 1914. fs4 Aug 1914. 1 reel. Keystone Film Company (pro). Mutual Film Corporation (dist). *Roscoe Arbuckle (dir).* Roscoe Arbuckle, Ford Sterling. Referred to variously as 1 reel, 2 reels.

62
Those Country Kids. (The Rural Rivals). r20 Aug 1914. fs5 Aug 1914. 1 reel. Keystone Film Company (pro). Mutual Film Corporation (dist). *Roscoe Arbuckle (dir).* Roscoe Arbuckle, Mabel Normand.

63
Fatty's Gift. (His Baby). r24 Aug 1914. fs8 Aug 1914. 1 reel. Keystone Film Company (pro). Mutual Film Corporation (dist). *Roscoe Arbuckle (dir).* Roscoe Arbuckle.

64
The Masquerader. (Queen of the Movies). r27 Aug 1914. fs12 Aug 1914. 1 reel. Keystone Film Company (pro). Mutual Film Corporation (dist). *Charles Chaplin (dir).* Roscoe Arbuckle, Charles Chaplin, Charles Parrott, Harry McCoy, Minta Durfee, Cecile Arnold, Charles Murray, Fritz Schade, Vivian Edwards, Chester Conklin. Also known as *Putting One Over*; *The Female Impersonator; The Picnic*; *His New Profession*; *Charlie at the Studio*; *Charlie the Actor*.

65
A Brand New Hero. (The Chief's Daughter). r5 Sep 1914. fs18 Aug 1914. 1 reel. Keystone Film Company (pro). Mutual Film Corporation (dist). *Roscoe Arbuckle (dir).* Roscoe Arbuckle.

66
The Rounders. (The Two Drunks). r7 Sep 1914. fs21 Aug 1914. 1 reel. Keystone Film Company (pro). Mutual Film Corporation (dist). *Charles Chaplin (dir).* Roscoe Arbuckle, Charles Chaplin, Minta Durfee, Phyllis Allen, Al St John, Charles Parrott, Fritz Schade, Dixie Chene, Edgar Kennedy, Wallace MacDonald. Also known as *Revelry; Two of a Kind; Oh, What a Night.*

67
Lover's Luck. (The Three Lovers). r19 Sep 1914. fs29 Aug 1914. 1 reel. Keystone Film Company (pro). Mutual Film Corporation (dist). *Roscoe Arbuckle (dir).* Roscoe Arbuckle. Variant: *Lovers Luck.*

68
Fatty's Debut. (Saving Lizzie). r26 Sep 1914. fs4 Sep 1914. 1 reel. Keystone Film Company (pro). Mutual Film Corporation (dist). *Roscoe Arbuckle (dir).* Roscoe Arbuckle. Also known as *Fatty Butts In.*

69
Fatty Again. (The Star). r3 Oct 1914. fs10 Sep 1914. 1 reel. Keystone Film Company (pro). Mutual Film Corporation

(dist). *Roscoe Arbuckle (dir)*. Roscoe Arbuckle, Minta Durfee, Charles Murray. Also known as *Fatty the Four-flusher*.

70
Their Ups and Downs. (The Baloon). r5 Oct 1914. fs12 Sep 1914. 1 reel. Keystone Film Company (pro). Mutual Film Corporation (dist). *Roscoe Arbuckle (dir)*. Roscoe Arbuckle.

71
Zip, the Dodger. (The African Dodger). r17 Oct 1914. fs19 Sep 1914. 1 reel. Keystone Film Company (pro). Mutual Film Corporation (dist). *Roscoe Arbuckle (dir)*. Roscoe Arbuckle. Variant: *Zip the Dodger*.

72
Lovers' Post Office. (Lover's Postoffice). r2 Nov 1914. c2 Nov 1914. fs15 Oct 1914. 1 reel. Keystone Film Company (pro/cc). Mutual Film Corporation (dist). *Roscoe Arbuckle (dir)*. Roscoe Arbuckle, Mabel Normand. First Arbuckle Keystone comedy to be copyrighted. Variants: *Lovers' Post-office*; *Lover's Postoffice*; *Lovers Post Office*.

73
An Incompetent Hero. (The Wrong Room). r12 Nov 1914. c12 Nov 1914. fs25 Oct 1914. 1 reel. Keystone Film Company (pro/cc). Mutual Film Corporation (dist). *Roscoe Arbuckle (dir)*. Roscoe Arbuckle, Minta Durfee. Variant: *In Incompetent Hero*.

74
Fatty's Jonah Day. (Park Troubles). r16 Nov 1914. c16 Nov 1914. fs29 Oct 1914. 1 reel. Keystone Film Company (pro/cc). Mutual Film Corporation (dist). *Roscoe Arbuckle (dir)*. Roscoe Arbuckle, Mabel Normand, Phyllis Allen. Variant: *Fatty's Hoodoo Day*.

75
Fatty's Wine Party. (Only a Dollar). r21 Nov 1914. c21 Nov 1914. fs6 Nov 1914. 1 reel. Keystone Film Company

(pro/cc). Mutual Film Corporation (dist). *Roscoe Arbuckle (dir)*. Roscoe Arbuckle, Mabel Normand, Syd Chaplin.

76
The Sea Nymphs. (Catalina Story). r23 Nov 1914. c21 Nov 1914. fs12 Sep 1914. 2 reels. Keystone Film Company (pro/cc). Mutual Film Corporation (dist). *Roscoe Arbuckle (dir)*. Roscoe Arbuckle, Mabel Normand, Mack Swain. Variant: *Sea Nymphs*.

77
Leading Lizzie Astray. (The Country Girl). r30 Nov 1914. c30 Nov 1914. fs18 Nov 1914. 1 reel. Keystone Film Company (pro/cc). Mutual Film Corporation (dist). *Roscoe Arbuckle (dir)*. Roscoe Arbuckle, Minta Durfee, Mack Swain, George 'Slim' Summerville. Variant: *Leading Lizzie Estray*.

78
Shotguns That Kick. (Fatty's Birthday Present). r3 Dec 1914. c3 Dec 1914. fs20 Nov 1914. 1 reel. Keystone Film Company (pro/cc). Mutual Film Corporation (dist). *Roscoe Arbuckle (dir)*. Roscoe Arbuckle.

79
Fatty's Magic Pants. (The Borrowed Dress). r14 Dec 1914. c14 Dec 1914. fs2 Dec 1914. 1 reel. Keystone Film Company (pro/cc). Mutual Film Corporation (dist). *Roscoe Arbuckle (dir)*. Roscoe Arbuckle, Minta Durfee, Bert Roach, Harry McCoy, Charles Parrott, Al St John, George 'Slim' Summerville. Variant: *Fatt's Magic Pants*. Also known as *Fatty's Suitless Day*.

80
Fatty and Minnie-He-Haw. (The Squaw's Man). r21 Dec 1914. c19 Dec 1914. fs8 Oct 1914. 2 reels. Keystone Film Company (pro/cc). Mutual Film Corporation (dist). *Roscoe Arbuckle (dir)*. Roscoe Arbuckle, Minta Durfee, Princess Minnie. Variant: *Fatty and Minnie He-Haw*.

81
Mabel and Fatty's Wash Day. (Mabel's Flirtation). r14 Jan 1915. c14 Jan 1915. fs4 Jan 1915. 1 reel. Keystone Film Company (pro/cc). Mutual Film Corporation (dist). *Roscoe Arbuckle (dir).* Roscoe Arbuckle, Mabel Normand. Original title, *Mabel's Flirtation*, changed to *Mabel and Fatty's Wash Day*. Variant: *Mabel's and Fatty's Wash Day.*

82
Fatty and Mabel's Simple Life. (The Runaway Auto). r18 Jan 1915. c16 Jan 1915. fs4 Jan 1915. 2 reels. Keystone Film Company (pro/cc). Mutual Film Corporation (dist). *Roscoe Arbuckle (dir).* Roscoe Arbuckle, Mabel Normand. Variants: *Fatty's and Mabel's Simple Life*; *Mabel and Fatty's Simple Life.*

83
Fatty and Mabel at the San Diego Exposition. (Fatty & Mabel at the Fair). r23 Jan 1915. c23 Jan 1915. fs11 Jan 1915. 1 reel. Keystone Film Company (pro/cc). Mutual Film Corporation (dist). *Roscoe Arbuckle (dir).* Roscoe Arbuckle, Mabel Normand, Frank Hayes. Variants: *Fatty and Mabel; Fatty and Mabel (At the San Diego Exposition)*; *Fatty and Mabel at San Diego Expo.*

84
Mabel, Fatty and the Law. (No Flirting Allowed). r28 Jan 1915. c28 Jan 1915. fs18 Jan 1915. 1 reel. Keystone Film Company (pro/cc). Mutual Film Corporation (dist). *Roscoe Arbuckle (dir).* Roscoe Arbuckle, Mabel Normand, Minta Durfee, Harry Gribbon, Frank Hayes, Al St John. Variants: *Mabel, Fatty and the Law*; *Fatty, Mabel and the Law.* Also known as *Fatty's Spooning Days.*

85
Fatty's New Role. (German Saloon Story). r1 Feb 1915. c1 Feb 1915. fs22 Jan 1915. 1 reel. Keystone Film Company (pro/cc). Mutual Film Corporation (dist). *Roscoe Arbuckle*

(dir). Roscoe Arbuckle. Referred to variously as 1 reel, 2 reels.

86
Mabel and Fatty's Married Life. (Monkey Scare). r11 Feb 1915. c11 Feb 1915. fs29 Jan 1915. 1 reel. Keystone Film Company (pro/cc). Mutual Film Corporation (dist). *Roscoe Arbuckle (dir)*. Roscoe Arbuckle, Mabel Normand. Variant: *Fatty and Mabel's Married Life*.

87
Fatty's Reckless Fling. (Disappearing Bed Story). r4 Mar 1915. c4 Mar 1915. fs24 Feb 1915. 1 reel. Keystone Film Company (pro/cc). Mutual Film Corporation (dist). *Roscoe Arbuckle (dir)*. Roscoe Arbuckle, Ted Edwards. Variant: *Fatty's Wreckless Fling*.

88
Fatty's Chance Acquaintance. (Fatty's Wife's Husband). r8 Mar 1915. c8 Mar 1915. fs27 Feb 1915. 1 reel. Keystone Film Company (pro/cc). Mutual Film Corporation (dist). *Roscoe Arbuckle (dir)*. Roscoe Arbuckle, Minta Durfee, Frank Hayes.

89
Love in Armor. (Suit of Armor Story). r11 Mar 1915. c11 Mar 1915. fs3 Mar 1915. 1 reel. Keystone Film Company (pro/cc). Mutual Film Corporation (dist). *Roscoe Arbuckle (dir)*. Roscoe Arbuckle, Charles Parrott, Max Davidson.

90
That Little Band of Gold. (Before and After Marriage). r15 Mar 1915. c13 Mar 1915. fs17 Feb 1915. 2 reels. Keystone Film Company (pro/cc). Mutual Film Corporation (dist). *Roscoe Arbuckle (dir)*. Roscoe Arbuckle, Mabel Normand, Alice Davenport, Ford Sterling, May Emory, Phyllis Allen, Vivian Edwards, Al St John, Dora Rodgers, Dixie Chene. Filmed at a local court house, the interior of the Republic Theatre in Los Angeles, and at the Keystone studio.

91
Fatty's Faithful Fido. (Fatty the Tough). r20 Mar 1915. c20 Mar 1915. fs14 Mar 1915. 1 reel. Keystone Film Company (pro/cc). Mutual Film Corporation (dist). *Roscoe Arbuckle (dir)*. Roscoe Arbuckle, Minta Durfee, Al St John, Glen Cavender, Frank Hayes, Ted Edwards, Luke (dog). Variants: *Fatty's Faithful Wife*; *Fatty's Fatal Fido*.

92
When Love Took Wings. (Fatty's Fast Ride). r1 Apr 1915. c1 Apr 1915. fs25 Mar 1915. 1 reel. Keystone Film Company (pro/cc). Mutual Film Corporation (dist). *Roscoe Arbuckle (dir)*. Roscoe Arbuckle.

93
Wished on Mabel. (Golden Gate Park Story). r19 Apr 1915. c19 Apr 1915. fs9 Apr 1915. 1 reel. Keystone Film Company (pro/cc). Mutal Film Corporation (dist). *Roscoe Arbuckle (dir)*. Roscoe Arbuckle, Mabel Normand.

94
Mabel and Fatty Viewing the World's Fair at San Francisco, Cal. (The Frisco Story). r22 Apr 1915. c22 Apr 1915. fs16 Apr 1915. 1 reel. Keystone Film Company (pro/cc). Mutual Film Corporation (dist). *Roscoe Arbuckle (dir)*. Roscoe Arbuckle, Mabel Normand, Ernestine Schumann-Heink. Variant: *Fatty and Mabel Viewing the World's Fair at San Francisco*.

95
Mabel's Wilful Way. (Idora Park Story). r1 May 1915. c1 May 1915. fs23 Apr 1915. 1 reel. Keystone Film Company (pro/cc). Mutual Film Corporation (dist). *Roscoe Arbuckle (dir)*. Roscoe Arbuckle, Mabel Normand.

96
Miss Fatty's Seaside Lovers. (By the Sea). r15 May 1915. c15 May 1915. fs7 May 1915. 1 reel. Keystone Film Company (pro/cc). Mutual Film Corporation (dist). *Roscoe*

Arbuckle (dir). Roscoe Arbuckle, Harold Lloyd. Variant: *Miss Fatty's Seaside Lover*.

97
The Little Teacher. (Small Town School). r21 Jun 1915. c21 Jun 1915. fs25 May 1915. 2 reels. Keystone Film Company (pro/cc). Mutual Film Corporation (dist). *Mack Sennett (dir)*. Roscoe Arbuckle, Mabel Normand, Owen Moore, Mack Sennett, Harry McCoy. Also known as *Small Town Bully*.

98
Fatty's Plucky Pup. (Dog and Villian Story). r28 Jun 1915. c28 Jun 1915. fs10 Jun 1915. 2 reels. Keystone Film Company (pro/cc). Mutual Film Corporation (dist). *Roscoe Arbuckle (dir)*. Roscoe Arbuckle, Luke (dog). Also known as *Fatt's Plucky Pup*; *Foiled by Fido*.

99
Fatty's Tintype Tangle. (Caught on the Screen). r26 Jul 1915. c26 Jul 1915. fs14 Jul 1915. 2 reels. Keystone Film Company (pro/cc). Mutual Film Corporation (dist). *Roscoe Arbuckle (dir)*. Roscoe Arbuckle, Louise Fazenda, Edgar Kennedy, Luke (dog). Variants: *Fatty's Tin Type Tangle*; *Fido's Tin-Type-Tangle*; *Fido's Tintype Tangle*.

TRIANGLE-KEYSTONE (1915)

Triangle-Keystone comedies were produced by the Keystone Film Company under the supervision of Mack Sennett and distributed by the Triangle Film Corporation on a block-booking basis. Arbuckle's Triangle-Keystone comedies of 1915 were produced at the Keystone studio at 1712 Allesandro Street in Los Angeles (Edendale), California, and filmed at the studio and in the general Los Angeles vicinity.

100
Fickle Fatty's Fall. (Fatty's Way). r14 Nov 1915; and 28

Nov 1915. c1 Nov 1915; and 15 Nov 1915. fs12 Oct 1915. 2 reels. Keystone Film Company (pro). Triangle Film Corporation (dist/cc). *Roscoe Arbuckle (dir).* Roscoe Arbuckle (husband), Minta Durfee (his wife), Phyllis Allen (her mother), Al St John (butcher boy), Glen Cavender (cook), Ivy Crosthwaite (maid), Fritz Schade (music celebrity), Bobby Dunn (small man at bath-house).

101
The Village Scandal. r12 Dec 1915. c18 Nov 1915; and 13 Dec 1915, 2 reels. Keystone Film Company (pro). Triangle Film Corporation (dist/cc). *Roscoe Arbuckle (dir).* Roscoe Arbuckle (village fat boy), Raymond Hitchcock (travelling magician), Flora Zabelle (village belle), Al St John (boarder), Harry McCoy (lounger).

102
Fatty and the Broadway Stars. (Fatty's Dream). r19 Dec 1915. c15 Dec 1915; and 20 Dec 1915. fs23 Nov 1915. 2 reels. Keystone Film Company (pro). Triangle Film Corporation (dist/cc). *Roscoe Arbuckle (dir).* Roscoe Arbuckle (janitor), Ivy Crosthwaite (leading lady), Al St John (stage manager), Mack Sennett, Joe Weber, Lew Fields, William Collier, Sr, Joe Jackson, Sam Bernard, Bert Clark, Fred Mace, Chester Conklin, Charles Murray, Mack Swain, Mae Busch, Ford Sterling, Hank Mann, Alice Davenport, Harry Gribbon, Glen Cavender, Wayland Trask, Minta Durfee, Edgar Kennedy, Harry Booker, Louis Hippe, Polly Moran, George 'Slim' Summerville, Bobby Vernon. Keystone Cops (as it was usually spelled then).

TRIANGLE-KEYSTONE (1916)

Arbuckle's Triangle-Keystone comedies of 1916 were produced at the Keystone studio at 1712 Allesandro Street in Los Angeles (Edendale), California, and at the Eastern Triangle studios in Fort Lee, New Jersey; their production locations are identified in the filmography at the end of each entry.

103
Fatty and Mabel Adrift. (House at Sea). r9 Jan 1916. c10 Jan 1916; and 14 Jan 1916. fs24 Dec 1915. 3 reels. Colour (tinted and toned). Keystone Film Company (pro). Triangle Film Corporation (dist/cc). *Roscoe Arbuckle (dir).* Roscoe Arbuckle (farm boy), Mabel Normand (his sweetheart and bride), Frank Hayes (her father), May Wells (her mother), Al St John (Fatty's hated rival), Wayland Trask (chief of the robbers), James Bryant (first robber), Joe Bordeau (second robber/chauffeur), Glen Cavender (real estate agent), Luke (dog). Filmed at Pacific Ocean and at Keystone studio in Los Angeles, California.

104
He Did and He Didn't. (Love and Lobsters). r30 Jan 1916. c9 Feb 1916. 2 reels. Keystone Film Company (pro). Triangle Film Corporation (dist/cc). *Roscoe Arbuckle (dir).* Roscoe Arbuckle (doctor), Mabel Normand (his wife), William Jefferson (her old school-mate), Al St John (burglar), Joe Bordeau (burglar). Filmed at Eastern Triangle studios in Fort Lee, New Jersey. Also known as *Love and Lobsters.*

105
The Bright Lights. (The Lure of Broadway). r20 Feb 1916. c14 Feb 1916; and 10 Mar 1916. 2 reels. Keystone Film Company (pro). Triangle Film Corporation (dist/cc). *Roscoe Arbuckle (dir).* Roscoe Arbuckle, Mabel Normand, Minta Durfee, William Jefferson, Al St John, Joe Bordeau. Filmed at Eastern Triangle studios in Fort Lee, New Jersey. Also known as *The Lure of Broadway.*

106
His Wife's Mistake. (The Wrong Mr Stout). r2 Apr 1916. c2 Apr 1916; and 19 Apr 1916; 2 reels. Keystone Film Company (pro). Triangle Film Corporation (dist/cc). *Roscoe Arbuckle (dir).* Roscoe Arbuckle (janitor), William Jefferson (city businessman), Minta Durfee (his wife), Arthur Earle (country businessman), Al St John (office boy), Betty Gray (telephone girl). Working title *The Wrong M.r Stout* was a Keystone inside joke referring to studio manager George

Walter Stout. Filmed at Eastern Triangle studios in Fort Lee, New Jersey.

107
The Other Man. r16 Apr 1916. c16 Apr 1916. 2 reels. Keystone Film Company (pro). Triangle Film Corporation (dist/cc). *Roscoe Arbuckle (dir).* Roscoe Arbuckle (wealthy young man/the hobo), Irene Wallace (fiancée), Minta Durfee, Horace J. Haine, Al St John, William Jefferson, Lillian Shaffner, Joe Bordeau (hobo friend). Filmed at Eastern Triangle studios in Fort Lee, New Jersey.

108
The Moonshiners. (The Moonshiner). r14 May 1916. No copyright. 2 reels. Keystone Film Company (pro). Triangle Film Corporation (dist). *Roscoe Arbuckle (dir).* Al St John, Alice Lake, Horace J. Haine, Joe Bordeau, Mike Eagan, Bert Franc. Filmed at Dover in the New Jersey countryside while at Eastern Triangle studios in Fort Lee, New Jersey. Variant: *The Moonshiner.*

109
The Waiters' Ball. (The Waiters Ball). r25 Jun 1916. No copyright. fs8 Aug 1916. 2 reels. Keystone Film Company (pro). Triangle Film Corporation (dist). *Roscoe Arbuckle, Ferris Hartman (dirs).* Roscoe Arbuckle (cook/belle of the ball), Corinne Parquet (cashier), Al St John (waiter), Joe Bordeau (cashier's bad brother), Robert Maximilian (proprietor), Kate Price (dishwasher), Alice Lake (customer). Filmed at Eastern Triangle studios in Fort Lee, New Jersey. Variants: *The Waiters Ball*; *The Waiter's Ball.*

110
A Reckless Romeo. (His Alibi). July? 1916. No copyright. fs13 Sep 1916. 2 reels. Keystone Film Company (pro). Triangle Film Corporation (dist). *Roscoe Arbuckle (dir).* Filmed at Keystone studio in Los Angeles, California.

111
A Creampuff Romance. July? 1916. No copyright. 2 reels.

Keystone Film Company (pro). Triangle Film Corporation (dist). *Roscoe Arbuckle (dir)*. Roscoe Arbuckle (baker), Alice Lake (cashier), Al St John (soda jerk). Filmed at Keystone studio in Los Angeles, California. Variant: *A Cream Puff Romance*. Also known as *His Alibi*; *A Reckless Romeo*.

COMIQUE (1917)

Paramount-Arbuckle Comedies were produced by the Comique Film Corporation under the supervision of Joseph M. Schenck and distributed through Famous Players-Lasky Corporation by Paramount Pictures (Famous Players-Lasky Exchanges) on an open-booking basis. Famous Players-Lasky considered Arbuckle an affiliate or allied producer. The Paramount-Arbuckle Comedies were produced at several studios in New York and California; their production locations are identified in the filmography at the end of each entry.

112
The Butcher Boy. r23 Apr 1917. c12 Apr 1917. 2 reels. Paramount-Arbuckle Comedy No. A-3101. Comicque [*sic*] Film Corporation (pro/cc). Paramount Pictures (dist). *Roscoe Arbuckle (dir/writ). Joe Roach (story). Herbert Warren (scen ed). Frank D. Williams (cam).* Roscoe Arbuckle (butcher boy/'girl' cousin), Buster Keaton (village pest), Al St John (rube clerk and rival lover), Josephine Stevens (daughter of proprietor and pupil at girls' boarding school), Arthur Earle (store proprietor), Agnes Neilson (principal of girls' boarding school), Joe Bordeau (rube accomplice), Luke (dog). Filmed at Norma Talmadge Film Corporation studios at 318 East 48th Street in New York, New York.

113
A Reckless Romeo. r21 May 1917. No copyright. 2 reels. Paramount-Arbuckle Comedy No. A-3102. Comique Film Corporation (pro). Paramount Pictures (dist). *Roscoe Arbuckle (dir/writ). Joe Roach (story). Herbert Warren (scen*

ed). Frank D. Williams (cam). Roscoe Arbuckle (flirting husband), Buster Keaton (rival), Al St John (rival), Alice Lake, Corinne Parquet, Agnes Neilson (husband's mother-in-law). Filmed at Palisades Park amusement resort and at Norma Talmadge Film Corporation studios at 318 East 48th Street in New York, New York.

114

The Rough House. r25 Jun 1917. c20 Jun 1917. 2 reels. Paramount-Arbuckle Comedy No. A-3103. Comicque [*sic*] Film Corporation (pro/cc). Paramount Pictures (dist). *Roscoe Arbuckle (dir/writ). Joe Roach (story). Herbert Warren (scen ed). Frank D. Williams (cam).* Roscoe Arbuckle (Mr Rough), Buster Keaton, Al St John, Alice Lake. Filmed at Norma Talmadge Film Corporation studios at 318 East 48th Street in New York, New York. Variants: *A Rough House; Rough House.*

115

His Wedding Night. r20 Aug 1917; and 30 Aug 1917. c20 Aug 1917. 2 reels. Paramount-Arbuckle Comedy No. A-3104. Comicque [*sic*] Film Corporation (pro/cc). Paramount Pictures (dist). *Roscoe Arbuckle (dir/writ). Joe Roach (story). Herbert Warren (scen ed). George Peters (cam).* Roscoe Arbuckle, Buster Keaton, Al St John, Alice Mann, Arthur Earle. Filmed at Selznick Studios (old Biograph studios) at 796 East 176th Street in New York, New York.

116

Oh, Doctor! r30 Sep 1917. c19 Sep 1917. 2 reels. Paramount-Arbuckle Comedy No. A-3105. Comicque [*sic*] Film Corporation (pro/cc). Paramount Pictures (dist). *Roscoe Arbuckle (dir/writ). Herbert Warren (scen ed). Jean Havez (scen). George Peters (cam).* Roscoe Arbuckle (doctor), Buster Keaton, Al St John, Alice Mann. Filmed at Selznick Studios (old Biograph studios) at 796 East 176th Street in New York, New York; and at Coney Island amusement park. Variants: *Oh Doctor*; *Oh Doctor!*

117
Fatty at Coney Island. r29 Oct 1917. c11 Oct 1917. 2 reels. Paramount-Arbuckle Comedy No. A-3106. Comicque [*sic*] Film Corporation (pro/cc). Paramount Pictures (dist). *Roscoe Arbuckle (dir/writ). Herbert Warren (scen ed). George Peters (cam)*. Roscoe Arbuckle, Buster Keaton, Al St John, Alice Mann, Agnes Neilson, James Bryant, Joe Bordeau. Filmed at Selznick Studios (old Biograph studios) at 796 East 176th Street in New York, New York; and at Coney Island amusement park. Variants: *Fatty in Coney Island*; *Coney Island*.

118
A Country Hero. r10 Dec 1917. c13 Dec 1917. 2 reels. Paramount-Arbuckle Comedy No. A-3107. Famous Players-Lasky Corporation (cc). Comique Film Corporation (pro). Paramount Pictures (dist). *Roscoe Arbuckle (dir/writ). Herbert Warren (scen ed). George Peters (cam)*. Roscoe Arbuckle (village blacksmith), Buster Keaton, Al St John, Alice Lake (schoolteacher), Joe Keaton. Filmed at Jazzville, a rural village set built for Arbuckle at Horkheimer Brothers' Balboa Amusement Producing Company studios on Sixth and Alamitos streets in Long Beach, California. Variant: *Country Hero*.

COMIQUE (1918)

119
Out West. r20 Jan 1918. c20 Feb 1918. 2 reels. Paramount-Arbuckle Comedy No. A-3108. Comique Film Corporation (pro/cc). Paramount Pictures (dist). *Roscoe Arbuckle (dir/writ). Herbert Warren (scen ed). Natalie Talmadge (scen). George Peters (cam)*. Roscoe Arbuckle (town stranger and new bartender), Buster Keaton (dude gambler), Al St John (outlaw), Alice Lake (Salvation Army girl). Filmed at Horkheimer Brothers' studios on Sixth and Alamitos streets Balboa Amusement Producing Company in Long Beach and at Mad Dog Gulch, a Western mining-camp set built for Arbuckle in the San Gabriel Canyon near Los Angeles, California.

120

The Bell Boy. r18 Mar 1918. c7 Mar 1918. 2 reels. Paramount-Arbuckle Comedy No. A-3109. Famous Players-Lasky Corporation (cc). Comique Film Corporation (pro). Paramount Pictures (dist). *Roscoe Arbuckle (dir/writ). Herbert Warren (scen ed). George Peters (cam).* Roscoe Arbuckle (hotel bellboy, barber and general helper), Buster Keaton (village pest), Al St John (night clerk), Alice Lake (manicurist), Joe Keaton (rube), Charles Dudley (hotel guest). Filmed at Ouchgosh, a rural village set built for Arbuckle at Horkheimer Brothers' Balboa Amusement Producing Company studios on Sixth and Alamitos streets in Long Beach, California.

121

Moonshine. r13 May 1918. c6 May 1918. 2 reels. Paramount-Arbuckle Comedy No. A-3110. Famous Players-Lasky Corporation (cc). Comique Film Corporation (pro). Paramount Pictures (dist). *Roscoe Arbuckle (dir/writ). Herbert Warren (scen ed). George Peters (cam).* Roscoe Arbuckle (revenue officer), Buster Keaton (his assistant), Al St John (moonshiner), Charles Dudley (his father and feud leader), Alice Lake (girl), Joe Bordeau. Filmed in the San Gabriel Canyon near Los Angeles, California; and at Horkheimer Brothers' Balboa Amusement Producing Company studios on Sixth and Alamitos streets in Long Beach, California. The Horkheimers' Balboa Amusement Producing Company ceased operations April 1918 while *Moonshine* was in production, but Arbuckle continued to use the studio for his own productions under the name Comique Film Corporation studios, Roscoe Arbuckle Comedy Company.

122

Good Night, Nurse! r8 Jul 1918. c22 Jun 1918. 2 reels. Paramount-Arbuckle Comedy No. A-3111. Famous Players-Lasky Corporation (cc). Comique Film Corporation (pro). Paramount Pictures (dist). *Roscoe Arbuckle (dir/writ). Herbert Warren (scen ed). George Peters (cam).* Roscoe Arbuckle (resort guest/'nurse'), Buster Keaton (visitor/doctor), Al St John (assistant), Alice Lake (patient), Kate

Price (nurse), Joe Keaton (assistant). Filmed at Arrowhead Hot Springs health resort and at Comique Film Corporation studios (old Balboa studios) on Sixth and Alamitos streets in Long Beach, California. Variants: *Good Night Nurse; Good Night, Nurse*; *Goodnight Nurse*.

123
The Cook. r15 Sep 1918. c20 Aug 1918. 2 reels. Paramount-Arbuckle Comedy No. A-3112. Comique Film Corporation (pro/cc). Paramount Pictures (dist). *Roscoe Arbuckle (dir/writ)*. Roscoe Arbuckle (cook), Buster Keaton (waiter and general helper), Al St John (rival lover), Alice Lake (cashier), Glen Cavender. Filmed at Comique Film Corporation studios (old Balboa studios) on Sixth and Alamitos streets in Long Beach, California. Original release date changed from 18 Aug 1918 to 15 Sep 1918.

124
The Sheriff. r24 Nov 1918. No copyright. 2 reels. Paramount-Arbuckle Comedy No. A-3113. Comique Film Corporation (pro). Paramount Pictures (dist). *Roscoe Arbuckle (dir/writ)*. Roscoe Arbuckle (sheriff), Betty Compson (schoolteacher), Mario Bianchi, Glen Cavender. Filmed at Diando Film Corporation studios (old Kalem studios) on Verdugo Road in Glendale, California.

FAMOUS PLAYERS-LASKY (1918)

125
United States Fourth Liberty Loan Drive. rNov 1918. Picture made by different studios to aid the Fourth Liberty Loan Drive; supervised by E. L. Hyman, Director of Pictures Division of the Commission on Training Camp Activities, for distribution to all Liberty Theatres throughout the United States. Roscoe Arbuckle, Douglas Fairbanks, Geraldine Farrar, Mary Pickford, Wallace Reid, William S. Hart, Elsie Ferguson, George M. Cohan, Lillian Gish, Dorothy Dalton, William Faversham, Mabel Normand, Harold Lockwood, Edith Storey, Emily Stevens, Alice

Brady, Norma Talmadge, William Farnum, Mae Murray, Pauline Frederick, Mae Marsh, Madge Kennedy, Tom Moore, Sessue Hayakawa.

126
Canadian Victory Loan Drive. rNov 1918. Picture produced by Famous Players-Lasky Corporation for the Canadian government's 1918 Victory Loan Campaign during October-November 1918. Roscoe Arbuckle, Elsie Ferguson, William S. Hart, Mary Pickford, Douglas Fairbanks, Wallace Reid, Lillian Gish, Dorothy Dalton, Mack Sennett players.

COMIQUE (1919)

127
Camping Out. r5 Jan 1919. c31 Dec 1918. 2 reels. Paramount-Arbuckle Comedy No. A-3114. Famous Players-Lasky Corporation (cc). Comique Film Corporation (pro). Paramount Pictures (dist). *Roscoe Arbuckle (dir/writ)*. Roscoe Arbuckle, Al St John, Alice Lake. Filmed in and around Avalon on Catalina Island. Also known as *Camping*.

128
The Pullman Porter. r16 Feb 1919. No copyright. 2 reels. No Paramount-Arbuckle Comedy Number assigned. Comique Film Corporation (pro). Paramount Pictures (dist). *Roscoe Arbuckle (dir/writ)*. Roscoe Arbuckle.

129
Love. r2 Mar 1919. c21 Feb 1919. 2 reels. Paramount-Arbuckle Comedy No. A-3115. Famous Players-Lasky Corporation (cc). Comique Film Corporation (pro). Paramount Pictures (dist). *Roscoe Arbuckle (dir/writ). Vincent Bryan (scen)*. Roscoe Arbuckle (farm boy), Al St John (rich boy and rival lover), Winifred Westover (farmer's daughter). Filmed at Comique Film Corporation studios at 1723 Allesandro Street in Los Angeles (Edendale), California.

Original release date changed from 16 Feb 1919 to 2 Mar 1919.

130
The Bank Clerk. r5 Apr 1919. No copyright. 2 reels. No Paramount-Arbuckle Comedy Number assigned. Comique Film Corporation (pro). Paramount Pictures (dist). *Roscoe Arbuckle (dir/writ).* Roscoe Arbuckle, Molly Malone. Filmed at Comique Film Corporation studios at 1723 Allesandro Street in Los Angeles (Edendale), California.

131
A Desert Hero. r1 Jun 1919; and 15 Jun 1919. c13 Jun 1919. 2 reels. Paramount-Arbuckle Comedy No. A-3116. Famous Players-Lasky Corporation (cc). Comique Film Corporation (pro). Paramount Pictures (dist). *Roscoe Arbuckle (dir/writ). Jean Havez (scen).* Roscoe Arbuckle (sheriff, the desert hero), Al St John (bad man), Molly Malone (young girl), Monte Collins (old man). Filmed in the hills near Glendale, California, and at the Comique Film Corporation studios at 1723 Allesandro Street in Los Angeles (Edendale), California.

132
Back Stage. r7 Sep 1919. c20 Aug 1919. 2 reels. Colour (tinted). Famous Players-Lasky Corporation (cc). Comique Film Corporation (pro). Paramount Pictures (dist). *Roscoe Arbuckle (dir/writ). Jean Havez (scen).* Roscoe Arbuckle (stage manager), Buster Keaton (stagehand), Al St John (stagehand), Molly Malone (young girl), John Coogan (dancer). Filmed at Comique Film Corporation studios at 1723 Allesandro Street in Los Angeles (Edendale), California.

133
The Hayseed. r26 Oct 1919. c13 Oct 1919. 2 reel. Famous Players-Lasky Corporation (cc). Comique Film Corporation (pro). Paramount Pictures (dist). *Roscoe Arbuckle (dir/writ). Jean Havez (scen).* Roscoe Arbuckle (rural mail carrier), Buster Keaton (general helper), Al St John (crooked sheriff),

Molly Malone (young girl). Filmed at Henry Lehrman studios (Thomas H. Ince studios) in Culver City, California.

COMIQUE (1920)

134
The Garage. r11 Jan 1920. c15 Dec 1919. 2 reels. Famous Players-Lasky Corporation (cc). Comique Film Corporation (pro). Paramount Pictures (dist). *Roscoe Arbuckle (dir/writ). Jean Havez (scen). Elgin Lessley (cam).* Roscoe Arbuckle (chief of fire department), Buster Keaton (assistant chief of fire department), Molly Malone (young girl), Harry McCoy (foiled lover), Daniel Crimmins (old man), Luke (mad dog). Filmed at Henry Lehrman studios (Thomas H. Ince studios) in Culver City, California. Also known as *Fire Chief*.

FAMOUS PLAYERS-LASKY (1920)

Paramount feature-length pictures starring Arbuckle were produced by the Famous Players-Lasky Corporation under the supervision of Jesse L. Lasky and distributed by Paramount Pictures (Famous Players-Lasky Exchanges). Famous Players-Lasky no longer considered Arbuckle an affiliate or allied producer. Arbuckle's feature pictures were produced at the Lasky ranch and the Lasky studio at 1520 Vine Street in Hollywood, California.

135
The Round Up. r10 Oct 1920. c26 Aug 1920. 7 reels. 6,417 feet. Paramount Production No. 323 (#2011). Famous Players-Lasky Corporation (pro/cc). Paramount Pictures (dist). *Jesse L. Lasky (pres). George Melford (pro/dir). Edmund Day (play). Tom Forman (scen). Paul Perry (cam).* Roscoe Arbuckle (Slim Hoover), Tom Forman (Jack Payson), Irving Cummings (Dick Lane), Mabel Julienne Scott (Echo Allen), Jean Acker (Polly Hope), Guy Oliver (Uncle Jim), Lucien Littlefield (Parenthesis), Fred W. Huntley (Sagebrush Charlie), Wallace Beery (Buck McKee), Jane

Wolfe (Josephine), George Kuwa (Chinese boy), Edward Sutherland (cowboy), Buster Keaton (bit as Indian). Picture produced between 22 Dec 1919 and 11 Feb 1920.

136
The Life of the Party. r12 Dec 1920. c8 Nov 1920. 5 reels. 4,944 feet. Paramount Production No. 342 (#2029). Famous Players-Lasky Corporation (pro/cc). Paramount Pictures (dist). *Joseph Henabery (dir). Dick Johnston (asst dir). Irvin S. Cobb (story: Saturday Evening Post). Walter Woods (scen). Karl Brown (cam).* Roscoe Arbuckle (Algernon Leary), Viora Daniel (Milly Hollister), Winifred Greenwood (Mrs Carraway), Roscoe Karns (Sam Perkins), Julia Faye (French Kate), Frank Campeau (Judge Voris), Allen Connor (Jake), Frederick Starr (Bolton), Ben Lewis (Clay). Picture produced between 15 Apr 1920 and 22 May 1920.

FAMOUS PLAYERS-LASKY (1921)

137
Brewster's Millions. rJan 1921. c4 Jan 1921. 6 reels. 5,502 feet. Colour (tinted and toned). Paramount Production No. 355. Famous Players-Lasky Corporation (pro/cc). Paramount Pictures (dist). *Jesse L. Lasky (pres). Frank E. Woods (sup). Joseph Henabery (dir). Dick Johnston (asst dir). George Barr McCutcheon (story: novel). Winchell Smith (play). Walter Woods (scen). Karl Brown (cam). Wilfred Buckland (art dir).* Roscoe Arbuckle (Montgomery Ingraham Brewster), Betty Ross Clark (Peggy Gray), Fred W. Huntley (Grandfather Brewster), Marian Skinner (Mrs Brewster), James Corrigan (Grandfather Ingraham), Jean Acker (Barbara Drew), Charles Ogle (Captain Drew), Neely Edwards (MacLeod), William Boyd (Harrison), L.J. McCarthy (Ellis), Parker J. McConnell (Pettingill), John McFarland (Blake), Walter A. Coughlin. This picture should not be confused with the *Brewster's Millions* produced by Jesse L. Lasky Feature Play Company and released

in 1914. Picture produced between 29 Jul 1920 and 20 Oct 1920.

138

The Dollar a Year Man. r3 Apr 1921. c3 Apr 1921. 5 reels. 4,606 feet. Colour (tinted and toned). Paramount Production No. 363 (#2061). Famous Players-Lasky Corporation (pro/cc). Paramount Pictures (dist). *James Cruze (dir). Vernon Keays (asst dir). Walter Woods (story/scen). Karl Brown (cam).* Roscoe Arbuckle (Franklin Pinney, a laundryman), Lila Lee (Peggy Bruce), Winifred Greenwood (Kate Connelly), Jean M. Dumont (Tipton Blair, a Socialist), Edward Sutherland (Prince Rupert), Edwin Stevens (Colonel Bruce, a Secret Service agent), Henry Johnson (General Oberano). Variant: *The Dollar-a-Year Man.* Picture produced between 16 Oct 1920 and 6 Nov 1920.

139

The Traveling Salesman. r5 Jun 1921. c2 Jun 1921. 5 reels. 4,514 feet. Paramount Production No. 350 (#2076). Famous Players-Lasky Corporation (pro/cc). Paramount Pictures (dist). *Joseph Henabery (dir). James Grant Forbes (play). Walter Woods (scen). Karl Brown (cam).* Roscoe Arbuckle (Bob Blake), Betty Ross Clark (Beth Elliott), Frank Holland (Franklin Royce), Wilton Taylor (Martin Drury), Lucille Ward (Mrs Babbitt), Jim Blackwell (Julius), Richard Wayne (Ted Watts), George C. Pearce (John Kimball), Robert Dudley (Pierce Gill), Gordon Rogers (Bill Crabb). This picture should not be confused with *The Traveling Salesman* produced by Famous Players Film Company, presented by Daniel Frohman and released by Paramount Pictures in 1916. Picture produced between 10 Jun 1920 and 12 Jul 1920; completed before *Brewster's Millions* and *The Dollar a Year Man*, but released later.

140

Gasoline Gus. r20 Aug 1921. No copyright. 5 reels. Colour (tinted and toned). Paramount Production No. 378 (#2112). Famous Players-Lasky Corporation (pro). Paramount Pictures (dist). *Jesse L. Lasky (pres). Frank E. Woods (sup).*

James Cruze (dir). Vernon Keays (asst dir). George Patullo (story: Saturday Evening Post). Walter Woods (adapt/scen). Karl Brown (cam). Roscoe Arbuckle (Augustus 'Gasoline Gus' Peeler), Lila Lee (Sal Jo Banty), Charles Ogle (Nate Newberry), Theodore Lorch ('Dry Check' Charlie), Wilton Taylor (Judge Shortredge), Knute Erickson ('Scrap Iron' Swenson), Fred W. Huntley (Don Rayburn). Adapted from two Patullo stories, 'Gasoline Gus' and 'Drycheck Charlie' which appeared in *Saturday Evening Post*. Picture produced between 21 Mar 1921 and 14 Apr 1921. Withdrawn from United States distribution in September 1921.

141
Crazy to Marry. (Three Miles Out). r28 Aug 1921; c28 Aug 1921. 5 reels. 4,693; 4,761; or 5,402 feet. Colour (tinted and toned). Paramount Production No. 372 (#2098). Famous Players-Lasky Corporation (pro/cc). Paramount Pictures (dist). *Jesse L. Lasky (pres). Frank E. Woods (sup). James Cruze (dir). Vernon Keays (asst dir). Frank Condon (story). Walter Woods (scen). Karl Brown (cam). Max Parker (art dir).* Roscoe Arbuckle (Dr Hobart Hupp), Lila Lee (Annabelle Landis), Lura Anson (Estrella De Morgan), Edwin Stevens (Henry De Morgan), Lillian Leighton (Sarah De Morgan), Bull Montana (Dago Red, a crook), Allen Durnell (Arthur Simmons), Sidney Bracy (Colonel Landis), Genevieve Blinn (Mrs Landis), Clarence Burton (Gregory Slade, a lawyer), Henry Johnson (Norman Gregory, his son), Charles Ogle (cement man), Jackie Young (cupid), Lucien Littlefield (minister). Picture produced between 17 Jan 1921 and 19 Feb 1921; completed before *Gasoline Gus*, but released later. Also known as *Three Miles Out*.

142
Leap Year. (Skirt Shy). r (scheduled) 1921. No copyright. 5 reels. 4,767 feet. Paramount Production No. 389 (#2128). Famous Players-Lasky Corporation (pro). Paramount Pictures (dist). *Adolph Zukor (pres). James Cruze (dir). Vernon Keays (asst dir). Sarah Y. Mason (story). Walter Woods (scen). Karl Brown (cam).* Roscoe Arbuckle (Stanley Piper),

Mary Thurman (Phyllis Brown), Lucien Littlefield (Jeremiah Piper), Harriet Hammond (Loris Keene), Maude Wayne (Irene Rutherford), Clarence Geldart (Scott Travis), Winifred Greenwood (Mrs Scott Travis), Allen Durnell (Tommy Blaine), Gertrude Short (Molly Morris), John McKinnon (Mumford). Picture produced between 16 May 1921 and 9 Jun 1921 under the working title *Should a Man Marry?* Picture completed and title changed to *Skirt Shy*, but not released in United States. Picture released in Europe 26 Mar 1922 as *Leap Year*. Also known as *This Is So Sudden.*

143
Freight Prepaid. (Via Fast Freight). r (scheduled) 1921. No copyright. 5 reels. Paramount Production No. 397 (#2176). Famous Players-Lasky Corporation (pro). Paramount Pictures (dist). *James Cruze (dir). Curtis Benton (story).* Roscoe Arbuckle (Erastus Berry), Lila Lee (Bonnie Daly), Nigel Barrie (John Hammond), Herbert Standing (Mr Hammond), Raymond Hatton (minister). Picture produced between 18 Jul 1921 and 13 Aug 1921 under the working title *Via Fast Freight.* Exterior scenes filmed on location in Chicago. Picture completed and title changed to *Freight Prepaid*, but not released in United States. Picture released in Europe 18 Jun 1922. Also known as *Fast Freight; The Fast Freight; Handle With Care.*

FAMOUS PLAYERS-LASKY (1922)
(Intended Arbuckle Pictures)

Famous Players-Lasky intended to star Arbuckle in the following feature-length pictures, which were given to other stars:

144
'The Melancholy Spirit.' r (scheduled) 1922. Famous Players-Lasky Corporation (pro). Picture begun with Arbuckle in September 1921 under the working title *The Melancholy Spirit.* Production under the supervision of Frank E. Woods, directed by James Cruze from an original

story by James Cruze and A. B. Barringer, scenario by Walter Woods, and camera by Karl Brown. Production was suspended, story revised under the title *Ek, A Fighting Soul*, and picture given to Will Rogers, with Lila Lee, Alan Hale, John Fox, George Nichols, Emily Rait, Knute Erickson. Title changed to *One Glorious Day* and picture released in 5 reels by Paramount Pictures on 5 Feb 1922.

145
'*Thirty Days*.' r (scheduled) 1922. Famous Players-Lasky Corporation (pro). Picture intended for Arbuckle, but given to Wallace Reid, with Wanda Hawley, Charles Ogle, Cyril Chadwick, Hershall Mayall, Helen Dunbar, Carmen Phillips, Kalla Pasha, Robert Brower. Picture produced between 24 Aug 1922 and 9 Sep 1922; released as *Thirty Days* in 5 reels by Paramount Pictures on 10 Dec 1922.

146
'*The Man From Mexico*.' r (scheduled) 1922. Famous Players-Lasky Corporation (pro). Picture intended for Arbuckle as remake of *Man From Mexico* (Paramount-Famous Players, 1914) starring John Barrymore and based upon the Henry A. Du Souchet stage play, *The Man From Mexico*. Picture given to Richard Dix, with Lois Wilson, Nat Pendleton, Douglas MacPherson, Gunboat Smith, Joseph Kilgour, Tom Findley, Edna May Oliver. Title changed to *Let's Get Married* and picture released in 7 reels by Paramount Pictures on 29 Mar 1926.

Famous Players-Lasky intended to star Arbuckle in the following feature-length picture, which was not produced.

147
'*Are You a Mason?*' r (scheduled) 1922. Famous Players-Lasky Corporation (pro). Picture intended for Arbuckle as remake of *Are You a Mason?* (Paramount-Famous Players, 1915) starring John Barrymore and based upon the Leo Ditrichstein stage play, *Are You a Mason?* Picture rights sold by Paramount to Twickenham Film Studios in London in 1934 for *Are You a Mason?* (Universal-Olympic, 1934).

Rights were bought back in 1941 for possible feature for Bob Hope or Jack Benny, but picture was not produced.

GAVIN McNAB (1923)

(Intended Arbuckle Picture)

Arbuckle's attorney Gavin McNab and associates financed the following two-reel picture to be Arbuckle's first starring role in films after the scandal.

148
'*Handy Andy.*' r (scheduled) 1923. No copyright. 2 reels. Gavin McNab (pro). *Herman Raymaker (dir).* Roscoe Arbuckle, Molly Malone. Arbuckle suspended work on this production in February 1923 and announced his return to the screen as director, not as comedian. Picture may have been completed but was not released in the United States.

FAMOUS PLAYERS-LASKY (1923)

149
Hollywood r19 Aug 1923. c10 Jul 1923. 8 reels. 8,100 feet. Paramount Production No. 477. Famous Players-Lasky Corporation (pro/cc). Paramount Pictures (dist). *Jesse L. Lasky (pres). James Cruze (dir). Frank Condon (story). Tom Geraghty (adapt). Karl Brown (cam).* Hope Drown (Angela Whitaker), Luke Cosgrave (Joel Whitaker), George K. Arthur (Lem Lefferts), Ruby Lafayette (Grandmother Whitaker), Harris Gordon (Dr Luke Morrison), Bess Flowers (Hortense Towers), Eleanor Lawson (Margaret Whitaker), King Zany (Horace Pringle), Roscoe Arbuckle (man in casting director's office). Also Gertrude Astor, Mary Astor, Agnes Ayres, Baby Peggy, T. Roy Barnes, Noah Beery, William Boyd, Clarence Burton, Robert Cain, Edythe Chapman, Betty Compson, Ricardo Cortez, Viola Dana, Cecil B. DeMille, William DeMille, Charles DeRoche, Dinky Dean, Helen Dunbar, Snitz Edwards, George Fawcett, Julia Faye, James Finlayson, Alec B.

Francis, Jack Gardner, Sid Grauman, Alfred E. Green, Alan Hale, Lloyd Hamilton, Hope Hampton, William S. Hart, Gale Henry, Walter Hiers, Mrs Walter Hiers, Stuart Holmes, Sigrid Holmquist, Jack Holt, Leatrice Joy, Mayme Kelso, J. Warren Kerrigan, Theodore Kosloff, Kosloff Dancers, Lila Lee, Lillian Leighton, Jacqueline Logan, Mae McAvoy, Robert McKim, Jeanie Macpherson, Hank Mann, Joe Martin, Thomas Meighan, Bull Montana, Owen Moore, Nita Naldi, Pola Negri, Anna Q. Nilsson, Charles Ogle, Guy Oliver, Kalla Pasha, Eileen Percy, Carmen Phillips, Jack Pickford, Chuck Reisner, Fritzi Ridgeway, Will Rogers, Sennett Girls, Ford Sterling, Anita Stewart, George Stewart, Gloria Swanson, Estelle Taylor, Ben Turpin, Bryant Washburn, Maude Wayne, Claire West, Laurence Wheat, Lois Wilson. Picture produced between 15 Feb 1923 and 3 May 1923.

EDUCATIONAL (1923)
(Disputed Arbuckle Pictures)

Educational Tuxedo Comedies were produced by Reel Comedies, Inc. and distributed by the Educational Film Exchanges. Arbuckle began his affiliation with Reel Comedies in February 1923 and may have worked as director, writer, supervising director and/or producer on the following pictures:

150
Easter Bonnets. r26 Aug 1923. No copyright. 2 reels. Tuxedo Comedies. Reel Comedies (pro). Educational Film Exchanges (dist). Ned Sparks, Harry Tighe, Marion Harlan, Doris Deane. First release in the Tuxedo Comedies series.

151
Front! r17 Oct 1923. No copyright. 2 reels. Tuxedo Comedies. Reel Comedies (pro). Educational Film Exchanges (dist). Poodles Hanneford.

152
No Loafing. r25 Nov 1923. No copyright. 2 reels. Tuxedo Comedies. Reel Comedies (pro). Educational Film Exchanges (dist). Poodles Hanneford.

EDUCATIONAL (1924)
(Disputed Arbuckle Pictures)

153
One Night It Rained. r20 Jan 1924. No copyright. 2 reels. Tuxedo Comedies. Reel Comedies (pro). Educational Film Exchanges (dist). Ned Sparks, Harry Tighe, Doris Deane.

154
The New Sheriff. r16 Mar 1924. No copyright. 2 reels. Tuxedo Comedies. Reel Comedies (pro). Educational Film Exchanges (dist). Poodles Hanneford.

METRO (1924)

155
Sherlock, Jr. r21 Apr 1924. c22 Apr 1924. 5 reels. Joseph M. Schenck (pro/cc). Metro Pictures Corporation (dist). *Buster Keaton (dir). Jean Havez, Joseph Mitchell, Clyde Bruckman (writs/adapts). Fred Gabourie (sets). Clare West (ward). Elgin Lessley, Byron Houck (cam).* Buster Keaton (Sherlock, Jr), Kathryn McGuire (girl), Joe Keaton (her father), Ward Crane (rival), Erwin Connelly (his henchman), Jane Connelly, Ford West, George Davis, Horace Morgan, John Patrick, Ruth Holley. According to Keaton, Arbuckle directed this picture's first few days of production until personal problems on set forced Keaton to assume full control as director. According to Doris Deane, Arbuckle wrote and directed this picture as well as other Keaton pictures for which he was not given screen credit.

EDUCATIONAL (1924)
(Disputed Arbuckle Pictures)

156
The Bonehead. r18 May 1924. No copyright. 2 reels. Tuxedo Comedies. Reel Comedies (pro). Educational Film Exchanges (dist). Poodles Hanneford.

Al St John received official credit as director and writer for his first four Tuxedo Comedies, and Grover Jones received credit as director for St John's three remaining Tuxedo Comedies. According to Doris Deane, Arbuckle was director on set and writer for all Tuxedo Comedies starring Al St John.

157
His First Car. r27 Jul 1924. No copyright. 2 reels. Tuxedo Comedies. Reel Comedies (pro). Educational Film Exchanges (dist). *Al St John (dir/writ)*. Al St John, Doris Deane, George Davis, Blanche Payson. Al St John's first picture in the Tuxedo Comedies series.

158
Never Again. r24 Aug 1924. c24 Aug 1924. 2 reels. Tuxedo Comedies. Reel Comedies (pro/cc). Educational Film Exchanges (dist). *Al St John (dir/writ)*. Al St John, Doris Deane, Blanche Payson.

159
Stupid But Brave. r26 Oct 1924. c27 Oct 1924. 2 reels. Tuxedo Comedies. Reel Comedies (pro/cc). Educational Film Exchanges (dist). *Al St John (dir/writ)*. Al St John, Doris Deane.

160
Lovemania. r28 Dec 1924. c28 Dec 1924. 2 reels. Tuxedo Comedies. Reel Comedies (pro/cc). Educational Film Exchanges (dist). *Al St John (dir/writ)*. Al St John, Doris Deane, George Davis, Glen Cavender.

EDUCATIONAL (1925)
(Disputed Arbuckle Pictures)

161
Dynamite Doggie. r Mar 1925. c6 Apr 1925. 2 reels. Tuxedo Comedies. Reel Comedies (pro/cc). Educational Film Exchanges (dist). *Grover Jones (dir)*. Al St John.

162
The Iron Mule. r12 Apr 1925. c4 May 1925. 2 reels. Tuxedo Comedies. Reel Comedies (pro/cc). Educational Film Exchanges (dist). *Grover Jones (dir)*. Al St John, Doris Deane, George Davis, Glen Cavender. Burlesque of John Ford's *The Iron Horse* (Fox, 1924).

163
Curses. r May 1925. c21 May 1925. 2 reels. Tuxedo Comedies. Reel Comedies (pro/cc). Educational Film Exchanges (dist). *Grover Jones (dir)*. Al St John.

EDUCATIONAL (1925)

Arbuckle adopted the pseudonym William Goodrich and used this name from 1925 to 1932. Tuxedo Comedies starring Johnny Arthur were produced by Goodwill Comedies, Inc.; Arbuckle worked as director and writer on this series, and may have been producer and/or supervising director. Lloyd Hamilton Comedies were produced by the Lloyd Hamilton Corporation and the Lupino Lane Comedies by Lupino Lane Comedy Corporation. These three series were distributed by Educational Film Exchanges and produced at the Educational studio at 7250 Santa Monica Boulevard in Los Angeles, California.

164
The Tourist. r20 Sep 1925. c24 Sep 1925. 2 reels. Tuxedo Comedies. Educational Film Exchanges (dist/cc). Goodwill Comedies (pro). *William Goodrich (dir)*. Johnny Arthur,

Helen Foster. First of the Tuxedo Comedies starring Johnny Arthur.

165
The Movies. r4 Oct 1925. c13 Oct 1925. 2 reels. Hamilton Comedies. Educational Film Exchanges (dist/cc). Lloyd Hamilton Corporation (pro). *William Goodrich (dir/writ)*. Lloyd Hamilton (country boy/screen comedy star), Marcella Daley (actress), Arthur Thalasso (villain), Frank Jonasson (director), Glen Cavender (traffic officer). Filmed at Montmartre Cafe on Hollywood Boulevard and at the Educational studio in Los Angeles, California.

METRO-GOLDWYN-MAYER (1925)

166
Go West. r1 Nov 1925. c23 Nov 1925. New York premiere 25 Oct 1925. 7 reels. 6,293 feet. Buster Keaton Productions (pro/cc). Metro-Goldwyn-Mayer (dist). *Joseph M. Schenck (pro/pres). Buster Keaton (dir/story). Raymond Cannon (scen). Elgin Lessley, Bert Haines (cam)*. Buster Keaton (Friendless), Howard Truesdale (owner of Diamond Bar Ranch), Kathleen Myers (his daughter), Ray Thompson (foreman), Roscoe Arbuckle (bit as big lady in department store), Babe London ('her' daughter), Brown Eyes (cow).

EDUCATIONAL (1925)

167
Cleaning Up. r22 Nov 1925. c2 Jan 1926. 2 reels. Tuxedo Comedies. Educational Film Exchanges (dist/cc). Goodwill Comedies (pro). *William Goodrich (dir/writ)*. Johnny Arthur, George Davis.

168
The Fighting Dude. r6 Dec 1925. c29 Dec 1925. 2 reels. Lupino Lane Comedies. Educational Film Exchanges (dist/cc). Lupino Lane Comedy Corporation (pro). *William*

Goodrich (dir/writ). Lupino Lane (hero), Virginia Vance (girl), Wallace Lupino (villain), Glen Cavender (referee), George Davis.

EDUCATIONAL (1926)

169
My Stars. r17 Jan 1926. c17 Mar 1926. 2 reels. Tuxedo Comedies. Educational Film Exchanges (dist/cc). Goodwill Comedies (pro). *William Goodrich (dir/writ)*. Johnny Arthur, Virginia Vance, Florence Lee, Glen Cavender, George Davis.

170
Home Cured. r14 Mar 1926. c14 Mar 1926. 2 reels. Tuxedo Comedies. Christie Film Company [*sic*] (cc). Goodwill Comedies (pro). Educational Film Exchanges (dist). *William Goodrich (dir). Vernon Keays (asst dir). Donna Barrell (story). Byron Houck (cam)*. Johnny Arthur (hypochondriac husband), Virginia Vance (his wife), Glen Cavender, George Davis.

171
Fool's Luck, r21 Mar 1926. c22 Jun 1926. 2 reels. Lupino Lane Comedies. Educational Film Exchanges (dist/cc). Lupino Lane Comedy Corporation (pro). *William Goodrich (dir/writ). Bert Houck (cam)*. Lupino Lane (rich youth), Virginia Vance (his fiancée), George Davis (sissy valet), Jack Lloyd.

172
His Private Life. r16 May 1926. c10 May 1926. 2 reels. Lupino Lane Comedies. Educational Film Exchanges (dist/cc). Lupino Lane Comedy Corporation (pro). *William Goodrich (dir/writ)*. Lupino Lane (Army private, once a foppish young millionaire), Virginia Vance (girl), Glen Cavender (officer), George Davis (sergeant).

173
One Sunday Morning. r12 Dec 1926. c14 Dec 1926. 2 reels. Hamilton Comedies. Educational Film Exchanges (dist/cc). Lloyd Hamilton Corporation (pro). *William Goodrich (dir/writ). William Nobles (cam)*. Lloyd Hamilton.

EDUCATIONAL (1927)

174
Peaceful Oscar. r30 Jan 1927. c30 Jan 1927. 2 reels. Educational-Hamilton Comedy. Educational Film Exchanges (dist/cc). Lloyd Hamilton Corporation (pro). *William Goodrich (dir)*. Lloyd Hamilton.

METRO-GOLDWYN-MAYER (1927)

175
The Red Mill. r29 Jan 1927. c2 Mar 1927. 7 reels. 6,337 feet. Metro-Goldwyn-Mayer Corporation (dist/cc). Cosmopolitan Productions (pro). *William Goodrich, King Vidor (dirs). Victor Herbert, Henry Martyn Blossom (musical comedy play). Frances Marion (adapt/scen). Joe Farnham (titl). Hendrik Sartov (cam). Cedric Gibbons, Merrill Pye (sets). Daniel J. Gray (film ed). Andre-ani (ward)*. Marion Davies (Tina), Owen Moore (Dennis), Louise Fazenda (Gretchen), George Siegmann (Willem), Karl Dane (Captain Edam), J. Russell Powell (burgomaster), Snitz Edwards (Caesar), William Orlamond (governor), Fred Gambold (innkeeper), Ignatz (mouse). Due to William R. Hearst's dissatisfaction with Arbuckle's direction, King Vidor was brought on to the film and finished it with Arbuckle. Arbuckle alone received official credit as director.

FAMOUS PLAYERS-LASKY (1927)

176
Special Delivery. r6 May 1927. c26 Mar 1927. 6 reels. 5,524

feet. Paramount Production No. 630. Famous Players-Lasky Corporation (pro/cc). Paramount Pictures (dist). *Adolph Zukor, Jesse L. Lasky (pres). B. P. Schulberg (assoc pro). William Goodrich (dir). Henry Hathaway, Vernon Keays (asst dirs). Eddie Cantor (story). John Goodrich (adapt/cont/scen). George Marion, Jr (titl). Henry Hallenberger (cam). Louis D. Lighton (editor-in-chief).* Eddie Cantor (Eddie Beagle, the mail carrier), Jobyna Ralston (Madge Warren, the girl), William Powell (Harold Jones, get-rich-quick artist), Louis Stern (John Beagle), Mabel Julienne Scott (Mrs Jones), Donald Keith (Harrigan, the fireman), Jack Dougherty (Flannigan, cop on the beat), Victor Potel (Nip, a detective), Paul Kelly (Tuck, another detective), Mary Carr (the mother), Doris Deane. Picture produced between 27 Dec 1926 and 4 Feb 1927.

EDUCATIONAL (1930)

Lloyd Hamilton Talking Comedies (later Lloyd Hamilton Comedies), Ideal Talking Comedies (later Ideal Comedies), Mermaid Comedies and Cameo Comedies were produced by Educational Pictures, Inc., distributed by Educational Film Exchanges, and produced at the Educational studio at 7250 Santa Monica Boulevard in Los Angeles, California.

177
Won By a Neck. r5 Oct 1930. c5 Oct 1930; and 1 Mar 1931. 2 reels. Sd. Lloyd Hamilton Talking Comedies. Educational film Exchanges (dist/cc). Educational Pictures (pro). *William Goodrich (dir). Ralph Nelson (asst dir). Tom Whiteley (story). Harry McCoy, Walter DeLeon (cont/dia). Dwight Warren (cam).* Lloyd Hamilton.

178
Si, Si, Senor. r21 Sep 1930. c26 Oct 1930. 2 reels. Sd. Ideal Talking Comedies. Educational Film Exchanges (dist/cc). Educational Pictures (pro). *William Goodrich (dir).* Tom Patricola, Joe Phillips, Chiquita, Carmel Guerrox. Variant: *Si Si Senor.*

179
Up a Tree. r30 Nov 1930. c27 Dec 1930. 2 reels. Sd. Lloyd Hamilton Talking Comedies. Educational Film Exchanges (dist/cc). Educational Pictures (pro). *William Goodrich (dir/story). Ralph Nelson (asst dir). Harry McCoy, Jimmy Starr (cont/dia). Dwight Warren (cam).* Lloyd Hamilton, Dell Henderson, Addie McPhail.

EDUCATIONAL (1931)

180
Three Hollywood Girls. r4 Jan 1931. c4 Jan 1931. 2 reels. Sd. Ideal Comedies. Educational Film Exchanges (dist/cc). Educational Pictures (pro) .*William Goodrich (dir). Ralph Nelson (asst dir). Katharine Scola, Sherman L. Lowe (story). James Gleason, Ernest Pagano, Jack Townley (cont/dia). Dwight Warren (cam).* Leota Lane, Rita Flynn, Phyllis Crane, Eddie Nugent, Ford West, Florence Oberle. First picture in the 'Hollywood Girls' series.

181
Marriage Rows. r18 Jan 1931. c18 Jan 1931. 2 reels. Sd. Lloyd Hamilton Talking Comedies. Educational Film Exchanges (dist/cc). Educational Pictures (pro). *William Goodrich (dir/story). Ralph Nelson (asst dir). Walter Reed (cont/adapt). Dwight Warren (cam).* Lloyd Hamilton, Al St John, Addie McPhail, Doris Deane, Edna Marion.

182
Pete and Repeat. r1 Mar 1931. c1 Mar 1931. 2 reels. Sd. Ideal Comedies. Educational Film Exchanges (dist/cc). Educational Pictures (pro). *William Goodrich (dir). George Jeske, Joey Mack, A. Gold (story). Ernest Pagano, Jack Townley (cont/dia).* 'Bud' Harrison and Peenie Elmo ('Seben 'n' Leben', vaudeville blackface comics).

183
Ex-Plumber. r8 Mar 1931. c8 Mar 1931. 2 reels. Sd. Lloyd Hamilton Comedies. Educational Film Exchanges (dist/cc).

Educational Pictures (pro). *William Goodrich (dir/writ). Ralph Nelson (asst dir). Walter Reed (cont/dia). Dwight Warren (cam).* Lloyd Hamilton, Addie McPhail, Stanley Blystone, Mitchell Lewis, Amber Norman, Polly Christy.

184
Crashing Hollywood. r5 Apr 1931. c5 Apr 1931. 2 reels. Sd. Ideal Comedies. Educational Film Exchanges (dist/cc). Educational Pictures (pro). *William Goodrich (dir). Ralph Nelson (asst dir). Ernest Pagano, Jack Townley (story/cont/dia). Dwight Warren (cam).* Virginia Brooks, Rita Flynn, Phyllis Crane, Eddie Nugent, Wilbur Mack, Walter Merrill. Second picture in the 'Hollywood Girls' series.

185
Windy Riley Goes Hollywood. r3 May 1931. c3 May 1931. 2 reels. Sd. Mermaid Comedies. Educational Film Exchanges (dist/cc). Educational Pictures (pro). *William Goodrich (dir). Ken Kling (story). Ernest Pagano, Jack Townley (cont/dia).* Louise Brooks, Jack Shutta, William Davidson, Wilbur Mack, Dell Henderson, Walter Merrill, E.H. Allen. Picture based upon Ken Kling's syndicated comic strip, 'Windy Riley'. Picture included guest appearance by E. H. Allen, General Manager of Educational studio.

186
The Back Page. r24 May 1931. c24 May 1931. 2 reels. Sd. Mermaid Comedies. Educational Film Exchanges (dist/cc). Educational Pictures (pro). *William Goodrich (dir). Ernest Pagano, Jack Townley (story/cont/dia).* George Chandler, Virginia Brooks, Wheeler Oakman, George MacFarlane, Ethel Davis. Burlesque of *The Front Page* (United Artists, 1931).

187
The Lure of Hollywood. r5 Jul 1931. c5 Jul 1931. 2 reels. Sd. Ideal Comedies. Educational Film Exchanges (dist/cc). Educational Pictures (pro). *William Goodrich (dir). Ernest Pagano, Jack Townley (story/dia).* Virginia Brooks, Rita

Flynn, Phyllis Crane, George Chandler, Bryant Washburn. Third picture in the 'Hollywood Girls' series.

RKO PATHE (1931)

Traveling Man Comedies and *Gay Girls Comedies* were produced by RKO Pathé Pictures, Inc., distributed by RKO Pathé Distributing Corporation, and produced at the RKO Pathé studios at 9336 Washington Boulevard in Culver City, California.

188
That's My Line. r13 Jul 1931. c13 Jul 1931. 2 reels. Sd. Traveling Man Comedies. RKO Pathé Distributing Corporation (dist/cc). RKO Pathé Pictures (pro). *Lew Lipton (sup). William Goodrich (dir/story/adapt). Albert Benham (asst dir). Harry Forbes, Robert Palmer (cam). Fred Maguire (film ed)*. Louis John Bartels, Paul Hurst, Doris McMahon. First picture in the *Traveling Man Comedies* series (sometimes called *Traveling Salesman Comedies*).

EDUCATIONAL (1931)

189
Honeymoon Trio. r30 Aug 1931. c30 Aug 1931. 1 reel. Sd. Cameo Comedies. Educational Film Exchanges (dist/cc). Educational Pictures (pro). *William Goodrich (dir). Ernest Pagano, Jack Townley, Harrison Jacobs (story/dia)*. Walter Catlett, Al St John, Dorothy Granger.

190
Up Pops the Duke. r20 Sept 1931. c20 Sep 1931. 2 reels. Sd. Mermaid Comedies. Educational Film Exchanges (dist/cc). Educational Pictures (pro). *William Goodrich (dir). Ernest Pagano, Jack Townley (story/dia)*. George Chandler, Pauline Wagner, Helen Bolton.

RKO PATHE (1931)

191
Beach Pajamas. r21 Sep 1931. c21 Sep 1931. 2 reels. Sd. Traveling Man Comedies. RKO Pathé Distributing Corporation (dist/cc). RKO Pathé Pictures (pro). *Lew Lipton (sup). William Goodrich (dir/story/adapt). William Mull (asst dir). Dwight Warren (cam). Walter Thompson (film ed).* Louis John Bartels.

192
Take 'Em and Shake 'Em. r28 Sep 1931. c28 Sep 1931. 2 reels. Sd. Gay Girls Comedies. RKO Pathé Distributing Corporation (dist/cc). RKO Pathé Pictures (pro). *Lew Lipton (sup). William Goodrich (dir). Albert Benham (asst dir). Beatrice Van (story). Ted McCord (cam). John Link (film ed).* June MacCloy, Marion Shilling, Gertrude Short.

EDUCATIONAL (1931)

193
That's My Meat. r4 Oct 1931. c4 Oct 1931. 1 reel. Sd. Cameo Comedies. Educational Film Exchanges (dist/cc). Educational Pictures (pro). *William Goodrich (dir). Ernest Pagano, Jack Townley, Johnnie Grey (story/dia).* Al St John.

194
One Quiet Night. r25 Oct 1931. c25 Oct 1931. 1 reel. Sd. Cameo Comedies. Educational Film Exchanges (dist/cc). Educational Pictures (pro). *William Goodrich (dir). Ernest Pagano, Jack Townley, Harrison Jacobs (story/dia).*

195
Queenie of Hollywood. r8 Nov 1931. c8 Nov 1931. 2 reels. Sd. Ideal Comedies. Educational Film Exchanges (dist/cc). Educational Pictures (pro). *William Goodrich (dir). Ernest Pagano, Jack Townley (story/dia).* Virginia Brooks, Rita Flynn, Jeanne Flarrin. Fourth picture in the 'Hollywood Girls' series.

196
Once a Hero. r22 Nov 1931. c22 Nov 1931. 2 reels. Sd. Mermaid Comedies. Educational Film Exchanges (dist/cc). Educational Pictures (pro). *William Goodrich (dir). Ernest Pagano. Jack Townley (story/dia)*.Emerson Treacy.

197
The Tamale Vendor. r26 Nov 1931. c26 Nov 1931. 2 reels. Sd. Ideal Comedies. Educational Film Exchanges (dist/cc). Educational Pictures (pro). *William Goodrich (dir). Ernest Pagano, Jack Townley (story/dia)*. Tom Patricola.

198
Idle Roomers. r29 Nov 1931. c29 Nov 1931. 1 reel. Sd. Cameo Comedies. Educational Film Exchanges (dist/cc). Educational Pictures (pro). *William Goodrich (dir). Ernest Pagano, Jack Townley (story/dia)*.

199
Smart Work. r27 Dec 1931. c27 Dec 1931. 1 reel. Sd. Cameo Comedies. Educational Film Exchanges (dist/cc). Educational Pictures (pro). *William Goodrich (dir). Ernest Pagano, Jack Townley (story/dia)*. Billy Dooley, Addie McPhail.

EDUCATIONAL (1932)

200
Moonlight and Cactus. r10 Jan 1932. c10 Jan 1932. 2 reels. Sd. Ideal Comedies. Educational Film Exchanges (dist/cc). Educational Pictures (pro). *William Goodrich (dir). Ernest Pagano, Jack Townley (story/dia)*. Tom Patricola.

201
Keep Laughing. r24 Jan 1932. c24 Jan 1932. 2 reels. Sd. Mermaid Comedies. Educational Film Exchanges (dist/cc). Educational Pictures (pro). *William Goodrich (dir). Ernest Pagano, Jack Townley (story/dia)*. Monty Collins, Addie

McPhail, Bryant Washburn, Phyllis Crane, Jack Shaw, Dorothy Granger, Richard Malaby, George Davis.

202
Anybody's Goat. r24 Jan 1932. c24 Jan 1932. 1 reel. Sd. Cameo Comedies. Educational Film Exchanges (dist/cc). Educational Pictures (pro). *William Goodrich (dir). Ernest Pagano, Jack Townley (story/dia).*

203
Bridge Wives. r21 Feb 1932. c21 Feb 1932. 1 reel. Sd. Cameo Comedies. Educational Film Exchanges (dist/cc). Educational Pictures (pro). *William Goodrich (dir). Ernest Pagano, Jack Townley (story/dia).* Al St John.

204
Hollywood Luck. r13 Mar 1932. c13 Mar 1932. 2 reels. Sd. Ideal Comedies. Educational Film Exchanges (dist/cc). Educational Pictures (pro). *William Goodrich (dir). Ernest Pagano, Jack Townley (story/dia).* Virginia Brooks, Rita Flynn, Frances Dean, Clarence Nordstrom, Fern Emmett, Addie McPhail.

205
Mother's Holiday. r20 Mar 1932. c20 Mar 1932. 1 reel. Sd. Cameo Comedies. Educational Film Exchanges (dist/cc). Educational Pictures (pro). *William Goodrich (dir). Walter Catlett (story).*

206
It's a Cinch. r27 Mar 1932. c27 Mar 1932. 2 reels. Sd. Mermaid Comedies. Educational Film Exchanges (dist/cc). Educational Pictures (pro). *William Goodrich (dir). Ernest Pagano, Jack Townley (story/dia).* Monty Collins, Phyllis Crane.

207
Hollywood Lights. r8 May 1932. c8 May 1932. 2 reels. Sd. Ideal Comedy. Educational Film Exchanges (dist/cc).

Educational Pictures (pro). *William Goodrich (dir). Ernest Pagano, Jack Townley (story/dia).*

RKO PATHE (1932)

208
Gigolettes. r23 May 1932. c6 Apr 1932. 2 reels. Sd. Gay Girls Comedies. RKO Pathé Pictures (pro/cc). RKO Pathé Distributing Corporation (dist). *Lew Lipton (sup). William Goodrich (dir). Beatrice Van (story). Fred Maguire (film ed).*

209
Niagara Falls. r27 Jun 1932. c16 Jul 1932. 2 reels. Sd. Gay Girls Comedies. RKO Pathé Pictures (pro/cc). RKO Pathé Distributing Corporation (dist). *Lew Lipton (sup). William Goodrich (dir). Ewart Adamson (story). Walter Thompson (film ed).* June MacCloy.

VITAPHONE (1932)

Vitaphone's Big V Comedies starring Arbuckle were produced by the Vitaphone Corporation under the supervision of Sam Sax, distributed by Warner Bros, and produced at the Vitaphone studio in Brooklyn, New York.

210
Hey, Pop. r12 Nov 1932. c12 Dec 1932. 2 reels. Sd. Big V Comedies, No. 4. The Vitaphone Corporation (pro/cc). Warner Bros (dist). *Alf Goulding (dir). Jack Henley, Glen Lambert (story).* Roscoe Arbuckle, Billy Hayes, Florence Auer, Jack Shutta, Dan Wolheim, Milton Wallace, Leo Hoyt, Hershall Mayall.

211

Buzzin' Around. r4 Feb 1933. c22 Mar 1933. 2 reels. Sd. Big V Comedies, No. 9. The Vitaphone Corporation (pro/cc). Warner Bros (dist). *Alf Goulding (dir). Jack Henley, Glen Lambert (story). E. P. DuPar (cam).* Roscoe Arbuckle, Al St John, Dan Coleman, Alice May Tuck, Tom Smith, Al Ochs, Harry Ward, Gertrude Mudge, Fritz Hubert, Donald MacBride, Pete (dog).

212

How've You Bean? r24 Jun 1933. c3 Jul 1933. 2 reels. Sd. Big V Comedies, No. 11. The Vitaphone Corporation (pro/cc). Warner Bros (dist). *Alf Goulding (dir). Jack Henley, Glen Lambert (story).* Roscoe Arbuckle, Mildred Van Dorn, Fritz Hubert.

213

Close Relations. r30 Sep 1933. c12 Sep 1933. 2 reels. Sd. Big V Comedies (New Series), No. 2. The Vitaphone Corporation (pro/cc). Warner Bros (dist). *Ray McCarey (dir). Jack Henley, Glen Lambert (story).* Roscoe Arbuckle, Charles Judels, Mildred Van Dorn, Harry Shannon, Shemp Howard, Hugh O'Connell.

214

In the Dough. r25 Nov 1933. c15 Nov 1933. 2 reels. Sd. Big V Comedies (New Series), No. 5. The Vitaphone Corporation (pro/cc). Warner Bros (dist). *Ray McCarey (dir). Jack Henley (story). E. P. DuPar (cam).* Roscoe Arbuckle, Lionel Stander, Shemp Howard, Marc Marion, Fred Harper, Dan Coleman.

215

Tomalio. r30 Dec 1933. c13 Feb 1934. 2 reels. Sd. Big V Comedies (New Series), No. 7. The Vitaphone Corporation (pro/cc). Warner Bros (dist). *Ray McCarey (dir). Jack Henley, Glen Lambert (story).* Roscoe Arbuckle, Charles Judels, Phyllis Holden, Fritz Hubert.

BIBLIOGRAPHY AND SOURCES

This is not a bibliography in the normally accepted sense of the word. Some of the books listed below are riddled with errors, half-truths and lies, while others proved accurate and informative. I have listed the bad along with the good.

In general, where there are several editions of a title, I have listed them in this order: American hardcover edition, first; then American paperback edition, in parentheses; then English edition. I have incorporated here the list of books consulted in the preparation of the filmography; titles consulted for that purpose are followed by (F). Primary sources for the filmography are listed at the end of this section.

Books

Adams, Ramon F. *Western Words: A Dictionary of the American West*. University of Oklahoma Press, 1968.

Anger, Kenneth. *Hollywood Babylon*. Phoenix: Associated Professional Services, 1965 (first version); Stonehill Publishing Company, 1974.

Blesh, Rudi. *Keaton*. Macmillan, 1966; Secker & Warburg. (F)

Brownlow, Kevin. *The Parade's Gone By*. Knopf, 1968.

Canfield, Alyce. *God in Hollywood*. New York: Wisdom House, 1961.

Cantor, Eddie, as told to David Freedman. *My Life Is In Your Hands*. New York: Blue Ribbon Books, 1932. (F)

Carr, William H. A. *Hollywood Tragedy*. Lancer paperback, 1962; expanded version, Fawcett paperback, 1975.

Chaplin, Charles. *My Autobiography*. Simon & Schuster, 1964; Bodley Head. (F)
Chaplin, Charles. *My Life in Pictures*. Grossett & Dunlap, 1975. (F)
Chesterton, G. K. *Selected Essays*. London: Collins, 1936, 1953.
Chevalier, Jaques. *Le Cinéma Burlesque Americain, 1912-1950*.
Cuence, Carlos Fernandez. *Historia del Cine*.
Durgnant, Raymond. *The Crazy Mirror: Hollywood Comedy and the American Image*. London: Faber & Faber, 1969.
Edmonds, I. G. *Hollywood R.I.P.* Illinois: Regency Books, 1963 (paperback).
Fowler, Gene. *Father Goose: The Story of Mack Sennett*. New York: Covici-Friede, 1934; (Avon paperback, 1974).
Fowler, Gene. *Goodnight, Sweet Prince: The Life and Times of John Barrymore*. Viking, 1944; (Ballantine, 1971).
Gifford, Denis. *Chaplin*. Doubleday, 1974. (F)
Gish, Lillian with Ann Pinchot. *The Movies, Mr. Griffith and Me*. Prentice-Hall, 1969; (Avon paperback).
Glyn, Anthony. *Elinor Glyn*. London: Hutchinson, 1955.
Goldwyn, Samuel. *Behind the Screen*. New York: George H. Doran, 1923.
Goodman, Ezra. *The Fifty-Year Decline and Fall of Hollywood*. Simon & Schuster, 1961.
Goodwins, Leslie. *The Most Popular Man in the English-Speaking World*, Charlie Chaplin. Landmark.
Gordon, Rev. C. *Personal Impressions of the Famous Trial*. San Francisco, December 1921 (published privately).
Green, Abel and Laurie, Joe, Jr *Show Biz: from Vaude to Video*. Holt, 1951.
Guiles, Fred Lawrence. *Marion Davies*. McGraw-Hill, 1972; W. H. Allen.
Gussow, Mel. *Don't Say Yes Until I Finish Talking: A Biography of Darryl F. Zanuck*. Doubleday, 1971.
Halliwell, Leslie. *The Filmgoer's Companion*. Hill & Wang, 1967; Paladin.
Hampton, Benjamin B. *A History of the Movies*. London: Noel Douglas, 1931. (Reprint available from Arno.)
Hays, Will. *The Memoirs of Will Hays*. Doubleday, 1955.

Hellman, Lillian. *An Unfinished Woman.* Little, Brown, 1969; Macmillan.
Huff, Theodore. *Charlie Chaplin.* Schuman, 1951. (F)
Inglis, Ruth A. *Freedom of the Movies.* University of Chicago Press, 1947.
Jeanne, René, and Ford, Charles. *Histoire du Cinéma Americain.*
Kael, Pauline, Mankiewicz, Herman J. and Welles, Orson. *The Citizen Kane Book.* Atlantic-Little, Brown, 1971; Paladin.
Keaton, Buster with Samuels, Charles. *My Wonderful World of Slapstick.* Doubleday, 1960; Geo. Allen & Unwin. (F)
Knight, Arthur. *The Liveliest Art.* New American Library, 1959 (paperback).
Kobler, John. *Capone.* G. P. Putnam's Sons, 1971; (Fawcett paperback).
Koch, Howard. *The Panic Broadcast.* Little, Brown, 1970; (Avon paperback).
Lahue, Kalton C. and Gill, Samuel. *Clown Princes and Court Jesters: Some Great Comics of the Silent Screen.* A. S. Barnes, 1970; Thomas Yoseloff Ltd. (F)
Lahue, Kalton C. *Dreams for Sale: The Rise and Fall of the Triangle Film Corporation.* A. S. Barnes; Thomas Yoseloff Ltd., 1971. (F)
Lahue, Kalton C., and Brewer, Terry. *Kops and Custards: The Legend of Keystone Films.* University of Oklahoma Press, 1967. (F)
Lahue, Kalton C. *Mack Sennett's Keystone: The Man, the Myth and the Comedies.* A. S. Barnes; Thomas Yoseloff Ltd., 1971 (F)
Lahue, Kalton C. *Motion Picture Pioneer: The Selig Polyscope Company.* A. S. Barnes; Thomas Yoseloff Ltd., 1973. (F)
Lahue, Kalton C. *World of Laughter: The Motion Picture Comedy Short, 1910-1930.* University of Oklahoma Press, 1966. (F)
Lamarr, Hedy. *Ecstasy and Me.* Fawcett paperback, 1970.
Lasky, Jesse, with Weldon, Don. *I Blow My Own Horn.* Doubleday, 1957; Gollancz.
Latham, Aaron. *Crazy Sundays: F. Scott Fitzgerald in Hollywood.* Viking, 1971.

Lebel, Jean-Patrick. *Buster Keaton.* Paris: Classiques du Cinéma, Editions Universitaires, 1964, translated by P. D. Stovin, A. S. Barnes & Co., A. Zwemmer, 1967. (F)
Lee, Raymond. *Those Scandalous Sheets of Hollywood.* California: Venice Publishing Co., 1972.
Lee, Raymond. *Not So Dumb: Animals in the Movies.* A. S. Barnes, 1970.
Loos, Anita. *A Girl Like I.* Viking, 1966; Hamish Hamilton.
Macgowan, Kenneth. *Behind the Screen: The History and Techniques of the Motion Picture.* Delacorte, 1965.
McCaffrey, Donald W. *Four Great Comedians: Chaplin, Lloyd, Keaton, Langdon.* A. S. Barnes, 1968; A. Zwemmer.
McDonald, Gerald D., Conway, Michael, and Ricci, Mark. *The Films of Charlie Chaplin.* Citadel Press, 1965. (F)
Milner, Michael. *Sex on Celluloid.* McFadden, 1964.
Moore, Colleen. *Silent Star.* Doubleday, 1968.
Nuetzel, Charles. *Whodunit? Hollywood Style.* Beverly Hills: California Book Company of America, 1965.
O'Dell, Paul, with Slide, Anthony. *Griffith and the Rise of Hollywood.* A. S. Barnes, 1970; A. Zwemmer.
Parsons, Louella O. *The Gay Illiterate.* Doubleday Doran, 1944.
Ramsaye, Terry. *A Million and One Nights.* Simon & Schuster, 1964.
Randall, Richard. *Censorship of the Movies.* University of Wisconsin Press, 1968.
Robinson, David. *Buster Keaton.* Indiana University Press, 1969; Martin Secker & Warburg. (F)
Robinson, David. *The Great Funnies.* Dutton, 1969; Studio Vista.
Robinson, David. *Hollywood in the Twenties.* A. S. Barnes, 1968; (Paperback Library, paperback); A. Zwemmer.
Sadoul, Georges. *Le Cinéma Devient Un Art.*
St Johns, Adela (Rogers). *Final Verdict.* Doubleday, 1962; (New American Library paperback).
St Johns, Adela (Rogers). *The Honeycomb.* Doubleday, 1969.
Sann, Paul. *The Lawless Decade.* Crown, 1974; (Fawcett paperback).
Sarris, Andrew. *The American Cinema: Directors and Directions, 1929-1968.* Dutton, 1968.

Schumach, Murray. *The Face on the Cutting Room Floor*. Morrow, 1964.
Seldes, Gilbert. *The Seven Lively Arts*. Sagamore Press, 1957 (1924).
Sennett, Mack, as told to Shipp, Cameron. *King of Comedy*. Doubleday, 1954; Peter Davies. (F)
Slide, Anthony, with O'Dell, Paul. *Early American Cinema*. A. S. Barnes, 1970; A. Zwemmer.
Thomas, Bob. *Selznick*. Doubleday, 1970.
Thomas, Bob. *Thalberg*. Doubleday, 1969.
Turconi, Davide and Savio, Francesco. *Buster Keaton*. Venezia: Edizioni M.I.A.C., 1963. (F)
Turconi, Davide. *Mack Sennett. Il 'Re delle comiche'*. Roma: Edizioni dell'Ateneo Roma, 1961. (F)
Turconi, Davide. *Mack Sennett*. Traduction de Nicole Brunet. Cinéma d'Aujourd'hui, no. 41. Paris: Editions Seghers, 1966. (F)
Wagenknecht, Edward. *The Movies in the Age of Innocence*. University of Oklahoma Press, 1962; (Ballantine paperback).
Winkler, John. *William Randolph Hearst*. The Hearst Corp. (Avon, 1955).
Zukor, Adolph with Kramer, Dale. *The Public Is Never Wrong*. G. P. Putnam's Sons, 1953.

Shooting scripts for seventy-three of Arbuckle's movies

Legal Documents

Transcripts of the coroner's inquest on Virginia Rappe
Transcript of the grand jury hearing on the death of Virginia Rappe
Transcripts of the trials of *The People of the State of California v. Roscoe Arbuckle*
Sworn depositions made on behalf of the prosecution and the defence in the trials of *The People of the State of California v. Roscoe Arbuckle*
Transcript of Supreme Court Judgement in the Case of District Attorney Nathan A. Tufts

Newspapers and Periodicals

The American Weekly, 22 October 1950
Billboard
Bioscope
Boston Daily/Evening /Sunday *Globe*, 1921
Chicago *Examiner*, 1915
Chicago *Herald & Examiner*
Ciné Miroir, 1933
Close-Up
Collier's Weekly, 1906
Ciné Comoedia
Detroit *News*
Every British National/Evening/Sunday Newspaper, 1915 to 1933
Exhibitor's Herald, March 1927
Film Daily Year Books, 1917 to 1925
Films in Review
Fresno *Republican*
Kine Weekly
Literary Digest
Los Angeles *Examiner*, 1917 to 1933
Los Angeles *Mirror-News*
Los Angeles *Times*, 1916 to 1933
Manchester Guardian, 1951
Melbourne *Herald*, 1922
Motion Picture
Motion Picture Classic
Motion Picture Digest
Motion Picture Herald
Motion Picture Magazine
Motion Picture News
Motion Pictures Dramatic Mirror, 1919-1920
Movie Monthly
Moving Picture World
New York *Dramatic Mirror*, September 1909
New York *Herald*
New York *Telegraph*, 1915
The New York Times, 1917 to 1933
New York *World-Telegram*, 1932 to 1933
Outlook
Parkside *Journal* (Los Angeles)

Photoplay
Picture Play
Picture Show
Pictures and Picture Goer
San Francisco *Bulletin,* 1915 onwards
San Francisco *Call,* 1915 to 1922
San Francisco *Chronicle,* 1917 to 1933
San Francisco *Examiner,* 1915 to 1933
Toledo *Blade,* 1920 to 1923
Vanity Fair
Variety, 1906 to 1933
Wid's Daily/Film Daily

Press releases from Paramount (1917 to 1923) and Warner Brothers (1930 to 1933)

SOURCES FOR THE FILMOGRAPHY

Because we wanted an accurate filmography, the sources used in compiling it have consisted primarily of original studio production papers, studio journals and release advertisements, motion picture trade magazines, studio directories, casting directories, exhibitor booking guides, almanacs and production annuals, all from the period in which Arbuckle's films were originally released.

Books published in recent years which deal in part with Arbuckle's career have been consulted and are included in the general bibliography – but only facts that could be authenticated have been incorporated in the filmography.

Periodicals

The Bioscope. Nos 142-402. 1909-1914.
Camera! Vols 2-3. 1919-1920.
Exhibitors Herald. Vols 18-32. 1924-1927.
Exhibitors Herald-World. Vols 90-101. 1928-1930.
Exhibitors Trade Review. Vols 17-18. 1924-1925.
The Film Daily. Vols 29-64. 1933.
The Film Index. Vols 3-7. 1908-1911.
Film Fun. Vols 31-48. 1919-1928.
General Directory. Vols 1-2. 1930-1932.
Hollywood Filmograph. Vols 9-14. 1929-1934.
Motion Picture Herald. Vols 102-114. 1910-1934.
Motion Picture News. Vols 10-42. 1914-1930.
Motion Picture News Booking Guide. Vols 2-14. 1921-1928.
Motography. Vols 9-13. 1913-1915.
Moving Picture World. Vols 1-89. 1907-1927.
The New York *Dramatic Mirror*. Later: *Dramatic Mirror*;

Dramatic Mirror and Theatre World. Vols 60-82. 1908-1920.
Paramount Artcraft Progress-Advance. Vol 4. 1918.
Reel Life. Vols 3-6. 1913-1915.
Selig Polyscope News. Vol 1. 1910.
Selig Release Heralds. 1911-1913.
Selig Release Supplements. Nos 52-206. 1907-1909.
Standard Casting Directory. Vols 1-10. 1923-1933.
The Triangle. Vols 1-2. 1915-1916.
Variety. Vols 58-112. 1920-1933.

Annuals and Reference Works

American Film Institute Catalog: Feature Films 1921-1930. Executive Editor, Kenneth W. Munden. NY & London: R. R. Bowker Co., 1971.
American Film Institute Catalog: Feature Films 1921-1930. Credit and Subject Indexes. Executive Editor, Kenneth W. Munden. NY & London: R. R. Bowker Co., 1971.
Directors' Annual and Production Guide 1929. NY: The Film Daily, 1929.
Directors' Annual and Production Guide 1930. NY: The Film Daily, 1930.
Directors' Annual and Production Guide 1931. NY: The Film Daily, 1931.
Film Daily Year Book 1928. NY: The Film Daily, 1928.
Film Daily Year Book 1929. NY: The Film Daily, 1929.
Film Daily Year Book 1930. NY: The Film Daily, 1930.
Film Daily Year Book 1931. NY: The Film Daily, 1931.
Film Daily Year Book 1932. NY: The Film Daily, 1932.
Film Daily Year Book 1933. NY: The Film Daily, 1933.
Film Flashes. The Wit and Humor of a Nation in Pictures. NY: Leslie-Judge Company, 1916.
Film Flashes. The Wit and Humor of a Nation in Pictures. NY: Leslie-Judge Company, 1917.
The Film Index: A Bibliography. Editor, Harold Leonard. Vol 1, *The Film as Art*. NY: Museum of Modern Art Film Library & The H. W. Wilson Co., 1941.
Film Year Book 1922-1923. NY: Wids Films and Film Folks, 1923.
Film Year Book 1924. NY: The Film Daily, [1924].

Film Year Book 1926. NY: The Film Daily, [1926].
Film Year Book 1927. NY: The Film Daily, [1927].
Keystone Releases. Inventory List, 1913-1917. Unpublished.
Library of Congress. *Motion Pictures 1894-1912*. Identified from the Records of the United States Copyright Office by Howard Lamarr Walls. Washington, DC: The Library of Congress, 1953.
Library of Congress. *Motion Pictures 1912-1939*. Catalogue of Copyright Entries. Washington, DC: The Library of Congress, 1951.
The Motion Picture Almanac 1929. Martin J. Quigley, ed. Chicago: The Quigley Publishing Co., 1929.
The Motion Picture Almanac 1930. Martin J. Quigley, ed. Quigley, 1930.
The Motion Picture Almanac 1931. Martin J. Quigley, ed. Quigley, 1931.
The Motion Picture Almanac 1932. Martin J. Quigley, ed. Quigley, 1932.
The Motion Picture Almanac 1933. Martin J. Quigley, ed. Quigley, 1933.
Motion Picture Blue Book 1925. NY: Exhibitors Trade Review, 1924.
Motion Picture News Blue Book 1929. NY: Motion Picture News, 1929.
Motion Picture News Blue Book 1930. NY: Motion Picture News, 1930.
Motion Picture News Studio Directory. 29 January 1916. NY: Motion Picture News, 1916.
Motion Picture News Studio Directory. 21 October 1916. NY: Motion Picture News, 1916.
Motion Picture News Studio Directory. 12 April 1917. NY: Motion Picture News, 1917.
Motion Picture Studio Directory 1918. NY: Motion Picture News, 1918.
Motion Picture Studio Directory 1919. NY: Motion Picture News, 1919.
Motion Picture Studio Directory and Trade Annual 1920. NY: Motion Picture News, 1920.
Motion Picture Studio Directory and Trade Annual 1921. NY: Motion Picture News, 1921.

Motion Picture Studio Directory and Trade Annual 1923-24. NY: Motion Picture News, 1924.
National Film Archive Catalogue. Part III: *Silent Fiction Films 1895-1930*. London: The British Film Institute, 1966.
Paramount Produced Properties and Releases. Including all pictures released up to 1 January 1957. NY: Paramount Pictures, 1957.
Story of the Famous Players-Lasky Corporation. NY: Famous Players-Lasky Corporation, 1919.

INDEX